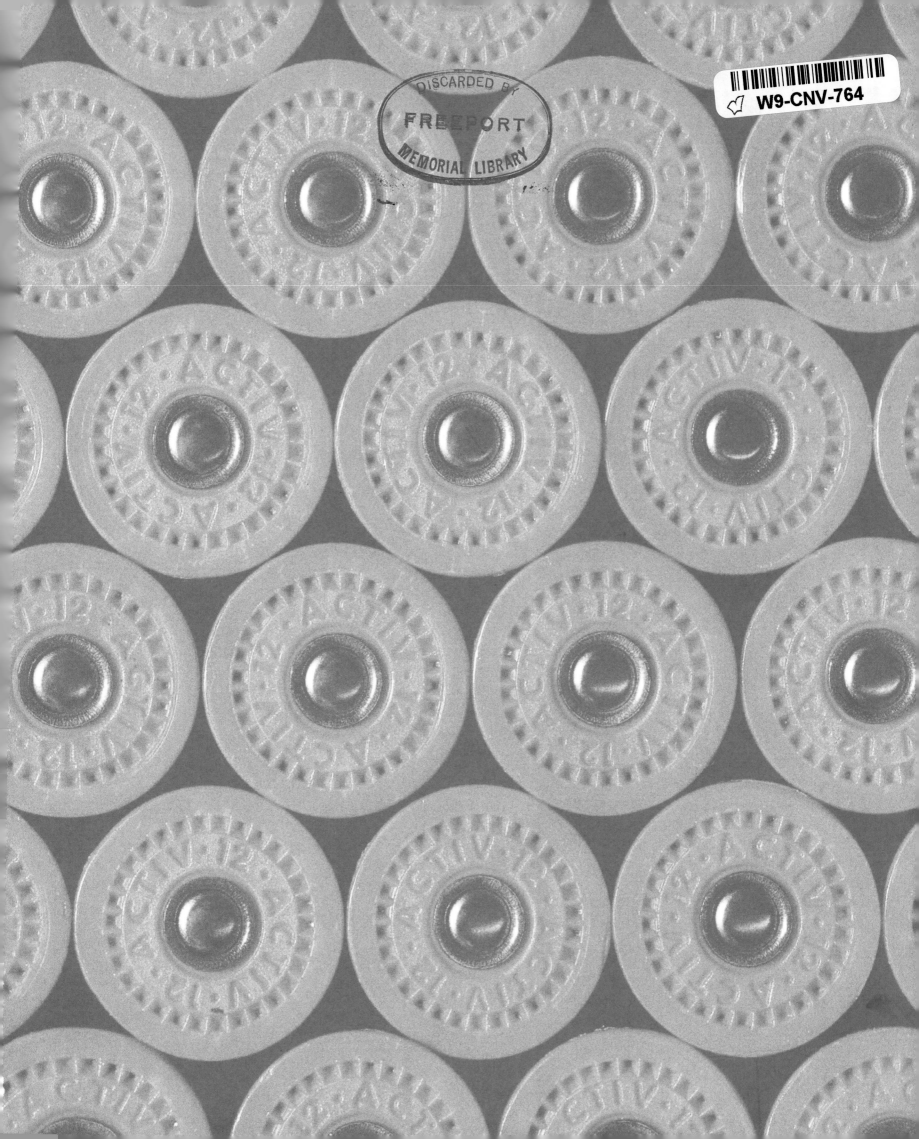

FIREARMS
AN ILLUSTRATED HISTORY

DK SMITHSONIAN

FIREARMS

AN ILLUSTRATED HISTORY

**LONDON, NEW YORK, MELBOURNE,
MUNICH, AND DELHI**

DK INDIA

Senior Art Editor	Anis Sayyed
Editorial team	Suneha Dutta, Deeksha Saikia, Rupa Rao, Bharti Bedi, Priyanka Kharbanda, Sonia Yooshing
Art Editors	Pooja Pipil, Mahipal Singh
Assistant Art Editors	Vidit Vashisht, Tanvi Sahu
DTP Designers	Sachin Singh, Vishal Bhatia, Nand Kishor Acharya
Picture Researcher	Aditya Katyal
Deputy Managing Editor	Kingshuk Ghoshal
Deputy Managing Art Editor	Govind Mittal
Production Manager	Pankaj Sharma
DTP Manager	Balwant Singh
Jacket Designer	Govind Mittal
Managing Jackets Editor	Saloni Talwar
Senior DTP Jacket Designer	Harish Aggarwal

DK LONDON

Senior Editors	Rob Houston, Christine Stroyan
Senior Art Editor	Gillian Andrews
US Senior Editor	Margaret Parrish
Photographer	Gary Ombler
DK Picture Library	Claire Bowers
Pre-Production Producer	Adam Stoneham
Producer	Linda Dare
Managing Editor	Stephanie Farrow
Managing Art Editor	Lee Griffiths
Jacket Editor	Manisha Majithia
Jacket Designers	Mark Cavanagh
Jacket Design Development Manager	Sophia MTT
Publisher	Andrew Macintyre
Art Director	Phil Ormerod
Associate Publishing Director	Liz Wheeler
Publishing Director	Jonathan Metcalf

CONTRIBUTORS

Primary Consultant	Graeme Rimer
Consultants	Herbert G. Houze, Peter Smithurst, Philip Wilkinson, Christopher Henry

First American Edition, 2014
Published in the United States by
DK Publishing
4th floor, 345 Hudson Street, New York, New York 10014

14 15 16 17 18 10 9 8 7 6 5 4 3 2 1
001—187518—04/14

Published in Great Britain by Dorling Kindersley Limited.

A catalog record for this book is available from the Library of Congress.
ISBN: 978-1-4654-1605-6

DK books are available at special discounts when purchased in bulk for sales
promotions, premiums, fund-raising, or educational use. For details, contact:
DK Publishing Special Markets, 345 Hudson Street, New York, New York 10014
or SpecialSales@dk.com.

Printed and bound in China by Leo Paper Products

Includes material previously published in *Gun*, *Weapon*, and *Military History*.

Discover more at
www.dk.com

CONTENTS

THE AGE OF CHANGE (1830–80)

A WORLD IN CONFLICT (1880–1945)

THE MODERN ERA (1945–PRESENT DAY)

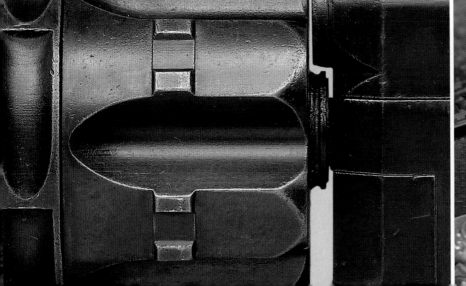

INTRODUCTION

THROUGHOUT THEIR HISTORY, firearms have had a profound effect on human activity. Created to wage war, guns soon provided a means for hunting and defending life and property. They also helped sustain traditions of target shooting that began with bows and arrows.

The first firearms appeared in China in the Middle Ages. At the time, gunpowder was already being used to create explosives. The Chinese discovered that by putting some of this powder, and a projectile, into a metal tube, and then igniting the powder, they could propel the projectile with enormous force. So, as far as we can tell, the first guns were born. While the earliest guns were artillery pieces, portable handguns were not far behind. Personal arms would never be the same again.

For several centuries, guns remained simple metal tubes, loaded at the muzzle and firing spherical balls of lead or stone, propelled by burning gunpowder. At first, they were fired manually by smoldering match-cord, but later, mechanical devices called locks ignited the powder, freeing the hands to concentrate on aiming. Matchlocks, and then wheel-locks and flintlocks, made guns quicker and simpler to fire.

The 19th century saw the greatest advances in the development and manufacture of firearms in their entire history. Muskets developed into rifles, smoothbore artillery evolved into rifled weapons, gunpowder was replaced by smokeless powder, and muzzle-loading gave way to breech-loading. Fulminates—compounds that exploded when struck—were discovered, and for the first time, guns would fire reliably even in the rain. Fulminates would eventually be incorporated into self-contained metal cartridges, loadable in an instant from magazines.

Arms manufacturers such as Samuel Colt pioneered technologies for mass-producing guns with precision-made interchangeable parts, creating a blueprint for how firearms would come to be manufactured. The turn of the 20th century saw the almost universal adoption of repeaters, self-loading pistols, and machine-guns. With evolving firearms technology, military tactics also changed forever.

Firearms development has consistently pushed the limits of available manufacturing technology and spurred the creation of new materials. Modern manufacturers utilize materials such as plastics and pressed steel to build guns using computer-controlled production processes.

Today's designs still owe much to earlier periods. Many modern revolvers, pistols, and rifles are rooted in the genius of their 19th-century designers. This book provides a fascinating visual survey of firearms, from their earliest forms until the present day. It celebrates the inspiration of great firearms designers and also the traditional craftsmanship that is still vital for the creation of fine sporting guns.

GRAEME RIMER

CONSULTANT

**COLT MODEL 1911
(TOOLROOM MODEL,
DISASSEMBLED VIEW)**

GERMAN WHEEL-LOCK RIFLE

BEFORE THE FLINTLOCK

UP TO 1650

A gunlock, or firing mechanism, ignites propellant—gunpowder—to fire a projectile down the barrel of a gun. At first, firearms had no special mechanism for igniting the charge, just a smoldering hemp-cord to light the gunpowder. Then the development of gunlocks such as the matchlock and wheel-lock—and ultimately the flintlock—mechanisms made guns quicker and easier to fire.

EARLY CANNON

The gun was first developed in medieval China. With the invention of gunpowder, blacksmiths there attempted to create a tube strong enough to contain its explosions. In the early 14th century, craftsmen in China, and then in Europe, made cannon by casting them in bronze. Shortly afterward, blacksmiths began to build cannon by assembling them from strips of wrought iron. The strips, or staves, ran lengthwise, and heated iron bands were placed around them. On cooling, the bands shrank, binding the strips tightly to form the bore of the cannon, a little like wooden staves form a wooden barrel. Early cannon were mostly loaded at the muzzle, with gunpowder and balls carved from stone. A vent in the barrel of the cannon allowed the gunpowder to be ignited, usually with a smoldering match-cord.

Vent for igniting gunpowder

Lifting ring

Muzzle

▲ FLEMISH BOMBARD

Date	Early 15th century
Origin	Flanders
Length	Not known
Caliber	Not known

In the 1400s, large siege guns were known as bombards. The stone balls they hurled were loaded through the muzzle after the gunpowder charge. Flanders, where this bombard was made, had a strong tradition of gunmaking, particularly during the reign of Charles the Bold (1433–77).

▶ BOXTED BOMBARD

Date	c.1450
Origin	England
Length	7¾ft (2.4m)
Caliber	13in (230mm)

As with most types of early gun, bombards had a narrow powder chamber and a wider bore. This helped to concentrate the force of the exploding gunpowder and to focus it behind the center of the ball.

Lifting ring

Wrought-iron barrel made of bands and staves

Powder chamber in breech

Towing eye

Astragals (decorative moldings)

▲ GREAT TURKISH BOMBARD

Date 1464

Origin Turkey

Length (Barrel) 11½ft (3.5m)

Caliber 25in (635mm)

Cast in bronze, this remarkable weapon was built to defend the Dardanelles, the narrow strait connecting the Sea of Marmara with the Aegean Sea. It was made in two parts, either so the gun could be moved, or perhaps to place the powder charge in the breech, making it an enormous early breech-loader. The barrel of the gun is seen here. Together with its breech section, this bombard would have been more than 16½ft (5m) long.

Swollen breech region   Reinforcing ring

Muzzle

▲ CHINESE IRON CANNON

Date c.1500

Origin China

Length 1½ft (0.47m)

Caliber 4in (100mm)

This small cannon was fired from a trestlelike stand. It was cast with a bulbous breech region to resist pressure. Rather than firing a single projectile, it was loaded with a number of smaller missiles.

Muzzle bands

Barrel

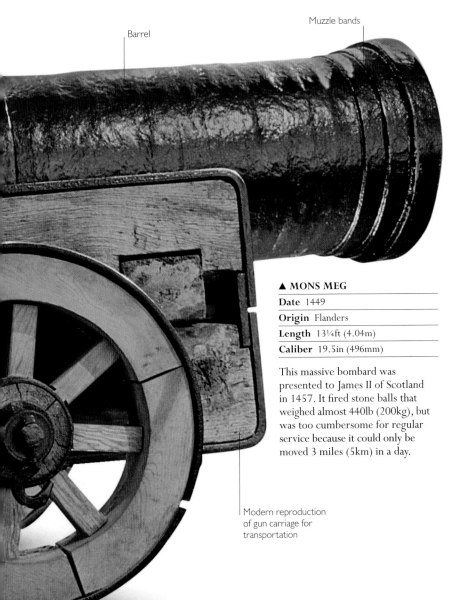

Wide muzzle

Fixing ring to attach to carriage

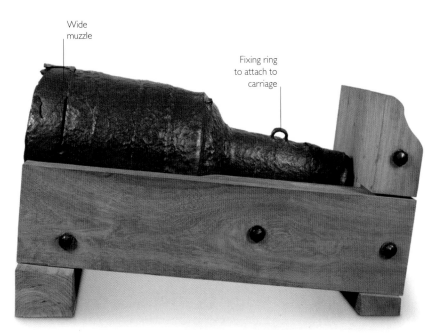

▲ MONS MEG

Date 1449

Origin Flanders

Length 13¼ft (4.04m)

Caliber 19.5in (496mm)

This massive bombard was presented to James II of Scotland in 1457. It fired stone balls that weighed almost 440lb (200kg), but was too cumbersome for regular service because it could only be moved 3 miles (5km) in a day.

Modern reproduction of gun carriage for transportation

▲ EARLY MORTAR

Date 15th–16th century

Origin England

Length 4ft (1.2m)

Caliber 14.2in (360mm)

A mortar was a muzzle-loading siege gun that fired projectiles such as stones or perhaps incendiaries at high angles over the walls of fortifications. This mortar was found in the moat of Bodiam Castle, England. It is pictured here in a resting state at a low angle.

FIELD AND NAVAL ARTILLERY

Artillery—guns that are too big and heavy to be fired by hand—include not only cannon but also smaller weapons such as swivel guns. While the design of early artillery used on land or at sea was similar, guns made for ships had to meet special requirements—space aboard ships is limited and the risk of fire considerable. Guns mounted on a pivot—swivel guns—were developed to increase the maneuverability of artillery. Light versions of swivel guns were created for naval use, and these guns could be fit onto sockets on the sides of ships. This helped to stabilize the guns when firing and to absorb recoil. Although most naval guns were muzzle-loading, loading the charge in the breech of the gun's barrel rather than in the muzzle, or breech-loading, made these guns easier to load. This was a useful feature, because it was impractical to reload a muzzle-loader whose muzzle projected from the side of the ship. Field and naval artillery gradually began to use balls of iron and lead rather than stone.

▶ **SWEDISH SWIVEL GUN**

Date	c.1500
Origin	Sweden
Material	Iron
Shot	Round or grapeshot

Swivel guns first appeared in the late 14th century. Unlike fixed cannon, which could only fire in one direction, they provided an arc of fire, and were mainly breech-loading. This model would have been mounted on a boat or a building and would often be loaded with grapeshot—small balls of iron and lead.

Muzzle lost through corrosion

Forged-iron barrel

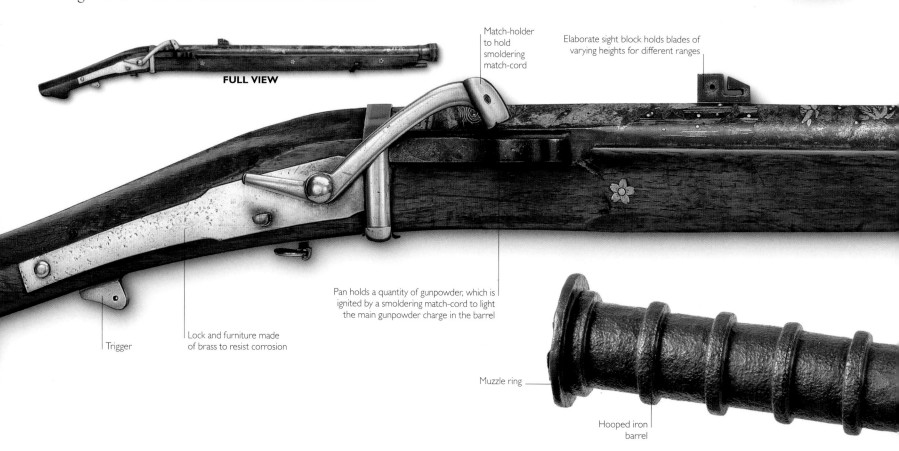

Match-holder to hold smoldering match-cord

Elaborate sight block holds blades of varying heights for different ranges

FULL VIEW

Pan holds a quantity of gunpowder, which is ignited by a smoldering match-cord to light the main gunpowder charge in the barrel

Trigger

Lock and furniture made of brass to resist corrosion

Muzzle ring

Hooped iron barrel

▼ **ENGLISH HAND-CANNON**

Date	1480
Origin	England
Barrel	Not known
Caliber	Not known

Hand-cannon were really small-scale versions of cannon and were deployed in the same way, but unlike true artillery they were small enough to be carried and fired by one user. Their muzzle-loading barrels were attached to wooden tillers. Small hand-cannon were used in naval and land warfare, but they were difficult to aim. The user had to hold the gun, look where he was aiming, direct the gun using a tiller, and then place a burning match-cord into a small amount of gunpowder around a touchhole—a vent at the rear of the barrel. On ignition, this priming powder would fire the main gunpowder charge in the breech of the barrel.

Cord binding

Touchhole

Wrought-iron barrel

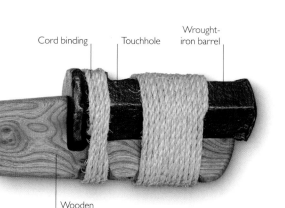

Modern reproduction of wooden tiller, used to aim the weapon

Wooden stock

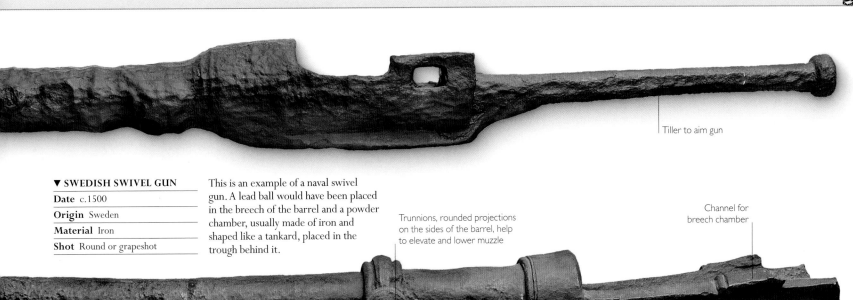

Tiller to aim gun

▼ SWEDISH SWIVEL GUN

Date	c.1500
Origin	Sweden
Material	Iron
Shot	Round or grapeshot

This is an example of a naval swivel gun. A lead ball would have been placed in the breech of the barrel and a powder chamber, usually made of iron and shaped like a tankard, placed in the trough behind it.

Trunnions, rounded projections on the sides of the barrel, help to elevate and lower muzzle

Channel for breech chamber

Joint of barrel and breech

Barrel decorated with a dragon in silver

Decorative expanded muzzle

Stock of red oak

▲ KAKAE ZUTSU

Date	17th–19th century
Origin	Japan
Barrel	2½ft (0.67m)
Caliber	.73in (18.7mm)

Kakae zutsu (hand-cannon), some with bores of up to ¾in (2cm) in diameter, were heavy guns that could be used as light artillery—to provide extra firepower in the battlefield or to batter down the wooden doors used in Japanese fortifications. Because they were heavy, they had to be shot from the waist, or from a support. These guns used a firing mechanism called a matchlock (see p.22). The matchlock in this example has an internal spiral spring to operate a match-holder.

Tankard-shaped powder chamber

Elevating bar

Iron breech wedge placed behind powder chamber to stabilize it during firing

Tiller to change direction of fire

▲ ENGLISH SWIVEL GUN

Date	Late 15th century
Origin	England
Length	4½ft (1.36m)
Caliber	2in (51mm)

Swivel guns were frequently employed for naval use. This model was mounted on the gunwales (upper edges of the sides) of a ship, where the superior arc of fire could be used to rake enemy vessels. Like most swivel guns, it is a breech-loader. As pictured, the breech chamber was wedged to hold it in place at the time of firing. This was true of almost all breech-loaders until the end of the 17th century.

Mounting podium

Chain secures breech wedge in place

NAVAL CANNON

The barrels of cannon used at sea differed little from those used on land until the 19th century, although carriages for naval service were often more compact. Naval cannon were either cast in bronze or built by forging together pieces of wrought iron (see p.12), until cast iron was perfected in the late 16th century. Bronze was an expensive material, but very durable and impervious to corrosion, unlike iron. Decorative elements could be easily added to the pattern from which a bronze cannon would be cast, and many bronze cannon were decorated ornately. Wrought-iron cannon were relatively plain because wrought iron was a difficult material to embellish.

▲ BRONZE FALCON WITH 10-SIDED BARREL

Date	c.1520
Origin	England or Flanders
Length	9ft (2.78m)
Caliber	2.6in (66mm)

This falcon was cast by a Flemish master gun-founder for King Henry VIII of England as part of a consignment of 28 guns. It fired balls of lead weighing 2¼lb (1kg).

Octagonal barrel

▲ BRONZE FALCON

Date	c.1520
Origin	Flanders or France
Length	8¼ft (2.5m)
Caliber	2.5in (63mm)

The falcon was a light cannon typical of the early 16th century. This model was ordered by Henry VIII, possibly from Flanders, because England did not have an established gun-manufacturing industry at the time.

Tudor rose symbol

▲ BRONZE SAKER

Date	1529
Origin	England
Length	7¼ft (2.23m)
Caliber	3.75in (95mm)

Like many early guns, the Saker was named after a bird of prey—in this case, the Saker falcon. This one was acquired from an Italian master craftsman as part of Henry VIII's campaign to supply English forces with artillery of the best quality.

Figure of *wyvern* (mythical dragonlike creature)

Winged mermaid (facing outward)

▲ BRONZE ROBINET

Date	1535
Origin	France
Length	7¾ft (2.39m)
Caliber	1.7in (43mm)

This is an extremely ornate example of the robinet, a light cannon with a small caliber and a barrel weighing a little more than 400lb (181kg). This model was made in Metz, France. It was seized in Paris in 1815 by troops of the Seventh Coalition (Prussia, Russia, Austria, and Great Britain) fighting Napoleon's forces.

Tiller

Trunnion

▲ BRONZE MINION

Date	c.1550
Origin	Italy
Length	8¼ft (2.5m)
Caliber	3in (76mm)

Minions, light cannon that were particularly well adapted for use at sea, saw service on many English ships during their engagement with the Spanish Armada (1588).

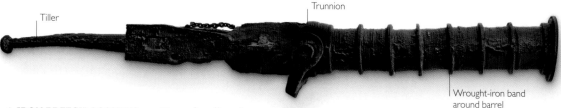

Wrought-iron band around barrel

▲ IRON BREECH-LOADING SWIVEL GUN

Date	16th century
Origin	Europe
Length	5¼ft (1.63m)
Caliber	3in (76mm)

Pivots that allowed a gun to fire across a wide arc turned a fixed barrel into a swivel gun (see p.14), especially useful aboard a ship when firing on moving vessels. This type was used in an antipersonnel role, shooting stone ammunition.

Bronze barrel

▼ **BRONZE DEMI-CULVERIN**

Date 1636

Origin France

Length 9½ft (2.92m)

Caliber 4.3in (110mm)

This naval version of a demi-culverin, a medium-sized cannon, was cast for Cardinal Richelieu, chief minister to King Louis XIII of France, who reorganized the French fleet and established a foundry at Le Havre.

Dolphin-shaped lifting handles

Trunnion

Astragals (decorative moldings)

Widely flared muzzle

Ornamental figure of pouncing lion

▲ **BRONZE DEMI-CANNON**

Date 1643

Origin Flanders

Length 10¼ft (3.12m)

Caliber 6in (152mm)

This demi-cannon, a heavy piece designed for naval use, was cast in the famous Flemish gun-foundry at Malines. It was capable of firing heavy shot, which could cause devastating damage at short range.

Elaborately decorated barrel

Small-bore barrel

▼ **MALAYSIAN BRONZE SAKER**

Date c.1650

Origin Malaysia

Length 7½ft (2.29m)

Caliber 3.5in (89mm)

Sakers were light cannon designed for long-range attack. This ornate model was cast in Malacca, Malaysia, by local craftsmen who probably followed a Dutch model.

Decoration depicting arms of Prince Maurice of the Netherlands

HARQUEBUSES

Simple hand-cannon remained in use into the 16th century. These evolved into harquebuses (hook guns)— muzzle-loaders with a recoil-absorbing hook on the underside to place over a wall or portable support for a steadier aim. Key to their development was a wooden shoulder stock that allowed the user to brace the gun with his shoulder, a feature that led to the evolution of the modern gun stock. Harquebuses were fired by a handheld match-cord, and they used lead balls. A harquebus modified by attaching a matchlock (see p.22) gave rise to the first musket.

Wooden stave inserted under armpit

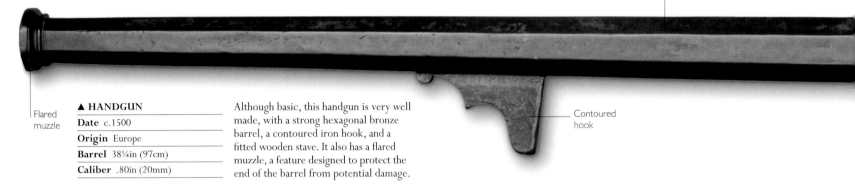

Hexagonal barrel

Contoured hook

Flared muzzle

▲ HANDGUN

Date	c.1500
Origin	Europe
Barrel	38¼in (97cm)
Caliber	.80in (20mm)

Although basic, this handgun is very well made, with a strong hexagonal bronze barrel, a contoured iron hook, and a fitted wooden stave. It also has a flared muzzle, a feature designed to protect the end of the barrel from potential damage.

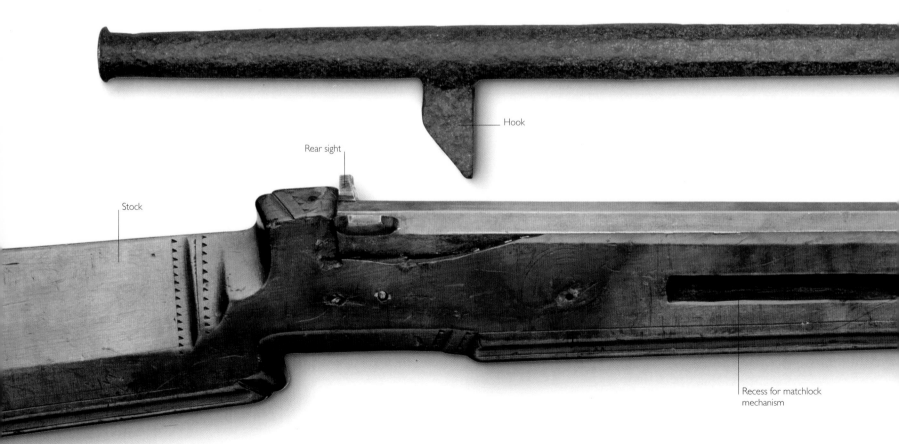

Hook

Rear sight

Stock

Recess for matchlock mechanism

▲ HOOK GUN

Date c.1500

Origin Germany

Barrel 39in (99cm)

Caliber .90in (23mm)

An improvement over earlier hand-cannon, although still undeniably simple, this hook gun consists of little more than an iron barrel fitted to a wooden stave, the stave being held under the armpit to stabilize the gun during firing. The wooden stave would evolve into the shoulder stock. The front hook beneath the barrel could be placed on a stable object to improve accuracy.

Hook for
stabilizing barrel

Stave

Iron tiller to
aim gun

Vent hole

▲ IRON HANDGUN

Date c.1500

Origin Netherlands

Barrel 28in (71cm)

Caliber .90in (23mm)

This early handgun does not have a wooden stock, but instead features a long iron tiller running out from the rear of the barrel. The weight and awkward shape of the weapon must have made it difficult to handle in the absence of a front support.

Foresight

Barrel

▲ EARLY MATCHLOCK HARQUEBUS

Date c.1560

Origin Germany

Barrel 29½in (75cm)

Caliber .59in (15mm)

This match-fired harquebus resembles a more modern firearm because its stock covers most of its body, a trend that would continue in muskets and other firearms. Note also the increased expectations of accuracy indicated by the front and rear sights, although the proportions of the gun (it weighed 50lb/22.7kg) must have affected accurate handling.

FULL VIEW

EARLY MATCHLOCK GUNS

The matchlock was an early firing mechanism for handheld guns. It featured a device—the serpentine—that held a piece of smoldering match-cord. Upon pulling the trigger, the serpentine plunged the match-cord into a pan carrying priming powder. Ignition of the priming powder produced a flash, which ignited the main charge via a vent in the side of the barrel. Firing the gun by just pulling a trigger or squeezing a lever allowed the firer to focus on the target by looking down the barrel. Early matchlock guns were muzzle-loading. A wooden rod called a ramrod was used to ram the gunpowder charge and ball into the breech.

Shoulder stock

▲ SNAPPING MATCHLOCK

Date	c.1540
Origin	Italy
Barrel	42in (105cm)
Caliber	.47in (12mm)

Henry VIII of England ordered 1,500 of these guns from the Venetian Republic in 1544. A year later, some of them were aboard his flagship, the *Mary Rose*, when it sank. Experiments have shown that their ammunition could penetrate up to 1/4in (6mm) of steel at 30 yards (27m).

Serpentine match-holder is shaped like an "S" and resembles a snake

Trigger

Brass serpentine match-holder is forward-facing

Brass lock plate

Decorative brass inlay

Brass serpentine spring

Trigger guard

Pan cover

Serpentine match-holder

Small of stock fits in hand

Lock plate

Trigger guard

Ramrod was carried in a hole drilled
along the forestock of the stock

Serpentine
match-holder

Stock extending to muzzle

▼ GERMAN
MATCHLOCK MUSKET

Date c.1580

Origin Germany

Barrel 46in (116.8cm)

Caliber Not known

Many matchlock mechanisms incorporated
a simple lever, like that on early crossbows.
The lever was squeezed to move the
serpentine holding the smoldering match-
cord into the priming pan. The military
musket shown here is typical of those used in
Germanic countries in the late 16th century.

▲ ENGLISH
MATCHLOCK MUSKET

Date c.1640

Origin England

Barrel 45½in (115cm)

Caliber .73in (18.7mm)

Muskets featured prominently in the English
Civil War, from the first encounter between
Royalists and Parliamentarians at Edgehill in 1642
to the war's conclusion at Worcester in 1651.
Because matchlocks took so long to load,
musketeers were vulnerable, particularly to
cavalry, and had to be protected by pikemen.

▼ HI NAWA JYU

Date 17th–19th century

Origin Japan

Barrel 36¾in (93.7cm)

Caliber .59in (15mm)

The *hi nawa jyu* was introduced to Japan by the
Portuguese from their base in India in 1543.
Within 25 years, manufacturing centers were
producing thousands of these guns for arming
foot soldiers, and the matchlock had become
a decisive weapon in battle.

FULL VIEW

Owner's heraldry

Cock   Frizzen   Serpentine match-holder

Trigger
guard

Frizzen spring causes
the frizzen to snap
forward as the cock falls

Ramrod pipe

Trigger

▲ DUTCH COMBINATION
LONG GUN

Date 17th century

Origin Netherlands

Barrel 46in (117cm)

Caliber .90in (23mm)

This unusual musket is equipped with both a
flintlock (see pp.38–39) and a matchlock
mechanism. The matchlock pan is part of the
top of the frizzen (pan cover combined with
a striking steel). The matchlock is operated
by the trigger guard, while the operation
of the flintlock is by means of the trigger.

Barrel is octagonal for first
third of length, then round

▲ BRITISH MATCHLOCK

Date 17th century

Origin England

Barrel 46in (117.2cm)

Caliber .70in (18mm)

By the end of their period of dominance, the best matchlocks
had acquired a degree of sophistication, at least in their finish.
They had also become much lighter, and thus were considerably
easier to handle. A high-quality piece such as this would have
been a prime contender for conversion into a snaphance
(see p.38) or flintlock (see pp.38–39), had it not been
preserved in a collection.

SHOWCASE

MATCHLOCK MUSKET

In the late 16th century, the harquebus (see p.20) developed into a type of matchlock musket that was widely adopted in western Europe. Matchlocks were more unwieldy and unreliable than the wheel-lock guns invented soon afterward (see p.27), but they continued to be popular until the end of the 17th century, largely due to their simplicity.

MATCHLOCK MUSKET	
Date	c. mid-17th century
Origin	Britain
Barrel	49½in (126cm)
Caliber	.75in (19mm)

Comb of stock assists in bringing shoulder to axis of recoil

Trigger

Nozzle without measuring device

▲ MATCHLOCK MUSKET
While the matchlock musket was a significant improvement over the hand-cannon, it was still a very clumsy weapon. Even in dry weather the match could be extinguished all too easily, and its glowing end was a giveaway at night. The best models were, however, surprisingly accurate and were capable of killing a man at 109 yards (100m) or more.

Trigger guard

Curled arm of rest

Sling is decorative as well as functional

▼ MUSKET REST
The earliest military matchlocks were very heavy and required the use of a rest. The rest itself had to be of sturdy design, and this increased the gunner's load. By about 1650, guns had become light enough that rests were no longer needed.

◄ POWDER FLASK
This flask is made of wood, covered in fabric, and has an outer iron frame. Originally its nozzle would have had a thumb-operated shutter at its base, which was used to measure the individual charges of gunpowder for a musket.

Socket for wooden staff

FULL VIEW

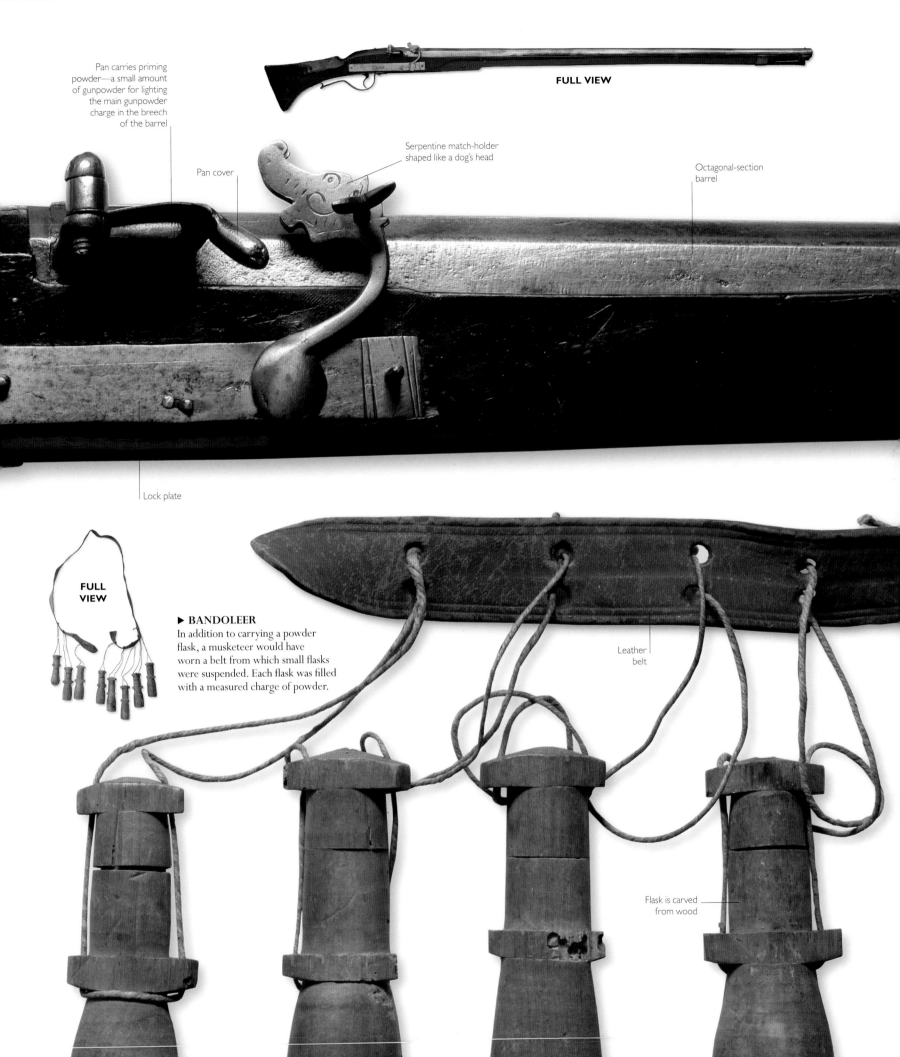

Pan carries priming powder—a small amount of gunpowder for lighting the main gunpowder charge in the breech of the barrel

Pan cover

Serpentine match-holder shaped like a dog's head

Octagonal-section barrel

FULL VIEW

Lock plate

FULL VIEW

▶ **BANDOLEER**
In addition to carrying a powder flask, a musketeer would have worn a belt from which small flasks were suspended. Each flask was filled with a measured charge of powder.

Leather belt

Flask is carved from wood

TURNING POINT

READY-TO-FIRE GUNS

Before 1500, all firearms had to be fired using a piece of
smoldering match-cord. The device to hold this match-cord—the
matchlock—was vulnerable to the effects of wind and rain, and
the match-cord could potentially burn the user. The wheel-lock
was the first mechanism to provide an internal system for igniting a
firearm, allowing guns to be carried, loaded, and ready to fire in an
instant. It made the development of an entirely new weapon—the
pistol—possible, and revolutionized the use of firearms by cavalry.

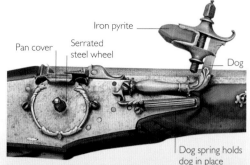

▲ WHEEL-LOCK MECHANISM
A spring-loaded steel wheel sits under a pan. A piece
of iron pyrite is held in jaws on a spring-loaded arm
called a dog. Before firing, the dog is placed onto the
pan cover. Pulling the trigger causes the wheel to spin
as the pan cover opens, bringing the iron pyrite in
contact with the wheel.

From their first appearance in Europe in the
14th century, firearms had to be lit and fired
with the help of direct heat. The only practical
source of this heat was hemp- or match-cord,
impregnated with saltpeter, or potassium
nitrate, which smoldered when lit. Early
handguns were fired by match-cord held
in the hand, which made supporting and
aiming the gun difficult. Matchlocks were
then devised to help place the lit match-cord
into a priming pan. Burning match-cord,
however, posed a constant risk to the shooter.
Plus, it could be extinguished in bad weather.

>> **BEFORE**

The match-cord and priming powder of
matchlock guns could be rendered damp
and useless in windy or rainy weather. The
smoldering match-cord was also a source
of danger to its user.

• **LARGE QUANTITIES OF MATCH-CORD** had
to be supplied to armies since soldiers had to keep
it burning in readiness, even if no gun was fired.

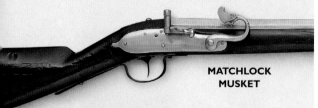

**MATCHLOCK
MUSKET**

• **THE MATCH-CORD POSED A RISK** to a
soldier because he kept it smoldering if his musket was
likely to be fired. The match-cord could either burn
him or set off his supply of gunpowder.

• **IMPOSSIBLE TO CONCEAL**, a matchlock
weapon with a smoldering match-cord would
easily give away the soldier's position at night.

• **ON HORSEBACK, IT WAS UNWIELDY AND
IMPRACTICAL** to load and fire a matchlock weapon,
and so cavalry, other than dragoons (mounted
infantry), were not equipped with firearms.

> "... **gun** that **men carry**... fires of its own action ... they are **small**... nobody **sees** them..."

ATTRIBUTED TO **DUCAL EDICT, BRESCIA, NORTHERN ITALY (1532)**

THE WHEEL-LOCK MECHANISM

The first gunlock to overcome these problems was based on a tinder-lighter—a simple device used to kindle fire. This "wheel-lock" demanded great skill to build. It consisted of a steel wheel that rotated against a piece of iron pyrite, a natural mineral, to produce sparks. One end of the lock's V-shaped mainspring was attached to a chain. By using a key to turn the wheel, the shooter wound this chain around the mechanism's axle, compressing the spring ("spanning" the lock). He then locked the spanned wheel in position, preventing it from spinning. At this point, the upper edge of the wheel entered the pan through a slot. Next, he placed gunpowder in the priming pan and closed the cover. When the gun was to be fired, the shooter moved the dog (the part of the lock that held the iron pyrite), bringing it over by hand, and placing it onto the pan cover. Pulling the trigger released the wheel, which automatically opened the pan cover. The iron pyrite hit the rotating wheel, producing sparks, which flashed through a touchhole on the side of the barrel to light the main gunpowder charge in the barrel's breech.

NEW WEAPONS

The wheel-lock design enabled the manufacture of firearms that could be carried primed and ready to fire. Because they did not require live fire, firearms could now be carried concealed. It made a brand new kind of small firearm—the pistol—a practical proposition by the 1520s. Single-handed operation of firearms became possible. The thought of a firearm small enough to be concealed under clothing alarmed European authorities, who considered it a threat to public safety. By the early 16th century, many European countries had introduced legislation against these new, portable firearms.

Thanks to the wheel-lock's portability, the cavalry at last had firearms that they could use effectively on horseback, without the need to dismount. Wheel-lock firearms, such as pistols and carbines (see p. 32), could be stowed away for use at a moment's notice. Each weapon could be fired only once during an engagement, which was why cavalry were issued with pairs of pistols, and sometimes carbines too. This, however, gave them the advantage of two or indeed three shots from the saddle, when previously none had been possible. This offered the cavalry firepower like never before.

◄ SHOOTING ON HORSEBACK
During the Thirty Years' War, at the Battle of Lützen (November 16, 1632), the Protestant Swedish king, Gustavus Adolphus, led his cavalry against Catholic Imperial forces. Shot by Imperial cavalrymen wielding wheel-lock pistols, he succumbed to his injuries.

Leonardo da Vinci
(1452–1519)

The earliest images of a mechanism resembling a wheel-lock appeared in the notes of Leonardo da Vinci's *Codex Atlanticus* in around 1495. It seems Leonardo was inspired by a tinder-lighter when he made drawings of a fire-striking device to attach to the side of a gun barrel.

AFTER »

Although the invention of the wheel-lock enabled the development of new handheld arms that could be portable, concealed, and used on horseback, there were still drawbacks. The wheel-lock was costly, easily put out of order, and hard to repair—problems in both military and hunting situations. A simpler, more reliable gunlock was still needed.

- **RARE LEVELS OF EXPERTISE** were needed to manufacture wheel-lock pistols, which made them expensive guns to buy.

- **THE SNAPHANCE LOCK** (see p. 38), a precursor to the flintlock, evolved in the 1560s.

FLEMISH FLINTLOCK PISTOL

- **THE FLINTLOCK** appeared during the 1570s (see pp. 38–39). It was cheaper, simpler, and more reliable than the wheel-lock or the matchlock.

SPORTING LONG GUNS

By the middle of the 16th century, some sporting guns had developed "rifled barrels" in which parallel spiral grooves were cut along the bore of the barrel. Firing these "rifles" imparted a spin to the round lead balls used as ammunition. This rotation made the balls fly straighter than those fired from a smoothbore (non-rifled) barrel. Smoothbore sporting guns could fire a solid lead ball or, for shooting at birds, a measured quantity of small lead pellets, or "shot." In almost all cases, early muskets and rifles were muzzle-loaders, but they used a variety of ignition systems to fire the main charge.

The guns shown here have matchlock (see p.22), wheel-lock (see pp.26–27), and flintlock (see pp.38–39) mechanisms. They have long barrels, which allows the gunpowder charge to burn fully, providing maximum power and greater accuracy.

Serpentine match-holder

Axle

Dog (the part of the wheel-lock mechanism that holds the iron pyrite)

Wheel

Lock plate

Trigger

Wooden butt stock

Flashguard limits flash produced by ignition of priming powder in pan

Short "cheek" stock

Decorative inlays

Exposed wheel-lock mechanism

Trigger

Top jaw screw

▲ **GERMAN WHEEL-LOCK TSCHINKE**

Date	c.1630
Origin	Germany
Barrel	37in (94cm)
Caliber	.33in (8.3mm)

Wheel-locks exist in three basic forms: fully enclosed; with the wheel exposed but the rest of the lock enclosed; and with the entire mechanism exposed. The last form, known as a "Tschinke," a German wheel-lock, is more easily damaged but easier to clean and maintain. This example was made in Silesia (a region spanning areas of present-day Germany, Poland, and the Czech Republic), and its stock is inlaid with horn and mother-of-pearl. It has a short butt forming a "cheek" stock which is braced against the face instead of the shoulder when firing. The gun has a heavy barrel to help absorb much of the recoil when it fires.

Short butt forming "cheek" stock

Cheek piece

Rear sight

FULL VIEW

Dog

Aperture
rear sight

Pin securing
barrel to stock

**▲ COMBINATION WHEEL-
LOCK/
MATCHLOCK MUSKET**

Date 1650 (mechanism)

Origin Germany

Barrel 46½in (118cm)

Caliber .70in (17.7mm)

In this gun, wheel-lock and matchlock
systems are set beside each other
on the same lock plate. The wheel-
lock mechanism and stock are typical
of those made in the Netherlands
and in parts of what is modern-day
Belgium and Germany around 1650.

Dog spring

FULL VIEW

**▼ SWEDISH
BALTIC FLINTLOCK**

Date c.1650

Origin Sweden

Barrel 38½in (98cm)

Caliber .4in (10mm)

This early flintlock rifle, with a characteristic
"Baltic" lock from the south of Sweden, has the
distinctive "Goinge" type short butt stock
reminiscent of weapons of a still earlier date.
Compared with later examples, its simple
lock is crudely made, but it features the frizzen
common to all flintlocks (see pp. 38–39).

Frizzen (pan cover
with swiveling steel)

Rear sight

Frizzen
spring

FULL VIEW

EUROPEAN HUNTING GUNS

Hunting guns were often built to popular regional styles that were in fashion at the time. Specific types of firing mechanism were preferred from place to place. The snaphance lock (see p.38), for instance, was preferred in Scotland and the wheel-lock (see pp.26–27) in German lands and in Italy. Hunting guns were often decorated with engraved and chiseled metalwork and inlaid stocks, to demonstrate the taste and wealth of their owner. In some regions of Europe where large game was hunted, hunters preferred rifles over smoothbore shotguns. Rifles had greater power and accuracy and were more capable of killing large animals.

Brass lock plate

Inlaid silver plaque and pins

Trigger

Decorated trigger guard

Silver butt plate

Axle

Wooden butt

Wheel

Rear tang of trigger guard

Trigger

Squared axle to span mechanism

Bone inlay

Lock plate

Serrated wheel

Trigger

Cheek piece

Steel on pivoting arm

Steel spring

Ramrod groove

FULL VIEW

▲ SCOTTISH SNAPHANCE

Date 1614

Origin Scotland

Barrel 38in (96.5cm)

Caliber .45in (11.5mm)

The name snaphance derives from the Dutch *schnapp-hahn*, meaning "pecking hen," which the mechanism was thought to resemble. It was the first attempt to simplify the wheel-lock's method of striking sparks from a piece of iron pyrite. This example is attributed to gunsmith Alison of Dundee, Scotland. It was a gift from King James VI of Scotland (and eventually of England) to Louis XIII of France.

Barrel-fixing pin

Ramrod

FULL VIEW

▲ ITALIAN WHEEL-LOCK

Date c.1630

Origin Italy

Barrel 31½in (80cm)

Caliber .45in (11.5mm)

By the 17th century, the northern cities of Brescia and Bologna had long been the centers for the fabrication of wheel-lock guns in Italy. This example is by Lazarino Cominazzo of Brescia, who was better known for his pistols.

Iron pyrite

Cocking ring works as a handle to help the shooter move the dog

Bone inlay

Ramrod

Spring holds dog firmly against wheel when gun is fired

FULL VIEW

▲ GERMAN WHEEL-LOCK

Date c.1640

Origin Germany

Barrel 34in (86.4cm)

Caliber .65in (16.5mm)

The wheel-lock mechanism appeared in both Italy and Germany in around 1500, and soon firearms using this revolutionary new ignition system were being made and used throughout much of Europe. This example has its serrated wheel mounted externally, to make it easier to clean, although the rest of the lock-work is protected within the stock behind the lock plate.

EARLY PISTOLS AND CARBINES

The advent of the wheel-lock (see pp. 26–27) not only made it possible to dispense with a lighted match-cord, but now firearms could also be made smaller, be fired with one hand, and carried around, instantly ready to fire. This gunlock made new types of firearms practical. Pistols and carbines appeared. These were lighter than cumbersome muskets and easier to handle. Carbines were shorter than muskets, but larger than pistols, and they provided cavalry with significant firepower.

Jaw to hold iron pyrite

Trigger guard

Scroll-work in steel wire

Jaw to hold iron pyrite

Pistol grip

Trigger guard

Pommel acts as a counterbalance

Dog spring

▶ WHEEL-LOCK PISTOL

Date 1590

Origin Germany

Barrel 12in (30.5cm)

Caliber .50in (12.7mm)

In northern Europe, pistols were known as dags (the origin of the name is obscure) until the late 16th century. The ball pommel, a common feature of dags, was designed to make the pistol easier to retrieve from a pocket or bag, instead of being used as a bludgeon.

▼ HOLSTER PISTOL

Date c.1580

Origin Germany

Barrel 12in (30.5cm)

Caliber .58in (14.7mm)

Ramrod

This holster pistol has a recognizably angular handgun layout, which meant it could be stored in a holster while on horseback. Every aspect of the gun is highly decorated, including a large pommel at the end of the grip.

Iron pyrite

Pan

Dog spring

Decorative ball pommel is attached to butt by a dowel

Dog is contacting the pan cover, as it does when the shooter is readying the gun to fire

Lock plate

Inlaid brass wire

Trigger

Trigger guard

Forestock

Ramrod

◄ WHEEL-LOCK CARBINE

Date 1650

Origin Germany

Barrel 20½in (52cm)

Caliber .50in (12.7mm)

Made by German gunmaker Hans Ruhr, this wheel-lock features a short, flattened butt. The steel butt plate is drilled with a cavity—possibly to contain a cartridge or powder measure. The stock is inlaid with scroll-work in steel wire featuring a cherub's head.

Top jaw screw

Ramrod

Mother-of-pearl inlay butt stock

Dog spring

Ramrod

▲ WHEEL-LOCK PISTOL

Date 17th century

Origin Germany

Barrel 20in (50.8cm)

Caliber .50in (12.7mm)

Military wheel-lock pistols were expensive (see p.27) and used only by cavalry. Pairs of these pistols were carried in holsters in front of the saddle. This example is more decorative than most, having mother-of-pearl inlay in the stock.

▼ ITALIAN WHEEL-LOCK

Date 1635

Origin Italy

Barrel 10¼in (26cm)

Caliber .52in (13.3mm)

This wheel-lock was produced in Brescia, Italy, by the famed gunmaker Giovanni Battista Francino. Francino built his reputation on the high quality of finish, fine balance, and superb lockwork of his guns, and he often made paired pistols for affluent customers.

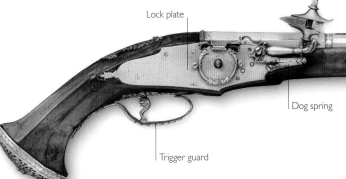

Lock plate

Dog spring

Ramrod

Trigger guard

Dog spring

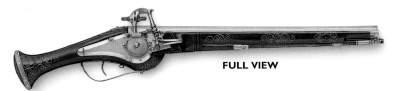

FULL VIEW

▲ GERMAN WHEEL-LOCK

Date 1620

Origin Germany

Barrel 17in (43cm)

Caliber .57in (14.5mm)

This pistol was made by Lorenz Herold, who is recorded as working in Nuremburg from 1572 until his death in 1622. This model is, however, stamped with the Augsburg control mark. Herold was, therefore, either working in both regions or buying in Augsburg-made barrels.

COMBINATION WEAPONS

Throughout history, arms-makers have tried to combine the benefits of more than one weapon. Sometimes these were attempts to produce practical military weapons, but often these hybrid weapons were made as objects of interest and technical curiosity. Combining two weapons would often compromise the effectiveness of both, but they could be splendidly decorative, even if they were not very practical. Firearms were frequently attached to other kinds of weapon, with the idea that a staff weapon, shield, or sword might gain additional potency.

▼ **HALBERD WITH TWO WHEEL-LOCK MECHANISMS**

Date	c.1590
Origin	Germany
Length	27¼in (69.1cm)
Caliber	.33in (.83cm)

This is a ceremonial halberd equipped with a double-barreled wheel-lock pistol. The pistol barrels are octagonal and mounted on either side of the leaf-shaped blade. The whole gun is etched and partly gilt with strap and scroll-work, the ax and fluke of the head having additional trophies of arms.

Gilt with strap and scroll-work

FULL VIEW

Hinged pommel

Shaft forms a second barrel

Dog

Trigger

Wheel-lock

Mace head composed of six pierced flanges

Ax blade

▲ **MACE WHEEL-LOCK**

Date	c.1560
Origin	Germany
Length	23in (58.5cm)
Caliber	.31in (.78cm)

The head of this wheel-lock pistol has six pointed flanges, each pierced with a trefoil shape. The lock incorporates a simple safety catch that engages with the sear, a part of the mechanism that holds back the dog before the trigger is pulled. The hollow shaft at the rear of the gun forms another barrel. It contains a compartment that can be accessed by opening the hinged pommel.

War hammer is missing the balancing hammer head

Dog

Barrel

Wheel

Shaft

Safety catch

Squared shaft takes the key that winds the action

Ramrod

FULL VIEW

Beak of war hammer

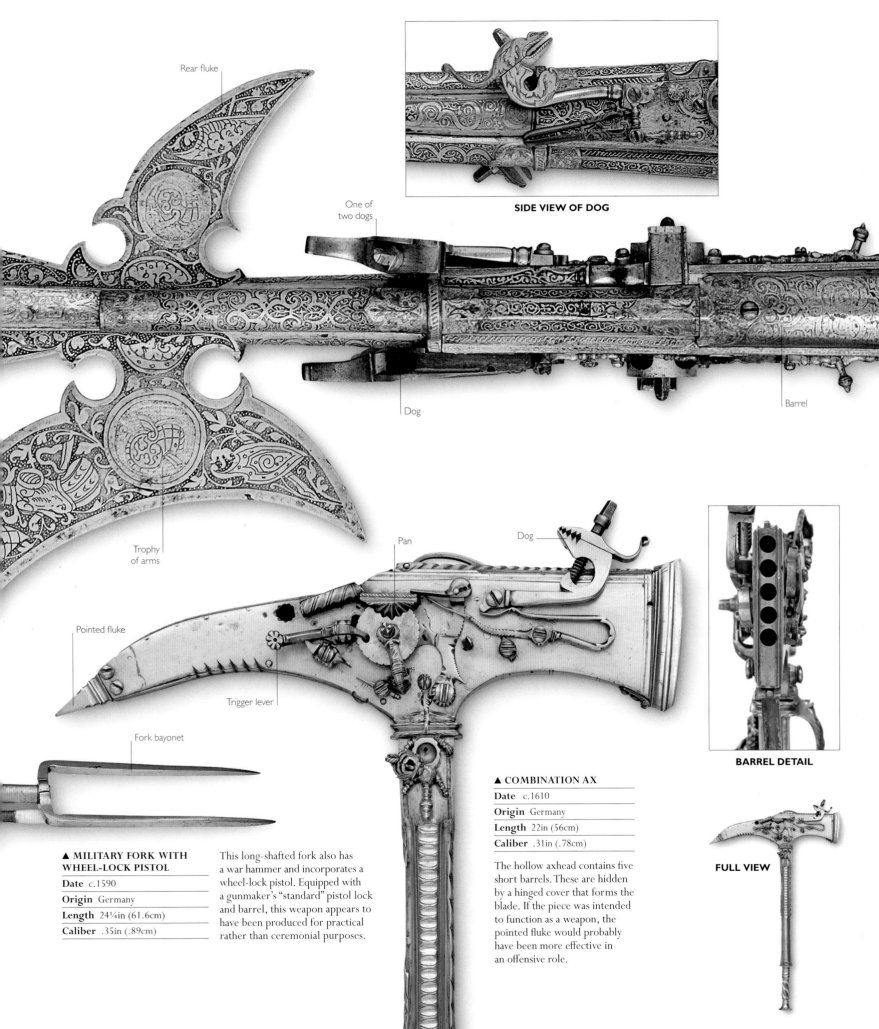

Rear fluke

One of
two dogs

SIDE VIEW OF DOG

Dog

Barrel

Trophy
of arms

Pointed fluke

Pan

Dog

BARREL DETAIL

Fork bayonet

Trigger lever

▲ MILITARY FORK WITH WHEEL-LOCK PISTOL

Date c.1590

Origin Germany

Length 24¼in (61.6cm)

Caliber .35in (.89cm)

This long-shafted fork also has a war hammer and incorporates a wheel-lock pistol. Equipped with a gunmaker's "standard" pistol lock and barrel, this weapon appears to have been produced for practical rather than ceremonial purposes.

▲ COMBINATION AX

Date c.1610

Origin Germany

Length 22in (56cm)

Caliber .31in (.78cm)

The hollow axhead contains five short barrels. These are hidden by a hinged cover that forms the blade. If the piece was intended to function as a weapon, the pointed fluke would probably have been more effective in an offensive role.

FULL VIEW

GERMAN FLINTLOCK SPORTING GUN

THE FLINTLOCK YEARS

1650–1830

The flintlock mechanism appeared in the late 16th century. It was cheaper and simpler than the wheel-lock, and produced sparks by striking a piece of flint onto a piece of hardened steel. By around 1650, it was being used widely in Europe and North America, although matchlock and wheel-lock guns remained in use. Employed on firearms ranging from pistols to artillery, the flintlock would continue to be the principal firing mechanism for more than 200 years.

TURNING POINT

GUNS FOR ALL

While the wheel-lock (see pp. 26–27) brought new opportunities for the creation of smaller, more portable firearms, it was a complex design and expensive to build. By the end of the 16th century, efforts to find a reliable but simpler and cheaper mechanism yielded a new lock. This "flintlock" utilized a piece of natural flint to strike hardened steel, generating sparks that ignited the priming powder. Due to their simple, robust working parts, flintlock guns were cheaper and more reliable than earlier arms and became the principal weapons for sporting and military purposes for the next two centuries.

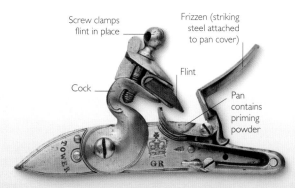

Screw clamps flint in place
Frizzen (striking steel attached to pan cover)
Flint
Cock
Pan contains priming powder

▲ **THE FLINTLOCK MECHANISM**
In this mechanism, the jaws of a spring-loaded cock hold a piece of flint. The cover of the priming pan and a striking steel are united to form a frizzen. A touchhole to the side of the pan connects to the barrel's breech.

The problems faced by users of matchlock weapons (see p. 26) were well-known—wind and rain could extinguish the match-cord or blow exposed priming powder away. As a result, matchlock guns were prone to misfire in bad weather. The smoldering match-cord was also unsafe and inconvenient for the user. An improvement on the matchlock, the wheel-lock, provided an internal system for igniting the priming powder, but it was

expensive to manufacture, prone to jam if left spanned (see p. 27) for any length of time, and difficult to maintain in the field. The iron pyrite used in the wheel-lock was soft, and wore out quickly. Soon after the wheel-lock evolved, it became clear that a less costly mechanism for firing a gun was needed. By the 1560s, new gunlocks began to appear. They worked on the principle of striking flint on hardened steel to create sparks.

THE FLINTLOCK MECHANISM

The snaphance, a precursor to the flintlock, was simpler than the wheel-lock. The snaphance's cock held a piece of flint. Pulling the trigger made the cock fall, pushing open the pan cover via an internal link. Simultaneously, the flint scraped against a steel held on a pivoting arm, which produced sparks. These sparks fell into the pan, igniting the priming powder inside. The

≫ BEFORE

Matchlock and wheel-lock firearms coexisted for a long time, despite the obvious advantages presented by the wheel-lock ignition system. Matchlock weapons were inexpensive and durable and so remained in military service until the latter part of the 17th century.

● **SINGLE-HANDED USE OF FIREARMS** was not possible using the matchlock. It was impractical for cavalry units to load and fire matchlock weapons on horseback.

THE WHEEL-LOCK MECHANISM

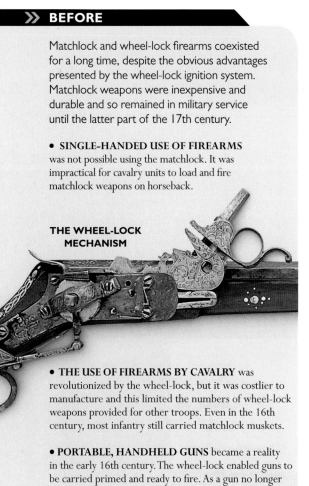

● **THE USE OF FIREARMS BY CAVALRY** was revolutionized by the wheel-lock, but it was costlier to manufacture and this limited the numbers of wheel-lock weapons provided for other troops. Even in the 16th century, most infantry still carried matchlock muskets.

● **PORTABLE, HANDHELD GUNS** became a reality in the early 16th century. The wheel-lock enabled guns to be carried primed and ready to fire. As a gun no longer required live fire, it was possible to carry a small weapon in a pocket, spurring the development of the pistol.

"... **easier** to use, **quicker** and of **less hindrance** to the user ... as well as **cheaper** ..."

FROM A LETTER MENTIONING SNAPHANCES TO THE VENETIAN AMBASSADOR IN ENGLAND
WRITTEN BY THE DOGE AND SENATE OF VENICE, NOVEMBER 6, 1613

touchhole relayed the ignition flash to the breech of the barrel, firing the main gunpowder charge.

The snaphance remained popular in parts of Europe until the 19th century but, while regional styles existed, the greatest influence on its design came from France. In the late 1600s, French gunmakers published design books depicting fashionable shapes for components and their decoration. Many gunmakers in western Europe adopted these enthusiastically.

The design of the snaphance was simplified to create the first true flintlock, in which the separate pan cover and steel were combined to create a part called the frizzen. This opened when struck by the flint (see p. 303). Uniting these parts into a single piece made the flintlock cheaper to manufacture and far more reliable. The flintlock had far fewer

parts than the wheel-lock—a late 17th-century flintlock might have just 16 parts compared to a wheel-lock's 40. This simplicity of design allowed flintlocks to be built more quickly.

THE FLINTLOCK IN USE

All three gunlocks—the matchlock, wheel-lock, and flintlock—remained in use throughout the 17th century, but the advantages of the flintlock were obvious. By the early 18th century, it had

▼ **FLINTLOCKS IN WAR**
By the 18th century, the flintlock musket was the main infantry weapon in Europe and North America, and featured prominently in the American Revolutionary War. At the Battle of Brandywine in 1777, American troops put up a stiff resistance before being defeated by British forces. Seen here are American soldiers firing their flintlock muskets in volleys.

been adopted widely. For the armies, it was cost-effective technology that could be applied toward manufacturing firearms in large numbers to standardized patterns. Gunmakers could fit a flintlock to all kinds of firearms, from a cavalry pistol to an artillery piece. Guns now became affordable for the civilian population, too. The flintlock provided travelers with useful firearms for self-defense, sportsmen with guns which were both efficient and fashionable, and duelists with weapons of deadly reliability.

Refinement of the flintlock technology continued into the 19th century, but even in its most efficient form, it had its drawbacks. Smoke produced by flintlock weapons could alert game to the presence of a hunter. The flint needed to be kept in precisely the right shape and place, and the touchhole needed to be kept clear of residue. The mechanism's exposed priming made it susceptible to bad weather. Gunmakers tried to keep the mechanism waterproof by designing a raised rib around the pan to keep out moisture, but this did not work completely. The solution to these problems came in the form of gunlocks using chemicals called fulminates (see p. 80) as primers. Chemical ignition systems heralded a new era for firearms development.

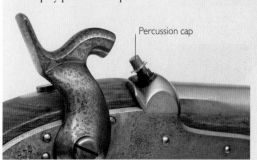

AFTER »

The flintlock mechanism continued to be used into the 1850s, but gradually gave way to a more reliable firing mechanism—the percussion cap (see pp. 80–81)—which rendered it obsolete.

- **FLINTLOCK MUSKETS** were produced en masse in the late 17th century to equip armies in Europe. Large-scale military firearms production became possible in the early 18th century, and standardized patterns of flintlock weapons became available to the armies.

- **FLINTLOCK PISTOLS** were used widely as weapons for self-defense and in dueling in the 18th century. These firearms continued to be standardized into the 19th century, resulting in plain-looking mass-produced guns.

- **PERCUSSION CAPS** began replacing the flintlock in most of Europe by the 1830s. Flintlock weapons were gradually upgraded by converting them to employ percussion caps.

Percussion cap

THE PERCUSSION CAP MECHANISM

EARLY FLINTOCK GUNS

Around the 1560s, a new form of gunlock was developed to overcome the inherent problems of the wheel-lock (see p. 38). Made out of fewer parts than its predecessor, it used the principle of striking a piece of flint against hardened steel to create sparks to ignite priming powder. The first form of this lock was the snaphance, which had a steel on the end of a pivoting arm. Movement of the cock opened the separate pan cover. A more efficient version, called the flintlock, was developed in the 17th century. This combined the pan cover and steel to form a frizzen, further simplifying the design. Early flintlock weapons came in a variety of shapes and sizes.

Frizzen for upper barrel

Barrel release catch

Frizzen for lower barrel

Flattened pommel

Steel

Cock spur

► **SCOTTISH SNAPHANCE PISTOL WITH LEMON BUTT**

Date	1627
Origin	Scotland
Barrel	8in (20cm)
Caliber	.60in (15.2mm)

This pistol is of classic Highland Scottish form. Snaphance locks were popular in Scotland for much of the 17th century and their stocks, with butts shaped like a lemon, heart, or ram's horns, were usually made of brass or steel.

Engraving on lock plate

Cock

Lock plate

Trigger

Lemon-shaped brass butt

Rounded butt

Trigger guard

▲ DUTCH DOUBLE-BARRELED FLINTLOCK

Date c.1650

Origin Netherlands

Barrel 19¾in (50.3cm)

Caliber .51in (13mm)

Multibarreled pistols gave travelers the advantage of additional firepower if attacked. The barrels on this pistol can be rotated by hand, in what is known as the Wender system. Once the upper barrel has been fired, a catch is drawn back to allow the two to be turned, bringing the unfired barrel up from beneath. Each barrel has its own pan and frizzen.

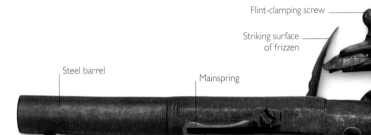

Flint-clamping screw

Cock

Striking surface of frizzen

Flint

Steel barrel

Mainspring

Tumbler

Steel stock

▲ FLINTLOCK PISTOL

Date c.1650

Origin England

Barrel 6in (15.3cm)

Caliber .59in (15mm)

This all-steel pistol is interesting because its mechanism is exposed on the outside of the stock. Even the spring-loaded tumbler, which is normally on the inside of a flintlock, is visible on the side of the gun. The tumbler governs the striking action of the cock via the mainspring when the trigger is pulled.

Engraved stock

Thin iron ramrod

Muzzle

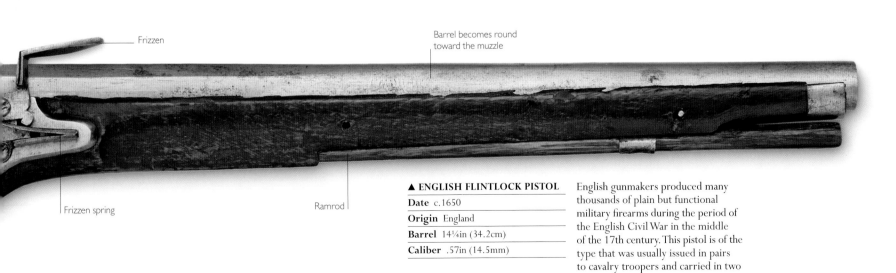

Frizzen

Barrel becomes round toward the muzzle

Frizzen spring

Ramrod

▲ ENGLISH FLINTLOCK PISTOL

Date c.1650

Origin England

Barrel 14¼in (34.2cm)

Caliber .57in (14.5mm)

English gunmakers produced many thousands of plain but functional military firearms during the period of the English Civil War in the middle of the 17th century. This pistol is of the type that was usually issued in pairs to cavalry troopers and carried in two holsters mounted on the front of the saddle. It has a lock plate and stock shaped like those of a wheel-lock, which was a fashionable design at this time.

FLINTLOCK PISTOLS (1650–1700)

In the second half of the 17th century, flintlock firearms in Europe were developed into the form they were to keep until well into the 19th century. Various flintlock mechanisms had been in use by the middle of the 17th century, but by 1700 the "French" design of lock had become the most common throughout Europe. Seen predominantly in the "sear" or cock-release mechanism underneath the lock plate of the gun, French influence was also considerable on the form and decoration of pistols and other firearms. However, regional styles, such as those in Austria and Silesia (in modern-day Poland, Germany, and the Czech Republic), continued to prosper.

Frizzen spring

Gilded steel decoration

Steel mountings on butt cap are selectively gilded

▲ AUSTRIAN HOLSTER PISTOL

Date c.1690

Origin Austria

Barrel 14in (35.5cm)

Caliber .64in (16.2mm)

Holster pistols were heavy, with long barrels and metal butt caps. Made in Vienna by Lamarre, this ornate example, although certainly atypical in the extent and high quality of its decoration, represents the state of the gunmaker's art as it was in the last decades of the 17th century.

Flint wrapped in leather patch to improve jaw's grip

Jaw

Frizzen

Staghorn inlay

Trigger

Pan

Twin cocks

▲ SILESIAN HOLSTER PISTOL

Date c.1680

Origin Silesia

Barrel 14in (35.5cm)

Caliber .54in (13.7mm)

This large, sophisticated holster pistol was made in the principality of Teschen (now divided between the Czech Republic and Poland), but shows considerable German influence in the angular shape and beveled edges of its lock. The staghorn inlaid decoration of the stock is also of German origin and indicates that the gun was made as a presentation piece.

FULL VIEW

Figured walnut stock

Lock plate

Metal-bound butt

Trigger for upper barrel

Trigger for lower barrel

Butt is brass-bound

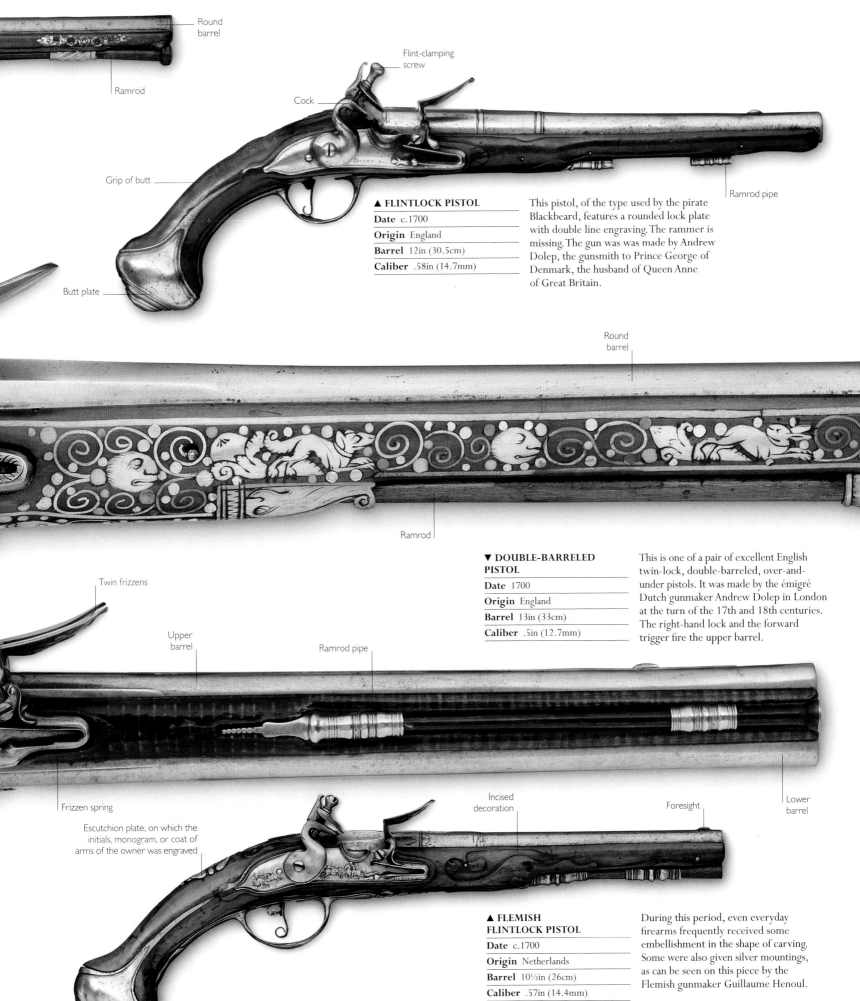

Round barrel

Ramrod

Flint-clamping screw

Cock

Grip of butt

Butt plate

Ramrod pipe

▲ FLINTLOCK PISTOL

Date	c.1700
Origin	England
Barrel	12in (30.5cm)
Caliber	.58in (14.7mm)

This pistol, of the type used by the pirate Blackbeard, features a rounded lock plate with double line engraving. The rammer is missing. The gun was was made by Andrew Dolep, the gunsmith to Prince George of Denmark, the husband of Queen Anne of Great Britain.

Round barrel

Ramrod

▼ DOUBLE-BARRELED PISTOL

Date	1700
Origin	England
Barrel	13in (33cm)
Caliber	.5in (12.7mm)

This is one of a pair of excellent English twin-lock, double-barreled, over-and-under pistols. It was made by the émigré Dutch gunmaker Andrew Dolep in London at the turn of the 17th and 18th centuries. The right-hand lock and the forward trigger fire the upper barrel.

Twin frizzens

Upper barrel

Ramrod pipe

Frizzen spring

Escutchion plate, on which the initials, monogram, or coat of arms of the owner was engraved

Incised decoration

Foresight

Lower barrel

▲ FLEMISH FLINTLOCK PISTOL

Date	c.1700
Origin	Netherlands
Barrel	10½in (26cm)
Caliber	.57in (14.4mm)

During this period, even everyday firearms frequently received some embellishment in the shape of carving. Some were also given silver mountings, as can be seen on this piece by the Flemish gunmaker Guillaume Henoul.

Metal-bound butt

FLINTLOCK PISTOLS (1701–75)

During this period, decorated silver mounts and the occasional use of inlaid wire became common on pistols for private use, while military pistols were still handsome pieces but rather plain. Although nearly all guns of the time were loaded through the muzzle, some pistols were breech-loading weapons, made with barrels that unscrewed for loading at the breech, which could be quicker and easier.

▲ ENGLISH HOLSTER PISTOL

Date	c.1720
Origin	England
Barrel	10in (25.4cm)
Caliber	.64in (16.2mm)

A pistol such as this would have been carried in a holster on the saddle of a horse (gun holsters worn by people were later inventions). After being discharged, holster pistols were often used as bludgeons.

Trigger guard

Unstocked round barrel

External mainspring

Screw-in breechblock

▲ SPANISH BREECH-LOADING PISTOL

Date	c.1725
Origin	Spain
Barrel	10in (25.4cm)
Caliber	.55in (13.9mm)

The miquelet lock, like the flintlock, had a combined steel and pan cover. But its mainspring, which powered the cock, was external, while that of a true flintlock was inside. This miquelet lock pistol is unusual in having a breechblock that screws out with one full turn of the trigger guard to which it is attached, allowing the ball and powder charge to be inserted.

Lock plate

Cock

Flint-clamping screw

Frizzen

Trigger has lost decorative finial ball at its tip

Silver medallion set into butt

Trigger guard

▲ WILSON PISTOL

Date	c.1730
Origin	UK
Barrel	5½in (13cm)
Caliber	.59in (15.1mm)

Robert Wilson was a maker of fine pistols during the 18th century. His firearms were sought-after collector's pieces and of the sort used by the famous highwayman Dick Turpin. Paired pistols were usually either for dueling or came in a boxed collector's set.

Heavy brass
butt plate

Ramrod

**▲ BRITISH HEAVY
DRAGOON PISTOL**

Date 1747

Origin England

Barrel 12in (30.5cm)

Caliber .65in (16.5mm)

Unlike pistols for private use, military pistols were quite plain. Officers in the French chasseurs, hussars, and dragoons generally carried flintlock pistols similar to this British example. One of a pair, it has a heavy brass butt plate that could be used as a club in hand-to-hand fighting.

Frizzen

▼ SCOTTISH PISTOL

FULL VIEW

Date c.1750

Origin Scotland

Barrel 9in (23cm)

Caliber .57in (14.4mm)

At this time, it was the fashion in Scotland to make pistols entirely of brass or iron, with their surface covered by intricate engraving. Typically, they lacked trigger guards. Most were snaphances; this example is unusual in that it is a flintlock. It was made by Thomas Cadell of Doune, who made some of the best iron pistols.

Frizzen spring

Barrel is engraved
all over

Cock has lost upper
jaw to flint clamp

Butt has incised
decoration

**◀ DOUBLE-BARRELED
TAP-ACTION PISTOL**

Date 1763

Origin UK

Barrel 2in (5.1cm)

Caliber .22in (5.6mm)

Tap

In this pistol, a rotating rod—operated by a small "tap" handle on the left side—lies beneath the cock. The pan is formed out of a shallow channel in the rod. A touchhole in the pan connects with the upper barrel. Once this barrel is fired, the tap is turned and another pan appears, whose touchhole is connected to the lower barrel. This enables two shots to be fired in quick succession.

Cock

Frizzen

Langets reinforced
wooden stock

Trigger guard

Brass butt plate

▲ LIÈGE PISTOL

Date 1765

Origin Belgium

Barrel 9in (23cm)

Caliber .62in (15.7mm)

Made in the city of Liège by M. Delince, this holster pistol appears to have been shortened at the muzzle, and shows signs of heavy use. This example lacks the internal reinforcing bridle, which was standard at the time, to stop the frizzen screw from breaking under the force of the falling cock.

FLINTLOCK PISTOLS (1776–1800)

In the late 18th century, flintlock firearms achieved a state of technical perfection and elegance that would last until the flintlock gave way to percussion weapons in the 19th century. Certain styles became popular, such as the "Queen Anne" pistol in UK, with its characteristic "cannon" barrel. Refinements in the flintlock mechanism were relatively few, but included a variant called the box-lock mechanism, in which the cock was placed centrally within the pistol, making the gun easier to carry.

Frizzen

Frizzen spring

Trigger guard

Brass-capped pommel

▲ RAPPAHANNOCK PISTOL

Date c.1776

Origin US

Barrel 9in (23cm)

Caliber .69in (17.5mm)

At the Rappahannock Forge near Falmouth, Virginia, Scottish émigré James Hunter produced the first American-manufactured military pistol. It was a copy of the British Light Dragoon pistol and was used by the Light Dragoons in the Continental Army.

Painted decoration

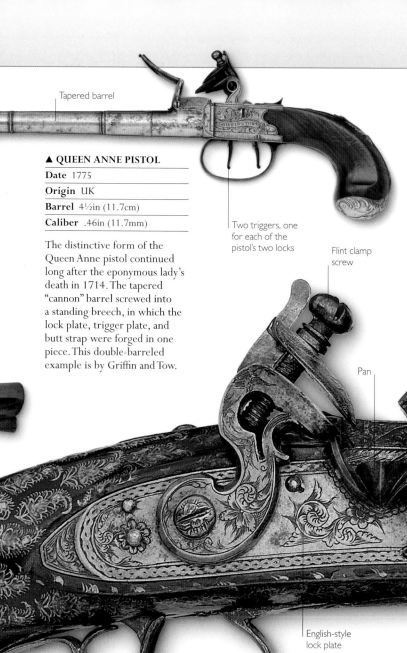

Tapered barrel

▲ QUEEN ANNE PISTOL

Date 1775

Origin UK

Barrel 4½in (11.7cm)

Caliber .46in (11.7mm)

The distinctive form of the Queen Anne pistol continued long after the eponymous lady's death in 1714. The tapered "cannon" barrel screwed into a standing breech, in which the lock plate, trigger plate, and butt strap were forged in one piece. This double-barreled example is by Griffin and Tow.

Two triggers, one for each of the pistol's two locks

Flint clamp screw

Pan

English-style lock plate

Trigger

Trigger guard

Checkered grip

▶ FOUR-BARRELED TAP-ACTION PISTOL

Date 1780

Origin UK

Barrel 2½in (6.35cm)

Caliber .38in (9.6mm)

A revolver is a gun with a number of chambers—each carrying a round—in a revolving cylinder. An alternative to this system was to multiply the number of barrels. Two barrels, each with its own lock, were quite common, and four—and even six—became feasible with the invention of the tap (see p.45). The taps, one for each vertical pair, presented priming for each of the two lower barrels when turned.

Wooden butt

Tap

Flint held in leather patch

Four barrels mounted side by side in vertical pairs

Ramrod

Tapered barrel

▲ FRENCH MODÈLE 1777 PISTOL

Date 1782

Origin France

Barrel 8½in (21.5cm)

Caliber .69in (17.5mm)

French military firearms were well constructed. This cavalry pistol has a lock mechanism built within a brass body and it lacks a forestock. Its ramrod passes through the lock body and into the wooden butt.

Jaw clamp screw

Frizzen

Box-lock mechanism

Brass barrel

Bell mouth ensures wide spread of shot at close range

Waters & Co

Spring-loaded bayonet

Rear trigger releases bayonet

Trigger

▲ JOHN WATERS BLUNDERBUSS PISTOL

Date 1785

Origin England

Barrel 7½in (19cm)

Caliber 1in (25.4mm) (at muzzle)

The blunderbuss (from the Dutch *donderbus*, or "thunder gun") was used in boarding ships during engagements with the enemy. A blunderbuss fired spherical shot (many lead balls) and the flared muzzle increased the spread of the shot over a short distance. This box-lock blunderbuss was made by John Waters of Birmingham. His name is legible on the mechanism.

Damascus barrel

Ramrod pipe

Ramrod

▲ PUNJABI FLINTLOCK PISTOL

Date c.1800

Origin Lahore (in modern-day Pakistan)

Barrel 8½in (21.5cm)

Caliber .55in (14mm)

This is one of a pair of superbly decorated pistols made in Lahore. By the early 19th century, Sikh gunmakers were able to fashion the components of a flintlock, although they were mostly devoted to making workaday muskets known as *jazails*. This pistol has a "Damascus" barrel, formed by a process of pattern-welding in which spirally welded tubes were made from specially prepared strips of iron.

Jaws to hold flint

Frizzen

Smoothbore barrel

Brass-plated butt

▲ SEA SERVICE PISTOL

Date c.1790

Origin England

Barrel 12¾in (30cm)

Caliber .56in (14.2mm)

Introduced in 1757, this pistol is of the type used in British naval service for the rest of the 18th century. Pistols issued to sailors were normally fired only once—in the initial attack or as a last resort. The pistol's brass-plated butt could also be used as a club.

Safety catch locks frizzen in closed position

Box-lock mechanism

Frizzen

Octagonal barrel

Bayonet

▲ POCKET PISTOL

Date 1800

Origin Belgium

Barrel 4¼in (11cm)

Caliber .59in (15mm)

Short-barreled pistols replaced the sword as the gentleman's weapon of self-defense. Box-locks were preferred to side-locks—in which the cock was mounted on the side of the gun—as they were less likely to catch in the clothing. Pistols often had a bayonet, which was released by pulling back the trigger guard.

Trigger guard retains bayonet in closed position

Catch locks bayonet in open position

FLINTLOCK PISTOLS (1801–30)

By the beginning of the 19th century, the flintlock mechanism had been in use for more than two hundred years but was still the principal ignition system for firearms. Flintlocks fitted to privately purchased weapons, such as the dueling pistol on this page, had some refinements, including the addition of prawls and steadying spurs on the trigger guard, to make the gun easier to aim, but the basic principle of flint on steel remained unchanged. Armies and navies in Europe and North America continued to use flintlock pistols well into the 1830s.

Safety catch
locks pan closed

Frizzen

Pulling trigger guard
releases bayonet

▲ FLEMISH POCKET PISTOL

Date 1805

Origin Netherlands

Barrel 4¼in (10.9cm)

Caliber .52in (13.2mm)

This box-lock pocket pistol has an integral spring-loaded bayonet, operated by pulling back on the trigger guard. The catch on its lock prevented the cock from falling accidentally. This kind of safety catch had been present in some pistols since the mid-16th century. This gun's lock plate is engraved and the butt is finely carved—the work of A. Juliard, a Flemish gunmaker of repute.

Jaw-clamp
screw

Butt

Brass trigger
guard

Prawl
aids grip

▲ HARPERS FERRY MODEL 1805 PISTOL

Date 1805

Origin US

Barrel 10in (25.4cm)

Caliber .54in (13.7mm)

The Model 1805 was the first pistol manufactured at the newly established Federal Armory and Arsenal at Harpers Ferry (in modern-day West Virginia). It was robust enough to be reversed and wielded as a club if required.

PATRICK

Hair
trigger

Steadying spur
of trigger guard

▲ FLINTLOCK DUELING PISTOL

Date 1815

Origin UK

Barrel 9in (23cm)

Caliber .51in (13.1mm)

Pistols specifically designed for dueling made their first appearance in Britain after 1780. They were invariably sold as a matched pair, cased, with all the accessories necessary for their use (see pp.106–07). "Saw handle" butts with pronounced prawls and steadying spurs on the trigger guard were later additions.

Octagonal barrel

Spring-loaded bayonet

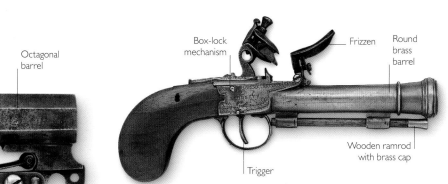

Box-lock mechanism

Frizzen

Round brass barrel

Trigger

Wooden ramrod with brass cap

◄ ITALIAN POCKET PISTOL

Date	1810
Origin	Italy
Barrel	4¾in (12.3cm)
Caliber	.85in (21.6mm)

Gunmaking flourished in post-Renaissance Italy (the English word "pistol" probably derives from Pistoia, a city famous for gun manufacture). Although the industry was in decline by the 19th century, craftsmen like Lamberti, creator of this pistol, still thrived.

Ramrod

Tower proof mark

Frizzen spring

Brass forestock cap

Brass-bound butt

▲ FRENCH HOLSTER PISTOL

Date	c.1810
Origin	France
Barrel	Not known
Caliber	Not known

Military pistols like this were often well made and robust, but because they were smoothbore, they were not accurate and had limited range. Most were intended for use in extremely close combat. Cavalry usually relied on the sword as the principal weapon, and only used pistols as a last resort.

▲ NEW LAND-PATTERN PISTOL

Date	1810
Origin	UK
Barrel	9in (23cm)
Caliber	.65in (16.5mm)

The British Army's New Land-Pattern Pistol, introduced in 1802, was a competent, sturdy design that remained in service until flintlocks gave way to percussion (see pp.80–81) in the 1840s.

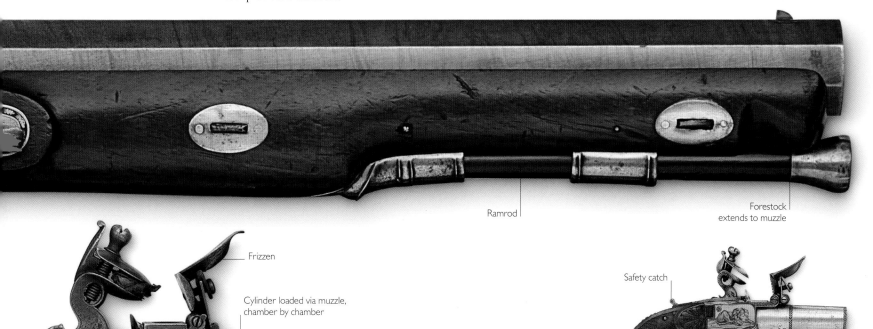

Ramrod

Forestock extends to muzzle

Frizzen

Cylinder loaded via muzzle, chamber by chamber

Safety catch

Ramrod

Butt

▲ FLINTLOCK REVOLVER

Date	c.1820
Origin	UK
Barrel	5in (12.4cm)
Caliber	.45in (11.4mm)

Around 1680, John Dafte of London designed a pistol with a revolving, multichambered cylinder that was indexed (each chamber rotated into position) manually by the cocking action. Elisha Collier of Boston gained a British patent for an improved version in 1814, and it was produced in London by John Evans in 1819. This slender pistol is less bulky than Collier's design, and was one of the many flintlock revolvers made by European gunmakers in the early 19th century.

▲ TURN-OFF POCKET PISTOL

Date	1810
Origin	France
Barrel	1½in (4cm)
Caliber	.52in (13.2mm)

Turn-off pistols were fitted with barrels that could be unscrewed, or "turned off," to reload at the breech. The screw-on barrel allowed this pistol to be loaded with a tighter-fitting ball and thus shoot both straighter and harder. Turn-off pistols were slow to reload, but their small size made them popular for self-defense.

THE FRENCH REVOLUTION
Flintlock muzzle-loaders were still common in France in the 1830s. Firing muskets produced thick, white smoke from burning gunpowder, as seen in this painting of the battle of the rue de Rohan (July 1830) in the French Revolution. At the center, a man in a top hat is priming his lock.

MUSKETS (1650–1769)

Throughout the 17th century, European armies purchased muskets mostly as complete weapons, rather than in parts from various companies that were then assembled by craftsmen. These muskets were made by commercial gunmakers working under contract to government authorities. There was little control over size, shape, and quality, which made maintaining large numbers of firearms a major logistical problem. Ammunition supply for firearms was particularly difficult if their barrels did not have bores of a regulated size. In the early 18th century, many European countries sought to overcome this problem by introducing officially approved standard muskets, manufactured to specifications that were much more strictly controlled, so that all weapons of that type, or "pattern," would be identical.

Comb of stock

Lock plate engraved with maker's name

Pan

Frizzen spring

Pivot screw

Trigger guard

Sling swivel

Cock

Comb of stock

Small of stock

TOWER

Trigger guard extension

Trigger

Rear sling swivel

Frizzen

Barrel-retaining pin holds barrel in place

Cock

Trigger

FULL VIEW

Forestock sized
to fit in the hand

Ramrod pipe

FULL VIEW

**▲ LONG LAND-PATTERN
FLINTLOCK MUSKET**

Date	1742
Origin	England
Barrel	46in (116.8cm)
Caliber	.76in (19.3mm)

The original Land-Pattern Musket, or "Brown Bess," was produced in the 1720s. This is a modified version, issued in 1742. It had a new trigger guard, a more pronounced comb to the stock, and a bridle extending from the pan to support the frizzen's pivot screw. This gun was made by Walter Tippin, a Birmingham gunmaker, and is a "sealed pattern," meaning that it was retained in the Tower of London Armoury as a model for other gunmakers producing this type of musket.

Ramrod pipe

Wooden ramrod

FULL VIEW

Front
sling swivel

▲ BRITISH MUSKET

Date	1750s
Origin	UK
Barrel	44in (111.7cm)
Caliber	.80in (20.3mm)

This musket has the furniture (parts such as butt plate, trigger guard, and ramrod pipe) of a Land-Pattern musket. It may have been produced for naval service rather than use on the battlefield, as sea service muskets were usually plainer and simpler than those used by infantry.

Iron barrel

Front sling swivel

Discharger cup for
launching grenade

▲ SEA-SERVICE MUSKET

Date	Mid-18th century
Origin	England
Barrel	37in (94cm)
Caliber	.75in (19mm)

This Sea Service flintlock is equipped with a discharger cup on the end of the muzzle. Developed in the mid-18th century, the discharger was used for firing cast-iron grenades and was an ideal weapon for close-range boarding actions.

MUSKETS (1770–1830)

In the later years of the 18th century, greater uniformity in shape, size, and bore diameter of muskets had evolved following the introduction of standard patterns of military musket. Most European countries adopted a robust and often handsome form of this weapon that formed the principal firearm for infantry. Some countries, such as Britain, favored a form of construction in which the barrel was held in place on the stock of the gun by iron pins, but many preferred the use of barrel bands, which made removal and reinstallation of the barrel much easier.

▶ AMERICAN MUSKET

Date	1770
Origin	US
Barrel	45in (114.3cm)
Caliber	.80in (20.3mm)

While the rifle is often seen as the archetypal American firearm of the American Revolutionary War (1775–83), many smoothbore muskets were used by American troops. Many of these, such as this one, resembled those used by British forces.

Trigger

Frizzen

Frizzen spring

Barrel-retaining pin holds barrel in place

Cock

Frizzen

Wooden butt

Wooden butt

Trigger guard

▲ AMERICAN MUSKET

Date	1770s
Origin	US
Barrel	46in (116.84cm)
Caliber	.80in (20.3mm)

In the 18th century, the US needed reliable military firearms, but supply was limited. Many were made using parts from other sources. This musket, with a butt resembling one from the 1720s, has a British lock made around 1750.

Flint clamping screw

Frizzen

Official British military ownership mark

Flint clamping screw

Small of stock is gripped in hand

Trigger guard

Brass flash guard

Frizzen

Barrel band

Cock

Frizzen spring

Muzzle

Ramrod

Ramrod pipe

Barrel band

Frizzen

Frizzen spring

Combined barrel band and forestock cap

▲ MUSKET MODEL 1795, TYPE I

Date 1795	
Origin US	
Barrel 49in (124.5cm)	
Caliber .69in (17.5mm)	

After the end of the Revolutionary War, the US adopted its own pattern of musket, based very closely on the French Charleville Model of 1763/66. This is the first type of the new pattern of US musket produced at Springfield Armory (see pp.62–63). During its service life, this musket underwent several internal mechanical modifications.

▲ MUSKET MODEL 1795, TYPE II

Date 1799	
Origin US	
Barrel 46¾in (119cm)	
Caliber .69in (17.5mm)	

This is a modification of the Type I musket. Examples of the Type I and II muskets were carried by members of the Lewis and Clark Expedition of 1804–06. They were also in general issue to US troops during the War of 1812, between the US and Britain. Built originally at Springfield Armory, Massachusetts, this musket was later also produced at Harpers Ferry (in modern-day West Virginia).

Foresight

Ramrod pipe

Ramrod

▼ INDIA-PATTERN MUSKET

Date 1797 onward	
Origin UK	
Barrel 39in (99cm)	
Caliber .75in (19mm)	

Before the outbreak of war with France in 1793, Britain had been planning a new pattern of musket, but this was not yet in production. To overcome a shortage of weapons, Britain bought British East India Company muskets as an emergency measure. These saw service throughout the Napoleonic Wars (1803–15).

FULL VIEW

Barrel-retaining pin

Front sling swivel

Combined barrel band and forestock cap has a trumpet-shaped pipe that allows the user to house the ramrod easily in the stock

Ramrod

▲ AUSTRIAN MODEL 1798 MUSKET

Date 1798	
Origin Austria	
Barrel 45in (114.3cm)	
Caliber .65in (16.5mm)	

When Emperor Leopold of Austria and King Frederick William of Prussia declared their intention to restore Louis XVI of France to his throne in 1791, Austria found itself outgunned by the French. Eventually, Austria commissioned a new musket, a copy of the French Model 1777, but with some improvements, notably in the way the ramrod could be housed easily in the stock.

Bayonet socket

Retaining notch

Triangular stabbing blade

Front sling swivel

Combined barrel band and forestock cap

◄ SPANISH MUSKET

Date c.1800	
Origin Spain	
Barrel 43½in (110.5cm)	
Caliber .72in (18.3mm)	

This musket resembles French patterns, but it is one of very few muskets of the time that has a flash guard. The guard is a metal (in this case, brass) disk fixed to the end of the pan. When a soldier fired a musket, a jet of hot gas from the exploding main charge shot out sideways from the touchhole. The flash guard helped to deflect this jet of gas upward, preventing it from hitting a neighboring soldier in the face.

FLINTLOCK RIFLES, CARBINES, AND SHOTGUNS (1650–1760)

Rifles had greater accuracy than smoothbore weapons and were used successfully in hunting. This spurred their military use, in which specialized marksmen, or "sharpshooters," could select and eliminate a particular target. A carbine was usually a lighter version of a military musket, or later, rifle, often of smaller caliber and shorter barrel. Some were specially developed for cavalry, or other troops where a lighter, handier weapon was an advantage.

Cock

Notch on cock

Dog-catch engages with notch on cock to prevent accidental firing

Trigger

Cock

Frizzen

Revolving chambers

Stock inlaid with silver

▲ FLINTLOCK REVOLVING SPORTING GUN

Date c.1670

Origin France

Barrel 31¼in (79.5cm)

Caliber .59in (15.1mm)

French gunmakers produced some of the finest sporting guns of the 17th century. This rifle has three revolving chambers, each equipped with its own striker and spring. All revolvers, and other multibarrel guns, of the muzzle-loading type were at risk from a dangerous chain reaction, in which firing one chamber could accidentally set off all the others.

Butt is bound with brass

Small of stock is gripped in hand

Cock

Frizzen

Forestock

Cock

Butt plate

Frizzen spring

Trigger guard

▼ PRUSSIAN RIFLED FLINTLOCK CARBINE

Date 1722

Origin Prussia

Barrel 37in (94cm)

Caliber .66in (16.7mm)

This carbine was manufactured until 1774 at the Prussian state arsenal at Potsdam (in modern-day Germany). The name of the armory is engraved on the lock plate.

Barrel band is cut partially at the top to act as rear sight

Ramrod

Small of stock is gripped in hand

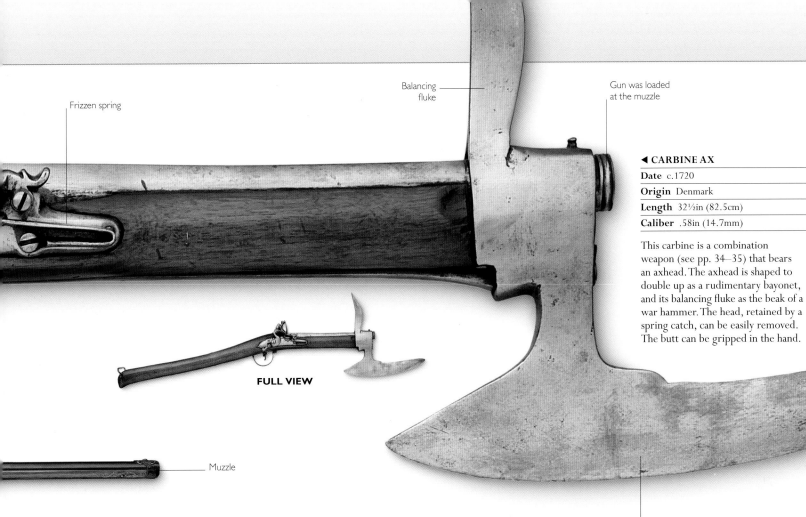

Frizzen spring

Balancing fluke

Gun was loaded at the muzzle

◄ CARBINE AX

Date c.1720

Origin Denmark

Length 32½in (82.5cm)

Caliber .58in (14.7mm)

This carbine is a combination weapon (see pp. 34–35) that bears an axhead. The axhead is shaped to double up as a rudimentary bayonet, and its balancing fluke as the beak of a war hammer. The head, retained by a spring catch, can be easily removed. The butt can be gripped in the hand.

FULL VIEW

Muzzle

Axhead serves as a stabbing bayonet

▼ LIGHT DRAGOON FLINTLOCK CARBINE

Date 1756

Origin England

Barrel 36in (91.4cm)

Caliber .66in (16.7mm)

British dragoons carried this carbine during the Seven Years' War (1756–63). It was a scaled-down version of the Long Land-Pattern musket (see pp.52–53), with a shorter barrel and in a smaller caliber.

Foresight

Ramrod pipe

Ramrod

◄ PENNSYLVANIA RIFLE

Date 1760

Origin Colonial America

Barrel 45in (114cm)

Caliber .45in (11.4mm)

This flintlock weapon is an ancestor of the celebrated Kentucky long rifle (see p.97) of later American frontiersmen. In trained hands, it was accurate at up to 1,200ft (365m). The long, rifled barrel made it far more accurate than the muskets used by European armies.

Maker's name is inscribed

Barrel-retaining pin

Blade-shaped foresight

Cocking levers

Ramrod

▲ FLINTLOCK DOUBLE-BARRELED GUN

Date c.1760

Origin France

Barrel 32in (81.3cm)

Caliber .59in (15.1mm)

This unusual double-barreled shotgun bears the name of its maker, Bouillet of Paris. The firing mechanism, including the flint, is concealed in a box to try to make it waterproof. The two levers in front of the trigger guard cocked the piece ready for discharging the barrels.

FLINTLOCK RIFLES, CARBINES, AND BLUNDERBUSSES (1761–1830)

During the 18th century, rifled weapons first made their mark on the battlefield. Military rifles were not only accurate, they also allowed soldiers to fire at long-range targets. However, muskets and carbines, all smoothbore weapons at the time, continued to be the most common firearms in most armies, with rifles still being supplied only to elite sharpshooter companies. Blunderbusses, which fired lead shot that spread out over a wide area in just a short distance, provided an excellent weapon for self-defense. In Europe, these were often carried by guards on mail coaches.

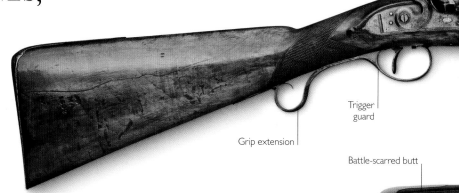

Trigger guard

Grip extension

Battle-scarred butt

▲ ENGLISH FLINTLOCK RIFLE

Date	1791
Origin	England
Barrel	32in (81cm)
Caliber	.68in (17.3mm)

Innovative London gunsmith Henry Nock made several volley guns (see p.83) for the Royal Navy and numbered Ezekiel Baker (see pp.60–61) among his apprentices. Nock designed this flintlock rifle—possibly an officer's private purchase—with nine-groove rifling.

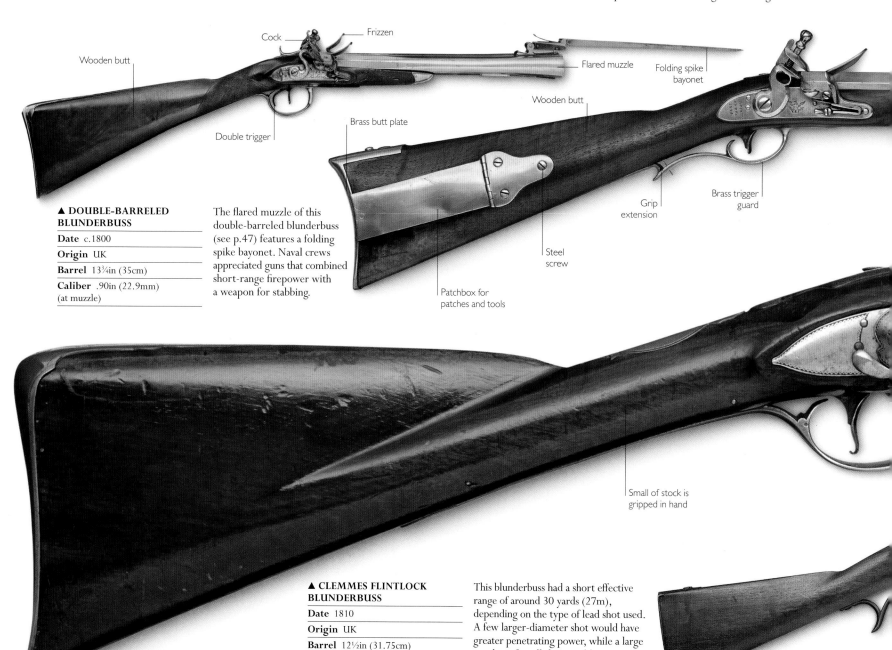

Cock

Frizzen

Wooden butt

Double trigger

Flared muzzle

Folding spike bayonet

Wooden butt

Brass butt plate

Grip extension

Brass trigger guard

Steel screw

Patchbox for patches and tools

▲ DOUBLE-BARRELED BLUNDERBUSS

Date	c.1800
Origin	UK
Barrel	13¼in (35cm)
Caliber	.90in (22.9mm) (at muzzle)

The flared muzzle of this double-barreled blunderbuss (see p.47) features a folding spike bayonet. Naval crews appreciated guns that combined short-range firepower with a weapon for stabbing.

Small of stock is gripped in hand

▲ CLEMMES FLINTLOCK BLUNDERBUSS

Date	1810
Origin	UK
Barrel	12½in (31.75cm)
Caliber	1.2in (30.5mm) (at muzzle)

This blunderbuss had a short effective range of around 30 yards (27m), depending on the type of lead shot used. A few larger-diameter shot would have greater penetrating power, while a large number of small shot would cover a target area more completely, leaving fewer chances of missing the target.

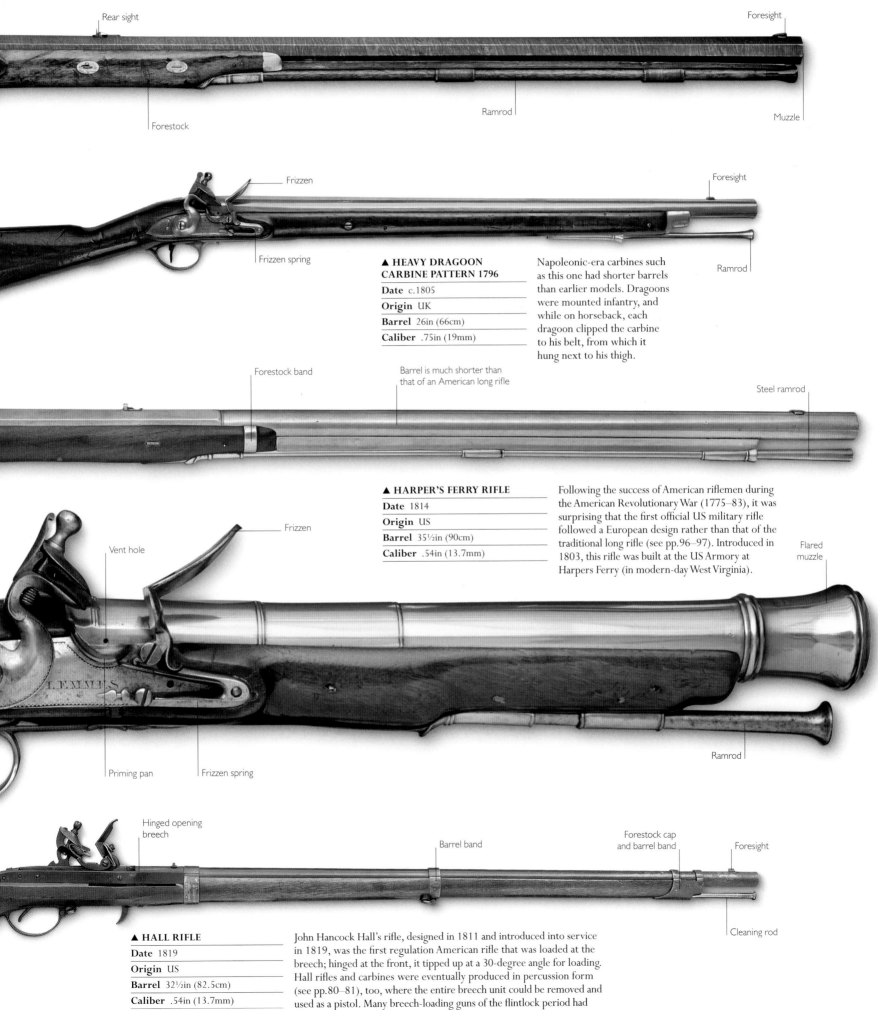

Rear sight

Foresight

Forestock

Ramrod

Muzzle

Frizzen

Foresight

Frizzen spring

Ramrod

▲ HEAVY DRAGOON CARBINE PATTERN 1796

Date	c.1805
Origin	UK
Barrel	26in (66cm)
Caliber	.75in (19mm)

Napoleonic-era carbines such as this one had shorter barrels than earlier models. Dragoons were mounted infantry, and while on horseback, each dragoon clipped the carbine to his belt, from which it hung next to his thigh.

Forestock band

Barrel is much shorter than that of an American long rifle

Steel ramrod

Frizzen

Vent hole

▲ HARPER'S FERRY RIFLE

Date	1814
Origin	US
Barrel	35½in (90cm)
Caliber	.54in (13.7mm)

Following the success of American riflemen during the American Revolutionary War (1775–83), it was surprising that the first official US military rifle followed a European design rather than that of the traditional long rifle (see pp.96–97). Introduced in 1803, this rifle was built at the US Armory at Harpers Ferry (in modern-day West Virginia).

Flared muzzle

Priming pan

Frizzen spring

Ramrod

Hinged opening breech

Barrel band

Forestock cap and barrel band

Foresight

▲ HALL RIFLE

Date	1819
Origin	US
Barrel	32½in (82.5cm)
Caliber	.54in (13.7mm)

John Hancock Hall's rifle, designed in 1811 and introduced into service in 1819, was the first regulation American rifle that was loaded at the breech; hinged at the front, it tipped up at a 30-degree angle for loading. Hall rifles and carbines were eventually produced in percussion form (see pp.80–81), too, where the entire breech unit could be removed and used as a pistol. Many breech-loading guns of the flintlock period had cleaning rods instead of the ramrods seen in muzzle-loaders.

Cleaning rod

SHOWCASE

BAKER RIFLE

In February 1800, the Baker rifle won a competition organized by the British Army's Board of Ordnance and became the first rifle officially adopted by the British Army. Its novel feature lay in its barrel. With shallow or "slow" rifling—in which the grooves turn by just a quarter along the length of the barrel—it stayed clean, and thus usable, for longer. The Baker rifle was issued to select men at first, and remained in service for more than 35 years.

BAKER RIFLE	
Date	1802–37
Origin	England
Barrel	30in (76cm)
Caliber	.62in (15.8mm)

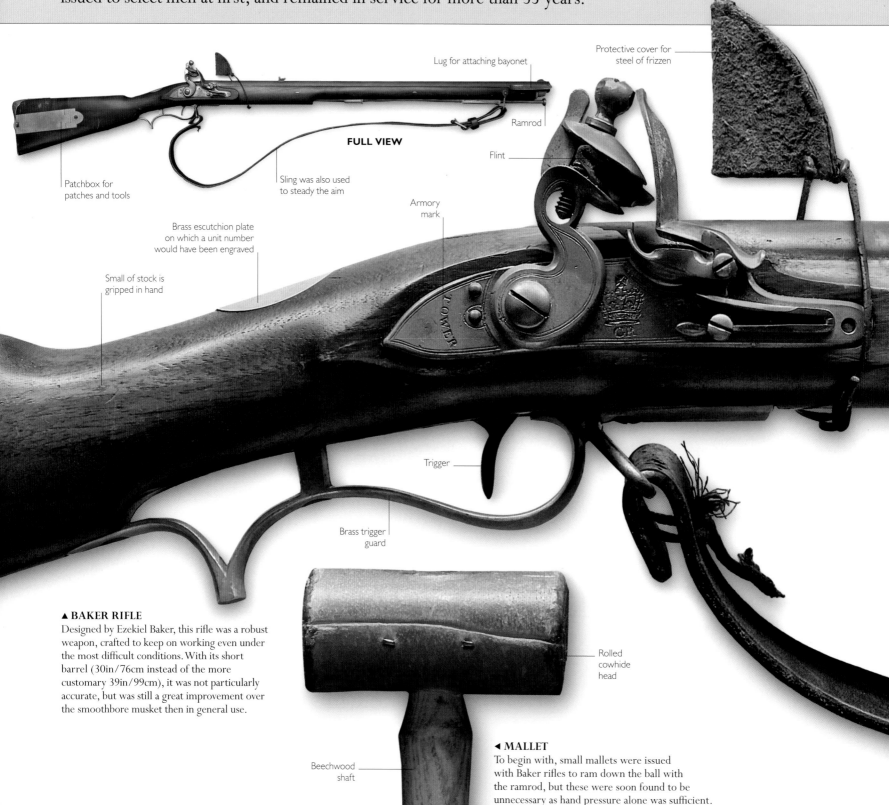

Lug for attaching bayonet

Protective cover for steel of frizzen

Ramrod

FULL VIEW

Flint

Patchbox for patches and tools

Sling was also used to steady the aim

Armory mark

Brass escutchion plate on which a unit number would have been engraved

Small of stock is gripped in hand

Trigger

Brass trigger guard

Rolled cowhide head

▲ **BAKER RIFLE**
Designed by Ezekiel Baker, this rifle was a robust weapon, crafted to keep on working even under the most difficult conditions. With its short barrel (30in/76cm instead of the more customary 39in/99cm), it was not particularly accurate, but was still a great improvement over the smoothbore musket then in general use.

Beechwood shaft

◀ **MALLET**
To begin with, small mallets were issued with Baker rifles to ram down the ball with the ramrod, but these were soon found to be unnecessary as hand pressure alone was sufficient.

Guard-retaining screw

Brass grip

Armory stamp

Release
stud

**Hand
guard**

▲ SWORD BAYONET
The Baker rifle was supplied with
a sword bayonet that could be used
alone or mounted on the rifle. At 24in
(61cm) long, it was unwieldy, but it
was necessary to compensate for the
rifle being so much shorter than other
weapons then in use.

FULL VIEW

Single-edged,
straight blade
for hacking
and thrusting

300-yard (274-m) sight

200-yard (183-m) sight

Ramrod pipe

Large head to
help a user ram
in a tight-fitting ball

▲ RAMROD
The steel rod was used
to ram the charge and
projectile into the barrel.

Gunpowder
wrapped in paper

Lead ball
wrapped in paper

Leather sling

▲ PAPER-WRAPPED CARTRIDGE
Each cartridge contained a charge of powder and the ball.
It was torn open with the teeth, with the ball held in the
mouth. A small portion of the charge was poured into the
primer pan and the rest down the muzzle. The paper would
then be rammed down to form a wad, and the ball, wrapped
in a patch taken from the patchbox, rammed down on top.

GREAT GUNSMITHS

SPRINGFIELD ARMORY

The Springfield Armory was the most important manufacturer of military firearms in the US between 1794 and 1968. Established in 1777 as the country's key weapons store during the Revolutionary War, the Armory became famous for pioneering the kind of mass-production techniques that allowed precision-engineered products to be built in large numbers. Led by Roswell Lee between 1815 and 1833, the armoury's mechanized production techniques had a huge impact, not only on the firearms business but also on American industry as a whole.

ROSWELL LEE

George Washington himself recommended Springfield, Massachusetts, as the location for an arsenal. He appreciated the high, defensible site near the Connecticut River, and the proximity of the river and roads was convenient for transportation. In 1777, the arsenal was founded to store a range of ammunition and arms. When the move was made to weapons manufacture in the 1790s, there was an expansion to lower-lying land to the south and west, near water that could provide a source of power. Here a foundry and workshops were built, beginning a tradition of firearms manufacturing in the area.

AN INDUSTRIAL PIONEER

In 1794, the Springfield Armory began to manufacture firearms, starting with muskets. As a major arms producer it made weapons for the US forces in the War of 1812, for Union troops during the American Civil War (1861–65), and in the Spanish–American War (1898). The Armory became a center for innovation as engineers and craft workers found ways of making better weapons and improving the efficiency of the production process. Some of these developments were groundbreaking, placing the Armory at the forefront of the Industrial Revolution. For

▼ BLANCHARD'S "LATHE"

This lathe, or shaper, invented by Thomas Blanchard, was a key development in the history of gunmaking. Installed at the Springfield Armory in the early 1820s, the lathe allowed the duplication of the irregular shapes of wooden stocks. Although the shaper shown is no longer in use, this technology is still used in some parts of the world.

example, in 1819, inventor Thomas Blanchard devised a machine on which workers could produce rifle stocks. Blanchard's machine, usually known as a lathe, was strictly a shaper, working in a way similar to a modern key-cutting machine in which an original shape is copied on to a stock blank. It enabled gun stocks to be mass-produced for the first time. Springfield also pioneered the

production of guns using interchangeable parts (a field also developed by Samuel Colt and many others), allowing firearms to be assembled at speed and repaired with ease. This method of production not only relied on new machinery but also depended on the division of labor, with separate workshops for different parts of the production process, precise measuring and gauging of components, and good quality control. By the time of the Civil War, the Armory was using state-of-the-art machines for milling, turning, grinding, and shaping, some driven by water, others by newly installed steam engines. These technological advances were accompanied by up-to-date management and accounting methods, introduced by Colonel Roswell Lee, who became superintendent of the Armory in 1815.

VOLUME PRODUCTION

The Armory's production facility was adaptable, producing a range of muzzle-loading weapons. In the 1840s, the Armory achieved the goal of producing firearms with interchangeable parts, and was able to build guns in large numbers during many conflicts of the 19th century. From about 85,000 Charleville Pattern smoothbore muskets (without interchangeable parts) produced between 1795 and 1815, the Armory's volume of production jumped to 800,000 Springfield Model 1861 rifled muskets (with interchangeable parts) during the Civil War. The techniques of mass production developed at Springfield during the 19th century made the Armory well placed to produce firearms in the huge numbers needed for major 20th-century conflicts. New improvements, such as the arrival of electrical power, also helped the Armory in this respect.

The early 20th century saw the production of bolt-action repeating rifles, including the

MODEL 1863 TYPE II MUSKET

MODEL 1873 TRAPDOOR RIFLE

M1 GARAND RIFLE

1777 The Springfield Arsenal is founded. As a store for weapons and ammunition, it plays a key role in the Revolutionary War.

1787 Daniel Shays and a group of rebels attempt to capture the arsenal in protest against unfair taxation and the debt collection practices of the Massachusetts state government, but are repelled by the state militia.

1795 Weapons production at the Armory begins with the Springfield "Charleville Pattern" Musket.

1815 Roswell Lee becomes superintendent of the Armory and leads efforts to mechanize production and improve management.

1863 The Model 1863 Type II is the last muzzle-loading long gun produced by the Armory.

1873 The US Army adopts the breech-loading Model 1873 "Trapdoor" rifle.

1936 The semiautomatic M1 Garand rifle is launched. It becomes the first general issue self-loading rifle to be accepted for military service in the US.

1968 Springfield Armory is closed; its buildings are preserved as the Springfield Armory National Historic Site.

Krag rifle, designed in Norway, and the Model 1903, which was designed in Springfield. The retooling and adaptation required to produce these new weapons was a challenge, but thanks to machine upgrades and a reorganization of the workforce, they were successfully put into production and demonstrated that the Armory could build quality firearms en masse. The Armory's Model 1903 was used in both world wars. It was followed by a new generation of semiautomatic firearms, including the famed Garand rifle of 1936, which made US infantrymen much better equipped than those in other parts of the world who were issued with slower bolt-action rifles. Such products kept the Armory going through the mid-20th century, until the US government decided to rely solely on private manufacturers and shut down the facility in 1968.

"It has long been considered a **privilege** to be employed at **Springfield Armory**."

G. TALCOTT, LT. COL. OF ORDNANCE, **ADDRESSING THE US SENATE, 1842**

▼ **SHARPENING CUTTERS**
A woman sharpens cutters for a milling machine at Springfield Armory in around 1943. The cutters were not only used for manufacturing rifle parts but also for building the tools used to make those parts.

EUROPEAN HUNTING GUNS

By the beginning of the 18th century, gunmakers in most parts of Europe were making sporting firearms in popular styles based originally on French designs. The flintlock now predominated in most of Europe. While a more austere style emerged, the remaining ornamentation became more sophisticated, with minimal decorative inlaying and emphasis placed on the natural qualities of the wood. The flintlock mechanism in these guns had become efficient enough that sportsmen could shoot not only stationary targets but also birds in flight. A breakthrough invention in this period was a repeating breech-loading flintlock gun.

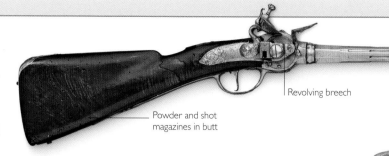

Revolving breech

Powder and shot magazines in butt

▲ ITALIAN REPEATING FLINTLOCK

Date	c.1690
Origin	Italy
Barrel	35in (89cm)
Caliber	.53in (13.5mm)

Italian gunmaker Michele Lorenzoni lived in Florence from 1683 to 1733 and invented an early form of repeating flintlock breech-loader. Paired magazines, one for powder and the other for shot, were located in the butt, and the breechblock was rotated for charging by means of a lever on the left side of the gun.

Barrel band

Cock

Ornate pierced brass barrel band

Lock plate

▲ FLINTLOCK SPORTING GUN

Date	1700
Origin	England
Barrel	55in (139.5cm)
Caliber	.75in (19mm)

This full-stocked sporting gun, by John Shaw, bears a remarkable resemblance to military firearms of the time. However, the attention that has been paid to the selection of the wood for its stock immediately sets it apart, as does the care that has been lavished on its finishing.

▲ ENGLISH SPORTING GUN

Date	1760
Origin	England
Barrel	36in (91.4cm)
Caliber	.68in (17.3mm)

The gunmaker Benjamin Griffin worked in fashionable Bond Street in London from 1735 to 1770, and was joined in 1750 by his son Joseph. Both father and son were renowned for their excellent pistols and long guns. Many of these, such as the example seen here, were graced with ornate engraving to the metal parts, decorative brasswork, and silver-wire inlay.

Jaw clamp screw

Frizzen

Cock

Pan

Silver-wire inlay

FULL VIEW

▲ ENGLISH FLINTLOCK SPORTING GUN

Date	1690
Origin	England
Barrel	38in (96.5cm)
Caliber	.75in (19mm)

Walnut stock

Andrew Dolep was a Dutch gunmaker who settled in London and set up shop near Charing Cross. He produced this magnificent flintlock—its walnut stock extensively inlaid with silver wire—toward the end of his career. Dolep is credited with the design of the "Brown Bess" musket (see p.53), which this gun resembles.

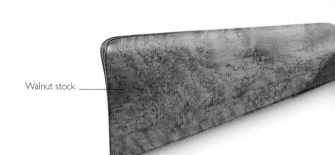

Walnut stock

Muzzle

Barrel lacks forestock

Foresight

Cock

Frizzen

Small of stock is gripped in hand

Ramrod pipe

Ramrod

Jaw clamp screw

Gold-plated pan

Silver-mounted forestock cap

Ramrod

Silver-mounted trigger guard

Abbreviated forestock

Trigger for firing left barrel

Trigger for firing right barrel

Forestock

Ramrod pipe

Frizzen spring

External mainspring

Trigger guard

Ramrod

Rear sling swivel

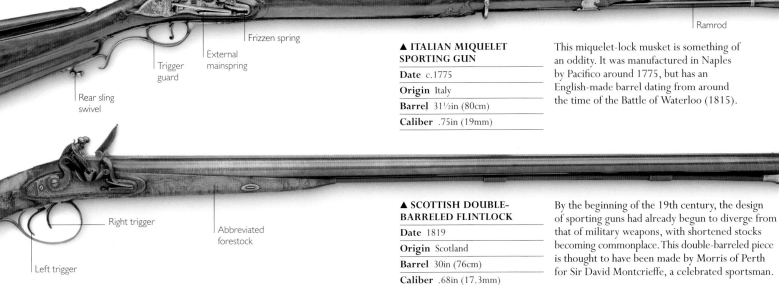

Right trigger

Abbreviated forestock

Left trigger

▲ RUSSIAN FLINTLOCK

Date	1770
Origin	Russia
Barrel	35in (89.8cm)
Caliber	.35in (8.9mm)

This beautifully decorated sporting gun was made by Ivan Permjakov, one of the most accomplished Russian gunmakers. It may have been recovered after the Battle of Alma River in 1854, during the Crimean War. Perhaps it was lost from the gear of one of the officers in the Russian force.

▲ DOUBLE-BARRELED FLINTLOCK SHOTGUN

Date	c.1770
Origin	England
Barrel	35½in (90.2cm)
Caliber	.60in (15.2mm)

This side-by-side double-barreled flintlock shotgun, attributed to the gunmaker Hadley, is typical of high-class fowling pieces of the latter part of the 18th century. Not only is its short stock silver mounted, but both its pans and its touchholes are gold-plated to fend off corrosion.

▲ ITALIAN MIQUELET SPORTING GUN

Date	c.1775
Origin	Italy
Barrel	31½in (80cm)
Caliber	.75in (19mm)

This miquelet-lock musket is something of an oddity. It was manufactured in Naples by Pacifico around 1775, but has an English-made barrel dating from around the time of the Battle of Waterloo (1815).

▲ SCOTTISH DOUBLE-BARRELED FLINTLOCK

Date	1819
Origin	Scotland
Barrel	30in (76cm)
Caliber	.68in (17.3mm)

By the beginning of the 19th century, the design of sporting guns had already begun to diverge from that of military weapons, with shortened stocks becoming commonplace. This double-barreled piece is thought to have been made by Morris of Perth for Sir David Montcrieffe, a celebrated sportsman.

FIELD AND SIEGE ARTILLERY (1650–1780)

Different types of artillery had become well-established by the mid-17th century. Field artillery was portable, and was towed into battle alongside infantry and cavalry. These guns were known as 6-, 9-, and 12-pounders, referring to the weight of the iron balls they fired. Siege artillery was composed of 18-pounders and even heavier guns, designed to break down fortifications. Mortars, short-barreled guns set at a high angle of elevation for use during sieges, had also been developed. Most large cannons were muzzle-loading. Cannon made of wrought iron were rarely being built, as guns could now be made more cheaply and quickly from cast iron, which had recently been perfected.

▲ INDIAN 6-POUNDER

Date	1693–1743
Origin	India
Length	12½ft (3.86m)
Caliber	3.74in (95mm)

Like many artillery pieces of the time, this gun is described by the weight of its ammunition—6-lb (2.72-kg) iron balls. The caliber of such weapons is based on the diameter of the shot they fired. The 6-pounder's cast bronze barrel has a bore lined with strips of iron, to make it more durable.

Decoration molded in relief

Cascabel to secure cannon with ropes for managing recoil when it is fired

▲ SINHALESE BRONZE GUN

Date	1699
Origin	Ceylon (modern-day Sri Lanka)
Length	4ft (1.19m)
Caliber	2.1in (53.3mm)

This small field gun is decorated with bands of stylized foliage and has the badge of the Dutch East India Company. The name Jaffanapatnam (a town in northern Ceylon) is written around the breech.

Highly ornate cast barrel

Relief decoration includes scrolls

Third barrel sits on top of the other two

Trunnion

▲ BRONZE THREE-BARRELED GUN

Date	1704
Origin	France
Length	5¼ft (1.62m)
Caliber	.04in (1.15mm)

Three barrels, two side by side with the third above, were cast in one piece and could be fired one at a time or simultaneously. The intriguing design did not prove successful in practice, because this field gun was difficult to reload and very heavy to maneuver.

Spokes carved as flames from the Sun

Monogram of King George I

Wooden bed

◀ COEHORN MORTAR

Date	c.1720
Origin	England
Length	1ft (0.32m)
Caliber	4.5in (114.3mm)

The Coehorn Mortar was a small, portable mortar used to despatch grenades. Swiss-born Andrew Schalch, first Master Founder of the Royal Brass Foundry at Woolwich in England, cast this one. It is mounted on its original wooden bed, which is just 12in (30cm) wide and 20in (51cm) long.

Studded iron tires

Panel of floral decoration

Barrel supported at set elevation

Derrick used to lift heavy shell and lower it into muzzle

Astragals (decorative moldings)

Wooden bed

▶ BRONZE 13-IN SEA SERVICE MORTAR

Date 1726

Origin UK

Length 5¼ft (1.6m)

Caliber 13in (330mm)

Mortars could be fired over the walls of fortifications to cause large-scale destruction, or into enemy troop formations to injure many soldiers at once. Sea service mortars were used to bombard fortifications on shore.

Trunnion

▶ MODEL BRITISH MORTAR

Date 1760

Origin England

Length (model) 2½ft (0.7m)

Caliber 13in (330mm)

This detailed model of a mortar was used in military training academies to instruct artillerymen on the correct use of such guns. It shows how the barrel on such pieces would be placed at a high angle (usually 45 degrees). The cast iron shell could be loaded by using a small derrick (a lifting device) to hoist it and place it into the muzzle.

Brass bed of model (original gun had an iron or wooden bed)

Lifting ring

Trail placed on the ground for balance

▲ BRONZE CANNON (FALCON) AND CARRIAGE

Date 1773

Origin Rome

Length Not known

Caliber Not known

This exceptionally fine field gun and ornate carriage was made for Francisco Ximenez de Texado, Grand Master of the Order of St. John of Jerusalem. The barrel was modeled by Filippo Lattarelli, of Rome, on a mold by the earlier master gun-founder Orazio Antonio Alberghetti.

FIELD AND SIEGE ARTILLERY (1781–1830)

In the 17th century, many gunmakers in Europe decided to make muzzle-loading guns rather than breech-loaders, as improvements in gunpowder made it more difficult to build breech-loading guns that could withstand the pressure of firing. As a result, by the 18th century, almost all types of large-caliber artillery was muzzle-loading. Deployed on battlefields, field artillery fired solid shot, explosive shells, or canister shot (shot made of smaller balls). Siege artillery was employed for consistent bombardment of fortifications and fired larger types of shot and shell from prepared emplacements.

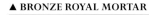

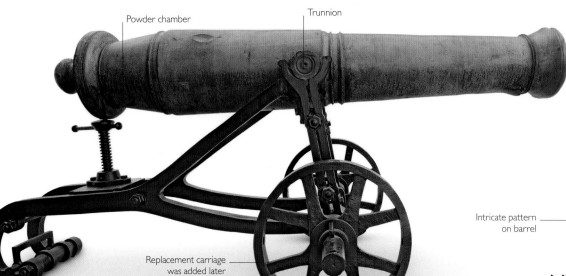

Powder chamber

Trunnion

Replacement carriage was added later

▲ BRONZE ROYAL MORTAR

Date	1800
Origin	England
Length	1¼ft (0.39m)
Caliber	5.7in (144.8mm)
Range	800 yards (730m)

A standard mortar in British field service, this weapon was cast at the Woolwich Royal Brass foundry. It fired a spherical, cast iron explosive shell at a high angle. Although transported by cart, it was placed on the ground during firing.

Intricate pattern on barrel

▲ RUSSIAN LICORNE

Date	1793
Origin	Russia
Length	9ft (2.8m)
Caliber	8.07in (205mm)
Range	1,800 yards (1.6km)

This gun, which saw action in the Crimean War (1853–56), could fire horizontally or at an elevated trajectory. It carried gunpowder in a powder chamber shaped like a cone. It could shoot spherical explosive shells as well as cannonballs.

▶ INDIAN BRONZE FIELD GUN

Date	1800
Origin	India
Length	6ft (1.8m)
Caliber	3.9in (99mm)
Range	1,600 yards (1.4km)

This finely decorated barrel was cast in the late 18th century and later fitted to its handsome carriage. It was captured by British forces from Maharaja Ranjit Singh of Punjab (a kingdom that spanned regions in modern-day India and Pakistan) during the first Anglo-Sikh War, which was fought in 1845–46.

Barrel shows battle scarring

▶ FRENCH 12-POUNDER FIELD GUN

Date	1794
Origin	France
Length	6¾ft (2.1m)
Caliber	4.8in (122mm)
Range	2,000 yards (1.8km)

This 12-pounder was named "Voltaire" after the French Enlightenment philosopher François-Marie Arouet de Voltaire (1694–1778), whose name is engraved into the forward part of the gun's barrel. The barrel exhibits battle damage, possibly caused by British guns at the Battle of Waterloo (1815).

Original carriage has been rebuilt

Muzzle

Carriage wheel

▲ FRENCH 6-POUNDER FIELD GUN

Date 1813

Origin France

Length 5½ft (1.68m)

Caliber 3.78in (96mm)

Range 1,600 yards (1.4km)

This field gun could fire two rounds a minute. Its carriage is marked "taken at Waterloo." It fired 6-lb (2.72-kg) iron balls.

▼ CHINESE SILK GUN

Date c.1825

Origin China

Length 2¾ft (0.83m)

Caliber 2.5in (63.5mm)

Range 200 yards (180m)

This unusual cannon, designed for portability, was made from a copper tube wrapped with iron wire and silk cord. It derived from some earlier guns which were made from bamboo wound with cord. Chinese paintings show soldiers lying on the battlefield firing similar guns.

Breech

Touchhole

Carrying handles

Muzzle

Trunnion

Muzzle

Wrought and cast iron garrison carriage

▲ CHINESE 18-POUNDER

Date 1830

Origin China

Length 10½ft (3.2m)

Caliber 5.25in (133.4mm)

Range 2,000 yards (1.8km)

This 18-pounder has inscriptions on top of its breech. It is mounted on a Russian wrought and cast iron carriage, which dates to 1853.

Carriage wheel

Trail

NAVAL GUNS

Although most artillery pieces were muzzle-loading by the 18th century, some naval guns continued to be breech-loading. In naval warfare, different types of gun could be useful in different situations, so special pieces of artillery were developed. For longer ranges, conventional cannon were used, mounted on carriages with wooden wheels, or "trucks," while for close-in attacks, a short-barreled type of gun called a carronade was very effective. Sometimes known as the "smasher," the carronade was built in different sizes and could fire solid shot or explosive shells with great power, although it did not have great range. Mortars could be used to attack ships, but were more often used to shell defenses or troops on shore.

▲ BRONZE BREECH-LOADING SWIVEL GUN

Date c.1670

Origin Netherlands

Length 4ft (1.22m)

Caliber 2.91in (74mm)

This swivel gun was owned by the Dutch East India Company and was most probably used as an antipersonnel weapon.

Reinforce ring

Muzzle

▶ FOUR-POUNDER SWIVEL GUN

Date 1778

Origin Scotland

Length 1ft (0.32m)

Caliber 3.30in (84mm)

This short, heavy swivel gun was one of the prototypes for the carronade made by the Carron Ironworks. Its trunnions—used to elevate and lower the gun—are equipped with pivots, and the cascabel—used to secure the gun against recoil—is connected to a long, curved tiller for directing the gun.

Carrying handles

▼ BRITISH 13-IN MORTAR

Date 1726

Origin England

Length 5½ft (1.6m)

Caliber 13in (330mm)

The reinforce ring of this sea service mortar shows the royal arms of the British king George II. The mortar may have been made for HMS *Thunder*, which saw action at the Siege of Gibraltar in 1727.

Replacement bed for land service, 8½ft (2.64m) long

Reinforce ring

Trunnion inscription reads "Carron 1778"

Slots for wedge to secure breech chamber

Trigger

Wooden butt

Iron swivel post

▲ **FLINTLOCK SWIVEL GUN**

Date c.1800

Origin UK

Barrel 2ft (0.61m)

Caliber 1.10in (28mm)

Fired with a flintlock mechanism more common on muskets or pistols, this swivel gun was fired at enemy ships prior to a boarding attempt. Because it could be swiveled, the gun—moving from side to side—had a wide arc of fire.

Recess in muzzle ring

Raised sight

Reinforce ring

Muzzle

Gun made of iron

Platform carriage

Carriage wheel

Fluted cascabel

Tiller used to rotate gun on its swivel to direct fire

▲ **CAST-IRON CARRONADE**

Date 1808

Origin Scotland

Length 3½ft (1.1m)

Caliber 5.7in (145mm)

This 24-pounder carronade was made with a raised sight in the reinforce ring and a recess in the muzzle ring for a removable sight. The muzzle was recessed for easy loading.

ASIAN FIREARMS (1650–1780)

Firearms arrived in Japan in 1543 with Portuguese traders who had traveled from their base in India. The Japanese initially resisted the use of gunpowder weapons, preferring their traditional bows and swords, but eventually saw the advantages of a coordinated use of matchlock muskets in battle, notably at Sekigahara in 1600. Until the late 19th century, Japanese muskets retained the Portuguese snap-matchlock design, a mechanism in which the serpentine was held back by a catch and fell forward under spring pressure when a user pulled the trigger. Matchlock muskets in other parts of Asia varied in style between regions although the matchlock used was the squeeze-type (see p. 74). In India, matchlock guns had been present from as early as 1531, when the Ottomans used them against the Portuguese in the Siege of Diu.

Serpentine match-holder

Brass inlay

Serpentine match-holder

Pan

Rear sight

Butt is of the form developed in Sakai

Lock plate

Mainspring

Decorative floral washer

Trigger

Hole in butt bordered by elaborate floral washer and eight-bucket waterwheel design

Serpentine match-holder

Gold decoration

Pentagonal-section butt

Prawl

Iron side plates cover lock

Trigger

Decorated leather-and-fabric pan cover

Serpentine match-holder

Silver inlay

Butt is covered in red fabric secured by embossed silver nails

Trigger

Rest terminates in forked antelope horn

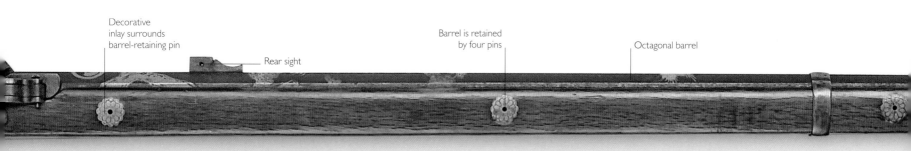

Decorative
inlay surrounds
barrel-retaining pin

Rear sight

Barrel is retained
by four pins

Octagonal barrel

FULL VIEW

▲ HI NAWA JYU

Date	Early 18th century
Origin	Japan
Barrel	40½in (103cm)
Caliber	.52in (13.3mm)

Japanese *hi nawa jyu* (matchlocks) could fire three bullets a minute and pierce typical samurai armour at 165ft (50m). This matchlock was made by Kunitomo Tobei Shigeyasu of Omi, western Japan. The influence of the Sakai school (below) is evident in its red oak stock although it has limited decoration.

Gold lacquering
over red oak

Barrel band

Lacquerwork *mon*
(family badge) is a
pine tree in a circle

Octagonal barrel

FULL VIEW

▲ HI NAWA JYU

Date	c.1700
Origin	Japan
Barrel	39¼in (100cm)
Caliber	.44in (11.4mm)

This early 18th-century matchlock musket is the work of the Enami family of Sakai, widely held to be among the finest Japanese gunmakers of the preindustrial era. The stock is made of red oak, and its decoration may have been added at a later date.

Barrel band

Decorative
gold band

▲ INDIAN CARNATIC TORADAR

Date	18th century
Origin	India
Barrel	44½in (113cm)
Caliber	.629in (16mm)

The barrel of this simple, straight-stalked matchlock musket, or toradar, is exquisitely decorated with incised flowers and foliage, and entirely gilded. Made in Mysore, southern India, the musket's incised side plates are made of iron, and on its trigger it has a tiger in *koftgari*—a method of inlaying gold into steel or iron.

FULL VIEW

Damascus barrel forged from
specially prepared strips of iron

Ramrod

▲ TIBETAN MEDA

Date	c.1780
Origin	Tibet
Barrel	43¾in (111cm)
Caliber	.66in (17mm)

Tibet was largely isolated from the rest of the world, but carried out trade with India and China. This *meda* (matchlock) shows Chinese influence in form and decoration. Attached to the forestock is an unusual rest, while the ramrod is a modern replacement.

FULL VIEW

ASIAN FIREARMS (1781–1830)

In Asia, guns remained technically simple for more than 500 years. The matchlock mechanism used, similar to that in Europe, persisted well into the late 19th century. While the snap-matchlock mechanism was used in Japan (see p.72), in India and elsewhere in Asia, gunmakers commonly employed the squeeze-type matchlock. This type of matchlock was concealed almost fully within the stock. The serpentine was linked to a trigger bar, which released it when a user pulled the trigger. In India, the guns varied between regions in the form of their stocks, and in their chiseled and gilded decoration. Matchlock pistols were made only in Asia, while people in Europe were using pistols driven by flintlocks and wheel-locks—mechanisms that would reach some parts of Asia only later and never be used in other parts.

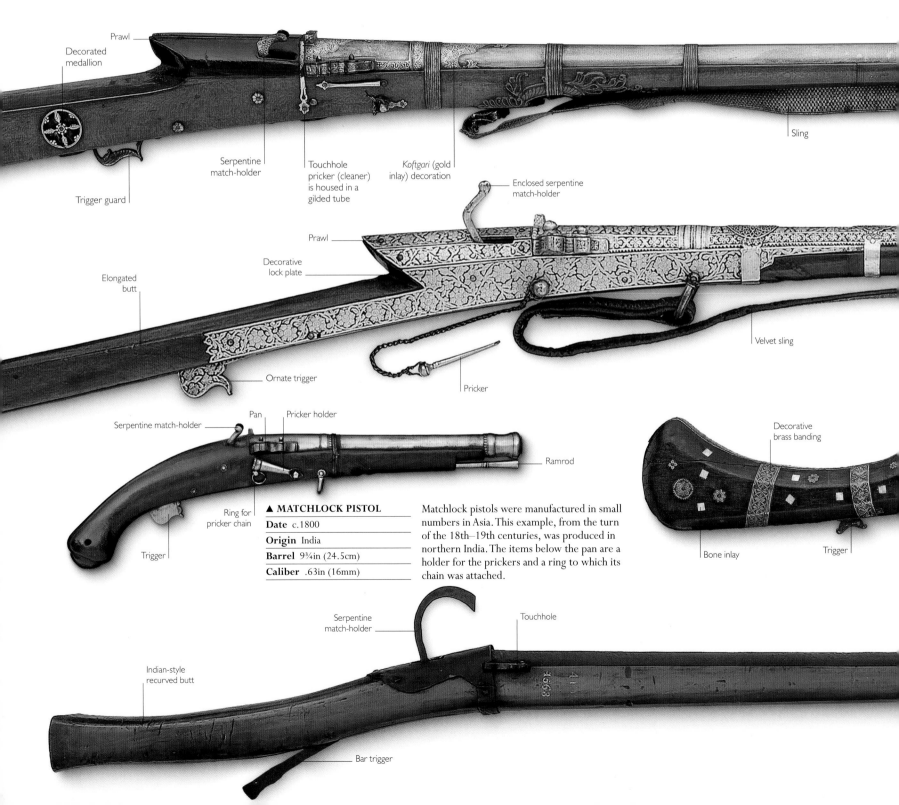

▲ MATCHLOCK PISTOL

Date	c.1800
Origin	India
Barrel	9¾in (24.5cm)
Caliber	.63in (16mm)

Matchlock pistols were manufactured in small numbers in Asia. This example, from the turn of the 18th–19th centuries, was produced in northern India. The items below the pan are a holder for the prickers and a ring to which its chain was attached.

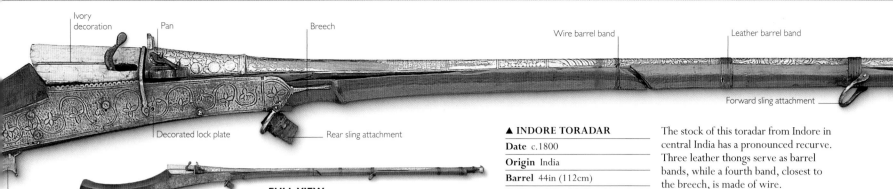

Ivory decoration
Pan
Breech
Wire barrel band
Leather barrel band
Forward sling attachment
Decorated lock plate
Rear sling attachment
Trigger

FULL VIEW

▲ INDORE TORADAR

Date c.1800

Origin India

Barrel 44in (112cm)

Caliber .55in (13.9mm)

The stock of this toradar from Indore in central India has a pronounced recurve. Three leather thongs serve as barrel bands, while a fourth band, closest to the breech, is made of wire.

Barrel bands of leather thongs

Tiger's-head muzzle

▲ INDIAN TORADAR

Date 19th century

Origin India

Barrel 49¾in (126cm)

Caliber .55in (14mm)

This toradar has a stock of polished red wood with circular pierced medallions on each side of the butt of iron, with gilding and *koftgari* applied over red velvet. The barrel has an elaborate arabesque decoration in gold *koftgari* at the breech, and the muzzle is fashioned into the shape of a tiger's head.

FULL VIEW

Gilded barrel band
Ornate barrel

FULL VIEW

▲ BUNDUKH TORADAR

Date c.1800

Origin India

Barrel 45¼in (115cm)

Caliber .55in (13.9mm)

This very ornate matchlock musket was probably made in Gwalior, central India. Like all matchlocks, it was supplied with a touchhole pricker, although since this, too, is gilded, it can hardly be considered to be entirely functional. Guns with such elongated butts were normally held beneath the arm, not against the shoulder.

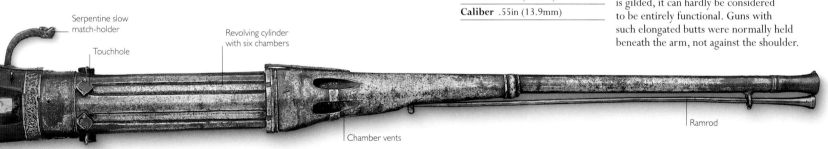

Serpentine slow match-holder
Revolving cylinder with six chambers
Touchhole
Ramrod
Chamber vents

▲ MATCHLOCK REVOLVING MUSKET

Date c.1800

Origin India

Barrel 24½in (62cm)

Caliber .60in (15.2mm)

An unusual matchlock revolving musket from Indore, central India, this gun uses a mechanical sophistication sometimes seen in European flintlocks—the use of a revolving cylinder to create a multi-shot weapon (see p.49). The chambers were rotated into position manually.

▼ CHINESE WALL GUN

Date c.1830

Origin China

Barrel 63in (160cm)

Caliber Not known

Wall guns were designed to be fired from a rest, and they were far too long and unwieldy to be used in any other way. This example is extremely simple in both design and execution, and it is completely devoid of decoration.

KYRGYZ HUNTING PARTY

In Kyrgyzstan, the nobility used matchlock guns for hunting. These arms were used widely in Central Asia well into the 20th century. Some guns, such as the one seen on the far right of this illustration from 1830, had a forked rest below the muzzle to assist aiming.

OTTOMAN FIREARMS

The military forces of the Ottoman Empire appreciated the value of muskets in warfare. At the end of the 17th century, the Ottoman Empire's occupation of large portions of southwest Europe ensured an inflow of military technology from the West. Fine examples of Ottoman snaphance, miquelet, and flintlock handguns were produced in the 18th century. Ornate decoration defines many of these pieces, with Islamic and Indian influences apparent in the use of inlaid precious metal and stones, and the sumptuous application of floral and geometric designs.

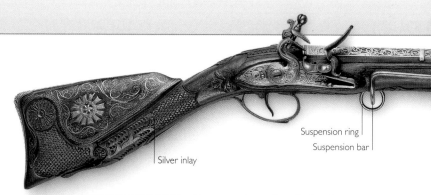

Suspension ring

Suspension bar

Silver inlay

▲ FLINTLOCK BLUNDERBUSS

Date	Early 18th century
Origin	Turkey
Barrel	13½in (34.3cm)
Caliber	1.2in (30.5mm) (at muzzle)

Despite its being furnished with a shoulder stock that is incised, carved, and inlaid with silver, this blunderbuss (see p.47) is actually a large cavalry pistol. The work of "the Dervish Amrullah," according to an engraved inscription, it was clearly made for use by a cavalryman, as it has a bar and ring for suspension from a saddle.

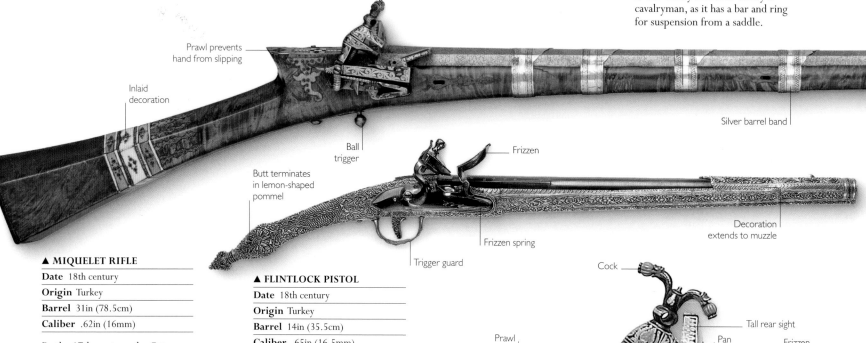

Prawl prevents hand from slipping

Inlaid decoration

Ball trigger

Butt terminates in lemon-shaped pommel

Frizzen

Frizzen spring

Trigger guard

Silver barrel band

Decoration extends to muzzle

Cock

Prawl

Tall rear sight

Pan

Frizzen

Trigger

▲ MIQUELET RIFLE

Date	18th century
Origin	Turkey
Barrel	31in (78.5cm)
Caliber	.62in (16mm)

By the 17th century, the Ottoman army had adopted a version of the Mediterranean miquelet lock (see p.44) for its firearms. Most of these guns were of high quality, with rifled barrels and elaborately inlaid stocks. The lock and mounts of this example are lavishly decorated with gold inlay, while the barrel bands are silver.

▲ FLINTLOCK PISTOL

Date	18th century
Origin	Turkey
Barrel	14in (35.5cm)
Caliber	.65in (16.5mm)

With the gentle fall to the butt and the slim "lemon" pommel, this pistol is reminiscent of European pieces of a century or more earlier. This gun also displays the common trademark of Ottoman gunmakers: gilded decoration surrounding the muzzle.

Shoulder stock is pentagonal in section

Striking steel integral with pan cover

Cock

Shoulder stock is inlaid with brass and precious stones

Trigger

External mainspring

Inlaid decoration on butt

Flared muzzle

Frizzen

Barrel is blued (heated to protect against rust) and inlaid with gold

Ramrod

Frizzen spring

▲ FLINTLOCK PISTOL

Date Late 18th century

Origin Turkey

Barrel 12½in (31.75cm)

Caliber .62in (15.7mm)

A pistol such as this—stocked all the way to the muzzle, with its woodwork copiously inlaid and its lock, barrel, and trigger guard decorated with silver and gold— would have graced many arms cabinets in the Ottoman world. The flintlock firing this weapon appears to be of European origin.

Narrow butt

Barrel is left unblued

Decoration extends to muzzle

▲ FLINTLOCK PISTOL

Date 1788

Origin Caucasus

Barrel 12in (30.5cm)

Caliber .60in (15.2mm)

The stocks and muzzle of this all-metal, ball-butt pistol (one of a pair) are covered with cast and chiseled silver gilt. The lock plate is inscribed "Rossi," the maker's name, suggesting that the lock, at least, was imported from Italy.

Octagonal barrel

Cock

Lock plate

Frizzen

Saddle bar

Muzzle flares to spread shot and facilitate loading

Pan

Trigger guard

Cast and chiseled decoration on stock

▲ FLINTLOCK BLUNDERBUSS

Date Late 18th century

Origin Turkey

Barrel 17in (43.18cm)

Caliber 1.5in (38.1mm) (at muzzle)

Ornate, even by Ottoman Empire standards, this silver-gilt blunderbuss carbine was most likely made as a presentation piece. Upon its lock plate is the inscription "London warranted," which suggests that the lock is a copy of an English flintlock.

Barrel bands made of twine

Octagonal barrel

FULL VIEW

▲ MIQUELET LOCK RIFLE

Date Late 18th century

Origin Turkey

Barrel 32in (81.3cm)

Caliber .60in (15.2mm)

This rifle is of classic Turkish form. Its stock has the typical pentagonal-section butt, and fine inlaid decoration incorporating panels of metal wire and colored and natural ivory. The rifled "Damascus" barrel (see p.47) has a marked grain pattern and a tall aperture rear sight. The lock is decorated with gold and panels of coral.

Ramrod

Entire stock is covered in engraved and decorated ivory

▲ BALKAN MIQUELET TÜFENK

Date Early 19th century

Origin Turkey

Barrel 36in (91.4cm)

Caliber .55in (13.9mm)

This piece is reminiscent of Indian muskets. The stock is entirely covered in ivory and further embellished with inlays of precious stones and brass. The miquelet lock, common in Spain and Italy, is thought to have made its way to the Ottoman Empire via Africa.

TURNING POINT

FAILSAFE GUNS

Matchlocks, wheel-locks, and flintlocks used a small amount of gunpowder to prime the propellant (main gunpowder charge). In 1807, the Reverend Alexander Forsyth patented a way of igniting the propellant by using a different substance—a sensitive chemical primer that detonates when struck. Joshua Shaw later patented the percussion cap as the simplest way of making Forsyth's invention work. Firearms could now use chemical ignition. This key development in firearms technology enabled guns to fire instantaneously and reliably, unlike earlier guns with exposed gunpowder priming. It also enabled the development of the revolver and the self-contained metallic cartridge (see pp.122–23), now used by nearly every modern firearm.

▲ **PERCUSSION CAPS**
Percussion caps were small copper or brass cups containing a minute quantity of fulminate. A cap was held in place on a hollow plug, or nipple, that was attached to the breech of the gun.

In the early 19th century, Alexander Forsyth, an avid duck hunter, was frustrated by the shortcomings of the flintlock system. Although reliable, it suffered from the occasional "flash in the pan" when the priming powder would ignite but the gun would fail to fire. Along with the noise of the flint striking the frizzen and the puff of smoke, the "flash" alerted potential game, which would quickly disappear.

>> **BEFORE**

At the beginning of the 19th century, most guns were fired by the flintlock mechanism. In this, a piece of flint was struck against steel to create sparks that ignited some priming powder in a small pan alongside the barrel. The flame from this passed through a vent in the barrel and ignited the main charge.

● **LOOSE POWDER PLACED IN A PRIMING PAN** in small quantities was not efficient. Wind could blow it away and rain could make it wet. The powder could also ignite but fail to detonate the main charge.

● **DELAYS BETWEEN PULLING THE TRIGGER** and the gun actually discharging gave time for birds and animals, startled by the flash and smoke of the ignited priming powder, to escape.

**FLINTLOCK
MECHANISM**

● **FLINTS NEEDED TO REPLACED** after 15 shots or so, and the quality of flints often varied. The hard steel face of the frizzen also wore out, reducing its ability to create a spark.

THE "SCENT-BOTTLE" LOCK

Forsyth set about devising a simpler, faster, and more effective means of ignition. He designed a mechanism that could be attached to any firearm. It used a detonating compound called mercury fulminate as a primer to ignite the main powder charge. The fulminate was held in a vessel shaped like a perfume bottle, which gave this mechanism the name "scent-bottle" lock. It was mounted on a hollow, cylindrical spindle and screwed into a flintlock gun's vent that had been specially enlarged.

Forsyth's invention embodied the fundamental principles of chemical ignition upon which all future gun and ammunition development would be based.

PERCUSSION DESIGN EVOLVES

Although revolutionary, the "scent-bottle" lock was unsafe as it carried a large quantity of a detonating compound, which could explode accidentally and injure the user. Many people attempted to adapt Forsyth's idea to design a variety of safer percussion systems that would use a tiny, isolated quantity of primer—just enough to prime the gun once. The gunmaker

▼ **THE THIN RED LINE**
Armed mainly with Pattern 1851 percussion rifles, the 93rd Highlanders regiment of the British Army bravely formed an unmoving line of defense against the Russian cavalry in the Battle of Balaclava in 1854. From a distance, they appeared to onlookers as a "thin red line" because of their red coats.

KEY **FIGURE**

Alexander John Forsyth
(1768–1843)

Alexander Forsyth graduated from King's College, Aberdeen, Scotland, in 1786, and in 1791, he was licensed as a minister in Belhelvie, Aberdeenshire. He was a game shooter as well as an amateur chemist and mechanic. His frustration with the flintlock's weaknesses spurred him to devise a better ignition system.

Joe Manton designed the "tube-lock"—in this, he placed the fulminate in a thin copper tube, which was inserted into a vent on one side of the barrel and struck with a hammer. Other systems included the "pellet-lock" and Edward Maynard's tape primer. The tape primer had the fulminate in a series of "caps" in a long tape and was popular in the US for a while. Even in recent times this was the "ammunition" for toy cap guns.

"… one of the most **ingenious**… one of the most useful **inventions** in modern times…"

ATTRIBUTED TO **COMMITTEE OF PATENTS ON JOSHUA SHAW'S CLAIM (FEBRUARY 1846)**

THE PERCUSSION CAP

The breakthrough, however, was made in 1822 by Joshua Shaw, an English artist. He designed a tiny copper cup, put fulminate in it, and held it in place with a drop of varnish. Shaw placed this cuplike cap on a hollow plug, or nipple, screwed into the breech of a gun, ready to be struck by the hammer. Striking the cap ignited the primer, producing a flash that was relayed to the propellant via a vent in the barrel.

As the percussion system evolved, ultimately resulting in the percussion cap, guns were transformed by having a means of ignition that was reliable and easy to use. Reloading times for these guns decreased dramatically. Rifles employing percussion caps were common in the Crimean War (1853–56). An important battle in this war was the Battle of Balaclava, in which a small number of British troops armed with percussion rifles stood their ground against a Russian cavalry onslaught, firing at the larger force in a volley. The percussion rifles were precise and reliable, and they could be reloaded quickly, which allowed the British forces to repel the Russians. Percussion weapons were also used widely in the American Civil War (1861–65). The 1861 Springfield Rifled Musket

was used to devastating effect by Union soldiers. The guns fired three shots per minute and, in the hands of skilled marksmen, could consistently hit targets within 500 yards (457m).

AFTER »

The percussion cap rendered all other ignition systems obsolete. It simplified the loading and firing process and made the revolver a viable proposition. It also paved the way for the development of the self-contained metallic cartridge and breech-loading firearms.

- **MAYNARD'S TAPE PRIMER** was one of the few percussion variations to enjoy a period of success, but it was flimsy and susceptible to damage compared to the copper cap.

MAYNARD'S TAPE PRIMER

Tape primer

- **THE REVOLVER** became a truly practical proposition. Early revolvers required a system to cover the pan to prevent the priming powder from falling out when the cylinder rotated. The cover also had to be moved when each chamber in the cylinder was in a firing position. Percussion caps solved these problems, allowing revolvers to be produced en masse.

- **BREECH-LOADING FIREARMS** such as the Dreyse needle-fire rifle (see pp. 108–09) were developed. These used combustible cartridges in conjunction with separate percussion-cap ignition.

- **SELF-CONTAINED METALLIC CARTRIDGES** evolved using the percussion cap. Guns could be reloaded by merely opening the weapon's breech end, loading the cartridge, closing the breech, and cocking the weapon.

EARLY METALLIC CARTRIDGE

EARLY PERCUSSION GUNS

A new way of priming a gun, by striking a small amount of chemical primer (a substance that ignites when struck), was invented in the 19th century. The first step toward this "percussion" system was taken by Alexander Forsyth, who developed a gunlock in which fulminate powder (the primer) was held in a magazine shaped like a scent bottle. Although this lock had advantages over the flintlock, loose fulminate was dangerous to use, so further devices were invented to contain just enough for priming a gun once. The evolution of percussion design culminated in the percussion cap (see pp.80–81). In the early 19th century, guns employed a variety of percussion locks, but the percussion cap had been almost universally adopted by the 1830s.

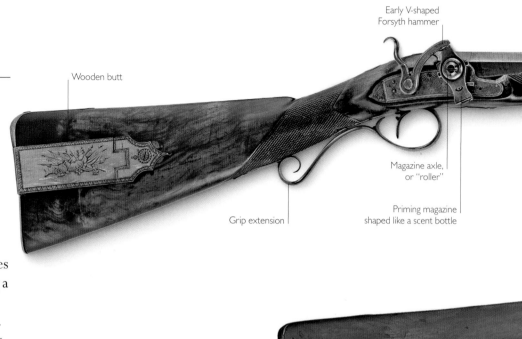

Early V-shaped Forsyth hammer

Wooden butt

Magazine axle, or "roller"

Grip extension

Priming magazine shaped like a scent bottle

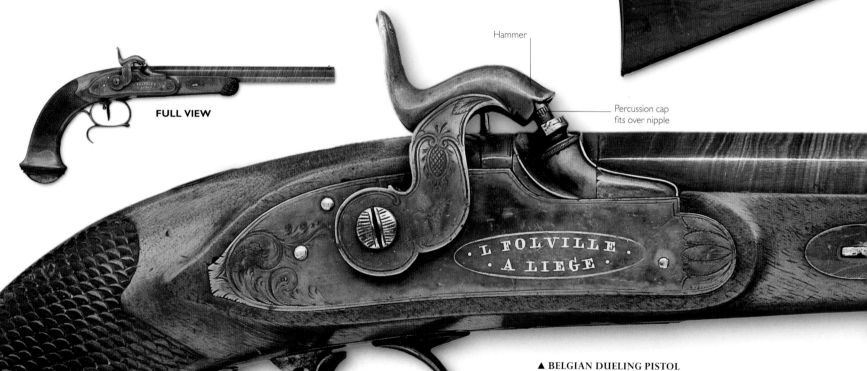

Hammer

Percussion cap fits over nipple

FULL VIEW

· L FOLVILLE ·
· A LIEGE ·

Incised checkering on butt

Steadying spur

Trigger guard

▲ **BELGIAN DUELING PISTOL**

Date 1830

Origin Belgium

Barrel 9¼in (23.8cm)

Caliber .31in (8mm)

Percussion-cap pistols were more reliable than even the best flintlocks, and one of their earliest uses was as dueling pistols. This half-stocked pistol by the gunmaker Folville, one of a cased pair, was made in Liège, Belgium, an internationally significant center of gunmaking at the time.

Barrel-retaining pin

▲ FORSYTH PATENT PERCUSSION SPORTING GUN

Date c.1808

Origin England

Barrel 32½in (82.2cm)

Caliber .73in (18.5mm)

This sporting gun was fired using Forsyth's "scent-bottle" lock. Loose fulminate powder (the chemical primer) was contained in a rotating magazine. This was fitted with a striker. To fire the gun, a user pulled the hammer back and then rotated the vessel backward, which deposited some fulminate in a small hole in the axle. Pulling the trigger released the hammer, which hit the striker in the vessel, detonating the primer.

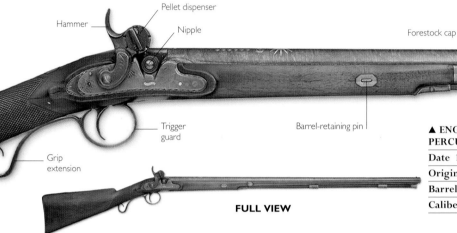

Hammer

Pellet dispenser

Nipple

Trigger guard

Grip extension

Forestock cap

Barrel-retaining pin

Ramrod pipe

Ramrod

FULL VIEW

▲ ENGLISH PELLET-LOCK PERCUSSION GUN

Date 1820

Origin England

Barrel 32¼in (82.2cm)

Caliber .73in (18.5mm)

This gun utilized a "pellet-lock" system, which was a major early step in the evolution of percussion (chemical ignition) technology. The detonating material in this gun was bound with gum or varnish, and the pellets thus formed were contained in a rotating drum attached to the cock. Each partial rotation of the drum brought a fresh, unfired pellet over the nipple, onto which the pellet was driven by the hammer.

Foresight

Octagonal barrel

Hammer

Seven barrels brazed together

Trigger guard

Trigger

Grip extension

▲ NOCK VOLLEY GUN

Date 1795, converted to percussion in c.1830

Origin England

Barrel 20½in (52cm)

Caliber .39in (9.9mm)

A version of this seven-barreled gun was used by the British Royal Navy in close-range fighting when boarding a ship or attempting to repel enemy boarders. This gun, like many flintlock weapons, was modernized by being converted to percussion ignition. Its central barrel was fired by the percussion cap. The exploding charge of the gunpowder in its breech was linked by radiating vents to those of the other six barrels, which fired simultaneously as a volley.

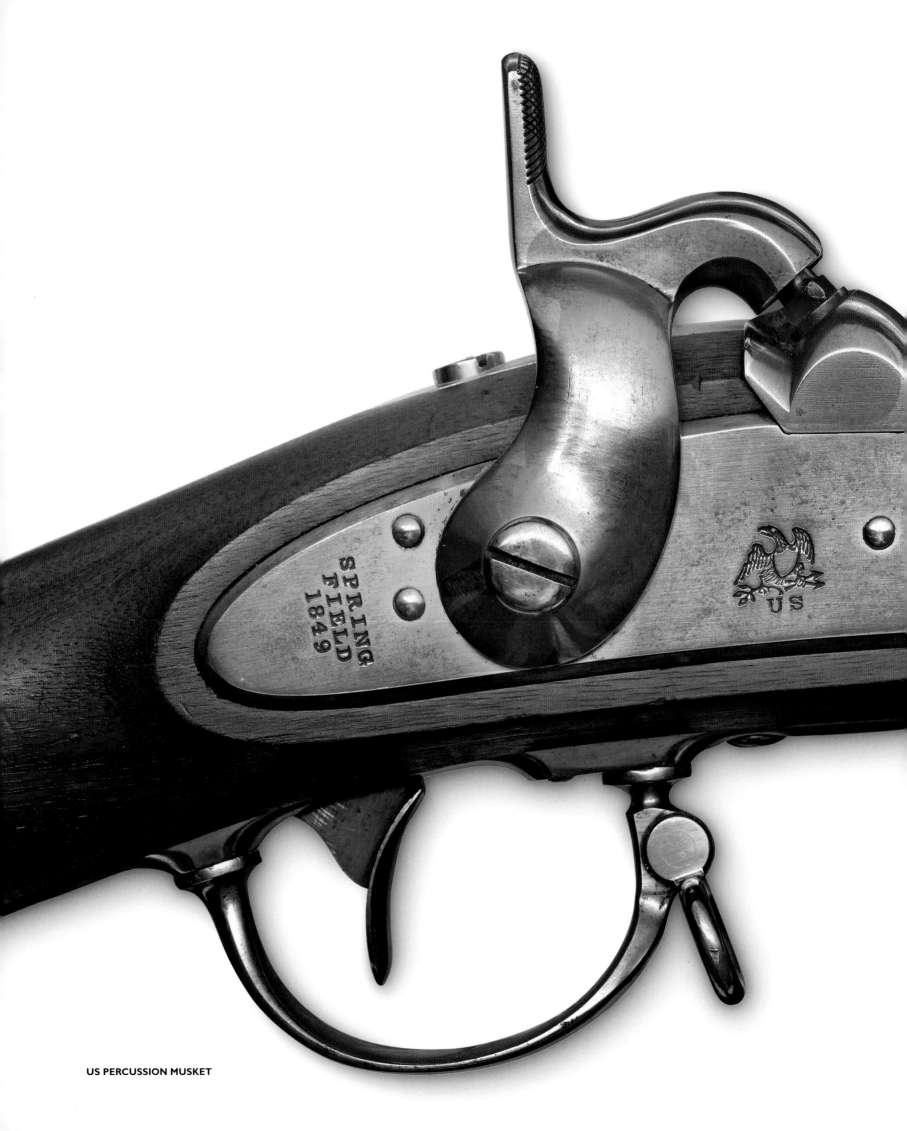

US PERCUSSION MUSKET

THE AGE
OF CHANGE

1830–80

Firearms technology leaped ahead in the 19th century. Around 1830, the flintlock
was still in almost universal military service, but the next 50 years saw the invention
and adoption of percussion ignition, successful breech-loading mechanisms, the
metallic cartridge, effective repeating firearms, and even machine-guns. Many of the
mechanisms developed during that time are still in use today.

PERCUSSION-CAP PISTOLS

The percussion cap (see pp.80–81) was simply a small cup containing primer, yet it enabled a revolution in the design of all handheld firearms. While flintlock pistols were bulky, the percussion cap made it possible to design sleeker and more compact handguns with fewer lock components. It made muzzle-loading pistols more reliable, and eventually spurred the development of more efficient breech-loading pistols. Among pistols, the revolver—with its chambers in a revolving cylinder—improved most significantly with the coming of percussion-cap technology.

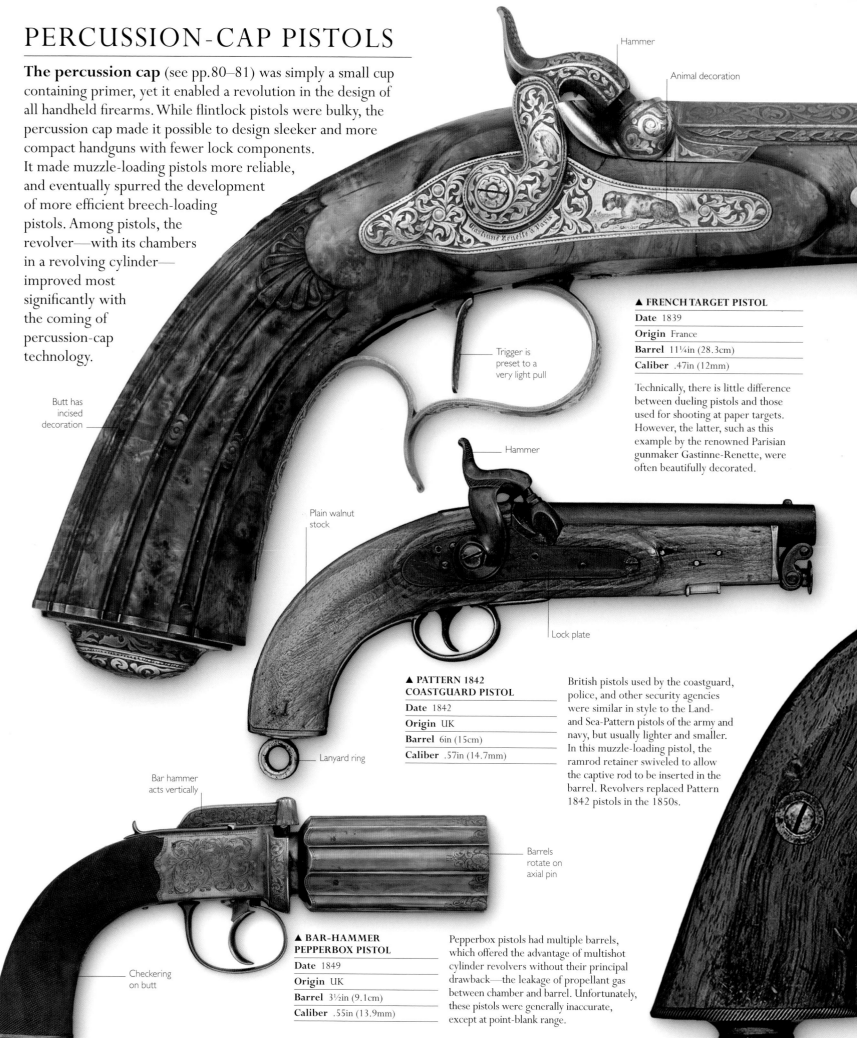

Hammer

Animal decoration

Butt has incised decoration

Trigger is preset to a very light pull

Hammer

Plain walnut stock

Lanyard ring

Bar hammer acts vertically

Lock plate

Barrels rotate on axial pin

Checkering on butt

▲ FRENCH TARGET PISTOL

Date	1839
Origin	France
Barrel	11¼in (28.3cm)
Caliber	.47in (12mm)

Technically, there is little difference between dueling pistols and those used for shooting at paper targets. However, the latter, such as this example by the renowned Parisian gunmaker Gastinne-Renette, were often beautifully decorated.

▲ PATTERN 1842 COASTGUARD PISTOL

Date	1842
Origin	UK
Barrel	6in (15cm)
Caliber	.57in (14.7mm)

British pistols used by the coastguard, police, and other security agencies were similar in style to the Land- and Sea-Pattern pistols of the army and navy, but usually lighter and smaller. In this muzzle-loading pistol, the ramrod retainer swiveled to allow the captive rod to be inserted in the barrel. Revolvers replaced Pattern 1842 pistols in the 1850s.

▲ BAR-HAMMER PEPPERBOX PISTOL

Date	1849
Origin	UK
Barrel	3½in (9.1cm)
Caliber	.55in (13.9mm)

Pepperbox pistols had multiple barrels, which offered the advantage of multishot cylinder revolvers without their principal drawback—the leakage of propellant gas between chamber and barrel. Unfortunately, these pistols were generally inaccurate, except at point-blank range.

Ornate octagonal barrel

Round barrel

Barrel-retaining slide

Butt is planed flat on the sides

Ring trigger is characteristic of Cooper's pistols

Combined mainspring and hammer

Hammer

Under-lever pivot bar

▲ COOPER UNDER-HAMMER PISTOL

Date	1849
Origin	England
Barrel	4in (10cm)
Caliber	.45in (11.4mm)

Joseph Rock Cooper was a prolific English firearms inventor. One of his patents was for this under-hammer pistol, which includes a hammer located under the barrel along with the percussion-cap plug, or nipple.

▲ SHARPS BREECH-LOADING PISTOL

Date	c.1860
Origin	US
Barrel	5in (12.7cm)
Caliber	.34in (8.6mm)

American inventor Christian Sharps was famous for his breech-loading rifles and carbines. His pistols were based on the same principles as his early rifles and carbines (see p.110).

Trigger

Trigger guard and breech under-lever

FULL VIEW

AMERICAN PERCUSSION-CAP REVOLVERS

Revolving pistols were made less cumbersome by the percussion cap (see pp.80–81), which improved the single-action revolver (in which the hammer is cocked manually) that had become a reality by the end of the 17th century. These revolvers were loaded with powder and projectile (bullet or ball) from the muzzle of each chamber with the help of a device called a compound rammer. Samuel Colt patented his revolver in the UK in 1835 and in the US in 1836. His revolver, and its later copies, mostly used an open-frame construction, while some other makers favored a solid frame, with a top strap of metal above the cylinder.

▶ **COLT MODEL 1849 POCKET REVOLVER**

Date	1849
Origin	US
Barrel	4in (10.2cm)
Caliber	.31in (7.87mm)

A revised version of his 1848 revolver, the Baby Dragoon, Samuel Colt's 1849 single-action Pocket revolver had a standard compound rammer, choice of three barrel lengths, and a five- or six-shot cylinder.

Walnut grips

Trigger

Octagonal barrel

Cutaway to facilitate placing of cap

Compound rammer lever

Cylinder axis pin

Compound rammer

Cylinder-retaining wedge passes through axis pin

Slot for cylinder-locking bolt

Nipple in recess

Brass back strap

Engraved cylinder

▲ **COLT MODEL 1851 NAVY REVOLVER**

Date	1851
Origin	England
Barrel	7½in (19cm)
Caliber	.36in (9.14mm)

At the Great Exhibition of 1851 in London, Samuel Colt introduced the Navy Model, a single-action, open-frame light revolver in .36in (9.14mm) rather than .44in (11.17mm) caliber. After the display, he obtained an order from the British government. This is one of the revolvers produced at his company's London factory.

Walnut grips

Trigger

Brass trigger guard

▶ **COLT MODEL 1855 POCKET REVOLVER**

Date	1855
Origin	US
Barrel	3½in (8.9cm)
Caliber	.28in (7.1mm)

Elisha Root, the Colt Works Superintendent, designed the 1855 Pocket revolver. This single-action revolver had a solid-frame design in which the cylinder was held in a rectangular frame made by the top and bottom straps, the standing breech end, and the part of the frame forming the rear of the barrel.

Hammer spur

Side-mounted hammer

Cylinder-locking screw

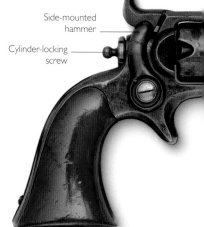

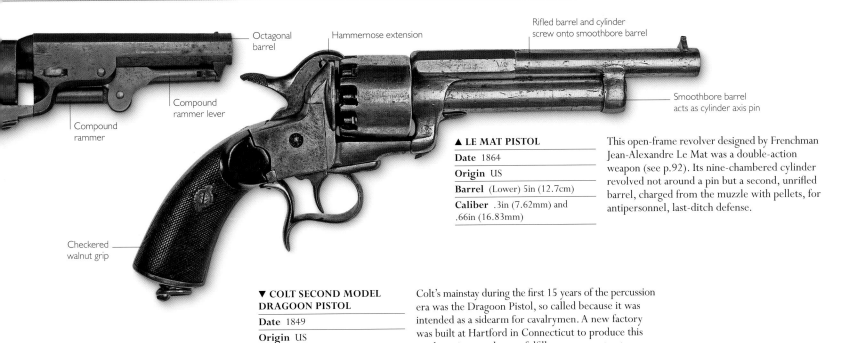

Octagonal barrel

Hammernose extension

Rifled barrel and cylinder screw onto smoothbore barrel

Compound rammer lever

Smoothbore barrel acts as cylinder axis pin

Compound rammer

Checkered walnut grip

▲ LE MAT PISTOL

Date	1864
Origin	US
Barrel	(Lower) 5in (12.7cm)
Caliber	.3in (7.62mm) and .66in (16.83mm)

This open-frame revolver designed by Frenchman Jean-Alexandre Le Mat was a double-action weapon (see p.92). Its nine-chambered cylinder revolved not around a pin but a second, unrifled barrel, charged from the muzzle with pellets, for antipersonnel, last-ditch defense.

▼ COLT SECOND MODEL DRAGOON PISTOL

Date	1849
Origin	US
Barrel	7½in (19cm)
Caliber	.44in (11.17mm)

Colt's mainstay during the first 15 years of the percussion era was the Dragoon Pistol, so called because it was intended as a sidearm for cavalrymen. A new factory was built at Hartford in Connecticut to produce this single-action revolver to fulfill an army contract.

Round barrel

Compound rammer lever

Rammer pivot pin

Compound rammer

Top strap

Cylinder-locking slot

Locking screw

Round barrel

Compound rammer

Top strap

Part of frame forms rear of barrel

Octagonal barrel

Compound rammer

Cutaway for bullet to pass under rammer

Bottom strap

▶ STARR ARMY MODEL

Date	1864
Origin	US
Barrel	7½in (19.2cm)
Caliber	.44in (11.17mm)

American gunmaker Nathan Starr was the pioneer of the break-open pistol, in which the barrel, top strap, and cylinder were hinged at the front of the frame before the trigger guard. The cylinder could be removed for cleaning or for replacing with another. The forked top strap of this solid-frame, double-action revolver passed over the hammer and was retained by a knurled screw.

Trigger

SHOWCASE

COLT NAVY REVOLVER

By the late 1840s, Samuel Colt had manufactured several models of single-action revolver fired by percussion caps. These were all variations on his open-frame design, which allowed the removal of the cylinder for cleaning, or to fit another ready-loaded one. Colt's most successful percussion revolver, the Model 1851 Navy Revolver, sold in huge numbers. Seen here is the improved Model 1861.

COLT NAVY REVOLVER	
Date	1861
Origin	US
Barrel	7½in (19.1cm)
Caliber	.36in (9.14mm)

▶ **COLT MODEL 1861 NAVY REVOLVER**
Colt was a firm believer in standardization in manufacture. One of the factors that made his pistols so sought-after was the interchangeability of their components, which meant that replacements for broken parts could be bought off the shelf, and that improvements could be easily incorporated. Some 38,843 examples of the Model 1861 Navy Revolver were produced before it was discontinued in 1873.

Nipple

Hammer nose has a notch to act as rear sight

Cylinder engraved with naval scene

Wedge passes through cylinder axis pin, retaining cylinder in frame

Cutaway allows caps to be placed on nipple

Brass backstrap

One-piece walnut grip

Cutaway to allow cartridges to be loaded without removing cylinder

Trigger guard

Box containing percussion caps

Percussion cap

▶ **PERCUSSION CAPS**
Percussion caps, so called because of their shape, were made of two layers of copper foil with a minute quantity of fulminate of mercury, oxidizer, and a sustaining agent sandwiched between them. They were introduced in this form in about 1822.

250 METAL-LINED CAPS, Made expressly for COLT'S Pt. Belt and Pocket PISTOLS. Manufacturers. London

Dispenser
nozzle

Body of lacquered
copper

Cutoff
shutter lever

Compound rammer to
force bullet into chamber

▲ POWDER FLASK
By the 1860s, the traditional powder horn
had given way to the flask, which incorporated
a dispenser for a measured amount of powder
as its spout. Most were ornamented with
hunting or martial scenes.

Foresight

Muzzle

Compound
rammer lever

Bullet mold
handle

▼ AMMUNITION
As in all percussion revolvers, powder and
projectile (bullet or ball) were loaded at the
muzzle of each chamber in turn, before a
percussion cap was placed over an external
nipple at the rear of each chamber. Measured
amounts of powder and projectile were made into
simple cartridges with combustible cases made
of fine animal membrane. The user placed each
cartridge into the muzzle of a chamber, powder
charge first, with the bullet facing outward. The
cartridge case was crushed when seated home in
the chamber by the compound rammer—a small
press permanently attached to the revolver.

Two bullets can
be cast at once

Excess lead
sheared by blade
when bullet was set

▲ LEAD BULLETS
By 1861, the cylindro-ogival form
(above) had replaced the ball to become
the standard shape for both rifle and
pistol bullets (see pp. 306–07). They
were still being made from pure lead,
without the addition of a hardening
agent such as antimony.

▶ BULLET MOLD
Even though calibers had by
now become standardized, it was
still almost unheard-of to buy loose
bullets. Instead, one bought a bar of lead
and made one's own bullets, using the
mold supplied with the pistol.

6 Combustible Envelope
CARTRIDGES,
MADE OF HAZARD'S POWDER
EXPRESSLY FOR
COL. COLT'S PATENT
REVOLVING BELT PISTOL
ADDRESS
COLT'S CARTRIDGE WORKS,
HARTFORD, CONN.

BRITISH PERCUSSION-CAP REVOLVERS

The American approach to revolver making, exemplified by the likes of Samuel Colt, sought to manufacture pistols in large numbers using machines to make interchangeable parts. In contrast, the British gun trade preferred to sustain traditional craft skills in the making of revolvers, as in all other aspects of revolver-making. By the mid-19th century, British companies were producing a variety of efficient revolvers, from those developed from earlier "pepperbox" (multiple-barrel) designs (see p.86), to models with sophisticated mechanisms that were either self-cocking (in which the hammer is cocked by pulling the trigger) or double-action (in which the hammer is cocked by single-action or self-cocking mechanisms).

Octagonal barrel

Cylinder axis pin can be withdrawn to remove cylinder from solid frame

▲ ADAMS DOUBLE-ACTION REVOLVER MODEL 1851

Date	1851
Origin	UK
Barrel	7½in (19cm)
Caliber	.50in (12.7mm)

This revolver—Robert Adams's first—is also called the Adams and Deane Model (they were in partnership at the time). The entire frame, barrel, and butt were forged out of a single iron billet, making the gun extremely strong. Adams's lock was later replaced by a superior design by a young army officer, F. B. E. Beaumont. The Beaumont-Adams was adopted by the British Army in 1855.

Trigger guard

Notched ridge forms rear sight

Fluted cylinder

Cylinder-locking wedge

Checkered walnut grip

Flash shield

Cylinder axis pin

Bar hammer

Cylinder

Engraved plate covers double-action lock

Octagonal barrel

Screw secures barrel to frame

▲ TRANSITIONAL BAR-HAMMER REVOLVER

Date	c.1855
Origin	UK
Barrel	5¼in (13.5cm)
Caliber	.4in (10.16mm)

Open-framed "transitional" pistols combined elements of both the pepperbox pistols they superseded and true revolvers. By the late 1850s, there was considerable demand in Britain for cylinder revolvers, but the best of them, by Colt, Deane, or Adams, were very expensive. Cheaper designs such as this open-frame example, with a bar hammer derived from a pepperbox revolver, were less satisfactory, with a tendency to discharge two cylinders at once because of the lack of partitions between the nipples.

Checkered walnut grip

Side-mounted hammer

Cylinder axis pin

Octagonal barrel

Lock plate

Trigger guard

▲ KERR DOUBLE-ACTION REVOLVER

Date 1856

Origin UK

Barrel 5¾in (14.7cm)

Caliber .44in (11.17mm)

James Kerr, Robert Adams's cousin, equipped his solid-frame revolver with a separate lock and a side-mounted hammer. The lock was held by two screws and could be easily removed. If a component broke, any gunsmith would have been able to repair it.

Octagonal barrel

Foresight

◀ JOSEPH LANG TRANSITIONAL REVOLVER

Date 1855

Origin UK

Barrel 6in (15.2cm)

Caliber .44in (11.17mm)

Transitional pistols continued to be produced, mostly in Europe, even after much more sophisticated designs had appeared. This open-frame, single-action revolver is of the type produced by one of the best-known proponents, Joseph Lang of London. Lang was more successful than most gunmakers of the time in solving the problem of propellant gas leaking between chamber and barrel. He designed the revolver in such a way that when the cylinder rotated and each chamber reached the end of the barrel, the mouth of the chamber engaged with the rear end of the barrel, mechanically sealing this connection between the two.

Articulated rammer head linked to lever

Combined cylinder locking catch and frame latch

Hammer

Compound rammer lever

Cylinder

Octagonal barrel

Prawl prevents pistol from slipping through hand

Compound rammer lever

▲ DEANE-HARDING ARMY MODEL

Date 1858

Origin UK

Barrel 5¼in (13.5cm)

Caliber .50in (12.7mm)

Trigger

Trigger guard

Checkered walnut grip

When Robert Adams broke with his partners in 1853, the elder of the Deane brothers, John, set up his own business. He later began manufacturing a revolver designed by William Harding with a new, simpler type of double-action lock—the forerunner of modern actions. The two-piece solid frame could be dismantled by removing the pin located in the top strap in front of the hammer nose. Considered unreliable, the pistol never achieved lasting popularity.

SAMUEL COLT

GREAT GUNSMITHS
COLT

American manufacturer Samuel Colt (1814–62) built his first revolver in 1831, when he was just sixteen. He perfected the design over a number of years, eventually founding the successful Colt's Patent Fire Arms Manufacturing Company. Colt's designs played a major role in the history of US firearms, leading the change from single-shot pistols to revolvers. As one of the first to make mass production work on a large, commercial scale, Colt also pioneered manufacturing methods that transformed industry worldwide.

In the first half of the 19th century, American inventors made attempts at developing the concept of the revolver, with its rotating cylinder that turns to bring one of several chambers in line with the barrel. Inventor Elisha Collier, who was attracted by the revolver's ability to fire several shots without reloading, designed a flintlock revolver (see p.49) in about 1814. It became popular, especially in Britain, but its unreliable mechanism was a drawback. Samuel Colt was the first to unite the revolver concept with the more reliable percussion-cap mechanism. In the 1830s and early 1840s, Colt made various attempts at manufacturing his revolver, which he patented in 1835. However, the quality of his products was uneven, and none of these enterprises was successful.

MASS PRODUCTION
In 1847, Colt made a new start, renting premises in Connecticut before opening a specially built factory by the Connecticut River

"Abe Lincoln may have freed all men, but Sam Colt made them equal"

POST-CIVIL WAR SLOGAN

in 1855. Here he developed mass production, building each gun from identical parts that could be put together on an assembly line. This kind of manufacturing had already been pioneered by other American industrialists, particularly other firearms producers and Connecticut clockmakers, but Colt was one of the first to adopt it on a large scale. His streamlined production methods enabled the Colt factory to fulfill large orders, not just in the US but also in Europe, where its sales increased during the Crimean War (1854–56).

Making the interchangeable parts for Colt's revolvers involved the development of specialized, state-of-the-art machinery. Colt

hired a skilled mechanic and inventor, Elisha K. Root, to oversee his manufacturing process and design the machinery needed. Soon Root was producing a host of mechanized tools, such as milling machines, drill presses, and specially built lathes. In the factory's first year, one observer counted no fewer than 400 different machine tools, most of which carried out processes that had previously been done by hand. This type of highly mechanized production of interchangeable parts was hugely influential in all kinds of industries, including the production of farm machinery, sewing machines, bicycles, steam engines, railroad locomotives, and automobiles. Manufacturers who used it found not only that they kept down their costs, but also that their products were reliable and easy to repair. The mass-production techniques pioneered by Colt transformed not just the firearms business but the whole of industry.

WINNING THE WEST
Colt's mass-produced revolvers were hugely popular. They sold not only to military users, but also to those involved in law enforcement and to individuals for self-defense. The Colt was especially popular among the settlers of the American West, and the most successful model

◄ CRIME CONFERENCE
The importance of the Colt company continued through the 20th century. Here, Newton D. Baker (left) attends a Crime Commission meeting in Chicago and examines the weapons used by the city's gunmen and bootleggers.

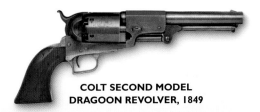

**COLT SECOND MODEL
DRAGOON REVOLVER, 1849**

**COLT NAVY MODEL
1861 REVOLVER**

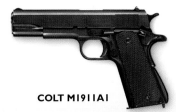

COLT M1911A1

1836 Samuel Colt founds his first company for firearms production.

1847 Colt produces the Walker Colt revolver with Samuel Hilton Walker.

1848 The Colt Dragoon revolver is introduced, initially for the US Army's Mounted Rifles.

1851 Colt opens a factory in England, increasing access to international markets.

1855 Colt incorporates the Colt's Patent Fire Arms Manufacturing Company, based at his newly built Connecticut factory.

1861 The Colt Navy Revolver is introduced and quickly sees service in the American Civil War.

1863 The Colt Single Action Army Model is introduced. Long-barreled versions produced in 1876 become known as "Buntline Specials," after a legend that author Ned Buntline presented them to lawmen, including Wyatt Earp.

1900 Colt becomes the first American manufacturer of automatic pistols.

1911 Browning designs the Colt M1911, which is adopted by the US Army. In 1924, it is modified into the M1911A1.

1994 After a difficult period involving bankruptcy proceedings, the Colt company is bought by new investors and begins a recovery.

▼ **THE GOOD, THE BAD, AND THE UGLY**
Clint Eastwood—as Blondie in the movie *The Good, The Bad, and The Ugly*—carries a Colt Single Action Army revolver. Colt revolvers appear widely in popular culture, particularly in movies depicting the American West.

of all was the Colt Single Action Army (SAA) Model, introduced in 1873. Well crafted and reliable, this revolver sold to everyone from ranchers to lawmen, peacemakers to outlaws. Texas cowboys, "forty-niners" joining the gold rush, and settlers on the trail through the West were among the hundreds of thousands of Americans who chose to carry a Colt revolver.

A SYMBOL OF THE FRONTIER

When Wild West shows began in the 19th century, many of the performers also used Colt revolvers, and the weapons became symbols of the opening up of the West and the exploits of cowboys and gunslingers. As a result, it was natural for the characters in TV and movie Westerns to carry Colts. The Lone Ranger, played by Clayton Moore, used Single Action Army guns with cream-colored grips, which he fired only as a last resort and never to kill. A host of other movie characters, including Clint Eastwood and Tim Holt, carried this celebrated revolver, cementing its reputation as one of the "guns that won the West." Building on this reputation, Colt continued to produce firearms into the 20th century, expanding during times of war, and trying, not always successfully, to diversify when demand dropped in peacetime. The company is still doing business today.

MUSKETS AND RIFLES (1831–52)

Many flintlock firearms remained in active use well into the 19th century. The iconic Kentucky long rifle was one of many civilian arms that saw sustained use as a flintlock, only gradually being converted to percussion ignition. European countries began to adopt rifles more widely for military use. Loading a rifle via the muzzle remained a problem. Rifles were loaded either using a shaped ball to mechanically fit the rifling grooves, or ramming a ball hard enough into the breech to deform the ball for gripping the rifling.

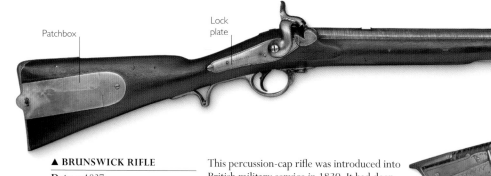

Patchbox

Lock plate

▲ BRUNSWICK RIFLE

Date	c.1837
Origin	UK
Barrel	32½in (82.5cm)
Caliber	.71in (18.03mm)

This percussion-cap rifle was introduced into British military service in 1830. It had deep, two-groove rifling and fired a lead ball with an integral band, or belt, around it. This belt fit into the grooves and caused the ball to spin as it was fired (see pp.98–99).

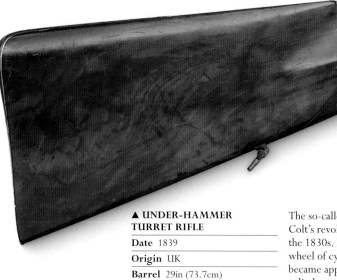

Catch for hinged upper frame strap

Trigger

Hammer

Small of stock has incised checkering

Disk is bored with seven radial chambers

Steel butt plate

▲ UNDER-HAMMER TURRET RIFLE

Date	1839
Origin	UK
Barrel	29in (73.7cm)
Caliber	.69in (17.6mm)

The so-called turret gun, an attempt to evade Colt's revolver patent (see p.94), appeared in the 1830s. Examples also exist in which the wheel of cylinders is set vertically. It soon became apparent that if flash-over from one cylinder to another occurred, the result would most likely be catastrophic to any bystanders, or even to the shooter himself.

Hammer

Comb of stock

Engraved lock plate

Nipple for lower barrel

Finger grip

Trigger

Barrel latch lever

Iron butt plate

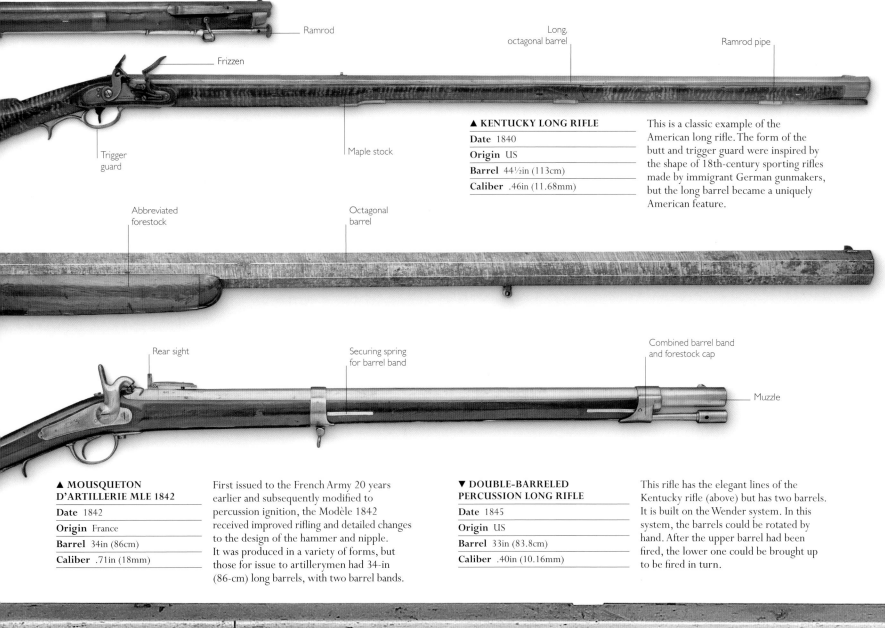

Ramrod

Frizzen

Trigger guard

Maple stock

Long, octagonal barrel

Ramrod pipe

▲ KENTUCKY LONG RIFLE

Date 1840

Origin US

Barrel 44½in (113cm)

Caliber .46in (11.68mm)

This is a classic example of the American long rifle. The form of the butt and trigger guard were inspired by the shape of 18th-century sporting rifles made by immigrant German gunmakers, but the long barrel became a uniquely American feature.

Abbreviated forestock

Octagonal barrel

Rear sight

Securing spring for barrel band

Combined barrel band and forestock cap

Muzzle

▲ MOUSQUETON D'ARTILLERIE MLE 1842

Date 1842

Origin France

Barrel 34in (86cm)

Caliber .71in (18mm)

First issued to the French Army 20 years earlier and subsequently modified to percussion ignition, the Modèle 1842 received improved rifling and detailed changes to the design of the hammer and nipple. It was produced in a variety of forms, but those for issue to artillerymen had 34-in (86-cm) long barrels, with two barrel bands.

▼ DOUBLE-BARRELED PERCUSSION LONG RIFLE

Date 1845

Origin US

Barrel 33in (83.8cm)

Caliber .40in (10.16mm)

This rifle has the elegant lines of the Kentucky rifle (above) but has two barrels. It is built on the Wender system. In this system, the barrels could be rotated by hand. After the upper barrel had been fired, the lower one could be brought up to be fired in turn.

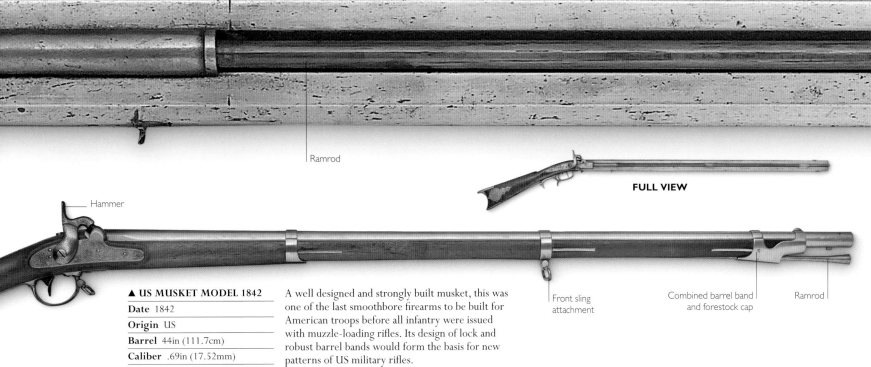

Ramrod

FULL VIEW

Hammer

▲ US MUSKET MODEL 1842

Date 1842

Origin US

Barrel 44in (111.7cm)

Caliber .69in (17.52mm)

A well designed and strongly built musket, this was one of the last smoothbore firearms to be built for American troops before all infantry were issued with muzzle-loading rifles. Its design of lock and robust barrel bands would form the basis for new patterns of US military rifles.

Front sling attachment

Combined barrel band and forestock cap

Ramrod

TURNING POINT

PRACTICAL RIFLES

In 1844, Captain Claude-Etienne Minié, a French military officer, developed a bullet that revolutionized firearms, making the rifle as simple to load as the common musket and increasing its firepower. Soon nearly every soldier in every nation had in his hands for the first time a weapon of almost undreamed of power, range, and accuracy. The first use of rifles on a large scale was in the Crimean War (1854–57), and it was there that the modern sniper emerged. A few years later, the use of rifles on an even larger scale helped make the American Civil War (1861–65) the deadliest in the country's history. In a short span of time, the "Minnie ball" bullet had dramatically transformed warfare.

▲ **MINIÉ BULLET**
Featuring a cavity in the base equipped with an iron cup, the original Minié bullets were plain, and tapered from base to point. Later versions, such as this one, had a cylindrical portion and grooves that were greased to lubricate the barrel, making it easier to clean. The bullet shown here is the American "Minnie ball."

The problem with rifles in the days of muzzle-loading had always been loading a ball that fit tightly enough to engage the rifling (see p.28). With a musket, the lead ball was a loose fit. With a rifle, the ball was wrapped in a patch made from greased paper or thin linen, which could be forced into the rifling grooves. After firing, gunpowder would leave thick residues in the grooves. The problematic process of loading rifles thus became even more difficult, and British riflemen in the Napoleonic Wars were issued with mallets to drive the ball down the bore after many shots had been fired.

Smoothbore muskets fired lead balls that were loose-fitting and might have been accurate only for an aimed shot of up to 50 yards (46m). They were more effective when used for volley-fire by ranks of men firing together, but beyond 300 yards (270m), an opponent could consider himself fairly safe, especially if moving.

• **A ROUND MUSKET BALL**, such as one made of lead, was a loose fit in the gun's bore. When fired, it would ricochet off the wall of the bore, its final direction depending upon the last point of contact.

LEAD MUSKET BALL

• **A LINEN OR PAPER PATCH** enveloping the round ball was an improvement. The ball would grip the grooves in the rifled barrel, making it spin and travel fairly accurately in flight. However, it was difficult to load.

• **THE BRUNSWICK BALL** was an example of a bullet designed to overcome existing problems. It was made to match the rifling and theoretically slide into the bore. The ball had a raised belt that fit into the two, deep rifling grooves in the Brunswick rifle. Brunswick balls could be damaged or deformed if knocked together in a pouch. Trying to align them correctly in the heat of battle also made loading difficult.

BRUNSWICK BALL

EARLY RIFLE SOLUTIONS

One route to overcoming this problem resulted in various breech-loading systems, some more successful than others. A famous example of a breech-loader was the Ferguson rifle. However, it was expensive to make and despite its superior design, only 100 units were manufactured. Other methods of loading used projectiles preformed to match the rifling. Loading rifles, however, continued to be difficult. Often, the force required to ram the ball down the bore was great enough to render the shooter's hands unsteady for accurate firing.

British officer John Jacob's rifles used four deep grooves and bullets with ribs to match. English engineer Sir Joseph Whitworth's rifle had spiral, hexagonal bores and used bullets made appropriately. Both were accurate and Whitworth's rifles were prized by sharpshooters in the American Civil War. However, they were too complex for general issue.

THE MINIÉ REVOLUTION

The solution to these problems lay in a simple bullet devised by Minié, based on his modification of a bullet created a few years earlier by fellow Frenchman Captain Henri-Gustave Delvigne. This new bullet could work with any conventional rifle. It could slide easily down the bore of a gun and at the instant of explosion, an iron cup in the bullet's base was driven into the cavity inside it, expanding the skirt of the bullet to grip the rifling grooves.

The muzzle-loading rifle evolved to become more effectual, and gradually warfare was transformed. Where once infantry could be safe beyond a distance of 300 yards (270m) from an

► **USING MINIÉ BULLETS**
At Fredericksburg, Virginia, in 1862, during the Civil War, the Union Army (seen here) and the Confederate defenders (entrenched outside the city) battled for weeks, many using rifles with Minié bullets.

"… conical ball… pass through the bodies of two men and lodge in the body of a third…"

ATTRIBUTED TO **GEORGE MACLEOD, CRIMEAN WAR SURGEON**

enemy, now danger lay up to a distance of 1,000 yards (914m) or more. In the US, the new Model 1855 Springfield rifle employed the Minié bullet, while in Britain, the first rifle to use the new bullet on a large scale was the Enfield Pattern 1853 (see pp.100–01). In the Crimean War, it was discovered that with these rifles, for the first time, infantry could outgun artillery, picking off the gunners from a safe distance. A few years later, almost a million

Pattern 1853 rifles would be shipped to serve both sides in the American Civil War. Battles, once close-quarter volleys followed by tides of bayonet or cavalry charges, now became long-range engagements from entrenched positions, against which a cavalry charge was almost suicidal. Judgment of distance and setting of sights now became paramount in making the rifle, in the hands of well-trained infantry, the new god of the battlefield.

KEY **FIGURE**

CLAUDE-ETIENNE MINIÉ
(1804–79)

Claude-Etienne Minié served as captain with the French Chasseurs (light infantry) in North Africa. He was frustrated with the shortcomings of the muskets issued to his troops. Following his invention of the Minié bullet, he was awarded 20,000 French francs and made an instructor at the Vincennes military establishment. In 1858, he retired as colonel, later becoming a military instructor for the Khedive of Egypt, and then manager at the Remington Arms Company, US.

AFTER »

The Minié bullet was critical in spurring on the development of long-range shooting. New military training regimes were needed. National Rifle Associations, such as those formed in Britain and the US, encouraged long-range target shooting as sport. Military sharpshooters became snipers—unseen long-range killers adding new levels of terror to an already fearsome business.

• **MILITARY TACTICS** had to be revised in the face of long-range accuracy, since close-range combat would increase the likelihood of soldiers being killed.

• **INDIVIDUAL SHARPSHOOTERS** and snipers picking off specific targets replaced the military tradition of "firing by numbers," or volley-fire.

• **DEADLY TEAMS OF SNIPERS** and "spotters" evolved; the spotters used telescopes to identify targets and passed details to the snipers.

• **HIGHER-VELOCITY BULLETS** inflicted greater damage than earlier bullets. Instead of repairable wounds to arms and legs, amputations became common.

• **NEW SNIPER RIFLES** in the 20th century, firing a .50in machine-gun cartridge, made it possible to aim at and hit human targets at ranges of more than 1 mile (1.7km), far greater than the ½-mile (0.9-km) range of an early muzzle-loading rifle.

.50IN BMG CARTRIDGE, 1910

SHOWCASE

ENFIELD RIFLED MUSKET

Adding grooves to a musket's bore, or replacing its smoothbore barrel with a rifled one, helped convert muskets into rifled weapons, or rifles. With the perfection of the expanding bullet (see pp.98–99), it became possible to issue rifles to all troops, not just to sharpshooters, because rifles could now be loaded as fast as muskets. The British Army adopted a key rifle in 1853. This gun—the Pattern 1853 Rifled Musket—remained in service until 1867.

ENFIELD RIFLED MUSKET	
Date	1853
Origin	UK
Barrel	33in (83.8cm)
Caliber	.57in (14.65mm)

FULL VIEW

Rear sling swivel

Forward sling swivel

Hammer

Nipple pierced to allow flash from cap to enter breech

Lock cover plate bears maker's name and insignia

▼ PATTERN 1853 RIFLED MUSKET
This rifled musket, produced by the Ordnance Factory at Enfield, London, was a highly successful weapon. In the hands of a competent infantryman, it was effective beyond its sighted distance (900yards/820m), and at 100yards (90m), the bullet could pass through a dozen ½-in (1.5-cm) planks. A soldier was expected to maintain a firing rate of three to four rounds per minute. For all its apparent simplicity, this rifled musket has a total of 56 parts.

Small of stock is gripped in hand

Attachment point for sling

Trigger

Socket fits over muzzle

◄ BAYONET
The socket bayonet, with its triangular-section blade, protruded almost 18in (46cm) beyond the muzzle. It alone required 44 separate manufacturing operations.

▼ CARTRIDGES
Cartridges were dipped in wax to lubricate the bore. For loading, soldiers tore off the twisted end of the cartridge with their teeth, poured the powder into the barrel, and rammed the lubricated end, carrying the projectile, down the muzzle. Rumors that cow or pig fat were used in the wax offended Hindu and Muslim soldiers because they were forbidden to eat beef or pork respectively; this is one suggested cause of the Indian Mutiny of 1857.

Triangular-section blade

TOMPION (MUZZLE PLUG)

SCREW-THREAD BALL REMOVER

BALL REMOVER

"WORM"

Pricker

▲ RAMROD ACCESSORIES
Ramrod accessories included a tompion (muzzle plug)—for preventing dust from entering the barrel—and the "worm" and ball removers that could be attached to the ramrod to remove dud cartridges and faulty balls respectively.

▲ COMBINATION TOOL
The combination tool included everything needed to care for the rifle in the field, including appropriately sized screwdrivers and wrenches, and a pricker to keep the nipple clear of residue.

Screwdriver

Rear sight set to 900yards (823m)

Barrel band retaining barrel to stock

Barrel

Barrel band-retaining spring

Grooves to keep cleaning patch in place

▲ RAMROD
In addition to being used to ram wadded cartridge paper onto the charge and ball, the ramrod served as a cleaning rod. It was threaded to take the double-helix "worm" (above) used to extract dud cartridges.

Packet of 10 cartridges

Cartridges twisted closed

Powder placed here

Ball placed here

Cartridges lubricated with wax

▶ AMMUNITION
The Pattern 1853 Rifled Musket was loaded with 2½ drams (4.43g) of gunpowder and a 530-grain (34.35g) bullet of .56in (14.42mm) caliber, which expanded to take the rifling of the barrel, whose bore was .57in (14.65mm) in diameter. Charge and bullet were packed into cartridges and issued in packets of 10, with a dozen percussion caps.

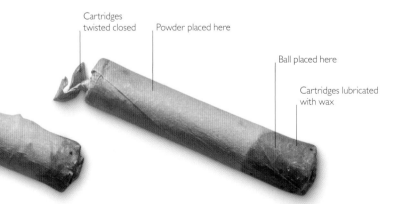

Rifle Musket /53
577.Bore
2½Drs.F.G.
PLUG
BALL
1856

MUSKETS AND RIFLES (1853–70)

Percussion ignition, whether using caps (see pp.80–81) or other devices, was a major improvement over the cumbersome flintlock. Not only was the percussion mechanism easier to use and maintain, it was also more weatherproof. In another key development, most European and American infantry had their smoothbore muskets replaced with muzzle-loading rifles, which had an accurate range several times greater than that of the musket.

▼ **FUSIL REGLEMENTAIRE MLE 1853**

Date	1853
Origin	France
Barrel	40½in (103cm)
Caliber	.71in (18mm)

For its final smoothbore musket, France maintained its established form of percussion firearms. This musket had a small spherical nipple seat on top of the breech of the steel barrel. It was fired by a strong and simple back-action lock—a percussion-cap variant in which the mainspring inside the lock plate lay behind the hammer, not in front of it, giving the lock a more slender appearance. This would be one of the last new patterns of smoothbore musket issued to European troops.

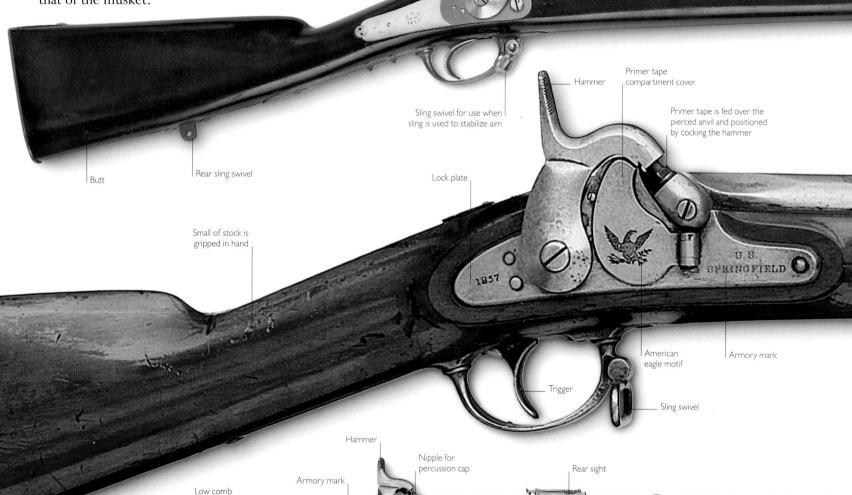

Nipple for percussion cap

Nipple seat

Butt

Rear sling swivel

Hammer

Sling swivel for use when sling is used to stabilize aim

Primer tape compartment cover

Primer tape is fed over the pierced anvil and positioned by cocking the hammer

Lock plate

Small of stock is gripped in hand

1857

U.S. SPRINGFIELD

American eagle motif

Armory mark

Trigger

Sling swivel

Hammer

Nipple for percussion cap

Rear sight

Low comb to butt

Armory mark

Barrel band

American eagle motif

Rear sling swivel

Hammer

Rear sling swivel

▲ **WHITWORTH RIFLE**

Date	1856
Origin	UK
Barrel	36in (91.45cm)
Caliber	.45in (14.3mm)

Sir Joseph Whitworth (see p.98) produced a rifle for a British Army trial with a hexagonal bore that fired a hexagonal bullet. It proved to be accurate over 1,500 yards (1.4km), but it was four times the price of an Enfield Model 1853 (see pp.100–01), and never adopted by the army.

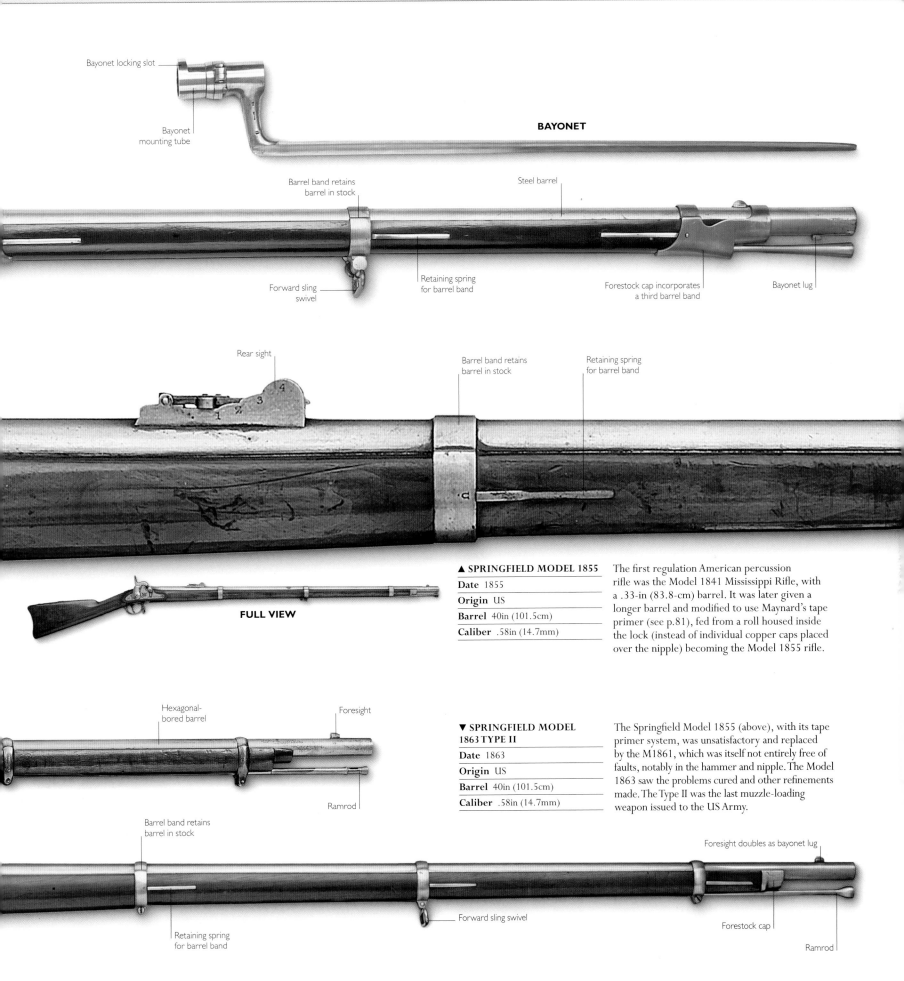

Bayonet locking slot

Bayonet mounting tube

BAYONET

Barrel band retains barrel in stock

Steel barrel

Forward sling swivel

Retaining spring for barrel band

Forestock cap incorporates a third barrel band

Bayonet lug

Rear sight

Barrel band retains barrel in stock

Retaining spring for barrel band

FULL VIEW

▲ **SPRINGFIELD MODEL 1855**

Date	1855
Origin	US
Barrel	40in (101.5cm)
Caliber	.58in (14.7mm)

The first regulation American percussion rifle was the Model 1841 Mississippi Rifle, with a .33-in (83.8-cm) barrel. It was later given a longer barrel and modified to use Maynard's tape primer (see p.81), fed from a roll housed inside the lock (instead of individual copper caps placed over the nipple) becoming the Model 1855 rifle.

Hexagonal-bored barrel

Foresight

▼ **SPRINGFIELD MODEL 1863 TYPE II**

Date	1863
Origin	US
Barrel	40in (101.5cm)
Caliber	.58in (14.7mm)

The Springfield Model 1855 (above), with its tape primer system, was unsatisfactory and replaced by the M1861, which was itself not entirely free of faults, notably in the hammer and nipple. The Model 1863 saw the problems cured and other refinements made. The Type II was the last muzzle-loading weapon issued to the US Army.

Ramrod

Barrel band retains barrel in stock

Foresight doubles as bayonet lug

Retaining spring for barrel band

Forward sling swivel

Forestock cap

Ramrod

SHOWCASE

LE PAGE SPORTING GUN

Pierre le Page set up in business as an arquebusier in Paris, perhaps as early as 1716, and was later appointed gunmaker to the king. He was succeeded by his nephew Jean in 1782, who was retained by the Emperor Napoleon to refurbish weapons from the royal gun-room for his own use. Jean's son Henri took over the firm in 1822, by which time Napoleon had died in exile. This sporting gun was made to commemorate the return of his ashes to France in 1840.

LE PAGE SPORTING GUN	
Date	1840
Origin	France
Barrel	31½in (80cm)
Caliber	.84in

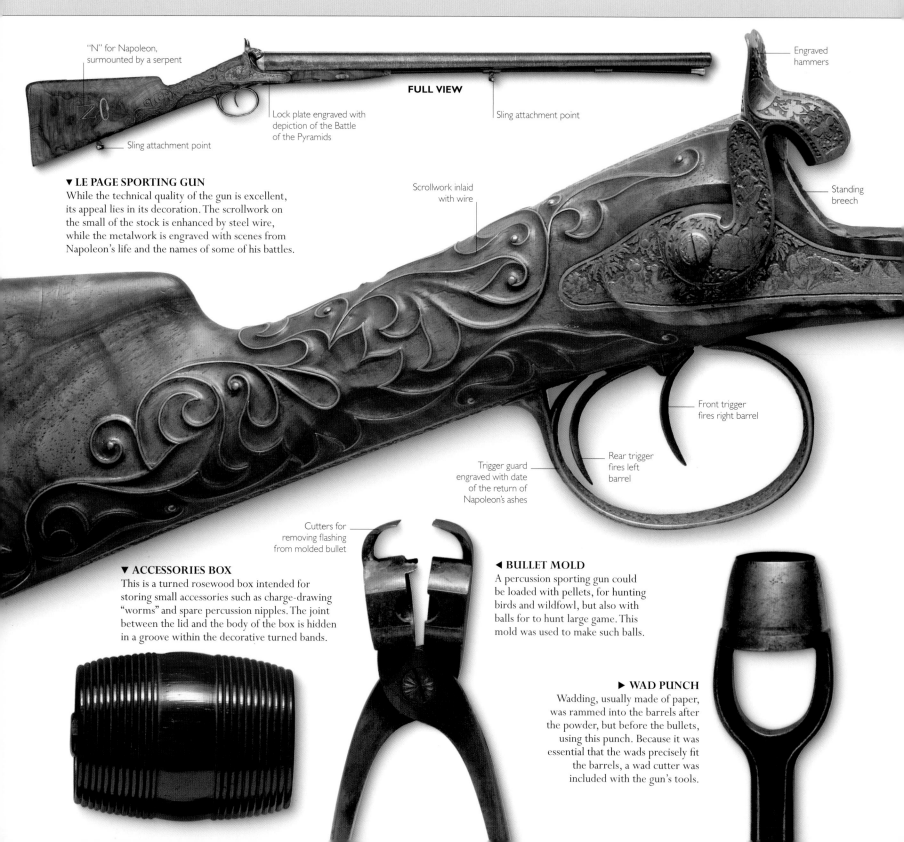

"N" for Napoleon, surmounted by a serpent

Engraved hammers

FULL VIEW

Lock plate engraved with depiction of the Battle of the Pyramids

Sling attachment point

Sling attachment point

Scrollwork inlaid with wire

Standing breech

▼ **LE PAGE SPORTING GUN**
While the technical quality of the gun is excellent, its appeal lies in its decoration. The scrollwork on the small of the stock is enhanced by steel wire, while the metalwork is engraved with scenes from Napoleon's life and the names of some of his battles.

Front trigger fires right barrel

Trigger guard engraved with date of the return of Napoleon's ashes

Rear trigger fires left barrel

Cutters for removing flashing from molded bullet

▼ **ACCESSORIES BOX**
This is a turned rosewood box intended for storing small accessories such as charge-drawing "worms" and spare percussion nipples. The joint between the lid and the body of the box is hidden in a groove within the decorative turned bands.

◄ **BULLET MOLD**
A percussion sporting gun could be loaded with pellets, for hunting birds and wildfowl, but also with balls for to hunt large game. This mold was used to make such balls.

► **WAD PUNCH**
Wadding, usually made of paper, was rammed into the barrels after the powder, but before the bullets, using this punch. Because it was essential that the wads precisely fit the barrels, a wad cutter was included with the gun's tools.

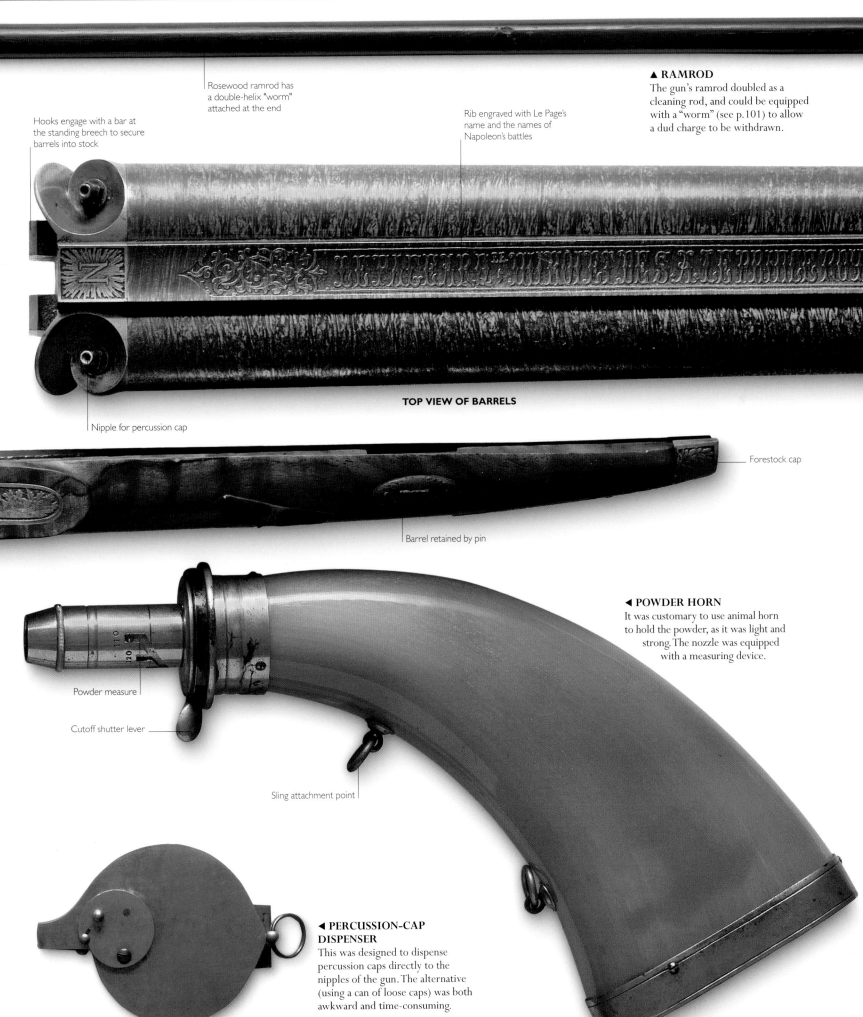

Hooks engage with a bar at
the standing breech to secure
barrels into stock

Rosewood ramrod has
a double-helix "worm"
attached at the end

Rib engraved with Le Page's
name and the names of
Napoleon's battles

▲ RAMROD
The gun's ramrod doubled as a
cleaning rod, and could be equipped
with a "worm" (see p.101) to allow
a dud charge to be withdrawn.

TOP VIEW OF BARRELS

Nipple for percussion cap

Forestock cap

Barrel retained by pin

Powder measure

Cutoff shutter lever

Sling attachment point

◀ POWDER HORN
It was customary to use animal horn
to hold the powder, as it was light and
strong. The nozzle was equipped
with a measuring device.

**◀ PERCUSSION-CAP
DISPENSER**
This was designed to dispense
percussion caps directly to the
nipples of the gun. The alternative
(using a can of loose caps) was both
awkward and time-consuming.

PISTOLS IN PAIRS
In the 18th and early 19th centuries, cased pairs of pistols were popular accessories for gentlemen. Each case contained tools to load and clean the pistols, which could be used for target shooting or dueling.

VISUAL TOUR

DREYSE NEEDLE-FIRE RIFLE

German gunsmith Johann Nikolaus von Dreyse invented the first rotating bolt for loading a rifle at the breech (see p. 304). It sealed the breech much more securely than previous breech-loaders did and ensured that the energy of the expanding gas propelled the bullet forward. The rifle was also revolutionary in using a long, thin firing pin to pierce a "self-consuming" paper cartridge, both drawn from the designs of Jean Samuel Pauly, Dreyse's employer.

3 Bolt handle

1 **2** Bolt

Firing pin catch

Bolt housing, or receiver

1859

4 Firing pin (inside the stock)

Hole for sling swivel

Trigger

Trigger guard

▶ BOLT AT REAR (BREECH OPEN)
Bolt action provides the rifle with an effective opening breech mechanism. The bolt was connected to a needle-shaped firing pin (opposite). Before the bolt could be unlocked, the firing pin would be retracted using the catch at the rear of the bolt. The bolt would then be rotated using the handle and pulled rearward, opening the breech. Once the breech was open, a cartridge was placed into it to load the gun.

▶ BOLT AT FRONT (BREECH CLOSED)
The bolt was closed by pushing the handle forward and rotating it. Doing this sealed the breech and also cocked the gun ready for firing. This gun fired paper cartridges that were not only self-contained (containing primer, charge, and bullet) but also "self-consuming." The cartridges would combust fully, leaving behind no shell or residue to eject, allowing the weapon to be reloaded very efficiently.

DREYSE NEEDLE-FIRE RIFLE

Date 1841

Origin Germany

Barrel 34in (86.5cm)

Caliber .60in (15.2mm)

Named after its needle-like firing pin, this revolutionary gun introduced bolt action (see p.304) in breech-loading rifles. Bolt-action rifles would lead to the development of repeaters and most automatic weapons. The Dreyse rifle helped to establish Prussia's military supremacy over its neighbors for more than two decades. It could be loaded lying down or kneeling behind cover, unlike muzzle-loaders, which had to be loaded standing up. Bolt action also provided the Dreyse rifle with a higher rate of fire than the muzzle-loaders.

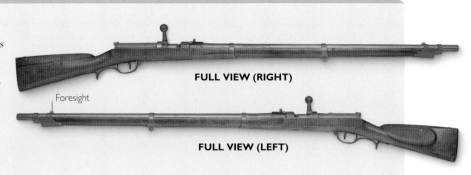

FULL VIEW (RIGHT)

Foresight

FULL VIEW (LEFT)

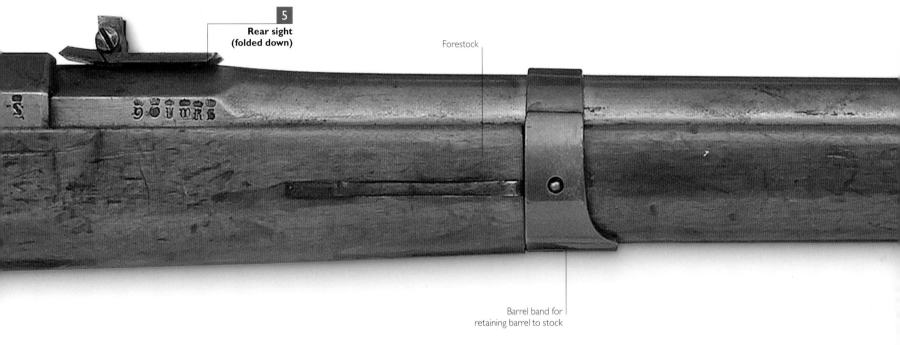

5
Rear sight (folded down)

Forestock

Barrel band for retaining barrel to stock

3

▲ **BOLT HANDLE**
The bolt was turned and moved with this lever, opening and closing the breech for loading. The bolt handle was placed on the right-hand side of the gun, a design feature that would come to be seen on most bolt-action rifles.

4

▲ **FIRING PIN**
This long pin is hidden within the bolt housing. On pulling the trigger, the firing pin pierced the case of the paper cartridge to strike a percussion cap buried within the gunpowder charge, at the bullet's base. Ignition of the cap detonated this charge inside the cartridge, firing the bullet. The cartridge residue burned away upon firing to leave an empty breech.

5

▲ **REAR SIGHT**
The rifle has a V-shaped rear sight, located in front of the bolt housing. It was used together with the foresight for aiming the gun.

BREECH-LOADING CARBINES

Muzzle-loading carbines were impractical to use on horseback as it was difficult to load them while riding. This was also a problem for muzzle-loading rifles, but infantry could manage these relatively inexpensive weapons. As a result, many military authorities recognized the potential benefits of a breech-loading carbine, and carbines became one of the first military arms to be converted to breech-loading. In the 1850s and 1860s, many types of breech-loading mechanism were developed. The availability of percussion ignition (see pp.80–81) technology and improved manufacturing methods fuelled a rapid increase in the conversion of carbines in the mid-19th century. These weapons fired a fully combustible paper cartridge carrying the powder charge and bullet.

▼ GREENE CARBINE

Date 1855

Origin US

Barrel 22in (56cm)

Caliber .54in

The Greene Carbine, produced in small numbers for the British Army during the Crimean War (1853–56), lost out to its rivals due to its cumbersome mechanism. The barrel had to be rotated through a quarter-turn: this unlocked the breech, which was then free to swing out so that a new cartridge could be introduced.

▲ SHARPS CARBINE

Date 1848

Origin US

Barrel 18in (45.5cm)

Caliber .52in

This breech-loader used a sliding breechblock to load a combustible cartridge, which was ignited by a tape primer (see p.81) or, in later models, a percussion cap.

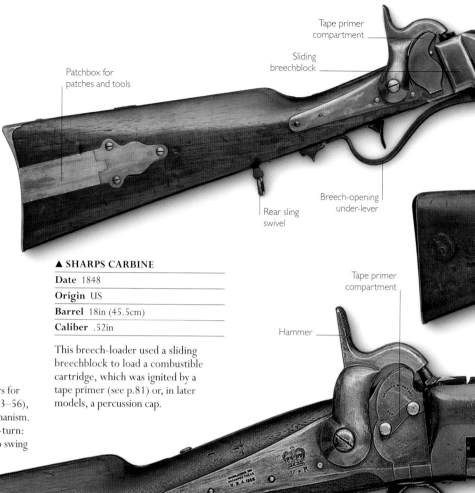

Tape primer compartment

Sliding breechblock

Patchbox for patches and tools

Breech-opening under-lever

Rear sling swivel

Tape primer compartment

Hammer

Trigger

Breech-locking catch lever

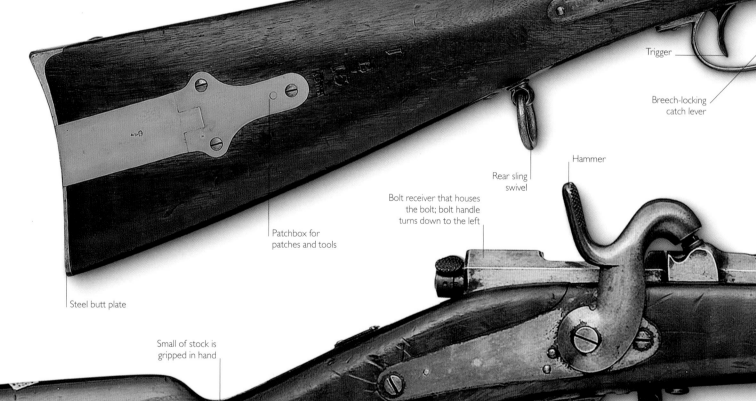

Patchbox for patches and tools

Steel butt plate

Small of stock is gripped in hand

Bolt receiver that houses the bolt; bolt handle turns down to the left

Rear sling swivel

Hammer

Rear sling attachment

Trigger

Foresight

Hammer

Nipple for percussion cap

Rear sight

Barrel band

Bolt

Trigger

Lock plate

▲ CALISHER AND TERRY CAPPING BREECH-LOADING CARBINE

Date 1861

Origin UK

Barrel 20in (51.2cm)

Caliber .54in

The Calisher and Terry carbine was the first bolt-action weapon adopted by the British Army. Its paper cartridge included a greased felt wad, which remained in the breech after firing and was pushed into the barrel by the insertion of the next round, lubricating and cleaning the bore when it was fired. In a trial, one carbine fired 1,800 rounds without requiring additional cleaning.

Breechblock

Rear sight

Foresight

Hammer

Barrel band

"Monkey Tail" breech lever

Lock plate

▲ WESTLEY RICHARDS "MONKEY TAIL" CARBINE

Date 1866

Origin UK

Barrel 18in (45.5cm)

Caliber .45in

Birmingham gunmakers Westley Richards produced two carbines for the British Army. This one had a front-hinged, tilting breech with a long, curved lever, which is how the weapon got its nickname.

Barrel band

Barrel band-retaining spring

FULL VIEW

▲ CHASSEPOT PERCUSSION CARBINE

Date 1858

Origin France

Barrel 28¼in (72cm)

Caliber 13.5mm

In the mid-1850s, gunmakers at the French Imperial Armories began experimenting with bolt-action, percussion-cap breech-loaders. Alphonse Chassepot produced a design using a rubber washer to seal the breech. He subsequently replaced the hammer with a needle striker within the bolt, which was accepted for use by the French Army as the Modèle 1866.

TURNING POINT

SELF-CONTAINED CARTRIDGES

In the early 19th century, the discovery of chemical primers and the invention of percussion ignition led to an even greater advance. It became possible to combine the key elements required for a gun to fire—primer, propellant, and projectile—into a single unit, the self-contained, or unitary, cartridge. Following a period of experimentation, the solid-drawn, center-fire metallic cartridge evolved in the 1870s, triggering a new era in firearms technology. The subsequent development of repeating rifles, self-loading pistols, and machine-guns ultimately culminated in the weapons seen today.

▲ **METALLIC CARTRIDGE**
All metallic cartridges, such as this .44in-40 Winchester cartridge, contain three main elements within a metal shell. These are a propellant (gunpowder), projectile (bullet), and chemical primer.

Although the percussion cap containing chemical primer (see pp.80–81) made muzzle-loaders far more reliable, inserting gunpowder and ball separately down the muzzle, and then adding a primer, was a laborious process. Early attempts to unite a breech-loading system with percussion-cap ignition resulted in the creation of some breech-loading guns in the mid-19th century. These guns suffered from the problem of leakage of gas at the breech because the paper or linen cartridge used did not form a gas-tight seal. However, the door to successful breech-loading guns had already been opened in the early 19th century with the invention of a "self-contained" cartridge.

UNITARY CARTRIDGES

Patented by gunsmith Jean Pauly in France in 1812, the first self-contained cartridge had a paper casing and a metal base. It worked perfectly in careful hands but it was not rugged enough for military use. In the following years, the cartridge was reinvented in several ways to improve the ruggedness, the ease of loading, and ignition, and the gas seal. Pauly's ex-employee Casimir Lefaucheux created a "pin-fire" cartridge of cardboard and brass in 1836, in which a metal pin struck and ignited the chemical primer in the cartridge. In 1841, another of Pauly's former employees, Nikolaus von Dreyse, created a cartridge with a combustible paper case. They both worked and had limited success, but they had too many drawbacks for widespread adoption.

In 1846, Parisian gunsmith Benjamin Houllier took a major step by creating a cartridge case pressed from a disc of copper or brass. Its all-metal, single-piece design properly sealed the breech. American Benjamin Tyler Henry used the same construction, but added a hollow rim filled with chemical primer, creating the first rim-fire cartridge in 1860.

BEGINNINGS OF CENTER-FIRE

Rim-fire cartridges had to be handled carefully, because they were liable to accidental discharge and the rim could burst in use. A major breakthrough—the center-fire cartridge—held the chemical primer in a percussion cap fixed in the center of the cartridge's base. Designed in Britain by Colonel Boxer, the cartridge did not need to be aligned while loading, as with pin-fires, and could be reloaded easily, unlike rim-fires. However, it had a complex composite case. US inventor Hiram Berdan developed a one-piece brass case, which was to become the standard for most cartridges in the future. By the late 1870s, center-fire metallic cartridges, similar to today's, had taken hold.

Before the advent of the self-contained cartridge, the loading of a gun required a user to place the correct charge of propellant in the barrel, along with a projectile and some wadding to hold the propellant and projectile in place, in the correct sequence. Next, he had to employ an external means of ignition, as there was no primer inside the barrel.

• **SINGLE-SHOT WEAPONS** were the norm of the day.

EARLY PAPER CARTRIDGE

• **PAPER CARTRIDGES** contained the correct charge of gunpowder and a projectile. They needed to be torn open before loading a gun.

• **AN INCORRECT LOADING SEQUENCE** would leave the gun useless until it could be unloaded and then reloaded correctly.

• **AN INCORRECTLY RAMMED PROJECTILE**, one not placed firmly on top of the gunpowder, could cause the gun barrel to burst. The same could happen if a loaded gun was accidentally reloaded.

• **GAS LEAKAGE** was a problem with early breech-loading guns, which used cartridges made of paper and other combustible material. Leakage reduced the pressure of the exploding gas that propelled the projectile.

EARLY BREECH-LOADING PAPER CARTRIDGE

" … the invention of **paramount value**, appears to me to be this **cartridge**…"

CAPTAIN O'HEA, **THE JOURNAL OF THE SOCIETY OF ARTS (1867)**

Unitary metallic cartridges transformed conflicts in the late 19th century. They played a key role in the Battle of Hoover's Gap—a decisive engagement of the Tullahoma Campaign in the American Civil War (1861–65). The Union Army was outnumbered by Confederate forces, which were in a strong defensive position. Marching rapidly into Hoover's Gap, the Union forces surprised the Confederates who scattered initially. In the battle that ensued, the Confederate Army regrouped and charged at the Union soldiers. Despite facing a volley of gunfire, the Confederate soldiers continued to advance, not expecting the Union rifles to be reloaded quickly. However, the Union soldiers were armed with new Spencer repeating rifles loaded with .56in-caliber rim-fire cartridges. These weapons could fire more than 14 rounds per minute and proceeded to cut down almost one-quarter of the Confederate Army.

In the Anglo–Zulu War (1879), a small number of British soldiers used the new technology in a similar way. Armed with Martini-Henry rifles loaded with Boxer cartridges, they repelled a vast Zulu army against all odds, because they were able to reload and fire swiftly in the heat of battle. Armed with superior guns and ammunition, European powers scrambled to make forays into Africa at the turn of the 20th century.

These conflicts exemplified the advantages of the metallic cartridge, without which self-loading and automatic firearms would not have seen the light of day.

KEY **FIGURE**

Hiram Berdan
(1824–93)

Engineer and inventor Hiram Berdan was a colonel of the United States Volunteer Sharpshooter Regiments during the American Civil War. A sought-after weapons designer, he was commissioned by the Russian Army to update its infantry firearms. He created the Berdan cartridge, which would go on to become the standard for metallic cartridges seen today.

AFTER »

Once the idea of self-contained ammunition had taken hold, cartridges and their associated firearms underwent a long process of evolution, eventually resulting in the invention of repeating rifles (see p.116) and magazine feeding systems.

● **EARLY CENTER-FIRE CARTRIDGES,** such as the .450in Martini Henry Boxer cartridge, were composite assemblies. The flimsy bodies were easily distorted and forcible extraction, in the heat of battle, could pull off the disk forming the rim. These problems were overcome as the composite assembly cartridges were replaced by solid-drawn cartridges.

● **MUZZLE-LOADERS WERE CONVERTED** into breech-loading weapons to utilize metallic cartridges. This spurred the refinement of breech-loading systems, resulting in the growth of more efficient breech-loading weapons, and eventually, self-loading firearms.

.450IN MARTINI HENRY BOXER CARTRIDGE

● **THE DURABILITY** of solid-drawn metallic cartridges allowed them to be loaded from magazines on guns. Repeating weapons designed to accept cartridges in magazines developed rapidly, leading to the firearms of today.

◄ **DEFENDING RORKE'S DRIFT**
In the defense of Rorke's Drift (1879) in the Anglo-Zulu War, fewer than 150 British soldiers defended themselves against an overwhelming force of 4,000 Zulu warriors. The use of Martini rifles and coiled brass-cased cartridges enabled the British forces to load and fire quickly, saving them from almost certain slaughter. Some soldiers can be seen handling the cartridges in the picture.

SINGLE-SHOT BREECH-LOADING RIFLES

For many years, military authorities throughout the Western world had appreciated the benefits of breech-loading firearms. Muzzle-loading muskets and rifles were difficult to reload while a soldier was lying prone, and were also usually slower to load than a well-designed breech-loader. Breech-loading mechanisms continued to evolve. Many rifles began to be loaded at the breech using bolt action (see p.304), which would influence the future development of these arms. In the 19th century, a number of breech-loading weapons were taken into military service in Europe and North America. Many were efficient conversions of existing muzzle-loading rifles and would have a long service life.

▼ BALLARD RIFLE

Date 1862–66
Origin US
Barrel 28½in (72.4cm)
Caliber .54in

The Ballard rifle used a breech-loading mechanism called lever action, in which an under-lever was used to open the breech chamber. The rifle's scroll under-lever operated a pivoting breechblock.

Scroll under-lever

Action cocked/uncocked indicator

Hinged breechblock

Small of the stock is gripped in hand

Under-lever

Rear sling attachment

"Trapdoor" breech cover incorporates firing pin

Rear sight

Barrel band

Iron trigger guard

Bolt handle

Cleaning rod

Front
sling swivel

**▲ DREYSE NEEDLE-FIRE
RIFLE MODEL 1862**

Date 1868

Origin Germany

Barrel 32in (81.2cm)

Caliber 15.43mm

Prussia adopted Dreyse's revolutionary bolt-action design (see pp.108–09) into its military service in 1848. Soon, different models began to be built, each one for a different branch within the army, such as line infantry or cavalry. The Model 1862 was an infantry rifle first manufactured in 1862, but this particular piece was built in 1868.

Barrel band

Foresight

Front sling
swivel

FULL VIEW

Rear sight

▼ PEABODY-MARTINI RIFLE

Date c.1870

Origin US

Barrel 30in (76cm)

Caliber .45in

This lever-action military rifle was designed by Henry O. Peabody and produced by the Providence Tool Company of Providence, Rhode Island. It is equipped with a safety catch. Many units were bought by the government of Turkey for the Russo–Turkish War (1877–78).

Barrel band anchors
the barrel in the stock

Rear sight graduated
to 1 mile (1.6km)

Foresight

Cleaning
rod

**▲ MAUSER
MODEL 1871 RIFLE**

Date 1872 onward

Origin Germany

Barrel 32½in (83cm)

Caliber 11 × 60mm

Many single-shot breech-loading rifles of the time employed combustible cartridges. German manufacturer Waffenfabrik Mauser began modifying Dreyse guns, such as the Model 1862 (above), to accept brass cartridges, but Peter Paul Mauser produced a new design with a bolt-action breech mechanism stronger than that of the Dreyse rifle. It was modified to take metallic cartridges (see pp.112–13) rather than fully combustible paper ones, and could therefore fire more powerful ammunition (cartridges with a larger powder charge). Effective out to a range of 875 yards (800m), the *Infanteriegewehr* (infantry rifle) M71 established Mauser's preeminence among suppliers of military rifles.

Front sling swivel

**▲ SPRINGFIELD MODEL
1866 RIFLE ALLIN
"TRAPDOOR" CONVERSION**

Date 1874

Origin US

Barrel 32½in (83cm)

Caliber .45in

The perfection of the unitary cartridge left the world's armies with a dilemma: what should they do with their millions of redundant muzzle-loaders? The US Army modified its rifled muskets by milling out the top of the barrel, creating a chamber for the cartridge, and installing a front-hinged breech cover, or "trapdoor," incorporating a firing pin.

MANUALLY OPERATED REPEATING RIFLES

There had been attempts to produce "repeater," or multiple-shot, rifles and muskets as early as the 16th century. Notwithstanding the success enjoyed by the percussion revolvers of Colt and others (see pp.88–93), it took the unitary cartridge containing primer, charge, and projectile in one package (see pp.112–13) to make the repeating rifle a satisfactory reality in the mid-19th century. Contained in magazines carrying set numbers of cartridges, the ammunition of a repeating rifle was fed to its breech as part of the single action that cleared the chamber of a spent cartridge case, cocked the action, and readied the gun for firing.

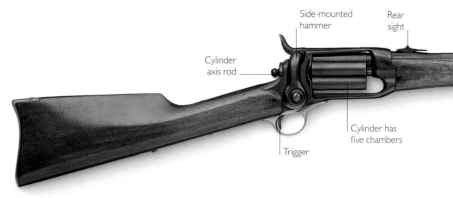

Side-mounted hammer

Rear sight

Cylinder axis rod

Cylinder has five chambers

Trigger

▲ COLT REVOLVING RIFLE

Date 1855

Origin US

Barrel 26¾in (68.2cm)

Caliber .56in

Of Colt's earliest revolving rifles (see pp.122–23), this one made a considerable impact, even though its loading procedure was cumbersome. The cylinder was removed, powder packed into the five chambers, a bullet packed on top, and the chambers sealed with wax in order to protect against the possibility of igniting all the chambers at once.

▼ HENRY MODEL 1860

Date 1860

Origin US

Barrel 20in (51cm)

Caliber .44in rim-fire

When Oliver Winchester set up the New Haven Arms Co. (see p.119), he brought in Benjamin Tyler Henry to run it. Henry's first act was to design a lever-action repeating rifle worked by an under-lever that ejected the spent round, chambered a new one, and left the action cocked. This rifle carried a magazine with 15 rounds. Magazines evolved various forms, the most common of which was tubular, with cartridges stacked in a horizontal row.

FULL VIEW

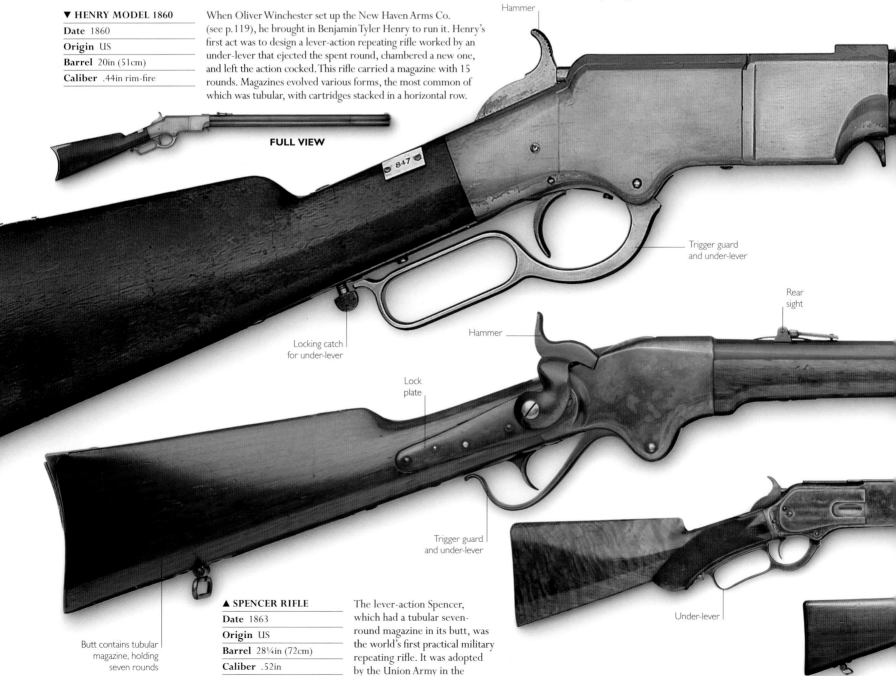

Hammer

847

Hammer

Trigger guard and under-lever

Rear sight

Locking catch for under-lever

Lock plate

Trigger guard and under-lever

Under-lever

Butt contains tubular magazine, holding seven rounds

▲ SPENCER RIFLE

Date 1863

Origin US

Barrel 28¼in (72cm)

Caliber .52in

The lever-action Spencer, which had a tubular seven-round magazine in its butt, was the world's first practical military repeating rifle. It was adopted by the Union Army in the American Civil War.

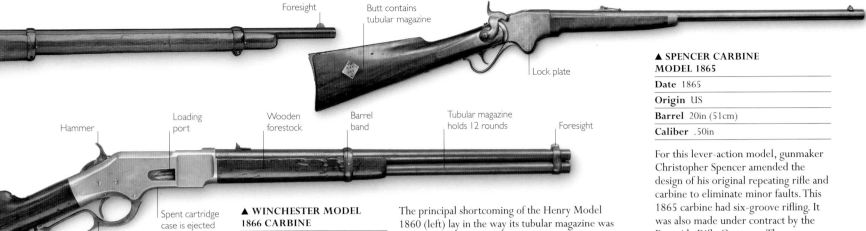

Foresight

Butt contains tubular magazine

Lock plate

▲ SPENCER CARBINE MODEL 1865

Date 1865

Origin US

Barrel 20in (51cm)

Caliber .50in

For this lever-action model, gunmaker Christopher Spencer amended the design of his original repeating rifle and carbine to eliminate minor faults. This 1865 carbine had six-groove rifling. It was also made under contract by the Burnside Rifle Company. The gun carried a tubular magazine in its butt. Some other guns of the time carried another common magazine type—the box form, in which cartridges were stacked one above the other.

Hammer

Loading port

Wooden forestock

Barrel band

Tubular magazine holds 12 rounds

Foresight

Spent cartridge case is ejected downward

Trigger guard and under-lever

▲ WINCHESTER MODEL 1866 CARBINE

Date 1866

Origin US

Barrel 23in (58.5cm)

Caliber .44in rim-fire

The principal shortcoming of the Henry Model 1860 (left) lay in the way its tubular magazine was charged. In 1866, an improvement was introduced to allow reloading via a port on the receiver, which doubled the rifle's rate of fire to 30 rounds a minute. The ammunition used by this rifle and the Model 1860 was a rim-fire cartridge in which the projectile and propellant were contained in the cartridge case and the primer was carried in its rim (see p.112).

Tubular magazine holds 15 rounds

Cylinder with nine chambers

.44in-caliber rifle barrel fires ball cartridges

.66in-caliber smooth barrel

Ejector rod

▲ LE MAT REVOLVER RIFLE

Date 1872

Origin France/US

Barrel 24¾in (62.8cm)

Caliber .44in and .66in

Based on a similar pistol, the Le Mat Revolver Rifle was an oddity. It boasted two barrels; the lower, charged with shot, acted as the axis pin for the nine-chambered cylinder, which was charged with ball cartridges. The gun was equipped with a loading/ejection gate and rod, similar to those found on Colt's early brass-cartridge pistols.

Small of the stock is gripped in hand

Trigger

Forward sling swivel

Barrel band

Bayonet lug

Foresight

◀ WINCHESTER MODEL 1876

Date 1876

Origin US

Barrel 28in (71cm)

Caliber .45in

Popular with frontier hunters, this lever-action model was designed to take a powerful .45in-75 caliber cartridge. In total, it took four types of high-powered cartridges reaching up to .50in-95 Express—a powerful cartridge with high-velocity propellant. Manufacturers had begun to use precise caliber designations for their cartridges—.50in is the caliber and 95 refers to the weight of charge in grains.

Bolt

Barrel band

Tubular magazine in forestock

Cleaning rod

Front sling swivel

▲ VETTERLI-VITALI 1880

Date 1880

Origin Italy

Barrel 34in (86cm)

Caliber 10mm

The Vetterli-Vitali 1880 was an experimental bolt-action rifle fitted with a tubular magazine and was an adaptation of earlier single-shot Italian rifles. Vetterli-Vitali eventually became better known for its box magazine system, which was introduced in 1886.

GREAT GUNSMITHS

WINCHESTER

The repeating rifle was an American invention—created initially in the 1840s by inventors Walter Hunt and Lewis Jennings. It was the Winchester Repeating Arms Company, owned by Oliver Winchester, that developed the idea, manufactured the firearms, and sold them both to American pioneers and hunters, and to armies all over the world. Known for producing high-quality firearms, this company was highly successful, especially in the period between the American Civil War and World War I.

OLIVER WINCHESTER

In 1857, entrepreneur Oliver Winchester found himself in control of the Volcanic Arms Company after many of the other investors pulled out. The repeating firearms produced by the company were impressive compared to the single-shot weapons that were then the norm, but they were not successful, mainly because the cartridges they fired lacked power. Winchester saw the need to improve the company's products and hired Benjamin Tyler Henry to develop a new repeating rifle. Patented in 1860, just before the outbreak of the Civil War, the weapon was the first practical lever-action gun (see p.116), and, when it came on to the market a year into the war, it made Winchester's name.

HENRY MODEL 1860

THE WINCHESTER AT WAR

During the Civil War, the US federal government bought about 2,000 of Winchester's firearms, which were then known as Henry rifles, after their designer. Individual soldiers purchased still more, realizing that the increased firepower provided by the repeating action gave them a better chance in battle. Soon, pioneers in the American West were using Henry rifles, too, but Winchester saw that the weapons could be improved, and subsequently introduced the Model 1866 (see p. 117), which had a better loading system and a wooden forestock to protect the user from the hot barrel. These improved rifles helped spread Winchester's fame far beyond the US, particularly when they were used in large numbers by the Ottoman Turks in the Russo–Turkish War of 1877–78. During this conflict, the repeating rifles helped the Turks at the

▼ RUSSO–TURKISH WAR

Russian riflemen (on the right) are seen here firing on Ottoman Turkish troops armed with swords at the battle of Stara Zagora, Bulgaria, in July 1877, during the Russo–Turkish War. Their guns were single-shot, however, and the Turkish forces also had Winchester repeating rifles, with which they eventually defeated the Russians.

> "… that damned **Yankee rifle** that they load on Sunday and fire all week…"
>
> ATTRIBUTED TO **CONFEDERATE SOLDIERS**

WINCHESTER MODEL 1876

WINCHESTER MODEL 1894

1860 The Henry rifle, designed by Benjamin Henry, is made by the New Haven Arms Company, under Oliver Winchester and John M. Davies.

1866 After the reorganization of the company as the Winchester Repeating Arms Company, the Winchester Model 1866 is launched.

1873 Winchester's first center-fire cartridge is used in the successful Model 1873.

1876 To celebrate the US Centennial, Winchester introduces the Model 1876, designed to take full-powered center-fire cartridges.

1883 Winchester begins to work in partnership with firearms designer John Browning.

1894 The Model 1894 is launched; it will eventually become one of the best-selling hunting rifles of all time.

1903 The company begins to produce the first of a series of self-loading rifles.

1914 Winchester produces firearms for the British government during World War I, including the Pattern 1914 Enfield rifle.

1931 After suffering poor sales during the postwar period and the Great Depression, the company goes into receivership.

siege of Plevna. They were outnumbered four to one but inflicted huge losses on the Russians because of the superior firepower of their Winchesters. Many European armies adopted repeating rifles in the years following the Russo–Turkish War.

ONE IN A THOUSAND

Further improvements to the line followed, including the Model 1873 and the Model 1876 (see p.117), the first Winchester rifle to be specially designed to fire full-powered center-fire cartridges for superior stopping power. It was the Model 1873 that made Winchester firearms especially popular in the American West, both for hunting and defense. Hunters found that they could bring down a buffalo at 200 yards (180m), and with a weapon as powerful as this they also believed that they

▶ **WINCHESTER '73**
James Stewart holds a Winchester rifle in the film *Winchester '73*. The movie in part tells the story of what happens when a "One in a thousand" Winchester passes from one owner to another.

could protect themselves and their families in the tough and dangerous frontier country. The Model 1873 also heralded an ingenious marketing campaign that showcased the high quality of many of the company's products. From 1875, Winchester tested its rifle barrels during manufacturing and selected the most accurate to be equipped with set triggers and engraved with the legend "One in a thousand." These weapons were sold at a premium price of $100 and were prized for their accuracy; they are still valued highly by collectors today.

To reinforce the link between Winchester products and the American West, the company introduced the slogan, "Winchester: the gun that won the West" from 1919. Many pioneers carried Winchester rifles and this phrase

certainly helped strengthen the link between Winchester and American history, underpinning the company's reputation as it continued to produce rifles, shotguns, and other firearms into the 20th century.

BREECH-LOADING SHOTGUNS

In 1835, a French inventor named Casimir Lefaucheux made a breakthrough in sporting gun design with his patent for a pin-fire cartridge (see p.112) and a gun with a break-open design (its barrels hinged downward for loading at the breech). Hinged barrels became almost universally adopted for sporting guns, although gunmakers created many designs for locking the breech. The pin-fire cartridge was eventually replaced by a center-fire cartridge (see pp.112–13). Guns using pin-fire cartridges typically had distinctively long hammers that needed to strike down onto each cartridge's pin. The use of center-fire cartridges meant that a gun's hammers could be made smaller. Gunmakers also realized that the opening of the breech could be used to cock the gun, and "hammerless" shotguns began to appear before the end of the 19th century. Shotguns generally lacked sights, since they were fired by accurate pointing rather than deliberate aiming.

Burr walnut stock

Pair of hammers

Barrel-retaining pin

Breech-locking lever

Abbreviated forestock

Lock plate

Paired triggers for two barrels

Pair of hammers

Lock plate

Checkered pistol grip

Left-barrel trigger

Right-barrel trigger

Under-lever

Paired triggers

Lock plate

Combined cocking and under-lever

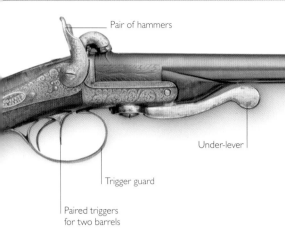

Pair of hammers

One of a pair of smoothbore barrels

Under-lever

Trigger guard

Paired triggers for two barrels

▲ FRENCH PIN-FIRE SPORTING GUN

Date 1835

Origin France

Barrel 25½in (64.7cm)

Caliber 18-gauge (.63in/16mm)

This was the breech-loading gun invented by Casimir Lefaucheux. Its break-open action was locked by a turning lever in front of the trigger guard. It was loaded with the pin-fire cartridge invented by Lefaucheux. This cartridge incorporated a short metal pin protruding from the case that detonated a fulminate charge placed within the cartridge.

One of a pair of smoothbore barrels

◄ ENGLISH PIN-FIRE SHOTGUN

Date c.1860

Origin UK

Length 30in (76.2cm)

Caliber 12-gauge (.73in/18.54mm)

Casimir Lefaucheux's pin-fire system remained popular with shotgun-armed hunters (particularly in Britain and France), even after it had been outmoded by the center-fire cartridge. This example, with back-action locks and a side-mounted breech-locking lever, is finely finished, but with little in the way of decoration. It was the work of Samuel and Charles Smith of London.

One of a pair of smoothbore barrels

Barrel-retaining pin

Abbreviated forestock

FULL VIEW

▲ ENGLISH SHOTGUN

Date 1880s

Origin England

Barrel 30in (76.2cm)

Caliber Not known

This gun, built by gunmaker Thomas Horsley of York, is one of the earliest sporting arms to employ center-fire cartridges. Similar to the pin-fire sporting guns shown above, it had strikers operated by external hammers, two triggers for quick barrel selection, and a break-open under-lever set beneath the trigger guard. The external hammers were each drawn back by hand, and when a trigger was pulled, it connected with the outer part of the striker, which struck the center-fire cartridge in the breech.

Abbreviated forestock

One of a pair of smoothbore barrels

▲ HOLLAND AND HOLLAND SHOTGUN

Date 1878

Origin England

Barrel 30in (76.2cm)

Caliber 12-gauge (.73in/18.54mm)

Holland and Holland is known for the superb quality of its bird-hunting shotguns. This hammerless shotgun with an under-lever has a classic English-style stock—it has no pistol grip. It also has an unusual breech-loading mechanism—its under-lever not only opened and closed the breech, but also cocked the enclosed box-lock action.

SPORTING RIFLES

Sporting rifles were made in fascinating varieties, influenced by many factors. These included popular regional styles, new technologies, and the size and nature of the game the rifle was used to hunt—from birds and rabbits to deer and elephants. The taste and budget of the owner also affected the design of these rifles. Sporting rifles were often more technically sophisticated than contemporary military arms, since they were not going to be subjected to a harsh environment or extended use on the battlefield.

▼ PERCUSSION UNDERHAMMER RIFLE

Date 1835

Origin US

Barrel 29½in (75cm)

Caliber .44in

This underhammer rifle by Vermont gunmaker Nicanor Kendall was a percussion-cap muzzle-loader. Its stock is probably of American Cherry and the furniture (gun parts such as trigger guard and hammer) is of a high nickel-copper alloy which is cast and incised with decoration. The heavy octagonal barrel is fitted with four ramrod pipes, a leaf rear sight, and a blade foresight.

▲ COLT PATERSON REVOLVING RIFLE

Date 1837

Origin US

Barrel 32in (81.3cm)

Caliber .36in

Samuel Colt's first factory in Paterson, New Jersey, produced revolving rifles as well as pistols. However, it had limited facilities and went bankrupt. Paterson-built Colt rifles, such as this first-pattern concealed-hammer eight-shot rifle, are extremely rare. This muzzle-loading revolving rifle used percussion caps.

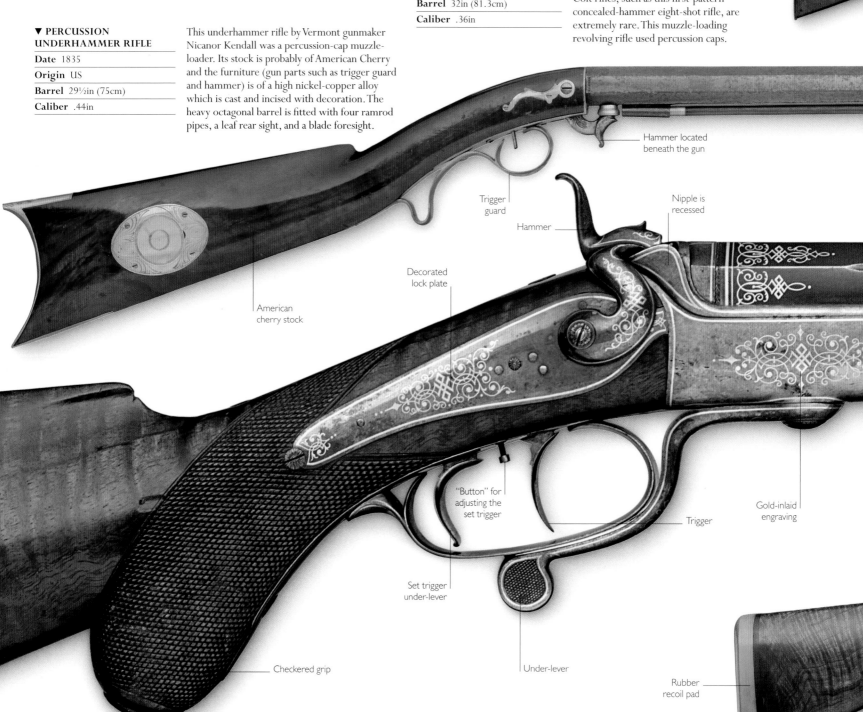

Recessed nipple for percussion cap

Cocking ring

Hammer located beneath the gun

Trigger guard

Hammer

Nipple is recessed

Decorated lock plate

American cherry stock

"Button" for adjusting the set trigger

Trigger

Gold-inlaid engraving

Set trigger under-lever

Under-lever

Checkered grip

Rubber recoil pad

Muzzle

Straight, "English-style" stock

Hammer

Rear sight

Barrel band

Trigger guard

Under-lever

Checkered grip

▲ PRINCE'S PATENT CAPPING BREECH-LOADING RIFLE

Date 1860

Origin UK

Barrel 25in (63.5cm)

Caliber .37in

This is also called the English rook and rabbit rifle. Rook and rabbit pies were popular meals in Victorian Britain, and the type of simple small-bore rifle used to shoot these animals took their name as its own. This example is a percussion-cap rifle that used paper cartridges that were loaded with a sliding barrel breech design. The breech was locked by the under-lever in front of the trigger guard using a method patented by London gunmaker Frederick Prince in 1855.

Leaf-shaped rear sight

Octagonal barrel

Blade-shaped foresight

Ramrod pipe

Ramrod

Incised checkering on the forestock to improve grip

Rear sight

Forestock cap shaped to fit the hand

▲ GERMAN UNDER-LEVER RIFLE

FULL VIEW

Date 1880

Origin Germany

Barrel 25½in (63.5cm)

Caliber .45in

Even after the perfection of the bolt-action magazine rifle, there were those who refused to embrace the new technology. Hunters, particularly of big and dangerous game, preferred to trust the simplicity of a break-open design, such as this center-fire rifle.

Ornate scroll work on lock plate

Checkered forestock

Under-lever

Checkered grip

▲ ENGLISH DOUBLE-BARRELED HAMMER RIFLE

Date 1870s

Origin England

Barrel 24in (61cm)

Caliber 10-gauge (.78in/19.81mm)

This fine Holland and Holland rifle has external hammers that were cocked by hand, ornate scroll-work decorating the lock plates, double triggers for quick barrel selection, and a checkered forestock characteristic of many English side-by-side guns. This gun fired center-fire cartridges.

METALLIC-CARTRIDGE PISTOLS (1853–70)

Pistol cartridges with metallic cases became practical through Lefaucheux's pin-fire design (see p.112). They were improved by Smith and Wesson's rim-fire cartridge (see pp.128–29) in 1860, and again by center-fire cartridges in the 1870s. In the US, manufacture of revolvers capable of using these cartridges was impeded by a patent taken out by Rollin White in 1859, later acquired by Smith and Wesson, which prevented others from making "bored-through" cylinders. These cylinders were bored all the way through for loading a cartridge from the rear, the cartridge case sealing the breech in the process. Once this patent expired in 1869, percussion revolvers were converted to utilize metallic cartridges, and new pistols were built to use them.

▶ **COLT NAVY CONVERSION**

Date	1861
Origin	US
Barrel	7½in (19cm)
Caliber	.36in

Colt replaced its angular 1851 Navy revolver (see p.88) with a new, streamlined version ten years later. This example has been converted to accept brass cartridges after the fashion of the Single Action Army (see p.95); many percussion revolvers were adapted in this way.

Loading (ejection) gate

Cylinder

Trigger

Trigger guard

Plain walnut grip

Wooden butt

Lanyard ring

Hammer

Cylinder

Round barrel

Loading (ejection) gate

Ejector rod helps remove spent cartridge cases

Steadying spur on trigger guard

▲ **LEFAUCHEUX PIN-FIRE REVOLVER**

Date	1853
Origin	France
Barrel	5¼in (13.5cm)
Caliber	12mm pin-fire

Eugène Lefaucheux produced a six-shot, double-action revolver in 12mm caliber for his father's 1835 pin-fire cartridge. This is a Cavalry model of 1853. An Army model, without a steadying spur, was also produced.

Round barrel

Extractor rod is pushed to remove spent cartridge cases

Extractor-rod housing

▼ DOUBLE-BARRELED PIN-FIRE PISTOL

Date	1860
Origin	Belgium
Barrel	7½in (19cm)
Caliber	.44in pin-fire

The modest quality of this inexpensive pistol is typical of the many tens of thousands of cheap weapons produced in Belgium, Germany, and elsewhere throughout the 19th century. The pistol breaks open like a shotgun for loading and has folding triggers that hinge downward when the hammers are cocked.

Hammer

Breech-locking catch

Octagonal barrel

Internal box-lock

Folding triggers

Foresight

Screw securing butt to pistol's frame

Hammer

Extractor rod is operated by pushing back the central rod in the center of the cylinder axle

▼ REMINGTON RIM-FIRE DOUBLE-BARRELED DERRINGER

Date	1865
Origin	US
Barrel	3in (7.6cm)
Caliber	.41in rim-fire

Henry Deringer was a Philadelphia gunmaker who specialized in pocket pistols; his name was ascribed—with the mysterious addition of a second "r"—to a genre of such weapons. The best-known of them was the rim-fire Remington Double Derringer, a top-hinged, tip-up, over-and-under design that was to remain in production until 1935.

Trigger guard

Hinge allowed barrels to tip up

Foresight

Hammer

▶ WEBLEY MARK 1 REVOLVER

Date	1870
Origin	UK
Barrel	4in (10.16cm)
Caliber	.455in

This was one of Webley and Scott's standard models of revolver and saw widespread commercial sale, as well as adoption by some police forces. It was produced in a number of different calibers and used center-fire cartridges.

Barrels positioned in over-and-under design (one above the other)

Barrel catch

Spur trigger

Lanyard ring

METALLIC-CARTRIDGE REVOLVERS (1871–79)

With the production of robust and reliable metallic cartridges, gun manufacturers could develop and improve upon all kinds of pistols and other guns to use them effectively. Revolvers continued to improve and were made in considerable variety. Some, like Colt and Remington revolvers, had fixed cylinders loaded through a rear gate, while others had cylinders that swung out sideways, or, like those made by Smith and Wesson, had frames that hinged open.

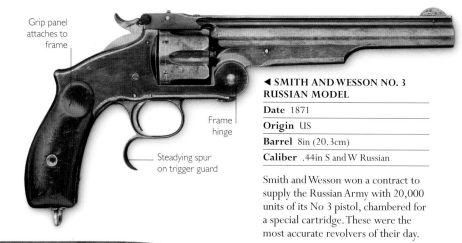

Grip panel attaches to frame

Frame hinge

Steadying spur on trigger guard

◀ **SMITH AND WESSON NO. 3 RUSSIAN MODEL**

Date 1871

Origin US

Barrel 8in (20.3cm)

Caliber .44in S and W Russian

Smith and Wesson won a contract to supply the Russian Army with 20,000 units of its No 3 pistol, chambered for a special cartridge. These were the most accurate revolvers of their day.

Hard rubber-composition grip

Six-chambered cylinder

Trigger

▲ **COLT SINGLE-ACTION ARMY (SAA) MODEL 1873**

Date 1873

Origin US

Barrel 7½in (19cm)

Caliber .45in

The Colt SAA ("Peacemaker") (see p.95) married the single-action lock of the old Dragoon model to a bored-through cylinder in a solid frame, into which the barrel was screwed.

Octagonal barrel

Foresight

Grip screw

Lanyard ring

▲ **DUTCH M1873 ARMY REVOLVER**

Date 1873

Origin Netherlands

Barrel 6¼in (16cm)

Caliber 9.4 × 21mm rim-fire

Two models of the M1873 were made for the Dutch Army. The earlier model had an octagonal barrel, while the later one had a round barrel.

Six-chambered cylinder

Distinctive web beneath barrel

Wooden butt

▲ **REMINGTON ARMY MODEL 1875**

Date 1875

Origin US

Barrel 7½in (19cm)

Caliber .45in

This gun was similar in build to the Colt Single Action Army Model of 1873. It had a web beneath the barrel to help guide it while being stored in its holster. It was also adapted for .40in and .44in cartridges.

Hammer

Five-chambered cylinder

Colt logo

▲ **COLT LIGHTNING DOUBLE ACTION**

Date 1877

Origin US

Barrel 5½in (14cm)

Caliber .38in

The Lightning was Colt's first double-action handgun. It was a small-frame revolver chambered for .38in cartridges, although Colt also produced an accompanying weapon, the Thunderer, in .44in caliber to cater to those preferring a heavier punch. Although the Lightning had some quality issues, sales were still respectable, and the total production run reached 166,000 guns.

Hammer

Barrel

Foresight

Cylinder arbor, or axle, on which cylinder rotates

Arbor catch

▲ REICHSREVOLVER M1879

Date 1879

Origin Germany

Barrel 7in (18cm)

Caliber 10.6 × 25mm rim-fire

This solid and reliable single-action six-shot revolver was used by the German Army until 1908. Some even saw service in World War I. The gun is unusual in having a safety catch, which helped prevent accidental discharges while on horseback.

Safety catch

Trigger guard

Diagonal slot

◀ MAUSER M1878 "ZIG-ZAG"

Date 1878

Origin Germany

Barrel 6½in (16.5cm)

Caliber .43in

The "Zig-Zag" was a six-shot revolver with a top-hinged frame. Diagonal slots cut into the cylinder face were used with a corresponding arm link to rotate the cylinder.

Checkered grip

Frame-opening catch

Fluted cylinder

Cylinder axis pin

Rib reinforces barrel

Checkered wooden grip

Frame pivot

▼ COLT FRONTIER DOUBLE ACTION

Date 1878

Origin US

Barrel 5½in (14cm)

Caliber .44in/.45in

After introducing the double-action Lightning (left) in 1877, Colt came up with a double-action version of the SAA "Peacemaker" (also left) in .44in and .45in calibers.

▲ WEBLEY-PRYSE NO. 4 REVOLVER

Date 1877

Origin UK

Barrel 6¼in (16cm)

Caliber .45in

In 1876, Charles Pryse designed a tip-down, break-open revolver with a rebounding-hammer action. It also featured simultaneous extraction of spent cartridges. Although uncommon in revolver design, automatic ejection of cartridges was desirable in military revolvers, which often needed to be reloaded quickly. This Fourth Model Webley-Pryse, recognizable by its fluted cylinder, was made in calibers ranging from .32in to .577in.

Ejector rod housing

Six-chambered cylinder

Trigger guard

Pearl grip

Lanyard ring

SMITH AND WESSON

DANIEL BAIRD WESSON

Horace Smith and Daniel Baird Wesson were two of history's most influential gunmakers. Their first major achievement was the Model 1, a revolver that was simple to use because it did away with separate powder, ball, and percussion cap—to load it, all that the user had to do was to drop self-contained metal cartridges (see pp.112–13) into the cylinder. This remarkable revolver, and the larger-caliber Model 2, established Smith and Wesson as one of the best-known firearms manufacturers in the United States.

Gunmakers Horace Smith and D. B. Wesson first collaborated in the early 1850s, when they worked on the production of a repeating pistol operated by lever action (see p.114) and based on an earlier design by Hunt and Jennings. The weapon had impressive fire power, earning it the name "Volcanic," but it proved unreliable. Its cartridges sometimes got stuck in the barrel and occasionally several of the volatile cartridges went off at once. Wesson devised an improved, self-contained metal cartridge for the gun, but the weapon still lacked a way of extracting the cartridge cases with ease and sales did not improve.

When the main investor pulled out, the business was bought by Oliver Winchester, who went on to develop his successful repeating rifle. Smith left the business, as eventually did Wesson.

COMBINING INNOVATIONS

By 1856, Samuel Colt's patent on the revolver, which he took out in 1835, was about to run out and Wesson wanted to design a revolver that fired the self-contained metal cartridge. Horace Smith was impressed with Wesson's plans and teamed up with him once again. The metal cartridge needed a bored-through revolver cylinder, allowing cartridges to be loaded from the rear. The bored-through cylinder had already been patented by a gunsmith named Rollin White, so Smith and Wesson made a deal with him. They licensed his patent, agreeing to pay White a royalty on each pistol they sold. White retained the patent and remained responsible for defending his patent rights should any other manufacturer try to produce a revolver with a similar cylinder. The Smith and Wesson Model 1, a seven-shot revolver incorporating White's cylinder and firing Wesson's self-contained .22in rim-fire cartridge, was launched in 1857. It became popular, heralding the end of percussion arms. Soon other manufacturers

> ## "The **Pistol**... proves to be one of the most powerful weapons I ever saw."

FROM A LETTER WRITTEN IN 1862 BY C. F. ACHENBACK, A GUN OWNER, TO SMITH AND WESSON **ON THE MODEL 1**

▼ **SMITH AND WESSON FACTORY**
A worker operates a rifling machine while others assemble revolver barrels and cylinders at the Smith and Wesson factory in Springfield, Massachusetts, in 1880.

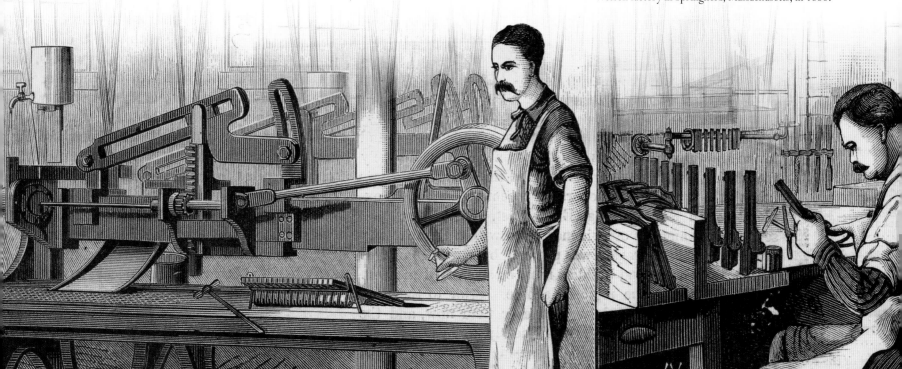

**SMITH AND WESSON
MODEL 3**

**SMITH AND WESSON
MILITARY AND POLICE**

**SMITH AND WESSON
MODEL 29**

1852 Horace Smith and D. B. Wesson form their first partnership to produce a lever-action pistol, but this venture is not successful financially.

1856 Smith and Wesson form their second company to manufacture the Model 1 revolver.

1869 The Model 3 is introduced, selling in large numbers in Russia and elsewhere.

1875 An order from the US military leads to the

Schofield revolver, named for the locking system devised by Major George W. Schofield.

1898 When the Spanish-American War comes to an end, the US Army sells off many surplus Schofield revolvers, bringing these onto the civilian market.

1913 The company introduces its first center-fire semiautomatic pistol, the Model 1913.

1919 Smith and Wesson produce a variant of the successful Military and Police revolver with a baton extension for police use.

1955 The Model 29, chambered for the .44in Magnum cartridge, is launched.

1971 Clint Eastwood sports a Model 29 in the film *Dirty Harry*, hugely increasing its popularity.

tried to make similar firearms, and so White had to defend his patent in court. While the inventor was embroiled in his legal battle, Smith and Wesson developed the Model 2, a similar design but with a larger .32in caliber, which was more suitable for use in combat. The launch of the Model 2 in 1861 coincided with the start of the American Civil War, and Smith and Wesson found that there was a huge demand for the new revolver—by 1865, the two gunmakers were rich men. When the war ended, many soldiers took home their weapons, and soon Smith and Wesson firearms were in use all over the American West.

NEW MARKETS

After the Civil War, there was a steep decline in demand for firearms in the US. Models 1 and 2 had sold in hundreds of thousands, but in 1867, the company sold only 15 guns per month. Smith and Wesson began looking for

new markets. The company started to sell guns in large numbers overseas, notably to Russia, where the 1869 Model 3 proved successful. The company also sold the Model 3 to the US Cavalry, who used a modified version that was easier to load while riding. In 1874, Horace Smith retired, selling his share of the company to Wesson. In the late-19th century, Wesson produced guns that proved especially attractive in another key market—police forces. A number of police departments bought Smith and Wesson firearms, such as the .38in Safety Hammerless of the 1880s. In 1899, Wesson brought out the revolver that was the most enduring of all Smith and Wesson's products— the Military and Police revolver. Prized for its power, accuracy, and ease of loading, the Military and Police revolver sold in huge numbers to law-enforcement agencies all over the world. Modified in various ways,

▲ **AUSTRALIAN POLICE**
A police officer from Victoria, Australia, fires a .40in-caliber Smith and Wesson automatic pistol. Such weapons were chosen by his force in 2009 to replace older revolvers.

it remains in production and was used very widely until police and military units replaced it with semiautomatic weapons. It has been estimated that around 6 million Military and Police revolvers have been produced, and large numbers are still in use, including many by target shooters. This unique record easily makes it the 20th century's best-selling center-fire revolver. Smith and Wesson is also known for introducing Magnum cartridges to handguns. These cartridges are very powerful and generate a lot of recoil. Popular examples are the .357in and .44in cartridges. The company continues to build on its heritage, carrying its innovations into the 21st century.

MUZZLE-LOADING ARTILLERY

Despite having been the earliest form of gunpowder weapon, muzzle-loading artillery remained a potent force until the very last years of the 19th century. Strong and mechanically uncomplicated smoothbore weapons, these muzzle-loaders fired round shot made of lead or iron. In the late 1850s, muzzle-loading artillery began to evolve into refined rifled steel weapons able to fire aerodynamic projectiles—huge shells capable of penetrating the thickest armor plate.

▲ CHINESE 32-POUNDER

Date	1841
Origin	China
Length	9ft (2.74m)
Caliber	7.5in (190mm)
Range	Just over 1 mile (1.8km)

Engravings on the breech indicate that this imposing bronze 32-pounder was cast in August 1841, during the reign of Chinese Emperor Daoguang (1820–50), for coastal defense duties.

Decorative molded bands on smoothbore barrel

▼ INDIAN BRONZE 24-POUNDER GUN

Date	Late 18th century
Origin	India
Length	10¾ft (3.27m)
Caliber	5.66in (142.2mm)
Range	Just over 1 mile (1.8km)

This gun barrel represents the many older pieces kept in regular and effective use in many parts of the world well into the 19th century. It is decorated on the muzzle and barrel with motifs resembling tiger's stripes. Tigers' heads also form the muzzle, the cascable button, and the ends of the trunnions.

Carriage

Trail hook

Smoothbore barrel

Muzzle

Cascable

Trunnion to help elevate or lower barrel

Rifled barrel made of hoops of steel

▼ BLAKELY 2.75-IN RML MOUNTAIN GUN

Date	1865
Origin	UK
Length	(Barrel) 3¼ft (1m)
Caliber	2.75in (69.85mm)
Range	Just over 1 mile (1.8km)

In mountainous terrain, armies required lighter, more maneuverable field guns, and mountain guns were developed to meet this need. This rifled muzzle-loader, or RML gun, manufactured by the innovative Blakely Ordnance Company, has a steel barrel with six-groove rifling and reinforcement at the breech in the form of an additional steel tube, or "jacket."

Rifled steel barrel

Carriage for land service

Original wooden carriage

Muzzle
molding

Rifled barrel

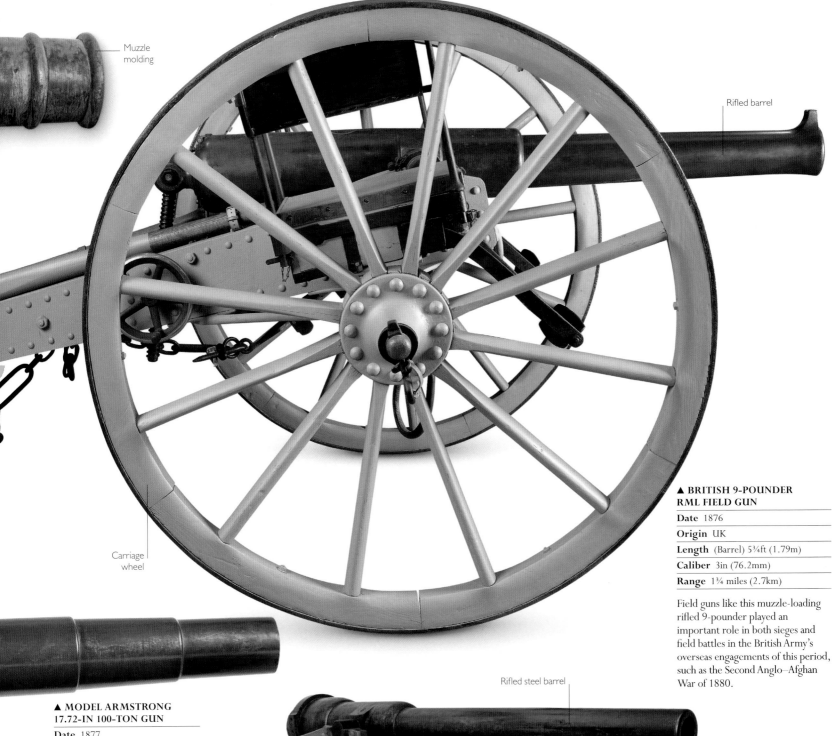

Carriage
wheel

▲ BRITISH 9-POUNDER RML FIELD GUN

Date	1876
Origin	UK
Length	(Barrel) 5¾ft (1.79m)
Caliber	3in (76.2mm)
Range	1¾ miles (2.7km)

Field guns like this muzzle-loading rifled 9-pounder played an important role in both sieges and field battles in the British Army's overseas engagements of this period, such as the Second Anglo–Afghan War of 1880.

▲ MODEL ARMSTRONG 17.72-IN 100-TON GUN

Date	1877
Origin	England
Length	31ft (9.44m)
Caliber	17.72in (450mm)
Range	3.7 miles (6km)

This is a model of one of the large 100-ton RML guns built by Sir William Armstrong. Eight were fitted to two Italian battleships, and others were installed in British batteries on Gibraltar and Malta.

Rifled steel barrel

Carriage

▲ ARMSTRONG 12-POUNDER RML

Date	1878
Origin	UK
Length	7¼ft (2.23m)
Caliber	3in (76.2mm)
Range	2 miles (3.1km)

This steel 12-pounder was manufactured by Armstrong in Newcastle, northern England, for use on an armed merchant ship. It fired 12-lb (5.4-kg) projectiles.

BREECH-LOADING ARTILLERY

New materials began to be used to build artillery—muzzle-loaders as well as rarer breech-loaders—in the second half of the 19th century, revolutionizing artillery design. Cast-iron and bronze barrels were replaced by stronger ones of wrought iron and steel. There were also improvements in gunpowder manufacture which translated into longer range, more accuracy, and greater penetration. This was especially important in the days of the development of ironclad warships. Breech-loaders had always proved more practical than muzzle-loaders on ships (see p.14). Breech-loading also meant that naval guns could now have long barrels, since it was no longer necessary to load at the muzzle, and this helped significantly to increase their range.

Trail

Carriage wheel

Rifled wrought-iron barrel

▶ ARMSTRONG RBL 12-POUNDER

Date	1859
Origin	UK
Length	(Barrel) 7ft (2.13m)
Caliber	7.62cm
Range	2 miles (3.1km)

This Armstrong rifled breech-loader, or RBL gun, required a crew of nine men to operate it. The gun that entered British Army service (shown here) in 1859 had a 7-ft (2.13-m) barrel, while the British Royal Navy used a 6-ft (1.83-m) barrel version. In 1863, the shorter version became standard.

▼ ARMSTRONG RBL 40-POUNDER

Date	1861
Origin	UK
Length	9¾ft (3m)
Caliber	12cm
Range	1½ miles (2.5km)

The Armstrong 40-pounder was used by the British Royal Navy as a broadside gun (a gun used in a battery on one side of a ship), and by the army as a defensive gun in military forts. It saw action in the Royal Navy's bombardment of Kagoshima, Japan, in August 1863.

Elevating mechanism

Rifled steel barrel

Rifled wrought-iron barrel has been reinforced

Cone mounting

▶ WHITWORTH 45-MM BREECH-LOADING BOAT GUN

Date	1875
Origin	UK
Length	3ft (0.94m)
Caliber	45mm
Range	¼ mile (0.3km)

This boat gun had hexagonal rifling with a Whitworth sliding-lock breech-loading mechanism. It was set on a cone mounting mostly used for small naval guns. This example was mounted on an armed yacht.

Leather water bucket for barrel cleaning

▼ MODEL 1896 FIELD GUN

Date	1896
Origin	Germany
Length	(Barrel) 7ft (2.13m)
Caliber	77mm
Range	3½ miles (5.5km)

This is a 77mm *Feldkanone M1896 Neue Art* (77mm Field gun, Model 1896, New Type), a standard German field gun of World War I. It used unitary ammunition (with projectile, propellant, and primer) with a brass case resembling a large rifle cartridge. This gun was used by German artillery against British tanks of the 7th Battalion, the Tank Corps, at Graincourt, France, in 1917. It was subsequently captured by the crews from the Tank Corps.

Splinter shield (barrier that protects the gun crew from enemy fire)

Breech

Recuperator helps return barrel to its firing position after recoil

Carriage wheel

Trail

EARLY MACHINE-GUNS

By the time of the American Civil War (1861–65), there was widespread military interest in the potential benefit offered by rapid-fire weapons during combat. Two designers in particular, Wilson Ager and Richard Gatling, developed guns which offered considerable potential. Ager and Gatling's early "machine-guns" used a primitive type of cartridge in the form of reloadable steel tubes fitted with percussion caps, and consequently suffered from ammunition problems. However, the development of reliable unitary, metallic-cased center-fire cartridges (see pp.112–13), carrying propellant, projectile, and primer in one package, enabled these guns, and a number of other effective hand-cranked repeating guns, to achieve high rates of fire.

Carriage trail

CARTRIDGE FOR AGER

FRONT AND REAR VIEW OF THE CARTRIDGE

▲ **AGER MACHINE-GUN**

Date c.1860

Origin US

Length (Barrel) 3ft (.88m)

Caliber .58in

This gun was developed by Wilson Ager, and advertised by him as "an army in six square feet" because of its ability to fire 120 rounds per minute. Sixty guns were ordered for the Union Army, but barrel overheating problems meant the guns saw little use.

Ammunition hopper (metal box on top of the gun containing cartridges)

Barrel group axle

Breech casing

Loading and firing lever

Elevating screw

Traversing wheel

▲ **EARLY GATLING CONVERTED TO METALLIC CARTRIDGE**

Date c.1862

Origin US

Length (Barrel) 4½ft (1.4m)

Caliber .50in

Richard Jordan Gatling patented his hand-cranked, multi-barrelled gun in 1862, and first used reloadable steel cartridges fired by percussion caps. Problems with misfires were common. In order to solve these issues, this early machine-gun was eventually modified to utilize the improved unitary cartridges.

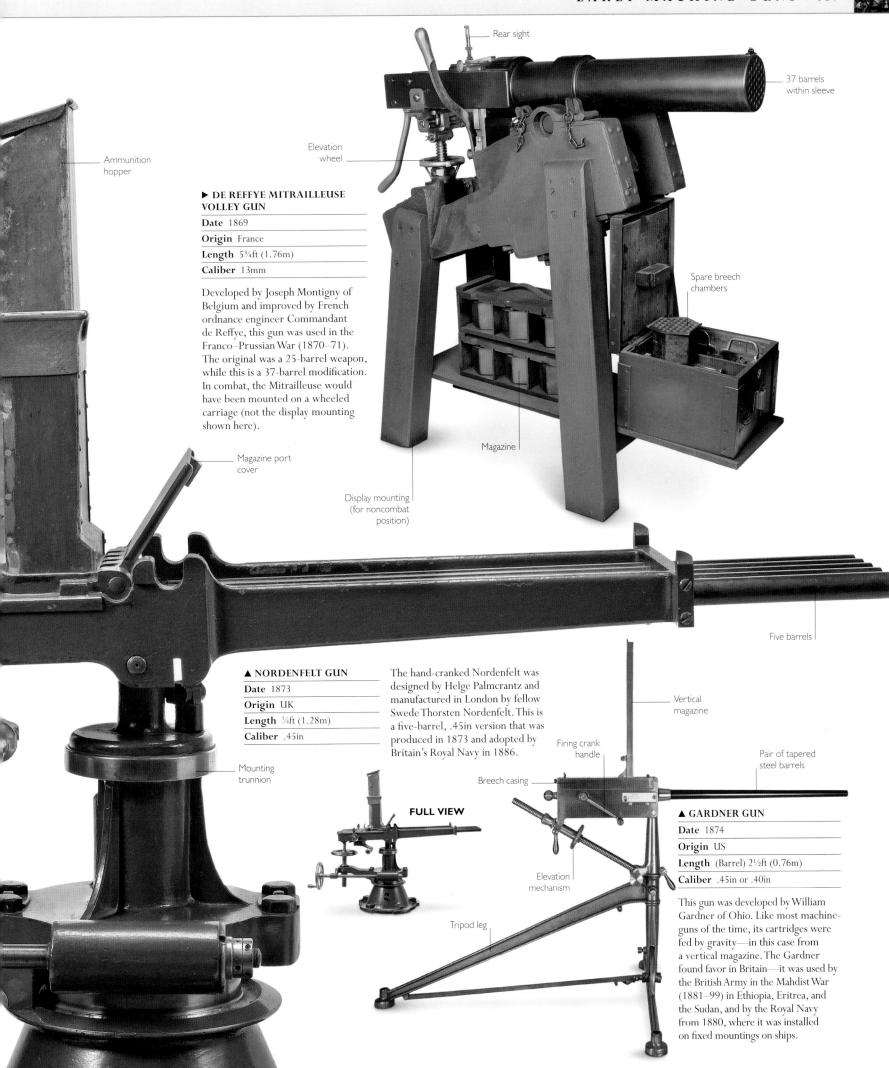

Rear sight

37 barrels
within sleeve

Ammunition
hopper

Elevation
wheel

▶ DE REFFYE MITRAILLEUSE VOLLEY GUN

Date 1869

Origin France

Length 5¾ft (1.76m)

Caliber 13mm

Developed by Joseph Montigny of
Belgium and improved by French
ordnance engineer Commandant
de Reffye, this gun was used in the
Franco–Prussian War (1870–71).
The original was a 25-barrel weapon,
while this is a 37-barrel modification.
In combat, the Mitrailleuse would
have been mounted on a wheeled
carriage (not the display mounting
shown here).

Spare breech
chambers

Magazine port
cover

Magazine

Display mounting
(for noncombat
position)

Five barrels

▲ NORDENFELT GUN

Date 1873

Origin UK

Length ¼ft (1.28m)

Caliber .45in

The hand-cranked Nordenfelt was
designed by Helge Palmcrantz and
manufactured in London by fellow
Swede Thorsten Nordenfelt. This is
a five-barrel, .45in version that was
produced in 1873 and adopted by
Britain's Royal Navy in 1886.

Vertical
magazine

Firing crank
handle

Pair of tapered
steel barrels

Mounting
trunnion

Breech casing

FULL VIEW

▲ GARDNER GUN

Date 1874

Origin US

Length (Barrel) 2½ft (0.76m)

Caliber .45in or .40in

Elevation
mechanism

Tripod leg

This gun was developed by William
Gardner of Ohio. Like most machine-
guns of the time, its cartridges were
fed by gravity—in this case from
a vertical magazine. The Gardner
found favor in Britain—it was used by
the British Army in the Mahdist War
(1881–99) in Ethiopia, Eritrea, and
the Sudan, and by the Royal Navy
from 1880, where it was installed
on fixed mountings on ships.

VISUAL TOUR

GATLING GUN

By the second half of the 19th century, improvements in engineering had made it possible to manufacture reliable rapid-fire weapons. This gun, patented by Richard Gatling in 1862, employed multiple barrels, as would all early machine-guns (see pp.136–37). It was first developed during the American Civil War and was deemed a success.

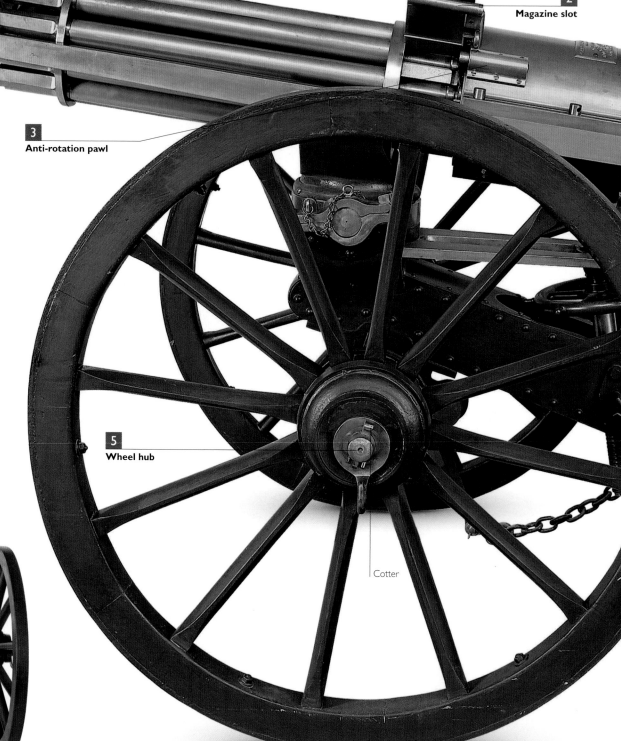

1
Foresight and barrels

2
Magazine slot

3
Anti-rotation pawl

▶ PROTOTYPE MACHINE-GUN
The gun's barrels—at first six, later 10 (as shown here)—were arranged around a cylindrical shaft. A hand-operated crank made the barrels revolve, and cartridges dropped into place from above as each barrel came around. A firing pin then struck and fired the bullet; the barrel turned and the process was repeated. As each barrel descended, its spent case was ejected. This is a prototype of one of Gatling's guns. It fired 400 rounds per minute.

GATLING GUN	
Date	1865
Origin	US
Barrel	26½in (67.3cm)
Caliber	.45in, .65in, or 1in

Magazine

Hand-operated crank

FRONT VIEW

5
Wheel hub

Cotter

◀ FORESIGHT AND BARRELS
The foresight enabled the gun to be kept on target. Ten barrels meant that each barrel fired only once in 10 rounds. Although each barrel would heat up considerably, the gun was able to achieve a higher rate of fire without serious overheating than was possible with a single-barreled gun.

▶ MAGAZINE SLOT
The 40-round magazine was constructed with a groove to help prevent the gun from jamming.

▶ ANTI-ROTATION PAWL
The anti-rotation pawl is the curved lever at the rear of the opening containing the channels for the breech bolts—one for each of the 10 barrels. The anti-rotation pawl was fitted to prevent the group of barrels being rotated in the wrong direction.

▶ WHEEL HUB
To make transportation easier, a towing ring was secured to the wheel hub by a cotter (a wedge-shaped fastener).

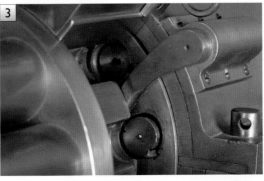

Elevating gear

Traversing handspike stowage (on the right side of the trail)

▲ ELEVATING GEAR
This wheel was used to raise and lower the barrels of the gun.

Riveted iron trail was placed on ground for stability during combat, and at other times could be attached to a horse-drawn limber containing ammunition

◀ TRAVERSING HANDSPIKE
Stored on the right side of the carriage trail, the handspike was used for additional grip when maneuvering the gun carriage. It is not visible on the main picture of the gun.

LUGER ARTILLERY PISTOL

A WORLD IN CONFLICT

1880–1945

Designers and manufacturers in Europe and North America continued to develop new and ever more efficient military firearms. The 1880s and 1890s saw the arrival of the modern machine-gun, smokeless powder, the first self-loading military rifle, self-loading pistols, and artillery of the types that would be responsible for the carnage of World War I. In the years between the world wars, and during World War II, many new types of rapid-fire, higher-velocity, and longer-range firearms were created and adopted into service throughout the Western world.

TURNING POINT

SMOKELESS POWDER

In 1884, the French chemist Paul Vieille invented a new propellant—"smokeless powder." Unlike gunpowder—the propellant used universally up to this point—smokeless powder did not obscure the battlefield or give away a concealed shooter's position. Being smokeless also meant that it left little residue to clog the barrels and actions of guns. Also, crucially, it burned more slowly and generated greater power. These advantageous properties combined to have a profound effect on the development of firearms. A key step was the creation of the first machine-gun—the Maxim gun (see pp.184–85).

5.56MM-CALIBER CARTRIDGE

▲ **SMOKELESS POWDER**
All modern cartridges, such as this 5.56mm NATO, contain smokeless powder as a propellant. Smokeless powder is composed of a mixture of nitrocellulose and other chemicals. It is shaped into thin flakes before being loaded into the cartridges.

Gunpowder, or black powder, was a mix of saltpeter, sulfur, and charcoal. It produced thick white smoke on burning, obscured targets, and clogged up the barrels and mechanisms of guns. Highly combustible, it could explode when unconfined, leading to accidents. These problems were overcome with Vieille's smokeless powder, with the added bonus of more power.

USING SMOKELESS POWDER

The French government was the first to take advantage of the remarkable ballistic properties of smokeless powder, developing the *Le fusil de 8mm Modèle 1886*—the Lebel rifle—named after the designer of its cartridge, Colonel

> " … as they used **smokeless** powder, it was **almost impossible** to see them…"

THEODORE ROOSEVELT, **ON THE SPANISH IN THE SPANISH–AMERICAN WAR (1898)**

Nicholas Lebel of France. This true modern rifle used Lebel's 8mm cartridge with a lead bullet encased in a jacket of cupro-nickel or copper, containing the smokeless propellant. It was faster and weighed less than its predecessors. The cartridge had a flat nose so that it would be safe nose-to-tail in the tubular magazine (see p.116) of the Lebel rifle.

NEW WEAPONS

In conjunction with the metallic cartridge (see pp.112–13), smokeless powder spurred the development of powerful firearms, notably machine-guns such as the Maxim gun (see pp.184–85), and new forms of artillery with greatly improved performance. It left little residue, which allowed the bore and workings of guns to be built to a perfect fit, making weapons such as infantry rifles more accurate. There was also less risk of a bullet jamming in the bore, which would be disastrous with a gun firing several rounds per second. Smokeless powder also provided more propulsive force than the same amount of gunpowder, which significantly increased the effective range of weapons as faster projectiles had a flatter trajectory. It burned clean with little smoke, giving shooters a clear field of vision and allowed them to fire shots with a fair amount of accuracy while hidden from view.

By the turn of the century, bullet designs had begun to be refined to exploit the properties of this new propellant. Captain Desaleux's solid brass pointed (spitzer) bullet used smokeless

powder and had a tapering "boat-tail," which increased its velocity, giving it a flatter trajectory and improving its long-range performance. It was the first bullet of its type to be placed into service by any army and it heralded the development of modern bullets.

Smokeless powder was seen in action in the battles in and around Colenso (1899–1900) on the Tugela River in the second Anglo–Boer War.

KEY **FIGURE**

Paul Marie Eugène Vieille
(1854–1934)

Paul Vieille was a chemistry graduate of Ecole Polytechnique. He became director of the "Laboratoire Central des Poudres et Salpetres" in Paris as well as a member of the French Academy of Sciences. In recognition of his invention of smokeless powder, he was awarded the Leconte prize of 50,000 Francs by the French Academy of Sciences in 1889.

≫ BEFORE

Gunpowder burned fast, coating the bores and actions of guns with a thick layer of "fouling." Also, when exposed to moisture in the air, this "fouling" corroded the insides of the barrels.

GUNPOWDER

• **DIFFICULTY IN PINPOINTING ENEMIES** on the battlefield through billowing smoke made it difficult to gauge tactics and plan countermeasures.

• **ACCUMULATION OF FOULING**, or residue, in a gun's barrel would make the gun increasingly inaccurate and reduce its range. Severe fouling could jam the gun's action, or cause a bullet to get jammed in its bore.

• **FURTHER DEVELOPMENT** of firearms was impeded by limitations in gunpowder's ballistic and chemical properties.

Its use by the Boers was a very important factor in the defeat of the British forces because it was impossible for the British to locate the Boers' weapons. Around the same time, in the Spanish–American War (1898), some of the US troops were still using mainly gunpowder-driven single-shot rifles and struggled against the Spanish, who were armed with magazine-loading rifles and smokeless-powder cartridges. While hidden from view, the Spanish were able to target the US soldiers easily, without giving away their own positions.

Smokeless powder prompted the development of guns large and small with power undreamed of a decade earlier. Long-range rifles and machine-guns became a reality and would change the face of warfare in the decades to come.

▼ WINNING SAN JUAN HILL

In the Battle of San Juan Hill in the Spanish–American War (1898), American soldiers (in the foreground) suffered heavy casualties under fire from Spanish forces, who stayed hidden with their use of smokeless powder. Tactical errors, however, eventually forced the Spanish to retreat.

AFTER »

Once it was found that smokeless propellant was not only smokeless but also more powerful, guns of all natures began to undergo a new revolution.

RUSSIAN MAXIM GUN M1910

● **RIFLES WITH FAR GREATER POWER** evolved, firing new bullets that traveled much faster, with ranges of 1 mile (1.6km) or more and the ability to inflict much more damage.

● **LONG-RANGE BATTLES** could be fought, and even though visibility was improved in the absence of thick smoke, enemies became more difficult to spot and concealment became more important.

● **A NEW BREED OF FIREARMS** evolved, made possible by smokeless powder. These included the first fully automatic weapon—the Maxim gun.

● **THE INCREASE IN FIREPOWER** combined with simplicity in function and manufacture began the age of modern firearms and artillery, which continues today.

MANUALLY OPERATED REPEATING RIFLES (1880–88)

By the end of the 1870s, military authorities in most of Europe and North America had realized the benefits of effective repeating rifles—those that fired multiple rounds from a magazine. Most of them had also recognized that the bolt-action breech mechanism (see p.114) offered the best design for military use, although lever-action rifles continued to be employed. Bolt-action designs were very robust, allowing the use of powerful metallic cartridges, and were not easily put out of action by adverse weather conditions or harsh use. Furthermore, they could be adapted to take different types of magazine. A fascinating variety of tubular and box magazines soon appeared.

Tubular magazine within forestock

Trigger guard

Small of stock is gripped in hand

▲ **KROPATSCHEK GENDARMERIE CARBINE**

Date	1878–79
Origin	Hungary
Barrel	29in (73.6cm)
Caliber	11mm

Designed by Alfred Ritter von Kropatschek, a general in the Austrian Army, this rifle was adopted by France and Hungary in 1878. It had a tubular brass magazine built within the forestock for holding six cartridges. Tubular magazines would gradually give way to box magazines, which became more popular.

FULL VIEW

Bolt is locked at the rear

Bolt handle

Trigger guard

▲ **MAUSER MODEL 71/84**

Date	1884
Origin	Germany
Barrel	33¾in (83cm)
Caliber	11 × 60mm rim-fire

Peter Paul Mauser made many attempts to turn the single-shot bolt-action M1871 rifle (see p.115) into a repeater, eventually creating the Model 71/84. Well-known flaws included weaknesses in the design of its magazine and its tendency to pull to the right. This gun eventually fell out of use in 1888.

Wooden butt

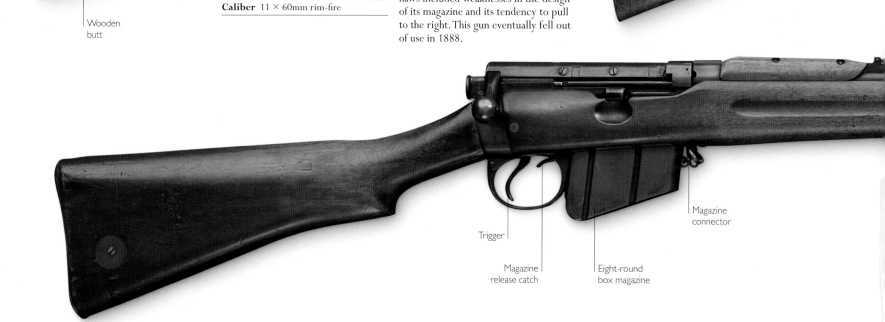

Magazine connector

Trigger

Magazine release catch

Eight-round box magazine

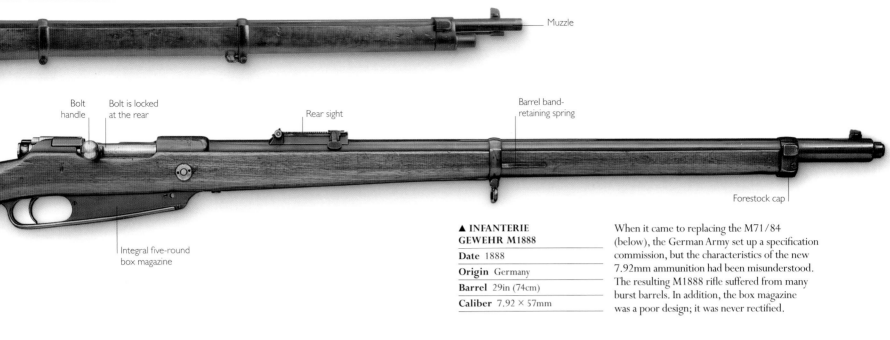

Muzzle

Bolt handle

Bolt is locked at the rear

Rear sight

Barrel band-retaining spring

Forestock cap

Integral five-round box magazine

▲ INFANTERIE GEWEHR M1888

Date	1888
Origin	Germany
Barrel	29in (74cm)
Caliber	7.92 × 57mm

When it came to replacing the M71/84 (below), the German Army set up a specification commission, but the characteristics of the new 7.92mm ammunition had been misunderstood. The resulting M1888 rifle suffered from many burst barrels. In addition, the box magazine was a poor design; it was never rectified.

Rear sight

Forestock holds eight-round tubular magazine

Barrel band-retaining spring

Forward sling attachment

Rear sight

Barrel band

Forward-hinged magazine cover

Rear sling attachment

▲ KRAG-JØRGENSEN M1888

Date	1888
Origin	Norway
Barrel	30in (76.2cm)
Caliber	6.5 × 55mm

Many held that the M1888 was obsolete before it was adopted by the Danish Army, because its five-round magazine had to be hand-loaded, one round at a time, and its bolt's single locking-lug limited it to low-velocity ammunition. It came as a surprise, even to its inventors, that it was also adopted by both the US and Norwegian armies.

Rear sight

Foresight

Forestock

▲ LEE-METFORD MARK 1

Date	1888
Origin	UK
Barrel	30¼in (76.9cm)
Caliber	.303in

The Lee-Metford began a prestigious lineage of British bolt-action rifles. The name derives from the inventor of its action, James Lee, and the designer of the rifled barrel, William Metford. It featured an eight-round box magazine and was chambered for the powerful .303in cartridge. The rifle also had a set of "Extreme Range Sights" on its left side, optimistically graduated out to 3,500 yards (3,200m).

MANUALLY OPERATED REPEATING RIFLES (1889–93)

By the final decade of the 19th century, the military authorities in all Western countries had adopted bolt-action repeating rifles for their infantry and other forces. These rifles were either of their own design or manufactured for them by major international arms companies. A reduction in caliber, and increase in range and velocity were features of this period. Rifles of this time, however, continued to use standard gunpowder, or "black powder," as the primary propellant. This caused difficulties, such as obscuring of targets and fouling of barrels when a gun was fired. The French Lebel rifle leaped ahead in being the first small-caliber, high-velocity military rifle to use smokeless ammunition.

FULL VIEW

▲ **CAVALRY CARBINE MODELLO 1891 TS**

Date	1891
Origin	Italy
Barrel	17¾in (45cm)
Caliber	6.5 × 52mm

This gun was often known as the Mannlicher-Carcano. It continued, in modified form, in Italian service until after World War II, and many units were sold to dealers in the US; one found its way to Lee Harvey Oswald, who allegedly used it to kill President John F. Kennedy in 1963.

Wooden butt

Cocking piece enabled the gun's action to be safely cocked and uncocked manually, if necessary

Trigger guard

▲ **SCHMIDT-RUBIN M1889**

Date	1889
Origin	Switzerland
Barrel	30¾in (78cm)
Caliber	7.5 × 55mm

In 1889, Colonel Rudolf Schmidt of the Swiss Army developed a straight-pull bolt-action rifle, similar to the M1895 (see p.149), with a 12-round box magazine. It was accepted as the regulation rifle and remained in service, only slightly modified, until 1931, when its bolt action was rejigged to operate in half the length. The modified version was only discarded in the late 1950s, and a sniper's version was in use until 1987.

Rear sling attachment

Wooden butt

Cocking piece

Bolt handle

Rear sight

Trigger

Trigger guard

Eight-round tubular magazine within the stock below the barrel

Muzzle

Bayonet lug

Front sling attachment

Barrel band

Rear sight

Integral six-round box magazine

Cleaning rod

Integral five-round box magazine

Finger groove

▲ MOSIN-NAGANT M91

Date	1891
Origin	Imperial Russia
Barrel	31½in (80.2cm)
Caliber	7.62 × 54mm

The "3-line," as it was called, was Imperial Russia's first repeater rifle and its first in a modern caliber. The "line" was a measure approximating one-tenth of an inch and refers to its caliber.

Barrel band

Detachable 12-round box magazine

Bolt handle

Rear sight

Cocking piece

Muzzle

Small of stock is gripped in hand

Magazine

Finger groove

Trigger guard

▲ STEYR M1893 CAVALRY CARBINE

Date	1893
Origin	Austria
Barrel	18in (46cm)
Caliber	6.5mm

The Austrian national arms factory, Steyr, produced 14,000 carbines of this design for Romania, which were delivered before the outbreak of World War I. Designed by Ferdinand Ritter von Mannlicher, they had a turning bolt, rather than Mannlicher's straight-pull breech mechanism (see p.149), and a single-column five-round box magazine, loaded by clip.

Stacking rod allowed rifle to be propped up on its butt (usually as part of a group of three) for storage

Barrel band-retaining spring

▲ LEBEL MLE 1886/93

Date	1893
Origin	France
Barrel	31½in (80cm)
Caliber	8 × 50mm

In 1885, Georges Boulanger was appointed to the ministry of war in Paris. One of his first priorities was to introduce a modern rifle. The result was the first rifle firing a small-caliber, jacketed bullet propelled by smokeless powder (invented by Meille in 1884.) Despite being mechanically unsophisticated, it rendered every other rifle in the world obsolete. This modified version followed in 1893.

MANUALLY OPERATED REPEATING RIFLES (1894–95)

Rifle designers constantly sought greater performance, accuracy, and durability, and continued to experiment with designs for breech mechanisms and magazines. Steyr Mannlicher (see pp.290–91), for example, designed a successful mechanism that required the handle only to be pulled directly backward in order to revolve and unlock the bolt. Meanwhile, in lever-action rifles, Winchester (see pp.116–17) developed a complex mechanism in which a box magazine descended with the under-lever.

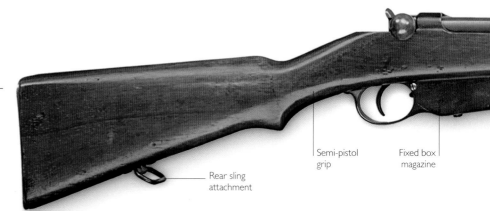

Semi-pistol grip

Fixed box magazine

Rear sling attachment

Five-round box magazine

Bolt handle

Bolt

Trigger

Under-lever was pulled down to eject a spent cartridge and returned to its place to load a new one and cock the weapon

Checkered small of stock

Wooden butt

Owner's personal badge

S.P.COETZEE

Rear sling attachment

Trigger

▶ **LEE-ENFIELD MARK I**

Date	1895
Origin	UK
Barrel	25in (63.5cm)
Caliber	.303in

A redesigned version of the .303in Lee-Metford of 1888 (see p.145), the Mark I had a detachable 10-round magazine, and, with the bolt handle near the trigger, was quite fast to operate. Officially known as the ".303in caliber, Rifle, Magazine, Lee-Enfield," its name was often shortened to MLE, sometimes spoken as "Emily."

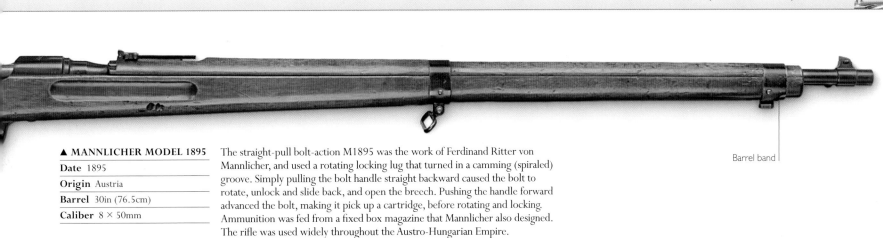

▲ MANNLICHER MODEL 1895

Date 1895

Origin Austria

Barrel 30in (76.5cm)

Caliber 8 × 50mm

The straight-pull bolt-action M1895 was the work of Ferdinand Ritter von Mannlicher, and used a rotating locking lug that turned in a camming (spiraled) groove. Simply pulling the bolt handle straight backward caused the bolt to rotate, unlock and slide back, and open the breech. Pushing the handle forward advanced the bolt, making it pick up a cartridge, before rotating and locking. Ammunition was fed from a fixed box magazine that Mannlicher also designed. The rifle was used widely throughout the Austro-Hungarian Empire.

Barrel band

▼ WINCHESTER MODEL 1895

Date 1895

Origin US

Barrel 30in (76cm)

Caliber .30in

Winchester joined the list of manufacturers making repeating rifles, and its repeaters used classic tubular magazines. This lever-action model, however, broke with tradition by having a box magazine. Military sales of the 1895 were strong, particularly to Russia, which bought over 290,000 between 1915 and 1917.

Rear barrel band with sling swivel

Forestock cap with sling swivel and bayonet lug

Sling

FULL VIEW

Rear sight

Steel barrel

Foresight

Front sling attachment

▲ MAUSER PLEZIER 1895–97 DELUXE

Date 1895–97

Origin Germany

Barrel 28in (71cm)

Caliber 7 × 57mm

The influential German manufacturer Mauser (see pp. 164–65) was a major supplier of rifles to the Boers in South Africa, and a very popular rifle was the Model 1895. Both military rifles and those made up as *Plezier* ("pleasure") sporting rifles saw combat in the hands of the Boers in the Second Boer War (1899–1902).

Bolt

Wooden forestock

Front sling attachment

Ten-round magazine

GREAT GUNSMITHS

LEE-ENFIELD

In 1895, the British Army adopted Lee-Enfield's bolt-action rifle. In various forms, this weapon was to remain the British Army's standard-issue rifle until 1957. It would see action in countless conflicts all over the world and is still used by police in some countries. This unique record is due largely to the brilliance of designer James P. Lee. The Lee-Enfield guns are named after him and the London borough of Enfield, where the original Lee-Enfield rifle was designed and where it and its various derivatives were produced at the Royal Small Arms Factory.

JAMES P. LEE

James P. Lee was a Scottish-born inventor and firearms designer who emigrated to Canada and worked in the US, where he made important advances in rifle and magazine design. His work came to the attention of the British Army in 1888, when they adopted the Lee-Metford rifle, which combined a bolt action designed by Lee and a barrel created by William Ellis Metford. Users were impressed with the Lee-Metford, which had a "cock-on-closing" action that allowed very rapid firing. When the weapon was used with smokeless powder (see pp.142–43), however, the rifling in the barrel wore rapidly. The search was soon on for a replacement.

RAPID FIRE

The problem with the Lee-Metford was that the smokeless propellant generated additional heat and pressure, which damaged the barrel's shallow, rounded rifling. The solution lay in a new type of rifling with a square shape, devised at the Royal Small Arms factory at Enfield. When barrels with

▼ **BRITISH SOLDIERS**
During World War I, hundreds of thousands of British infantrymen, on the Western front and elsewhere, carried Lee-Enfield rifles. Soldiers affectionately referred to their SMLEs as "smellies."

**SMLE MARK III WITH
WIRE-CUTTER ATTACHMENT**

**RIFLE NO 5 MARK 1
"JUNGLE CARBINE"**

1879 James P. Lee develops a bolt-action, magazine-fed rifle; successful in its own right, this design attracts the interest of the British Army in 1888.

1895 The British Army adopts the Magazine, Lee-Enfield (MLE) rifle.

1907 The SMLE Mark III is introduced.

1914 British Army Sergeant Instructor Alfred Snoxall sets the world record for rapid fire, with 38 aimed rounds in a minute.

1915 Because the SMLE Mark III is quite complex to manufacture, the simpler SMLE Mark III is developed to fulfill the high rate of demand during World War I.

1939 The No. 4 Rifle is designed to be easy to mass-produce; its spike bayonet is known to soldiers as the "pig-sticker."

1943 A very quiet, suppressed version of the Lee-Enfield rifle, the De Lisle Carbine, is produced for British commando troops during World War II.

1944 The need for a short, lightweight rifle spurs the creation of the Rifle No. 5 Mark I, known as the "Jungle Carbine."

the new-style rifling were combined with Lee's rapid-firing bolt action in 1895, the new Lee-Enfield rifle was born. Lee's cock-on-closing action, in which the forward thrust of the bolt cocks the action, was faster than that of the Mauser Model 1898, which cocked on opening. The Lee-Enfield design also placed the bolt handle over the trigger, near to the user's hand, again making it faster to operate. A detachable 10-round magazine kept the weapon supplied with ammunition. Military commanders were initially sceptical about the removable magazine—they feared that soldiers would lose this vital piece of equipment in the heat of battle, and some early Lee-Enfields had a length of thin chain to keep the magazine tethered to the gun. Subsequent versions had a charger, or "stripper clip," loading system that did away with the need for the detachable magazine, while allowing the operator to load and fire at speed. The rate of fire possible with Lee-Enfield rifles was impressive and surprised Britain's enemies in World War I. There are accounts of German troops attacked by fire from Lee-Enfields mistaking this for machine-gun fire. This was borne out in target shooting, when skilled marksmen could hit a target at 300 yards (270m) more than 30 times a minute, and even inexperienced soldiers could achieve a rapid rate of fire.

VERSATILITY AND USE

The original Lee-Enfields were impressive, but many wanted a more accurate weapon that was also lighter. The manufacturers at Enfield responded with shorter and lighter models offering charger-loading and improved sights. The Army designated these firearms Rifle, Short, Magazine, Lee-Enfield (SMLE rifle for short). The SMLE Mark III,

▲ MODERN CONFLICTS
An Afghan soldier holds a 1902 Lee-Enfield rifle found during a joint US and Afghan Army raid in 2002 in Kunar province, Afghanistan.

introduced in 1907 and used throughout World War I, was the best-known of them. The way these Lee-Enfields combined a user-friendly layout with the ability to fire rapidly piqued the interest of many users, and the guns spread around the British Empire and beyond. Users also realized that the basic design—and later models that were simpler and easier to manufacture—could be modified for a range of uses. Many were converted

to .22in caliber so that they could act as training rifles firing inexpensive ammunition. Others, with the addition of features such as cheek pieces and telescopic sights, became sniper rifles. Conversions to automatic or semiautomatic loading were also carried out. Both the versatility of the original rifles and the various conversions have helped to keep the Lee-Enfield popular globally. It is widely used by police forces, for hunting, and for target shooting, and Lee-Enfields (or copies of the weapons) are still found in combat. The history of the Lee-Enfield is one of the greatest success stories in the world of firearms.

"It was a **rifle light and handy,** accurate at short and at long ranges and... capable of a remarkable rate of fire."

LIEUTENANT-COLONEL LORD COTTESMORE **ON THE LEE-ENFIELD .303IN MAGAZINE RIFLE**

MANUALLY OPERATED REPEATING RIFLES (1896–1905)

Many countries designed and introduced into military service their own varieties of bolt-action repeating breech-loaders. Those of Mauser (see pp.164–65) from Germany, however, were regarded as especially robust, accurate, and serviceable. Countries sought to purchase their rifles from Mauser, from other manufacturers making Mauser rifles under license, or, as in the case of the US, were sufficiently influenced by the quality of the design that they acquired rights to manufacture their own version.

Regimental identification plate

Bolt handle

Trigger guard

Rear sling attachment

Bolt handle

Rear sight

Integral five-round magazine

Bolt handle protrudes horizontally

Dismounting disk

Semi-pistol grip

Trigger guard

Internal five-round box magazine

Cocking piece

Rear sling swivel

Experimental 25-round removable box magazine

Leaf-type
rear sight

Cleaning rod

▲ MAUSER MODEL 1896

Date 1896

Origin Germany

Barrel 29¼in (74cm)

Caliber 6.5 × 55mm

Waffenfabrik Mauser began exporting rifles to China in 1875; then came the Mauser-Koka, for Serbia; the Belgian M1889; the Turkish M1890; the Argentine M1891; and the Spanish M1893. The world's armies seemed to be beating a path to Mauser's door. Mauser began manufacturing the Model 1896 for Sweden in 1895. Licensed Swedish production of the rifle continued until 1944.

▼ ARISAKA MEIJI 30

Date 1897

Origin Japan

Barrel 31½in (79.8cm)

Caliber 6.5 × 50mm

At the conclusion of its war with China in 1895, the Japanese Army decided to adopt a modern rifle in a small caliber. Designed by Colonel Nariakira Arisaka, this gun was chambered for a 6.5mm semi-rimmed round and used a turning bolt of the Mauser pattern with forward-locking lugs. It came into service in the 30th year of the Emperor Meiji.

Leaf-type
rear sight

FULL VIEW

Sling

▼ MAUSER MODEL 1898

Date 1898

Origin Germany

Barrel 29¼in (74cm)

Caliber 7.92 × 57mm

By the time of the *Gewehr* (rifle) 98, Mauser had solved virtually every problem known to beset the bolt-action magazine rifle. It added a third rear-locking lug to reinforce the two forward-mounted lugs, as well as improving gas sealing and refining the magazine. If the rifle had a fault, it lay in the design of its bolt handle, which projected outward and tended to catch on clothing.

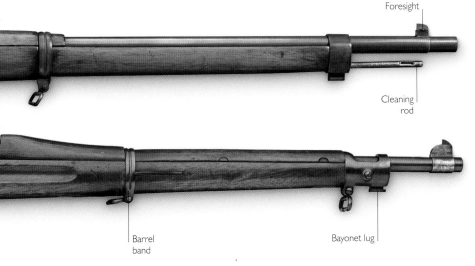

Foresight

Cleaning
rod

Barrel
band

Bayonet lug

◀ MAUSER MODEL 1893

Date 1900

Origin Germany

Barrel 29¼in (74cm)

Caliber 7 × 57mm

The Mauser 1893 was the seminal Spanish Mauser rifle of the late 1800s. Such was its effectiveness during the Spanish–American War that it pushed the US toward development of the Springfield rifle (below). The 1893 was fed from a five-round integral box magazine. The example shown here was manufactured in 1900.

◀ SPRINGFIELD MODEL 1903

Date 1903

Origin US

Barrel 24in (61cm)

Caliber .30in-03

Impressed by the Mauser rifles US troops encountered during the war against Spain, the United States Ordnance Department looked to replace its Krag rifles (see pp.62–63). Negotiating a license to build a Mauser design of its own, the result was the .30in Rifle, Magazine, M1903. The example shown here has an experimental 25-round magazine.

MANUALLY OPERATED REPEATING RIFLES (1906–16)

By the end of the 19th century, bolt-action repeating rifles were in almost universal military use, but each country sought to refine and improve its own rifle. France, for example, replaced the outmoded Lebel rifle with a more modern, but still flawed, design in the form of the Berthier. The British Lee-Enfield Mark I rifle was shortened to make it handier. Although France and Britain planned more refined smaller-caliber rifles, the arrival of World War I meant that the standard caliber of .303in was retained. Even before the outbreak of war in 1914, however, the trend was toward shorter-barreled rifles.

FULL VIEW

Wooden butt

Bolt handle

Trigger guard

Detachable 10-round box magazine

▲ SMLE MARK III

Date	1907
Origin	UK
Barrel	25¼in (64cm)
Caliber	.303in

A shorter version of the Lee-Enfield Mark I (see p.148) had been introduced in 1904 as the Short Magazine Lee-Enfield (SMLE, often nicknamed "Smellie"). The SMLE Mark III introduced improvements to the rear sight, magazine, and chamber.

Rear sling attachment

Cocking piece enabled the action to be safely cocked and uncocked manually if necessary

Integral five-round box magazine

Bolt handle

Bolt

Butt screw

Wooden butt

Experimental 20-round removable box magazine

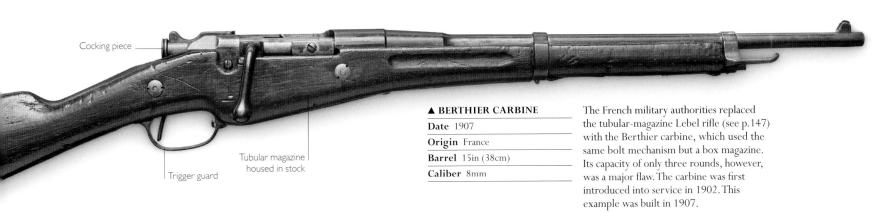

Cocking piece

Trigger guard

Tubular magazine
housed in stock

▲ BERTHIER CARBINE

Date	1907
Origin	France
Barrel	15in (38cm)
Caliber	8mm

The French military authorities replaced the tubular-magazine Lebel rifle (see p.147) with the Berthier carbine, which used the same bolt mechanism but a box magazine. Its capacity of only three rounds, however, was a major flaw. The carbine was first introduced into service in 1902. This example was built in 1907.

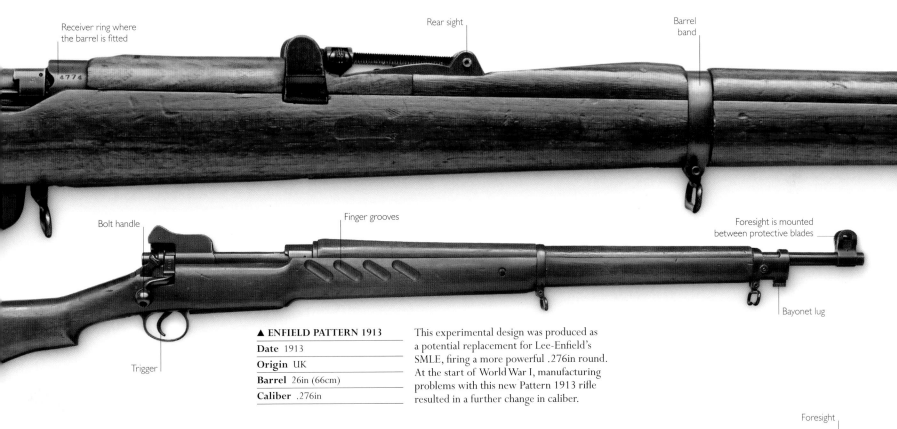

Receiver ring where
the barrel is fitted

Rear sight

Barrel
band

Bolt handle

Finger grooves

Foresight is mounted
between protective blades

Bayonet lug

Trigger

▲ ENFIELD PATTERN 1913

Date	1913
Origin	UK
Barrel	26in (66cm)
Caliber	.276in

This experimental design was produced as a potential replacement for Lee-Enfield's SMLE, firing a more powerful .276in round. At the start of World War I, manufacturing problems with this new Pattern 1913 rifle resulted in a further change in caliber.

Foresight

Barrel band

▲ BERTHIER MLE 1916

Date	1916
Origin	France
Barrel	31½in (79.8cm)
Caliber	8 × 50mm

Foresight is mounted
between protective blades

Although the Berthier carbine (above) continued to use the bolt action of the Lebel, it was outmoded in appearance, due to the length of its barrel. Its only serious defect lay in its limited magazine capacity. Seen here is an example of a modified version issued in 1916, with a five-round magazine.

Front sling
attachment

Bayonet lug

▲ ENFIELD PATTERN 1914

Date	1914
Origin	UK
Barrel	26in (66cm)
Caliber	.303in Mauser

Around the onset of World War I, the Pattern 1913 rifle was modified to use the .303in chambering, and the weapon was redesignated as the Pattern 1914. The Model 1917, a .30in-caliber version of the Pattern 1914, was later adopted by the US Army.

MANUALLY OPERATED REPEATING RIFLES (1917–45)

The experience of World War I had severely tested military rifles in service throughout the world. Most had stood up to combat conditions well, and when World War II loomed, most rifles still had the bolt-action mechanism recognizable from 50 years before. While the barrels of many had been reduced in length to make rifles lighter and handier, this had little adverse effect on their accuracy over fighting distances.

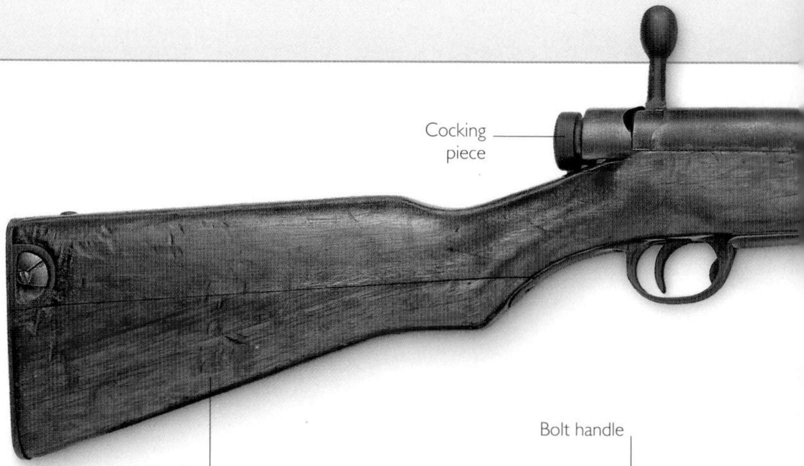

Cocking piece

Wooden butt

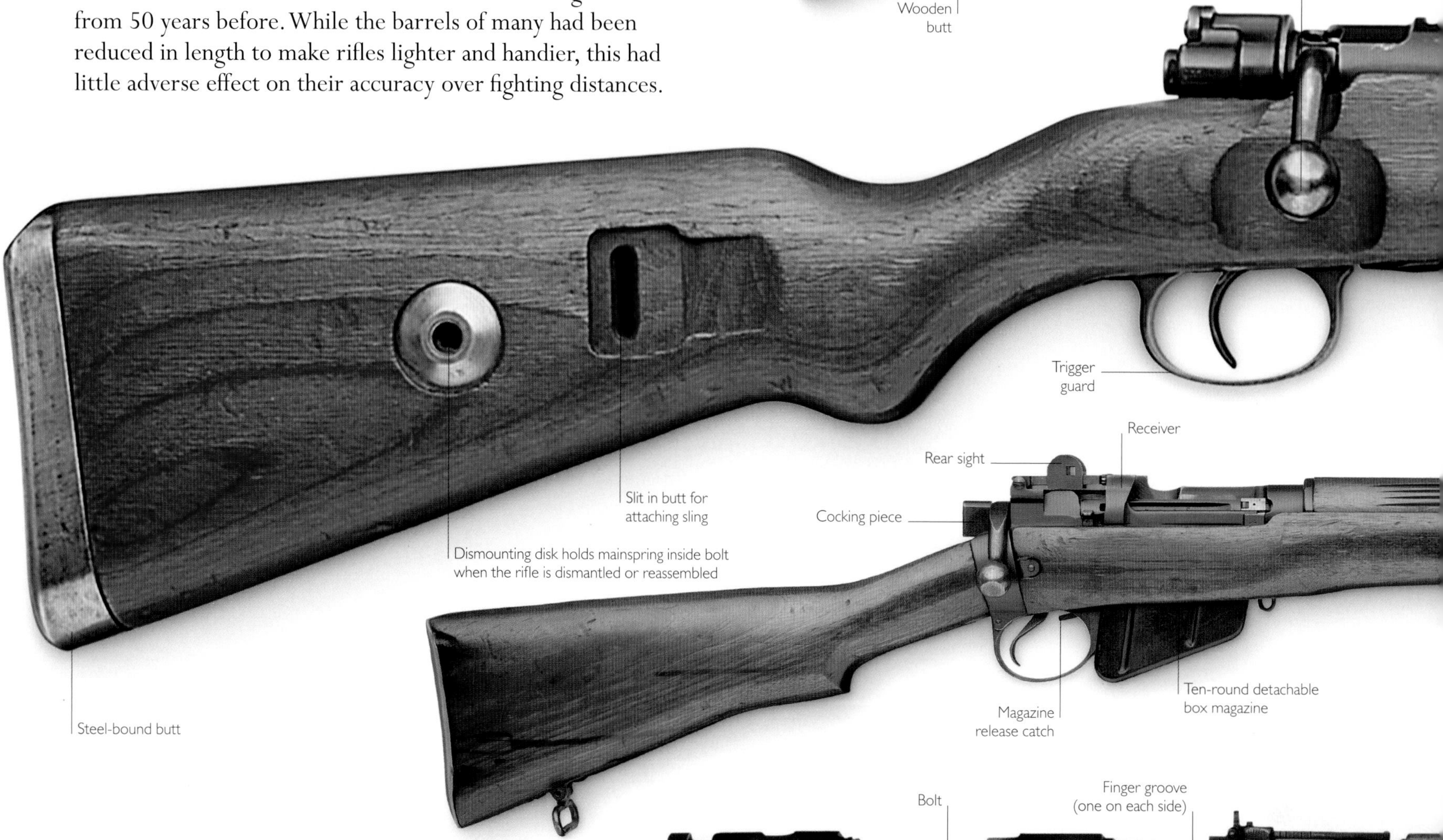

Bolt handle

Slit in butt for attaching sling

Dismounting disk holds mainspring inside bolt when the rifle is dismantled or reassembled

Steel-bound butt

Rear sight

Cocking piece

Receiver

Magazine release catch

Ten-round detachable box magazine

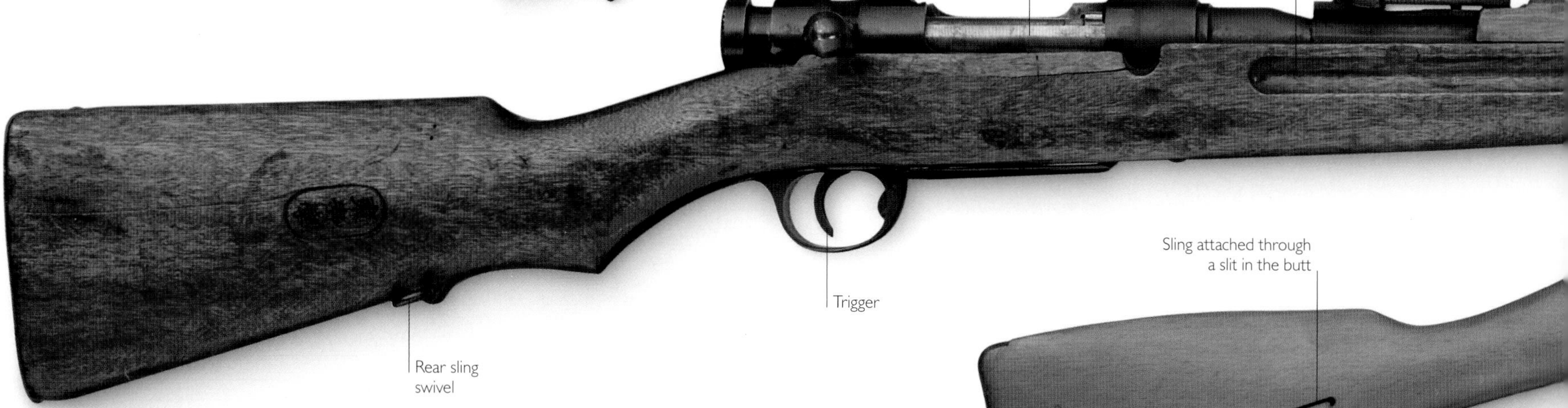

Bolt

Finger groove (one on each side)

Trigger

Rear sling swivel

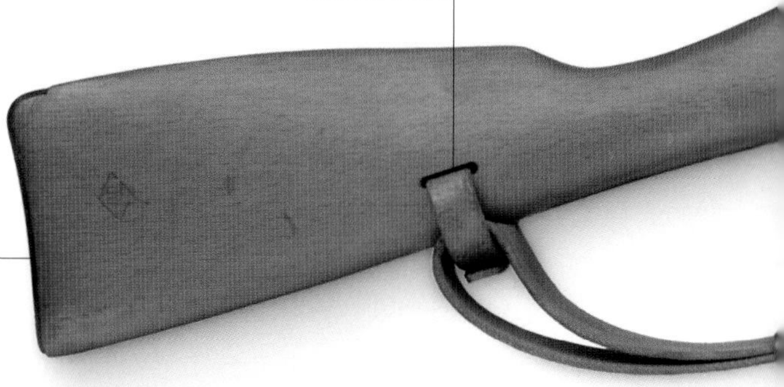

Sling attached through a slit in the butt

Butt plate

Foresight

Bayonet hinge

Folding bayonet

▲ ARISAKA YEAR 38/44 CARBINE

Date 1944

Origin Japan

Barrel 18in (45.72cm)

Caliber 6.5mm

Introduced to Japanese service in 1907, the Arisaka Year 38 rifle was upgraded during World War II. This model is called the Year 38/44 Carbine because it was made in the 38th year of the reign of the Emperor Meji and was updated in 1944. This short carbine has a folding bayonet hinged beneath the muzzle.

Rear sight

FULL VIEW

▲ MAUSER KAR 98K

Date 1935

Origin Germany

Barrel 23½in (60cm)

Caliber 7.92 × 57mm

The "Karabiner" 98K embodied improvements to the Mauser Gewehr 98 rifle (see p.153) and became the standard German service rifle of World War II. More than 14 million guns were manufactured between 1935 and 1945. A number of variations were produced, including those for mountain troops, paratroops, and snipers. During the war, the original design was simplified to speed up production.

Barrel band

Foresight protector

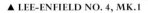

Muzzle

▲ LEE-ENFIELD NO. 4, MK.1

Date 1939

Origin UK

Barrel 25¼in (64cm)

Caliber .303in

The new Lee-Enfield, which appeared late in 1939, differed very little from the model it replaced – the SMLE Mark III (see p.154). The bolt and receiver (the central body of the firearm containing the operating parts) were modified; the rear sight was a new design and was placed on the receiver and the forestock was shortened, exposing the muzzle. The Number 4 remained in service until 1954.

▼ ARISAKA TYPE 99

Date 1939

Origin Japan

Barrel 25¾in (65.5cm)

Caliber 7.7mm

Japan's war experience showed that the 6.5mm round used in the Year 38 rifle was inadequate. The Type 99 used the more potent 7.7mm round. It was available in two versions, a short carbine (shown here) and a standard version, 6in (15.2cm) longer. An oddity of the Type 99 was a folding metal monopod support beneath the forestock (detached from this gun), although this was not rigid enough for its purpose.

Bolt handle protrudes horizontally

Folding cruciform bayonet

Foresight in protective shroud

Integral five-round magazine

▲ MOSIN-NAGANT CARBINE M1944

Date 1944

Origin USSR

Barrel 20¼in (51.7cm)

Caliber 7.62 × 54mm

In 1910, the 3-line Mosin-Nagant rifle (see p.147) was modified to produce a carbine by shortening its barrel. In 1938, it was revamped, largely to make it cheaper to manufacture, and in 1944, it attained its final form with the addition of a folding cruciform bayonet. Though it was obsolete by that time, the People's Republic of China began manufacturing copies in 1953.

LARGE-SCALE PRODUCTION
By the 1860s, the Colt factory in Hartford,
Connecticut, was the largest of its kind in the
world. Employees carried out specific tasks in
order, producing firearms on a large scale. Here,
revolvers are being assembled in around 1917.

RIFLES FOR SPECIAL PURPOSES

Difficulties encountered during World War I included barbed wire entanglements and the need to project grenades over longer distances than a man could throw. This spurred the combatant forces to develop new devices to deal with these challenges. Britain's Lee-Enfield rifle, for example, could be given special adaptations including cutters to enable infantrymen to penetrate barbed wire defenses, and a special cup to help fire a Mills Bomb (TNT-filled grenade) into enemy trenches.

Turned-down bolt handle

Butt plate

Butt marking disk to uniquely identify rifle

Magazine catch

Rear sight

Receiver

FULL VIEW

Ten-round box magazine

Bolt

Bolt handle

Wooden butt

Forestock

Ten-round magazine

Rear sling attachment

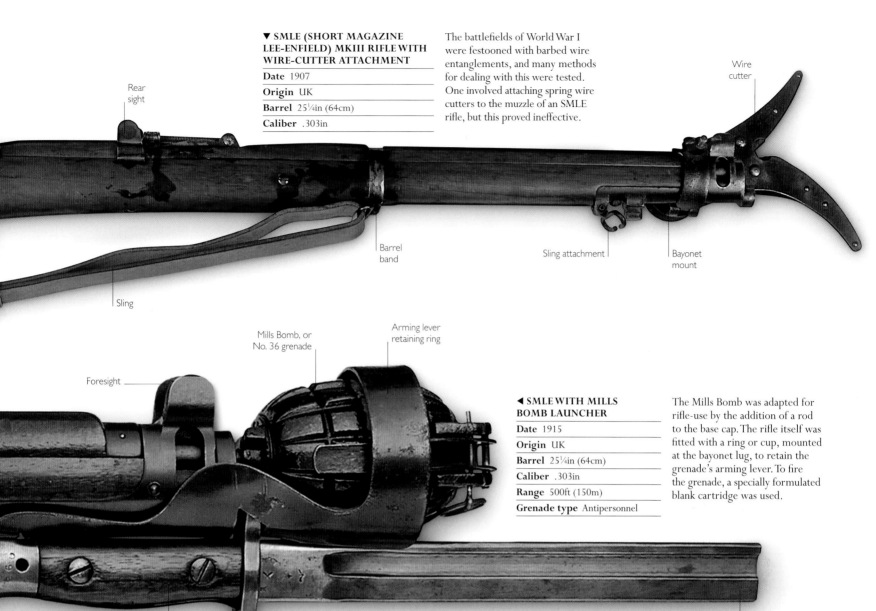

▼ SMLE (SHORT MAGAZINE LEE-ENFIELD) MKIII RIFLE WITH WIRE-CUTTER ATTACHMENT

Date	1907
Origin	UK
Barrel	25¼in (64cm)
Caliber	.303in

The battlefields of World War I were festooned with barbed wire entanglements, and many methods for dealing with this were tested. One involved attaching spring wire cutters to the muzzle of an SMLE rifle, but this proved ineffective.

Rear sight

Wire cutter

Barrel band

Sling

Sling attachment

Bayonet mount

Foresight

Mills Bomb, or No. 36 grenade

Arming lever retaining ring

◄ SMLE WITH MILLS BOMB LAUNCHER

Date	1915
Origin	UK
Barrel	25¼in (64cm)
Caliber	.303in
Range	500ft (150m)
Grenade type	Antipersonnel

The Mills Bomb was adapted for rifle-use by the addition of a rod to the base cap. The rifle itself was fitted with a ring or cup, mounted at the bayonet lug, to retain the grenade's arming lever. To fire the grenade, a specially formulated blank cartridge was used.

Bayonet could be detached to be used as a knife

Broken end of bayonet

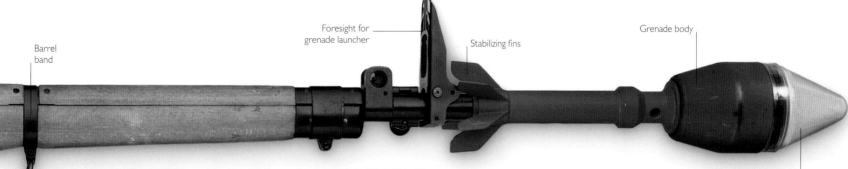

Barrel band

Foresight for grenade launcher

Stabilizing fins

Grenade body

Marker capsule

▲ LEE-ENFIELD NO. 4 RIFLE WITH GRENADE LAUNCHER

Date	1940s
Origin	UK
Barrel	30in (76.2cm)
Caliber	.303in
Range	330ft (100m)
Grenade type	Antitank

The No. 4 Rifle, used extensively in World War II, had an exposed muzzle, which enabled the British Army to develop a new style of tubular launcher. The rifle could launch a fin-stabilized antitank grenade, which was mounted over its muzzle on the bayonet lugs. Using a powerful blank cartridge, it was fired with the butt of the rifle grounded. This example is equipped with a later model L1A1 practice grenade.

CENTER-FIRE REVOLVERS

Once revolvers adopted center-fire metallic cartridges (see pp.112–13), invented in the 1860s–70s, several basic designs of frame became established, and these were to remain almost consistent for a very long period. Solid frames with cylinders that hinged out sideways for reloading were most common. The user pushed the extractor rod to eject the cartridges. Alternatives included the Webley and Scott system, which extracted all the cartridges at once as the frame swung open. The strength, simplicity, and durability of a revolver meant that it could be deployed reliably in military, sporting, and self-defense roles. Earlier self-cocking and single-action designs gave way to a more universal use of the double-action mechanism, which provided the option for rapid fire or for cocking the revolver manually to aim with more precision.

Trigger guard

Checkered walnut grip

▲ LEBEL MODÈLE 1892

Date 1892

Origin France

Barrel 11¼in (28.6cm)

Caliber 8 × 27mm rim-fire

The double-action, solid-frame Lebel Modèle 1892 was loaded by means of a gate. It was used by the French Army in World War I.

Foresight

Brand name inscribed on barrel

Barrel lug (attaches barrel to forestock)

▼ RAST AND GASSER M1898

Date 1898

Origin Austria

Barrel 8¾in (22.3cm)

Caliber .32in

This solid-frame, double-action pistol was issued to soldiers in the Austro-Hungarian Army in World War I. Around 200,000 of them were produced from 1898 to 1912. In this design, the cylinder revolved around a fixed axle and cartridges were loaded and extracted one at a time through a rearward-hinging gate.

Hammer

Checkered grip

Lanyard ring

Foresight

Extractor rod

Type and caliber stamped into barrel

Cylinder holds six .45in Colt rounds

Cylinder-releasing catch

Cylinder axis and extractor rod

▶ COLT NEW SERVICE

Date 1901

Origin US

Barrel 5½in (14.4cm)

Caliber .45in Colt

American officers were issued with Colt "automatics" beginning in 1902, but some felt that they were likely to jam. They preferred the last revolver produced for the US Army—the .45in-caliber double-action Colt New Service, which remained in service until 1941.

Lanyard ring

Cylinder contained six .455in Eley rounds

Recess for cylinder-locking bolt

▲ WEBLEY AND SCOTT MK VI

Date 1915

Origin UK

Barrel 6in (15.2cm)

Caliber .455in Eley

The last in a long line of service revolvers produced by the famous Birmingham, England, partnership, the Mark VI was introduced early in World War I. This revolver, which took Eley cartridges, was renowned for its sturdy reliability. Its frame could hinge open to expose the rear face of the cylinder for rapid reloading.

Trigger guard

▲ SMITH AND WESSON M1917

Date 1917

Origin US

Barrel 5½in (14.4cm)

Caliber .45in ACP

During World War I, Smith and Wesson was commissioned to produce a revolver that chambered the .45in ACP round. This was the M1917. Although it was a success, it faced extraction problems unless the ammunition was loaded in flat half-moon clips, each carrying three rounds.

Hammer

Cylinder-releasing catch

Cylinder holds six .45in ACP cartridges

▶ SMITH AND WESSON MODEL 27

Date 1938

Origin US

Barrel 8⅜in (21.3cm)

Caliber .357in Magnum

Smith and Wesson produced a huge variety of pistols chambered for the various Magnum cartridges—.357in and .44in are only the most common—on light, intermediate, and heavy frames. The heavy Model 27, which fired a .357in Magnum, was the most popular model, and was produced with 4in (10.2cm), 6in (15.2cm), and 8⅜in (21.3cm) barrels.

Recess for cylinder-locking bolt

Heavy N-Type frame

Foresight

Spurless hammer

Cylinder holds six .38in rounds

▲ ENFIELD NO. 2 MARK 1

Date 1938

Origin UK

Barrel 5in (12.7cm)

Caliber .38in

After World War I, the British Army decided to adopt a lighter caliber for its service side-arm. The revolver it chose was almost a copy of the Webley and Scott MK VI (left). The version shown was issued to tank crews, and lacks a hammer spur to prevent it catching from on clothing in the confined spaces of a tank.

Cylinder holds six rounds of ammunition

Hammer

Cylinder-releasing catch

Trigger

Grip-retaining screw

▲ SMITH AND WESSON MILITARY AND POLICE

Date 1900

Origin US

Barrel 5in (12.7cm)

Caliber .38in Special

Having championed the hinged-frame revolver, Smith and Wesson, with the advent of more powerful ammunition, was obliged to switch to a solid frame with a swing-out cylinder for its Military and Police pistol. This was chambered for the long .38in Special round.

Lanyard ring

PAUL
MAUSER

GREAT GUNSMITHS
MAUSER

Mauser is one of the most celebrated names in the history of firearms design. Although Paul Mauser, its creator, died in 1914, Mauser's influence was still clear in the design of many of the rifles in use during World War II. It was in the late 1800s and early 1900s that Paul Mauser developed a series of bolt-action rifles, weapons that became known for their ease of use and reliability. This helped them sell in large numbers, dramatically changing the way battles were fought.

Paul Mauser was born into a family of German gunsmiths and his father, Franz Andreas Mauser, worked at the Württemberg Royal Armory. Paul Mauser was drafted as an artilleryman in 1859 and did his military service at the arsenal at Ludwigsburg. Here, he was able to continue his trade as a gunsmith. At both the Royal Armory and at Ludwigsburg, the young Mauser found that the prevailing rifle was the Dreyse needle-fire rifle (see pp.108–09), a bolt-action weapon. Although the Dreyse rifle was widely used, Mauser wanted to improve it, in particular to eliminate problems such as gas blowback (caused by expanding gases created by the ignition of the propellant) and the gun's tendency to discharge accidentally. So from the 1860s onward, Mauser began to develop new bolt-action weapons to address these issues.

TRANSFORMING WARFARE
Bolt-action rifles began to become popular in the 1860s and Mauser patented his first one in 1868. The advantages of the bolt action for loading a gun at the breech were immediately

▲ MODEL 1898
German troops used this rifle very effectively in World War I. It replaced the Model 1888 rifle as the main rifle in service in Germany.

"The **pistol** was the best thing in the world."

clear—it was reliable and easy to use, and because it did not have a downward-moving lever it could be fired and loaded more easily in a prone position than a lever-action rifle. Also, unlike muzzle-loading guns, it did not have to be loaded while standing up, making it safer to use in battle. Bolt-action weapons would gradually become more widespread. Mauser's weapons also used metallic cartridges. This overcame

a major problem with the Dreyse needle-fire rifle, with its long, needlelike firing pin, which sometimes caused the weapon's paper cartridges to discharge accidentally when the bolt was being closed. However, all early Mausers were single-shot weapons and were at a marked disadvantage compared to the repeating rifles introduced by Winchester in 1866. Mauser began to design bolt-action rifles with a repeating action in which a cycle of the bolt loads the chamber for the next shot. The most successful of these was the Model 1898 (see p.153), which took five smokeless cartridges in a disposable charger (or stripper clip). Light and easy to use, the Model 1898 was one of the most successful rifles of its time, a reliable repeater that could be loaded and fired from a prone position and could stop an enemy advance in its tracks. Adopted by the German Army (where it was given the designation Gewehr 98), the rifle played a major part in World War I and set a high standard for other manufacturers to emulate.

◀ GERMAN TROOPS WITH MAUSER RIFLES
Seen here is a group of German troops in battle, in about 1916, aiming their Mauser Gewehr 98 rifles from a ruined building.

MAUSER MODEL 1871

MAUSER C.96

1871 The Model 1871 is the first rifle manufactured by Paul and his brother, Wilhelm Mauser.

1874 The Mausers purchase the Württemberg Royal Armory and begin to make 100,000 Model 1871 rifles for Württemberg's army.

1878 Mauser develops the Zig-Zag, the first German military revolver to employ modern brass cartridges.

1896 The distinctive grip of the C.96 semiautomatic pistol leads to its nickname, "Broom handle."

1898 The Model 1898, purchased by the German Army, becomes the most successful Mauser rifle.

1914 Paul Mauser dies, but the company continues to prosper, supplying weapons in large numbers during World War I.

1918 The Mauser 1918 T-Gewehr is the world's first antitank rifle.

1935 The K98k is adopted by German armed forces.

1948 The Mauser factory is dismantled after World War II, and engineers salvage some of the equipment for the company that will become known as Heckler and Koch.

▶ **YOUNG WINSTON**
The actor Simon Ward, playing Winston Churchill in the 1972 film *Young Winston*, carries a Mauser C.96 pistol. Winston Churchill used this gun in the Sudan and during the Boer War, and it became his favorite weapon.

THE PISTOLS OF MAUSER

When the first semiautomatic pistols (see p.166) were developed by German gunsmiths such as Hugo Borchardt in the 1880s and 1890s, Mauser also moved into this market. Mauser's first, the highly successful C.96 (see p.166), was a highly distinctive firearm with a box magazine in front of the trigger and a grip that looked like the handle of a broom. The gun also had a removable wooden shoulder stock that doubled as a carrying case or holster. Carried by Winston Churchill and Lawrence of Arabia, the C.96 became well-known, and Mauser manufactured more than a million of them. The C.96 also took the Mauser name to China, where large numbers of the weapon were manufactured. The name Mauser is almost synonymous with "pistol" in many countries in Asia.

WAR AND PEACE

After World War I, the Mauser company used its engineering and manufacturing skills to branch out into peacetime products, such as tools, sewing machines, and even cars. But when Germany began to rearm in the mid-1930s, the Mauser line of firearms continued with the KAR 98k (see p.157), a bolt-action rifle first produced in 1935 but descended from the Model 1898 (left). Like the older rifle, the KAR 98k took ammunition loaded in a stripper clip, but it had a down-turned bolt handle (in contrast to the straight bolt handle of the Model 1898), which made for faster operation. The KAR 98k was used widely by the German army in World War II, especially for providing covering fire for machine-gunners.

SELF-LOADING PISTOLS (1893–1900)

The final decade of the 19th century saw an extraordinary upsurge in the development of reliable self-loading, or "semiautomatic," pistols, which could fire one round with every pull of the trigger. They worked on recoil operation (see p.305)—by using a spring to harness the power in the recoil of the fired cartridge to reload the weapon. It was Hiram Maxim who had perfected recoil action in machine-guns (see pp.184–85), following which gunmakers began applying it to other weapons.

Recoil spring housing

Detachable stock

Leather holster combined with detachable wooden shoulder stock

FULL VIEW

Recoil spring housing

▲ **BORCHARDT C.93**

Date 1894

Origin Germany

Barrel 6½in (16.5cm)

Caliber 7.65mm

The C.93, developed by gunmaker Hugo Borchardt, was the first successful self-loading pistol. For its loading action, the C.93 drew on the design of Maxim's machine-guns, which Borchardt's employer, Ludwig Loewe, was producing under license in Berlin.

Hammer

Adjustable rear sight

Loading/ejection port

Blade-shaped foresight

Fixed magazine

Trigger

Lanyard ring

▲ **"MARS," BY GABBETT-FAIRFAX**

Date 1899–1902

Origin UK

Barrel 10½in (26.5cm)

Caliber 8.5mm Mars/.45in Webley

The "Mars" pistol was too big, expensive, complex—and too unforgiving—to succeed in the already congested and competitive weapons market of 1900.

▲ **MAUSER C.96**

Date 1896

Origin Germany

Barrel 5½in (14cm)

Caliber 7.63mm Mauser

Although complicated and slow to load due to its fixed magazine, the "Broom handle" Mauser *Selbstladepistole* (self-loading pistol) soon became popular in military circles thanks to its very powerful ammunition. It remained in production until 1937 and was copied the world over. It was usually supplied with a holster-cum-shoulder stock (like that of the C.93, above), which was essential for safely firing the gun. Fully automatic versions, which could fire continuously while the trigger was pulled, were also produced.

Ejection port, an opening in the receiver through which spent cartridge cases are ejected

Foresight

SYSTEM BORCHARDT. PATENT.

Trigger guard

Exposed hammer

Butt houses removable eight-round magazine

Recoil spring housing

Fixed magazine

▲ BERGMANN NO. 3

Date 1896

Origin Germany

Barrel 4½in (11.2cm)

Caliber 6.5mm Bergmann

The Louis Schmeisser-designed "No. 3" was among the simplest of pistols, with a small-capacity fixed magazine and a "blowback" breech. The blowback system used the combined weight of the breechblock and the resistance of the pistol's mainspring to counter the recoil force generated on firing a cartridge. This enabled the breechblock to move fully rearward, where it was held back by the sear. Pulling the trigger again made the breechblock fly forward under spring pressure, collecting a cartridge, chambering it, and firing it. The cycle would then repeat.

Cocking handle

Foresight

Rear sight

Recoil spring housing

Hammer pivot screw

▲ BROWNING MODEL 1900

Date 1900

Origin Belgium

Barrel 4in (10.2cm)

Caliber 7.65mm

Trigger guard

John Browning (see pp.180–81), probably the most prolific gun designer ever, moved to Belgium from his native US in 1895. There he produced an improved version of his first semiautomatic pistol, which became known as the Model 1900. It used a breech of the blowback type. Small and light, the Model 1900 was hugely popular, and over 700,000 units were sold before production ceased in 1911.

Butt houses removable seven-round magazine

Magazine release catch

SELF-LOADING PISTOLS (1901–24)

This period saw the appearance of several designs of self-loading pistol that are still familiar today. John Browning created a series of slide-action pistols produced by Colt, culminating in the Model 1911A1, which was carried by American forces through both world wars. Georg Luger perfected the toggle-bolt breech mechanism of Hugo Borchardt to produce the pistol which became the ubiquitous German military sidearm. Other pistols, while technically interesting, proved less successful.

Cutaway toggle knob

▲ LUGER P.08

Date 1902

Origin Germany

Barrel 4¾in (12cm)

Caliber 7.65mm

Georg Luger designed his iconic *Pistole '08* in 1900. It would remain instantly identifiable for its entire production life. This early model used 7.65mm ammunition, which lacked stopping power.

Safety catch

Trigger

Magazine grip

▲ WEBLEY-FOSBERY

Date 1901

Origin UK

Barrel 7½in (19cm)

Caliber .455in

In 1899, Colonel George Fosbery designed a self-cocking revolver in which recoil propelled the barrel and cylinder backward within a slide, indexing the cylinder (positioning each chamber in turn opposite the firing pin). It proved too fragile for battlefield conditions.

Foresight

Cylinder-indexing grooves

Hammer

Slide

Cylinder-retaining wedge

Safety catch

Foresight

4in (10cm) barrel, the longest permitted in Germany after World War I

Muzzle

Slide, drawn back manually to cock the pistol

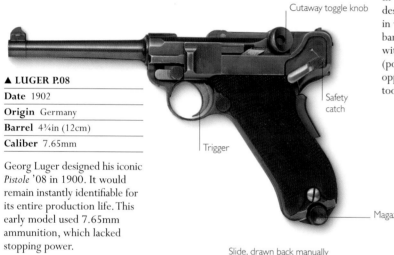

Barrel-locking lug

Trigger guard

Butt houses seven-round removable box magazine

◄ COLT MODEL 1902

Date 1902

Origin US

Barrel 6in (15.2cm)

Caliber .38in ACP

Browning produced a series of successful locked-breech pistols for the military market. However, the Model 1902 was not as popular. This gun featured a double-link mechanism. Its barrel was connected to the pistol frame at each end via pivoting links, which locked the barrel and slide together until the bullet left the muzzle.

Foresight

Loading/ejector port

Hammer

▲ STEYR M1905

Date 1905

Origin Austria-Hungary

Barrel 6½in (16cm)

Caliber 7.63mm Mannlicher

The M1905, designed by Austrian manufacturer Steyr-Mannlicher (see pp. 290–91), was chambered for a round generally thought too powerful for a recoil action, but succeeded due to the high standard to which it was manufactured. This pistol was never especially popular though.

Butt houses 10-round fixed box magazine

Foresight

Tapered barrel

▲ LUGER P.08 AMERICAN EAGLE

Date 1906

Origin Germany

Barrel 6in (15.2cm)

Caliber 9mm

International sales of Luger pistols grew enormously and in 1906, new models, in 9mm caliber, included one for commercial sale in the US. This finely finished version had the manufacturer's mark (DWM) and also an American eagle on the top of the receiver.

Action-locking pin

Trigger guard

Concealed hammer

Barrel locking lug

▶ STEYR-HAHN MODEL 1911

Date	1911
Origin	Austria
Barrel	5in (12.7cm)
Caliber	7.63mm Mannlicher

Austria tried for many years to produce a successful military pistol, and succeeded with the M1911. It was similar in concept to the Colt (below), except that its barrel rotates, rather than tips, to unlock it from the slide.

Butt houses eight-round fixed box magazine

▲ WEBLEY MODEL 1910

Date	1910
Origin	UK
Barrel	5in (12.7cm)
Caliber	.38in

Webley of Birmingham, England, produced a range of locked-breech, self-loading pistols from about 1904. They were all designed by J. H. Whiting, who collaborated with Hugh Gabbett-Fairfax on the "Mars" (see p.166), and were adopted by some police forces.

Butt houses seven-round removable box magazine

Foresight

Slide

Lever holds slide back for stripping

Recoil spring housing

Patent data

Ejection port

Toggle doubles up as cocking grip

Ramp breaks toggle joint upward

Butt houses seven-round removable box magazine

▲ COLT M1911A1

Date	1924
Origin	US
Barrel	5in (12.7cm)
Caliber	.45in ACP

Browning designed the Colt M1911 in 1911, following which it was accepted as the US Army's official sidearm. He designed it in response to a demand by US soldiers fighting Moro rebels in the Philippines for a pistol firing a heavy .45in round in place of the less-effective .38in caliber revolvers with which they had been issued. The example shown here is a later M1911A1.

Safety catch

Magazine catch

▲ LUGER P.08 9MM PARABELLUM

Date	1908
Origin	Germany
Barrel	4in (10cm)
Caliber	9mm Parabellum

The Luger P.08 is one of the best-known pistols in the world. Luger copied many features of Borchardt's C.93 pistol of 1893 (see p.166), but adopted a leaf recoil spring and moved it into the butt, improving the overall balance considerably. Luger also produced improved ammunition for his pistol, the Parabellum round, which was to become the world standard.

Safety catch

Butt houses 10-round removable box magazine

Magazine grip

Magazine grip

SHOWCASE

LUGER LANGE P.08 PISTOL

Recognized worldwide, this distinctive gun was used heavily by German forces in both world wars because of its reliability, accuracy, and light weight. It is one of the earliest self-loading pistols (see p.166), but unlike others, it is equipped with a recoil-operated toggle-lock instead of the slide action that later became standard. Firing the gun pushes the breechblock backward, folding the toggle and ejecting the spent cartridge.

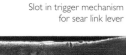

Loading indicator

▶ **LOADING INDICATOR WITH CARTRIDGE**
The extractor, or loading indicator, is attached to the breechblock. When a cartridge is in place, the extractor lifts upward at the front, exposing the word "*geladen*" (loaded) stamped on its side. It is easy to see, and feel, if a Luger pistol is loaded. Most Luger pistols used the Parabellum cartridge, which became the standard pistol round of armies across the world.

Breechblock contains a striker

Barrel

Sideplate fits here

Toggle assembly fits here

Sear

5928

Rear sight adjustment catch

Flat plate projects rearward

Barrel assembly-retaining lug

▲ **BARREL AND LOCK ASSEMBLY**
The barrel fits into a block that has two plates projecting rearward. The toggle assembly is fitted between these plates. The barrel and the toggle assemblies are attached to the main frame (receiver) of the pistol. To field-strip the gun for cleaning, the barrel assembly is pushed backward. This allows the user to turn the release lever clockwise and lift off the sideplate. The user can then pull out the release lever, allowing the barrel assembly to slide forward out of the receiver.

Slot in trigger mechanism for sear link lever

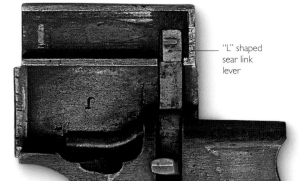

"L" shaped sear link lever

▲ **SIDEPLATE**
Unique to the Luger is an L-shaped lever located on the inner side of the sideplate. This lever connects the trigger with the sear. The sear in this gun holds back a striker until the trigger is pulled. Without the sideplate in place, the gun is inoperable.

Sideplate release lever

▶ **MAIN FRAME**
The main frame (receiver) of the gun houses the magazine, mainspring (inside the butt), and trigger, and provides the platform onto which the barrel and lock assembly fit.

▼ **TOGGLE ASSEMBLY**
The toggle assembly consists of the sliding breechblock and the hinged toggle. The toggle is a mechanical linkage between the breechblock and the mainspring, which runs down the back of the gun's butt. The mainspring is attached to the toggle by the coupling link.

2
Toggle (unfolded)

▼ **REAR TOGGLE PIN**
The toggle pin fixes the toggle assembly to the barrel frame.

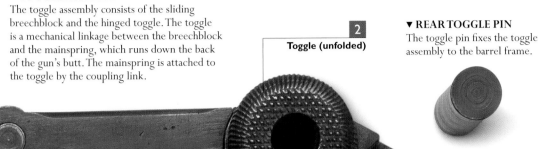

Hole for rear toggle pin

Coupling link

LUGER LANGE P.08 PISTOL

Date 1917

Origin Germany

Barrel 7in (17.8cm)

Barrel 2in (5cm)

Caliber 9mm Parabellum

This is a variation of Georg Luger's Luger P.08. It was available in calibers of 7.65mm or 9mm and with various barrel lengths. The "lange" in its name refers to its long barrel. This model was issued to artillerymen as a personal weapon, and is also known as the "artillery" model. It was equipped with either a standard 8-round magazine or a 32-round drum magazine, both detachable and using 9mm Parabellum cartridges. The gun has a rifle-type adjustable rear sight graduated to 875 yards (800m) and was supplied with a simple detachable shoulder stock to enable a more steady aim at longer ranges.

FULL VIEW

Hole for rear toggle pin

Ramp to fold toggle

Safety catch

Magazine catch

Mainspring is housed here, parallel to the magazine, which occupies most of the butt

2

▲ **TOGGLE (FOLDED)**
The user loads the gun by pulling the toggle, which folds upward, drawing the breechblock backward and compressing the mainspring (left, in the butt). As the toggle folds upward, the spring inside the magazine pushes a cartridge up. Then, as the mainspring extends, it straightens the toggle and pushes the breechblock and cartridge forward, sealing the breech and chambering the cartridge. On firing, the recoil sends the breechblock and toggle backwards, and the toggle folds as it runs up a ramp on the rear of the frame, triggering a cycle of automatic loading.

GREAT GUNSMITHS
BERETTA

UGO GUSSALLI
BERETTA

The world's oldest firearms manufacturer is the Italian company Fabbrica d'Armi Pietro Beretta SpA, which originated in the 16th century as a supplier of gun barrels to the arsenal in Venice. From these small beginnings, Beretta has expanded into a large business with a global reputation in a variety of fields—from small arms for military use to hand-made shotguns, often beautifully engraved. These guns continue to be recognized for their excellent design and high standard of quality under the able guidance of Ugo Gussalli Beretta and his sons.

In the 15th and 16th centuries, the city of Venice was a powerful and independent republic with lands in northern Italy and the Mediterranean. The Venetians grew rich through trade, and to help defend their empire, they developed the arsenal at Venice, originally a ship-building complex, as a major gun manufacturer. The arsenal called on craft workers from outside the city to supply parts for weapons. One of these craft workers was Mastro Bartolomeo Beretta, a gunsmith from

▼ BERETTA CRAFTSMAN
A worker assembles a hunting rifle at the Beretta factory in Italy in 1985. The stunning engraving on these premium weapons is done by hand and individually signed by the engraver.

Gardone Val Trompia in Lombardy, whose business began to prosper in 1526, when he supplied 185 arquebus barrels to the arsenal.

THE CRAFT TRADITION
The Venetians valued the work of gunsmiths such as Beretta and levied low taxes on them, giving them more power to run their own affairs and a ready market for their products. Mastro Bartolomeo Beretta, exploiting local deposits of high-grade iron ore to make his guns, did well, and he and his descendants handed down the techniques of gunsmithing from father to son from the 16th century to the present. Venice provided a strong market for Beretta's firearms until the city went into

decline in the 18th century. By this time, Beretta's weapons were well-known beyond the Venetian empire, so the company could still flourish as its initial market shrank. In the 19th century, Pietro Antonio Beretta and his son Giuseppe traveled up and down Italy demonstrating their company's products and collecting orders. Purchasers liked the quality, workmanship, and craft values of Beretta's products and the orders continued to flow in, especially for their finely crafted, ornately engraved rifles.

PRIZED FOR PRECISION
Throughout its history, the company has developed weapons for supply to a variety of military and civilian users. Its military weapons have moved with the times. For example, during World War I, the company developed the Model 1918, one of the first submachine-guns used by the Italian army. During the 20th century, Beretta handguns, especially its semiautomatic pistols, were widely employed by the military and police, and this has continued into the 21st century. Strength in this area is partly due to Pietro Beretta, who took over in 1903 and developed international sales, and partly to Tullio Marengoni, Beretta's chief designer from

MODEL 1934

MODEL S-686, 1982

1526 Mastro Bartolomeo Beretta supplies 185 arquebus barrels to the arsenal in Venice.

1915 Beretta begins to produce semiautomatic pistols—a type of gun that will become one of its most important products during the 20th century.

1918 Beretta's first submachine-gun, the Model 1918, is launched and taken up by the Italian Army.

1934 The Model 1934, a compact, semiautomatic pistol designed for the Italian Army, is created.

1935 The SO series of over-and-under shotguns is launched, beginning an enduring line of double-barreled shotguns, including the Model S-686, that lasts until today.

1953 In Ian Fleming's first James Bond novel, *Casino Royale*, the hero carries a Beretta 418 pistol.

1985 The semiautomatic M9 is ordered for the US Army as a replacement for the venerable M1911 pistol designed by John Browning.

> "We are **Beretta**. We don't want to make a copy of other shapes."
>
> *ATTRIBUTED TO* **FRANCO BERETTA, SON OF UGO GUSSALLI BERETTA**

◀ **TARGET SHOOTING**
Beretta weapons have found particular favor with competitive skeet shooters. Here, Australian shooter George Barton fires a Beretta during an event in Melbourne in 2006.

1904 until his death in 1965. Marengoni's work in small arms bore fruit in the form of the Model 34, which sold in huge numbers over a 40-year period. This tradition has continued with the M9, issued to the US Army, and the 92 series, bought widely by armed forces around the world. These weapons are valued for their precision of manufacture and reliability, as are Beretta's competition rifles and shotguns, especially the SO (*Sovrapposto*, indicating that the barrels are arranged one above the other) shotgun series launched in 1935. The firm's position in this area was also strengthened by the fact that Pietro Beretta's nephew, Carlo, was an avid competition marksman, giving the designers informed feedback on the firearms he used.

FOR THE ATHLETES

By 1956, the excellence of the weapons was confirmed at the Melbourne Olympics, at which a shooting competitor with a Beretta won gold for the first time; medals went to Beretta shooters in nearly all the following Olympics, and there were also successes in the World Championships from 1978 onward. The success enjoyed by the SO1 has continued to today, with the SO5 and the SO6—premium firearms that combine excellent balance and precision with beautiful design. In addition to these premium weapons, Beretta also produces many competition and hunting weapons designed for users on a budget that still maintain the quality and reliability that have made the company's name.

SELF-LOADING PISTOLS (1925–45)

In the years following World War I, military forces worldwide began adopting self-loading pistols for use by their officer corps. While some were intended solely for personal defense, others, such as the Browning High Power or GP35, were dual-purpose weapons suitable for offensive operations due to their caliber and magazine capacity.

▼ NAMBU TAISHO 14

Date	1920
Origin	Japan
Barrel	4in (12cm)
Caliber	8mm Nambu

The first Nambu pistols appeared in 1909. Although they were clearly influenced by the Luger P.08 (see p.168), they have nothing in common with it internally, the unlocking of the bolt from the barrel being achieved by the rotation of a linking block.

Safety catch

Foresight

Foresight

Trigger

Magazine catch

Cocking piece

Hammer

FULL VIEW

Removable butt

▲ ASTRA MODEL 901

Date	1927
Origin	Spain
Barrel	6¼in (16cm)
Caliber	7.63mm Mauser

This self-loading pistol was part of the Astra 900 series, a copy of the *Schnellfeuer* ("Rapidfire") version of the Mauser C.96 (see p.165). It could switch between semiautomatic and automatic firing modes. In fully automatic mode, the gun would keep firing as long as the trigger was kept pulled. The gun was, however, difficult to control in that mode.

Firing-mode selector switches between fully and semiautomatic modes

20-round fixed magazine

Foresight

Manufacturer's markings

Hammer

Slide grips

Recoil spring housing

▲ WALTHER PPK

Date	1931
Origin	Germany
Barrel	3¼in (8.3cm)
Caliber	7.65mm

The Walther PPK was popularized through its cinematic use by James Bond, and it did indeed find its way into many security service hands, mainly because of its compact dimensions. It was a simple recoil weapon most commonly produced in .32in ACP (7.65mm) caliber, and was fed from a seven-round magazine.

Trigger guard

Magazine base

Foresight

Semi-shrouded hammer

▲ TOKAREV TT MODEL 1933

Date	1933
Origin	Soviet Union
Barrel	4½in (11.6cm)
Caliber	7.62mm

The Tokarev TT was the first self-loading pistol on general issue to the Red Army. In design, it was similar to the Browning GP35 (right), with a similar recoil-driven self-loading action. It was simple and could be field-stripped without tools. It lacked a safety catch.

Butt houses eight-round removable box magazine

Safety catch

Recoil spring housing

▶ STAR MODEL M

Date	1932
Origin	Spain
Barrel	5in (12.5cm)
Caliber	9mm Largo

Manufactured by Echeverria in Eibar, the Star was one of the best of many copies of the Colt M1911 (see pp.178–79), although it lacked the grip safety of the original 1911 model. Various versions of this model were produced in a number of different calibers until the mid-1980s.

Foresight

Hammer

Recoil
spring
housing

▶ BERETTA MODEL 1934

Date 1934

Origin Italy

Barrel 6in (15.2cm)

Caliber 9mm short

Pietro Beretta SpA (see pp.172–73)
is the world's longest-established
gunmaker. Its M1934 became the
official Italian officer's side-arm
during World War II. The design
evolved from one executed two
decades earlier. This recoil-operated
weapon was restricted to firing a
reduced-power round, originally
in 7.65mm caliber.

Butt houses
removable
nine-round
box magazine

Manufacturer's
markings

▶ BERETTA 318

Date 1935

Origin Italy

Barrel 2¼in (5.7cm)

Caliber .25in ACP

The Beretta Modello 318
was produced in Italy from
1935 to 1943. It was one
of a developing line of
Beretta small-frame pistols in
.25in ACP caliber introduced
in 1919, and it was exported
in decent numbers to the US,
where it sold under the name
Bantam or Panther.

Trigger
guard

Polish eagle
proof mark

Manufacturer's
markings

Decocking
lever

Rear
sight

Hammer

Hold-open
notch

Milled
cocking grip

Hammer

Slide catch
lever

▲ RADOM M1935

Date 1935

Origin Poland

Barrel 4½in (11.5cm)

Caliber 9mm Parabellum

The Radom was similar in concept
to the Browning GP35 (left), but
it was more compact and had extra
security features. These included a
decocking device that pulled the firing
pin back and allowed the hammer to fall
forward safely without firing the pistol.

Safety
catch

Trigger

Butt houses
13-round
removable
box magazine

▲ BROWNING GP35

Date 1935

Origin Belgium

Barrel 4¾in (11.8cm)

Caliber 9mm Parabellum

Self-loading pistols were used only
occasionally by special forces before
the High Power (Grand Puissance)
GP35 became the first self-loading
pistol to be officially adopted into
British service in 1954. It replaced
the revolver as the official military
sidearm in Britain. This model
was the last Browning design.

Barrel
breech

Foresight

▶ WALTHER P38

Date 1938

Origin Germany

Barrel 4¾in (12.4cm)

Caliber 9mm Parabellum

Developed by the Walther company
just prior to World War II, the P38
has come to be recognized as one of
the finest semiautomatic pistols ever
designed. Simple in construction and
ruggedly built, it proved to be reliable
under all circumstances.

Grip made out of
Bakelite, one of the
early forms of plastic

SELF-LOADING RIFLES

Self-loading, or semiautomatic, rifles existed before the end of the 19th century. The first one was developed by Manuel Mondragon of Mexico in 1891, but like other early designs it proved too complex for military use. While some early self-loading rifles were recoil-operated (see p. 305), others began utilizing a system of gas-driven reloading (see p. 305). In 1917, French gunmakers introduced the St. Etienne self-loading rifle, while in the US, John M. Browning perfected his "automatic" rifle, the BAR (Browning Automatic Rifle). Both were in service in World War I. A later successful design was the M1 Garand rifle, designed by John Garand, which, with its numerous variations, saw widespread service in World War II. The German Sturmgewehr 44 had fully automatic firing capability, and led the way toward today's assault rifles (see pp. 250–51).

▼ M1 GARAND RIFLE	
Date	1932
Origin	US
Barrel	24in (61cm)
Caliber	.30in-06

Designed by John Garand, the M1 rifle was the first general issue self-loading rifle to be accepted for US military service. By the end of World War II, more than five million of them had been manufactured.

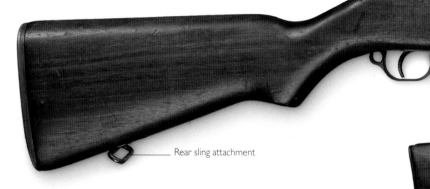

Rear sling attachment

Foresight

Threaded receiver cap

Integral magazine

▲ MONDRAGON RIFLE MODEL 1908	
Date	1908
Origin	Mexico/Switzerland
Barrel	24in (61cm)
Caliber	7mm

The Model 1908 Mondragon was the final version of a gas-operated, semiautomatic rifle first designed by Mexican General Manuel Mondragon in 1891. Though designed for infantry use, some rifles were issued to German air crew at the beginning of World War I.

Wooden butt

Rear sight

Cocking handle

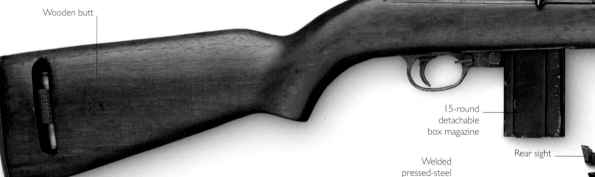

15-round detachable box magazine

Welded pressed-steel receiver

Rear sight

Wooden butt

Pistol grip

30-round detachable box magazine

Cocking handle

Forward
sling swivel

Foresight between
protective blades

Gas cylinder containing
a piston linked to the
breechblock

Bayonet
attachment

Bottom plate of
internal eight-round
box magazine

Cocking
handle

Perforated sheet-
steel hand guard

Muzzle compensator
deflects propellant gas
exhaust on firing to
reduce recoil

Trigger

10-round detachable
box magazine

▲ TOKAREV SVT40

Date	1940
Origin	Soviet Union
Barrel	24in (61cm)
Caliber	7.62 × 54mm

Fedor Tokarev designed a self-loading rifle with a
tilting bolt locking into the floor of the receiver, and
had it accepted by the Red Army in 1938. Two years later,
he produced a more robust weapon that was cheaper and
quicker to manufacture. The Samozaryadnaya Vintovka
Tokarev 40 (SVT40) was issued to noncommissioned
officers, and some were employed as sniper rifles.

Foresight

Rear sight

Cocking handle

Safety catch

Steel
butt plate

10-round detachable
box magazine

▲ GEWEHR 43

Date	1943
Origin	Germany
Barrel	22in (56cm)
Caliber	7.92 × 57mm

The German army's request
for a self-loading rifle to increase
infantry firepower spurred the
introduction of the successful
Gewehr rifle 43. A number of
them were fitted with telescopic
sights and used as sniper rifles.

Foresight in
protective shroud

▲ M1 CARBINE

Date	1941
Origin	US
Barrel	18in (46cm)
Caliber	.30in

Designed to be lighter and handier than an infantry rifle,
and employing cartridges more powerful than those used
by pistols, the M1 was intended as an alternative to the
rifle and the pistol. Issued from 1942, it was chambered
for an intermediate round developed by Winchester, and
had an action similar to that of the Garand (top), except
it had a short-stroke gas piston. It was also produced
with a folding butt (see pp.214–15).

Foresight

Stacking hook is part of the gas cylinder
cap and enabled groups of rifles to be
propped up on their butts and stacked

Perforated
pressed-steel
fore-end

**▲ STURMGEWEHR 44
(STG44)**

Date	1944
Origin	Germany
Barrel	16½in (41.8cm)
Caliber	7.92 × 33mm Kurz

In 1940, work began on a rifle capable of
selective fire—it could switch between
semiautomatic and fully automatic fire.
It was chambered for a new intermediate
7.92 × 33mm round. It was put into
production as the *Maschinen Pistole*
(machine-pistol) 43 and later renamed
the Sturmgewehr (assault rifle) 44. The
StG44 was an early example of a handheld
machine-gun, and used gas to reload
its mechanism.

FULL VIEW

SHOWCASE

COLT MODEL 1911

This all-time classic recoil-operated pistol (see p.305) has its origins in the work of John Browning in the 1890s. It used the .45in ACP (Automatic Colt Pistol) cartridge, which delivered a bullet with twice the energy of the 9mm cartridges favored in Europe. Adopted by the US government in 1911, it is still in limited service, a record for a military handgun.

Ejection port

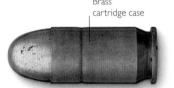

Brass cartridge case

▲ .45IN ACP CARTRIDGE
Designed by Browning in 1904, this powerful center-fire cartridge is also used by the Thompson submachine-gun (see p.212–13).

Slide houses firing pin and extractor

Barrel bushing

▲ SLIDE AND RECOIL SPRING HOUSING
The slide houses the barrel, recoil spring, and breechblock. When the bullet is fired, the slide recoils backward, extracting the empty case and cocking the hammer. Driven forward by the recoil spring, the slide then feeds a new cartridge into the chamber. The hammer remains cocked until the trigger is pulled, at which point it strikes the firing pin.

► RECOIL SPRING
After the gun is fired and the slide has moved backward, the recoil spring forces it forward again, feeding a new cartridge into the chamber and sealing the breech ready for firing.

Recoil spring

► REAR SIGHT
This steel block with a "V" notch is fixed into a dovetail slot on the slide. The rear sight is set in correct position at the factory and is not adjustable.

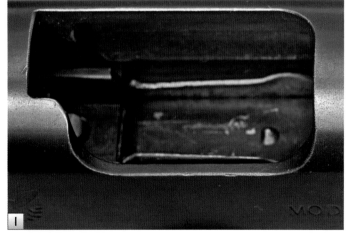

▲ RECEIVER, OR MAIN FRAME
The receiver houses the magazine and the main elements of the firing mechanism. These are the trigger, sear (not seen), hammer, mainspring (not seen, located in the butt), grip safety, safety catch, and a disconnector (not seen) to prevent full automatic fire. The receiver also houses the slide stop, which holds the barrel on the receiver independently of the slide. If removed, it allows the slide to move forward off the receiver.

▲ EJECTION PORT
The ejection port is an aperture cut in the upper portion near the rear end of the slide to allow the ejection of empty cases when the gun is fired.

COLT MODEL 1911

Date 1914

Origin US

Barrel 12in (30.5cm)

Caliber .45in ACP

With seven cartridges in the magazine and one in the chamber, this rugged gun was a formidable weapon to be confronted with. The Model 1911's use of the same ammunition as the Thompson submachine-gun made these two weapons ideal and deadly partners, not only for use in the battlefield by the military but also by law enforcement agencies, and "gangs" in their battles on the streets. The model shown here was made in 1914.

FULL VIEW

**FULL VIEW
(SLIDE PULLED BACK)**

Grip-retaining
screw

Breechblock
containing firing
pin and extractor

2
Rear sight

▼ BARREL ASSEMBLY

The barrel is fitted into the barrel bushing, and the recoil spring sits underneath the barrel. To field strip the gun, the recoil spring is pushed backward, allowing the barrel bushing to be rotated sideways. The slide stop can then be removed and slide and barrel taken apart from the main frame.

▼ MAGAZINE

A steel box magazine holds seven cartridges and is fitted inside the butt. When the last cartridge is fired, the platform inside the magazine engages with the slide stop, which holds the slide in an open position to show the magazine is empty. Inserting a full magazine and depressing the slide stop allows the slide to move forward and feed a cartridge into the chamber ready for firing.

Magazine platform
(opened up)

Slide stop is a "hold-open" device that retains the slide in a rearward position after the last round from the magazine has been fired

Barrel link pin,
which attaches
barrel assembly
to frame, fits here

Hammer
(cocked)

Safety catch

Trigger

Grip safety locks the
trigger so that it cannot be
pulled unless the user is
gripping the pistol and has
the safety pressed down

Magazine-release button

Magazine housed in butt

JOHN BROWNING

BROWNING

John Moses Browning was one of the most versatile and widely respected gunmakers in history. Although he began as a gunsmith, based in a small workshop in his native Utah, he built his reputation not as a manufacturer but as a designer of firearms. He sold his designs to gunmakers such as Winchester, Colt, and the Belgian firm Fabrique Nationale. He became famous for the build quality and practicality of his firearms, and for his innovations, especially in the field of automatic weapons.

From the age of seven, John Browning worked for his father, Jonathan, a gunsmith in Ogden, Utah. This is where he learned the basics of the gunsmith's craft and was soon experimenting and coming up with ideas of his own. Within a few years, he had built his first gun, a single-shot rifle for his brother, Matt, and by 1879, when John was 24, he and his brother set up their own workshop. The Brownings quickly established a reputation for efficient, well-made weapons. Their small workshop could not keep up with the demand, but the brothers did not have the capital to expand. So in 1883, Browning started to sell manufacturing rights to Winchester, beginning a fruitful business relationship that produced some of the best-known firearms made in the US.

THE BROWNING APPROACH

The 1880s and 1890s were fruitful decades for John Browning. During this time he produced many weapons in partnership with the Winchester Repeating Arms Company. His approach was to design guns that were simple in layout and therefore straightforward to manufacture and repair, as well as being robust enough to be reliable under the sometimes punishing conditions of the American West.

The first design Winchester bought from Browning was the single-shot rifle he was producing in his workshop in Ogden. This impressed Thomas G. Bennett, president and general manager of Winchester, when he visited Ogden in 1883. It became the Winchester Model 1885. The gun sold well, especially to users who wanted a rifle for long-range target shooting, and gained an excellent reputation. Its falling block action was so strong that Winchester used it for the punishing job of testing new cartridges. It cemented Browning's reputation as a creator of rugged, effective firearms.

Once he had sold the Model 1885 to Winchester, the young gunsmith was free to concentrate on designing new firearms for the company, and the Model 1886, a

◄ **TESTING A PROTOTYPE**
John Browning tests a prototype of his heavy machine-gun in around 1918. This firearm, a water-cooled .50in caliber weapon, was an enlarged version of the .30in caliber M1917 gun.

high-powered repeating rifle, soon appeared. This was followed by the Model 1892, a lighter gun popular with cowboys, the Model 1895, a bigger weapon designed for hunters, and the Model 1897 (see p.183), the first effective repeating shotgun, a weapon used by Wells Fargo bank guards and the US military. A total contrast was the Model 90, a lightweight weapon that was often given to young people who were learning to shoot. Altogether, Browning sold more than 40 designs to Winchester, 10 of which made it into production, along with designing weapons for other companies. It was an outstanding achievement that made Browning one of the most celebrated firearms designers in the world.

NEW BREAKTHROUGHS

Some of Browning's most notable breakthroughs came in the field of automatic weapons. In the late 1880s, he developed the first effective gas-operated automatic gun. Gas-operated firearms (see pp.194–95) use the high-pressure gas generated when a cartridge is fired to power a mechanism that extracts the spent cartridge case and delivers another one to the chamber. He offered his design to Colt and it eventually became the Colt M1895 machine-gun (see p.194), which could fire more than 400 rounds per

"If anything can happen in a **gun**, it probably will sooner or later."

GUNMAKER **JOHN BROWNING**

WINCHESTER MODEL 1887

**BROWNING
M1917**

**FN BROWNING
HP 35**

1883 Thomas G. Bennett of Winchester visits Browning and buys the patent of his single-shot rifle outright for $8,000.

1887 The lever-action Winchester Model 1887, designed by John Browning, is the first successful repeating shotgun.

1897 Browning signs a contract giving FN the right to manufacture and sell his .32in automatic pistol.

1900 Browning is granted a US patent for a semiautomatic rifle, which becomes the Remington Model 8 in the US and the FN Model 1900 elsewhere.

1917 The launch of the Browning M1917 heavy machine-gun is too late for widespread use in World War I, but the weapon will be used for decades afterward.

1918 The M1918 light machine-gun, also known as the Browning Automatic Rifle (BAR), begins its long service life of more than 40 years.

1935 Derived from Browning's last design, the FN Browning HP 35 also incorporates the work of FN designer Dieudonné Saive.

minute and used air-cooling to compensate for the heat produced by the action. The weapon sold in markets from Russia to countries in South America and saw service in the Spanish–American War (1898) and World War I. Having made a mark with this large automatic gun, Browning designed an automatic pistol. This type of weapon had been developed in Europe by manufacturers such as Mauser, but Browning was the first American to enter this market. First, he offered his design to Winchester, but he asked for a royalty on each weapon made, rather

than the single-fee payment he had accepted in the past. Winchester turned down Browning's request, and the designer instead went to the Belgian company Fabrique Nationale (FN). FN accepted, and its Browning-designed M1900 semiautomatic pistol (see p.167) was produced between 1900 and 1911. This was the beginning of a partnership that lasted until Browning's death.

In the final decades of his life, Browning continued his work, concentrating especially on automatic weapons. He produced such guns as

the Model 1917 (see p.190), a powerful recoil-operated machine-gun cooled with a water jacket, and the Browning Automatic Rifle (see p.194), a light machine-gun first produced in 1918. The latter remained in production, in various forms and via a number of manufacturers, into the 1950s. A tireless innovator, Browning continued working into his last years and died while working on a self-loading pistol at his bench in the FN factory in Liège, Belgium. His name lives on as the creator of some of the world's most successful firearms.

▼ **PUBLIC ENEMIES**
Leaning out of a car window, Stephen Dorff, playing Homer Van Meter, fires a Browning Automatic Rifle at FBI agent Purvis and his men in the 2009 film *Public Enemies*. The movie is about the notorious 1930s bank robber John Dillinger.

COMBAT AND POLICE SHOTGUNS

Shotguns have a long history as combat weapons, giving service in conflicts from the American Revolutionary War (1775–83) to World War I and beyond. Their cartridges are packed with shot—small lead pellets. The shotgun has always been an effective close-quarters weapon. US infantrymen recognized the value of the six-shot pump-action Winchester 1897 in trench warfare in World War I. Shotguns continued to evolve, with progress centering on increasing the capacity of the magazine and on new types of ammunition for both military and civilian security operations.

Shrouded hammer

Trigger guard

Under-lever

Wooden butt

External hammer

Ejection port

Loading gate in under side

Semi-pistol stock

Decocking lever

Rear sight

Under-lever

Cocked/ uncocked indicator

Tapered round barrel

Muzzle

Tubular four-round magazine

Abbreviated wooden forestock

▲ WINCHESTER MODEL 1887 UNDER-LEVER SHOTGUN

Date	1887
Origin	US
Barrel	19½in (50cm)
Caliber	12-gauge (.73in/18.54mm)

An action unique to shotguns is the lever-action rolling block of the Winchester Model 1887, designed by John M Browning. Produced in .73in and .79in chamberings (and a very few to accommodate .70in bulleted cartridges), the lever action proved unsuitable for shotgun cartridges, and was discontinued in favor of pump-action guns.

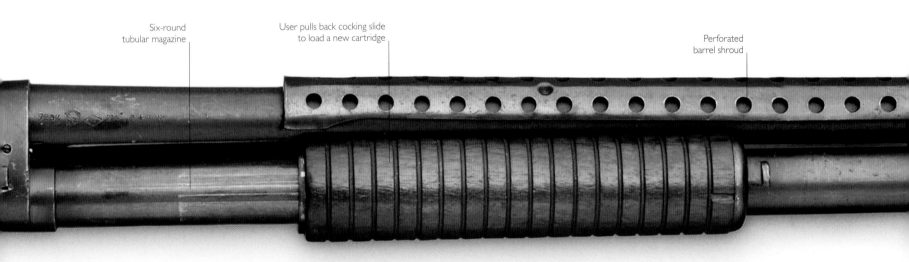

Six-round tubular magazine

User pulls back cocking slide to load a new cartridge

Perforated barrel shroud

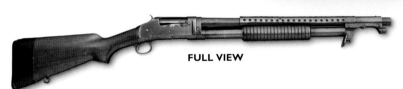

FULL VIEW

▲ WINCHESTER MODEL 1897 PUMP-ACTION SHOTGUN

Date	1897
Origin	US
Barrel	20in (51cm)
Caliber	12-gauge (.73in/18.54mm)

The Winchester Repeating Arms Company commissioned John M. Browning to develop a pump-action shotgun, and he produced the M1897. This gun's magazine made it extremely useful to the combat infantryman. Pump action is a type of slide-action mechanism in which the user first pulls the cocking slide backward, ejecting an empty case and cocking the hammer. Pushing the slide forward chambers a cartridge and closes the breech. The gun is then ready to fire.

Full-length wooden forestock

Sling swivel

▲ GREENER-MARTINI POLICE SHOTGUN

Date	1920
Origin	UK
Barrel	28in (71.2cm)
Caliber	12-gauge (.73in/18.54mm)

Developed after World War I for use by British colonial police forces, this single-shot weapon was unconventional in that it had a Martini falling-block action. In this action, the cocking lever is pivoted forward, causing the breechblock to hinge vertically downward into the receiver. This opens the breech for loading a new cartridge manually. Furthermore, this gun accepted only cartridges of an unusual form—to prevent stolen guns from being used by civilians.

TURNING POINT

MACHINE-GUNS

In 1883, a patent filed by Hiram Maxim covered a revolutionary concept in firearms—a gun in which energy from the explosion, in addition to driving the bullet, also drove the cycle of loading and firing and would continue to do so as long as there was a supply of ammunition. All the user had to do was point the gun and pull the trigger. This true machine-gun inspired the development of new "fully automatic" and "semiautomatic" firearms, which are the weapons used today by the world's armed forces and law enforcement agencies.

▲ MAXIM GUN
In the Maxim gun, the energy from the recoil was used to eject each spent cartridge and insert the next one and fire it. This made it less labor-intensive and more efficient than previous rapid-firing guns that relied on manual cranking.

Mechanized guns, or what were considered to be "machine-guns," first began to appear in the middle of the 19th century. Their operation involved feeding the cartridge into the chamber of a barrel, firing it, and then extracting the empty case by a manually powered mechanical process in a continuous cycle. The first of these guns to achieve real success was the Gatling, later followed by the Nordenfelt, Hotchkiss, and Gardner guns. All performed well in their own distinctive ways and were widely used by the major military and maritime nations of the world. However, all mechanical machine-guns suffered from the same drawback—they required human energy to operate them and stamina to maintain a continuous fire.

RECYCLING WASTED ENERGY

All guns obey the same law of nature—the force that drives the ammunition forward also drives the gun backward. This was considered an unavoidable nuisance by gunmakers. Hiram Maxim, however, recognized it as a source of energy and put it to better use. He also noted other flaws associated with machine-guns, which included cartridges that often suffered from a "hang-fire"—a delayed explosion of the main charge after the primer was detonated.

THEORY BECOMES REALITY

Maxim experimentally modified rifles to use their recoil energy to load and fire them. Satisfied that the idea could work, he built an experimental gun, which operated in the same way but used a specially designed lock mechanism. This mechanism extracted cartridges from a continuous belt, fed them into the chamber, and fired them. A hang-fire was not a problem in such a gun, because it could not continue its cycle until the explosion occurred.

Conscious of the heat generated by continuous

>> **BEFORE**

The third quarter of the 19th century saw the creation of guns capable of giving sustained fire. Often referred to at the time as "battery guns," they became thought of as "machine-guns" because the processes of loading and firing had been mechanized, turning them into "shooting machines." They were successful, but they had their drawbacks.

GATLING GUN

• **MOST GUNS WERE HEAVY** and often needed to be mounted on wheeled carriages for transport. Their use on land and at sea needed massive mountings fixed to the deck or other structures capable of supporting them.

• **A CREW OF SEVERAL MEN** was required to operate the guns, and a team of horses had to draw the gun carriage along with a limber to carry the ammunition.

• **LIGHTWEIGHT, PORTABLE MACHINE-GUNS**, such as the Nordenfelt gun, were developed. However, since they were hand-cranked, their aim was easily disturbed and not very accurate.

"**Whatever** happens, we **have got** The Maxim gun, and they have **not.**"

HILAIRE BELLOC, IN HIS POEM, "*THE MODERN TRAVELLER***" (1898)**

firing, Maxim fitted a jacket containing water around the gun's barrel to keep it cool. His creation was aided by the invention of smokeless powder (see pp. 142–43). This new propellant produced less residue to clog a barrel, and developed its explosive pressure more gradually, thereby imparting less shock to the mechanism. Maxim had observed that the guns, operated by a crank handle or a lever, were hard to train onto moving targets. With his new gun, all the user had to do was aim and shoot—the gun would continue to fire until its ammunition supply was exhausted. Maxim's genius had conceived a new way to use explosion energy for operating a gun and created a true machine-gun.

On the battlefield, the Maxim gun brought shocking carnage and prompted a change in military tactics. It was an ideal weapon for defending a position, whether a building or a trench, and Maxim-equipped armies began to lure enemies into "charging," at which point

they could be mown down. This was seen for the first time when British colonial forces used the Maxim in the Matabele War (1893–94) in modern-day Zimbabwe. In a nation where firearms were not in common use by non-Europeans, its impact was as much psychological as physical. In one battle, it is said that 50 British soldiers with just four Maxim guns fought off 5,000 Ndebele warriors. Pitched battles and charging began to become obsolete. This weapon was again used to devastating effect in Sudan in the Battle of Omdurman (1898), fought between the British and Arab Mahdist forces. Used successfully against the charging tactics of the Arabs, the Maxim enabled the British forces to kill more than 10,000 of the enemy while losing only about 50 soldiers.

Maxim's patent became a blueprint for many modern self-loading firearms that followed and have become icons of their type, bringing with them a new level of horror to armed conflict.

KEY FIGURE

HIRAM STEVENS MAXIM
(1840–1916)

American-born Hiram Maxim emigrated to Britain in 1881 and became a British subject in 1900. His childhood experience of being knocked over by a rifle's recoil may have been instrumental in leading him to harness a gun's recoil energy, eventually designing the Maxim machine-gun. His inventions included, among others, his "Captive Flying Machine"—a very successful fairground ride, which helped fund his experiments. He was knighted in 1901.

▼ THE MAXIM IN CHITRAL
By the 1890s, the British Army decided to issue the Maxim gun to every battalion. Captain Alan L. Peebles of the Devonshire Regiment had seen the Maxim in action in Waziristan in 1894. In 1895, he brought a pair of Maxim guns to Chitral (in modern-day Pakistan) as part of a British expeditionary force sent to recapture a fort overtaken by Afghan tribesmen. Pictured here are some soldiers from the force with a Maxim Gun.

AFTER »

Maxim's gun turned the old, manual machine-guns into obsolete technology. Once it got into production and its capabilities became known, it provided the cutting edge every military power wanted in order to give themselves supremacy over a supposed enemy.

• **LIGHT MACHINE-GUNS** developed rapidly, leading to guns such as the Browning Automatic Rifle (see p.194). These could be carried by one man with a supply of ammunition and fired from the hip while moving.

BROWNING AUTOMATIC RIFLE

• **SUBMACHINE-GUNS** were lighter, more compact, and fired pistol ammunition. The most iconic gun of this period was the Thompson submachine-gun (see pp. 212–13).

THOMPSON SUBMACHINE-GUN

• **MODERN FULLY AUTOMATIC** and semiautomatic weapons are the offspring of these early developments, relying on the same basic recoil-operation principles for their action. The technology extended beyond heavy weaponry to handguns and spurred the development of self-loading, semiautomatic pistols using recoil energy.

RECOIL-OPERATED MACHINE-GUNS (1884–95)

In 1884, Sir Hiram Maxim invented a machine-gun (see pp. 184–85) that worked by recoil-action instead of being hand-cranked like earlier machine-guns (see pp.136–39). Maxim had initially tried to harness the energy of a gun's recoil to automate its action in rifles such as the Peabody-Martini and Winchester. He ultimately perfected the process in his machine-gun. The Maxim machine-gun was fully automatic, meaning it could fire continuously while the trigger was kept pulled. Within 10 years, armies in the UK, Germany, and Russia had adopted this weapon.

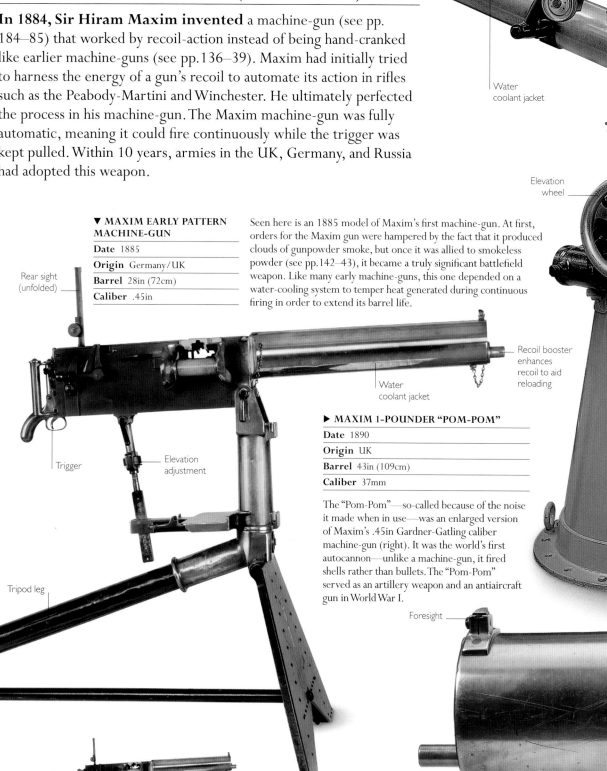

▼ MAXIM EARLY PATTERN MACHINE-GUN

Date	1885
Origin	Germany / UK
Barrel	28in (72cm)
Caliber	.45in

Seen here is an 1885 model of Maxim's first machine-gun. At first, orders for the Maxim gun were hampered by the fact that it produced clouds of gunpowder smoke, but once it was allied to smokeless powder (see pp.142–43), it became a truly significant battlefield weapon. Like many early machine-guns, this one depended on a water-cooling system to temper heat generated during continuous firing in order to extend its barrel life.

Rear sight (unfolded)

Trigger

Elevation adjustment

Tripod leg

Water coolant jacket

Recoil booster enhances recoil to aid reloading

► MAXIM 1-POUNDER "POM-POM"

Date	1890
Origin	UK
Barrel	43in (109cm)
Caliber	37mm

The "Pom-Pom"—so-called because of the noise it made when in use—was an enlarged version of Maxim's .45in Gardner-Gatling caliber machine-gun (right). It was the world's first autocannon—unlike a machine-gun, it fired shells rather than bullets. The "Pom-Pom" served as an artillery weapon and an antiaircraft gun in World War I.

Water coolant jacket

Elevation wheel

Gun on antiaircraft mounting

Naval pintle mounting, modified during World War I for a ship's defense against attacking aircraft

Foresight

Water coolant jacket

FULL VIEW

Grip

Elevation wheel

Operator's
seat

◀ **MAXIM .45IN GARDNER-
GATLING CALIBER**

Date 1892

Origin UK

Barrel 44in (112cm)

Caliber .45in

The British Army's .45in Maxim gun
had become the standard Maxim
gun by the late 19th century. It was
converted to .303in caliber from
1897–98 onward. The Royal Navy,
however, continued with the .45in
Gardner-Gatling caliber gun until
the end of World War I. This was
mainly because these machine-guns,
even the higher-caliber ones, would be
fixed to a ship's structure and did not
need to be moved. The .45in caliber
gave the naval Maxim guns greater range
and penetrating power. These weapons
fired about 450 rounds per minute.

Tripod
mounting

Tripod leg

Spike to
position gun
in soft ground

Rear sight
(unfolded)

▼ **MAXIM-NORDENFELT
MODEL 1893**

Date 1893

Origin UK

Barrel 42½in (108cm)

Caliber 11mm

Hiram Maxim and Swedish gunmaker Nordenfelt
entered into partnership in 1888. In this early
experimental model, intended for French trials,
steam pressure was used to operate the firing mechanism
of the gun when the trigger was pulled—an impractical
refinement that was soon discontinued. This model fired
450 rounds per minute. In 1896, their joint venture was
subsumed into Vickers, Sons and Maxim.

Cover for
breechblock mainspring

RECOIL-OPERATED MACHINE-GUNS (1896–1917)

Machine-guns built at the turn of the 20th century were either recoil-operated or gas-driven (see pp. 192–93). They were produced in Europe when the continent was devoid of conflict. Materials such as brass were plentiful and were used to make gun parts such as water jackets and spring housings. As Europe entered World War I, brass became scarcer, and steel—which was less expensive and also more durable—began to be employed for making gun parts. Gas-operated machine-guns could withstand greater pressure than recoil-operated ones and fire more powerful ammunition. However, recoil-operated machine-guns were more common, because their simple, reliable design found greater favor with troops.

Recoil booster enhances recoil to aid reloading

Connection for condenser hose

Muzzle cap

Sangster auxiliary tripod

Rear sight

Feedway for ammunition belt

Water jacket to cool barrel

Foresight

Feedway for ammunition belt

Tripod leg

Carrying handle

Operator's seat

FULL VIEW

Elevation wheel

Tripod leg

Foot of tripod leg fitted with cleat to stabilize the gun by preventing movement

▲ MAXIM MACHINE-GUN MODEL 1904

Date 1904

Origin UK

Barrel 28½in (72.3cm)

Caliber .30in-03

The Maxim gun was robust in construction and almost foolproof in design, taking on many forms after its introduction, including this upgraded model. This Maxim gun was the first rifle-caliber machine-gun formally adopted into US service. It was manufactured in .30in-03 caliber in the US by British gun manufacturer Vickers, Sons and Maxim. Later, some units were manufactured under licence in the US by Colt. Eventually, most Maxim models began to accept the newly introduced US .30in-06 cartridge. This gun fired 400–600 rounds per minute.

▶ BROWNING MODEL 1917

Date 1917

Origin US

Barrel 24in (61cm)

Caliber .30in

John Browning produced a poorly designed machine-gun for Colt, the gas-operated M1895 "Potato Digger" (see p. 194), but later reverted to recoil operation when creating the M1917. It fired 400–520 rounds per minute. This gun sported a water jacket to cool its barrel during operation. Water-cooled machine-guns usually required a two-man crew—one to fire the gun and the other to monitor the jacket and the fabric belt which loaded ammunition into the gun. Ammunition belts could carry a higher number of cartridges than standard magazines and they could be loaded easily via the feedways on these guns.

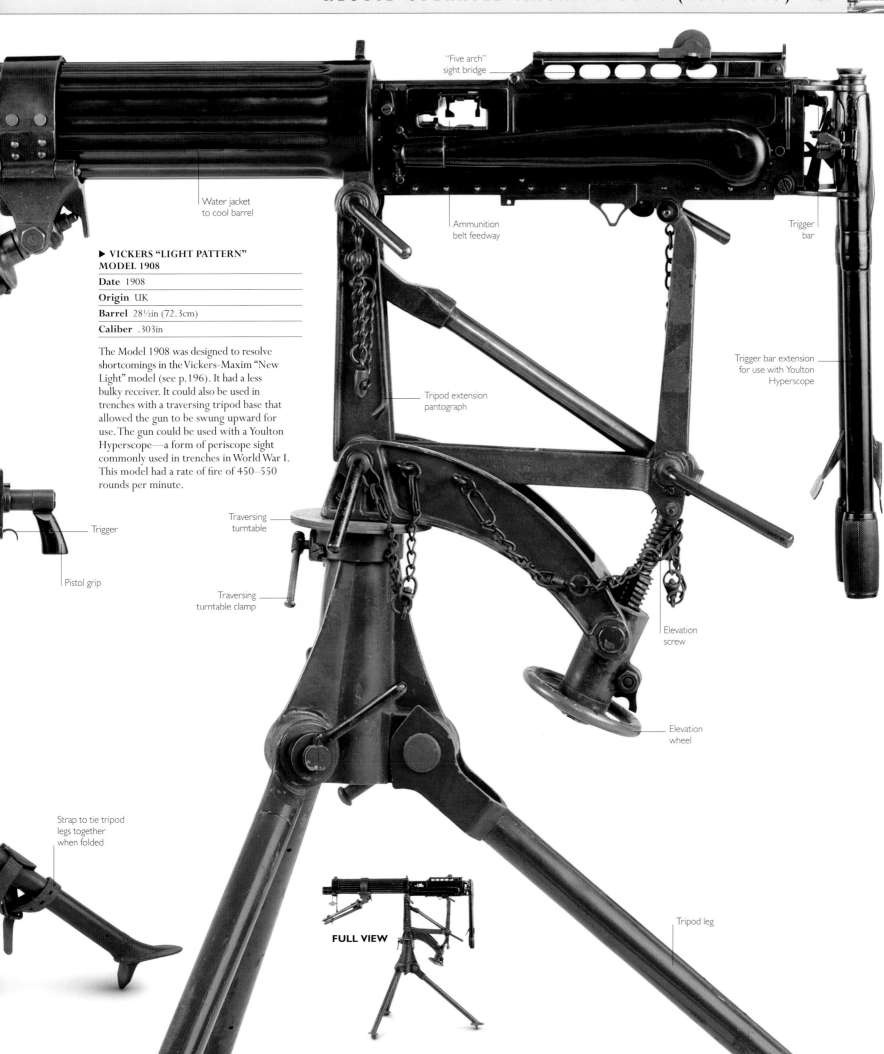

"Five arch"
sight bridge

Water jacket
to cool barrel

Ammunition
belt feedway

Trigger
bar

▶ **VICKERS "LIGHT PATTERN"**
MODEL 1908

Date 1908

Origin UK

Barrel 28½in (72.3cm)

Caliber .303in

The Model 1908 was designed to resolve
shortcomings in the Vickers-Maxim "New
Light" model (see p.196). It had a less
bulky receiver. It could also be used in
trenches with a traversing tripod base that
allowed the gun to be swung upward for
use. The gun could be used with a Youlton
Hyperscope—a form of periscope sight
commonly used in trenches in World War I.
This model had a rate of fire of 450–550
rounds per minute.

Trigger bar extension
for use with Youlton
Hyperscope

Tripod extension
pantograph

Trigger

Pistol grip

Traversing
turntable

Traversing
turntable clamp

Elevation
screw

Elevation
wheel

Strap to tie tripod
legs together
when folded

FULL VIEW

Tripod leg

TRENCH WARFARE
Machine-guns such as those made by Hotchkiss and Maxim caused great destruction in the trench warfare of World War I. This two-man French Hotchkiss crew is flanked by two infantrymen.

RECOIL-OPERATED MACHINE-GUNS (1918–45)

Without question, the most important advancements in machine-gun design were made by the American inventor John M. Browning (see pp.180–81). His designs stimulated the production of both medium (.30in caliber) and heavy (.50in caliber) machine-guns that could be operated by two men. The second advancement that allowed the effective use of recoil-operated guns was the introduction of barrel-locking systems that allowed the barrels to be changed quickly while in the field to prevent overheating. Perhaps the best of these systems was that developed for use on the German MG42, a design that remains in use to this day.

Rear sight

Ammunition belt feedway

Foresight

Trigger

Pistol grip

▲ BROWNING MODEL 1919

Date 1919

Origin US

Barrel 24in (61cm)

Caliber .30in

The M1919 was an air-cooled version of the earlier M1917 (see p.190), and it proved to be a first-rate medium machine-gun, supporting US infantrymen throughout World War II, and remaining in use until the 1960s. It had a firing rate of 400–600 rounds per minute.

Barrel-change handle

Perforated barrel shroud

▲ BROWNING M2 HB

Date 1933

Origin US

Barrel 3¾ft (1.14m)

Caliber .50in

The highly effective "fifty cal" M2 HB (heavy barrel) has been used as a key armament in aircraft, on armored vehicles, and as shown here, by ground troops. This gun can fire 485–635 rounds per minute, and remains in service today.

Flash hider concealed the flash of exploding propellant gases, helping to hide the firer's position

Rear sight

Ammunition belt feed

Butt

▲ MASCHINENGEWEHR 34

Date 1935

Origin Germany

Barrel 24¾in (62.7cm)

Caliber 7.92 × 57mm

The *Maschinengewehr* 34 (MG34) was a revolutionary design—light, yet robust enough to deliver sustained fire at 900 rounds per minute. However, it was difficult and expensive to manufacture and was subsequently replaced by the MG42.

Bipod

Double-crescent trigger

Perforated barrel shroud insulates the user's hands from the hot barrel and helps to air-cool the barrel

Flash hider

Perforated barrel shroud

Recoil-actuated automatic traverse mechanism

Bracing bar

Lafette 42 heavy tripod

▶ MASCHINENGEWEHR 42

Date 1942

Origin Germany

Barrel 21in (53.3cm)

Caliber 7.92 × 57mm

A successor to the MG34 (below), the MG42 had an extraordinarily high rate of fire—over 1,200 rounds per minute—and was capable of sustained long-range fire when used with a tripod. It featured a recoil-actuated automatic traverse mechanism, which moved the gun's butt slightly to the left and right when firing, allowing the weapon to spray bullets over a small arc and a large target area.

Belt feed mechanism

Trigger bar

Firing lever

Spade grips

Ammunition belt supporting box

Tripod leg

Tripod mount

GAS-OPERATED MACHINE-GUNS

Gas-operated machine-guns harness the energy of the gases produced by the exploding cartridge (see p.305) that propel the bullet down the barrel. A portion of these gases are bled off to reload the gun by driving a piston to the rear, which pushes the bolt backward. This extracts the spent cartridge and chambers a new one. Guns using this system can be made light and easily to control because the gas piston and springs inside the gun absorb much of the recoil. These machine-guns evolved in the 1880s and 1890s, and the first claim to a working design was the Colt–Browning "Potato Digger." A more sophisticated design belonged to the Hotchkiss company's hugely successful Hotchkiss machine-gun. Gas-operated systems have continued to proliferate.

Ejection port

Elevation/traverse controls

Spade grip

Tripod leg

▲ COLT-BROWNING M1895 "POTATO DIGGER"

Date	1895
Origin	US
Barrel	28¼in (72cm)
Caliber	.30in Krag

The Colt M1895 was the creation of John Browning; it was nicknamed the "Potato Digger" because of its innovative mechanics. Some of the gas produced by the exploding charge was tapped off from near the muzzle to drive an arm through a 170-degree action. Through a linkage, the arm, in turn, powered the opening and closing of the breech. The M1895 was reliable enough, and served with the US Army, Navy, and Marine Corps around the turn of the century.

▼ LEWIS GUN M1914

Date	1914
Origin	US
Barrel	26in (66cm)
Caliber	.303in

The air-cooled Lewis gun was the first light machine-gun (LMG) used on the Western Front. Taken up by the Belgians, then by the British, it remained in service on the ground, in the air (when it was usually stripped of its barrel shroud), and even at sea until World War II. It could fire 500–600 rounds in a minute.

Flash hider

Foresight

Pan magazine holds 47 rounds

Muzzle

Gunner's left hand grips stock here

Trigger

Cocking handle

Cooling fins continue inside barrel shroud

Barrel shroud and heat dissipator

Bipod leg

Carrying handle

Foresight guard

Ejection port

Gas tube

▲ BROWNING AUTOMATIC RIFLE (BAR)

Date	1918
Origin	US
Barrel	24in (61cm)
Caliber	.30in

John Browning responded to pleas to provide infantrymen with a weapon they could fire in bursts from the hip while advancing. The gas-operated Browning Automatic Rifle was too heavy and cumbersome ever to be a success in that role, but it survived as the US Army's stock LMG until the 1950s.

Rear sling attachment

Trigger guard with security lock in place

20-round detachable box magazine

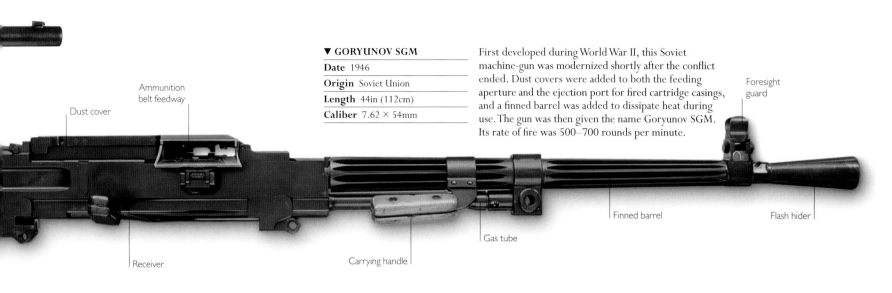

▼ GORYUNOV SGM

Date 1946

Origin Soviet Union

Length 44in (112cm)

Caliber 7.62 × 54mm

First developed during World War II, this Soviet machine-gun was modernized shortly after the conflict ended. Dust covers were added to both the feeding aperture and the ejection port for fired cartridge casings, and a finned barrel was added to dissipate heat during use. The gun was then given the name Goryunov SGM. Its rate of fire was 500–700 rounds per minute.

Dust cover

Ammunition belt feedway

Receiver

Carrying handle

Gas tube

Finned barrel

Foresight guard

Flash hider

▼ HOTCHKISS MLE 1914

Date 1914

Origin France

Barrel 50in (127cm)

Caliber 8mm Lebel

The Hotchkiss MLE 1914 was based upon a design originally conceived by Baron A. Odkolek von Augeza of Austria. It was improved by Lawrence V. Benet in association with Henri Mercie. The primary changes in the arm's construction involved the incorporation of fins to cool the barrel during firing—a design improvement that would be seen in many machine-guns— and a gas regulator to control the rate of fire, which was about 550 rounds per minute. Simple in construction, with only 32 parts, the MLE 1914 was fed with metallic ammunition strips that held 24 rounds.

Gas tube

Cooling fin

Elevation gear

Ammunition belt feedway

Optical sight

Trigger

Steadying grip

Traversing turn table

Elevation wheel

Gunner's seat

FULL VIEW

HEAVY MACHINE-GUNS (1900–10)

Viewed almost as artillery pieces, heavy machine-guns—some operating by recoil, others by gas pressure—were designed to provide covering fire for attacking forces or defensive fire from fixed positions. From the Maxim 1904 machine-gun (see p.188) to the Goryunov SGM (see p.195) and the Russian Maxim 1910, heavy machine-guns were cumbersome and needed crews of three to five soldiers for operation. Although these weapons were effective, they had limited mobility. During firing, they generated vibrations that made them unstable, and so they were best suited for use from static mounts fitted to vehicles or, later, aircraft.

Rear sight

Ammunition belt feedway

Receiver

▲ VICKERS-MAXIM "NEW LIGHT" MODEL 1906

Date 1906

Origin UK

Barrel 28½in (72.3cm)

Caliber .303in

The first departure from Maxim's original design (see p.186), the recoil-operated "New Light" saw the original brass fittings exchanged for much lighter steel, but continued to employ the downward-breaking locking toggle that made the receiver large. Its rate of fire was 450–500 rounds per minute. The Russians adopted it as the M1910 (below).

Flash hider

Cooling water jacket

Optical rear sight

Front legs of mount swiveled up and back

Cover for breechblock mainspring

Grip

▲ DWM MG08

Date 1908

Origin Germany

Barrel 28¼in (71.9cm)

Caliber 7.92 × 57mm Mauser

Soon after the German Army acquired its first Maxims in 1895, *Deutsche Waffen und Munitionsfabriken* (DWM) began modifying the design, and the final version was adopted as the *schweres Maschinengewehr* 08 (heavy machine-rifle), or MG08. It had a heavy sledge-style mount, known as the *schlitten*. This gun fired 500 rounds per minute.

Towing tongue

Sledge-style mount

Elevation screw

Wheeled carriage

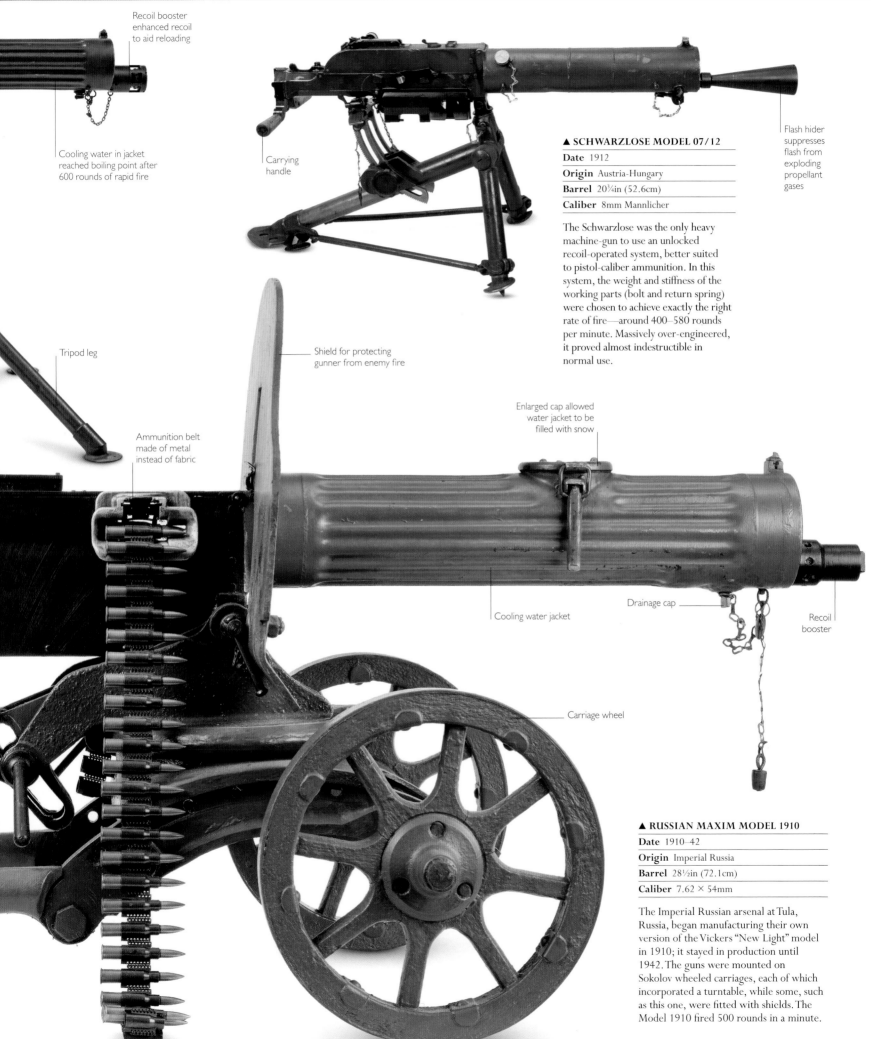

Recoil booster enhanced recoil to aid reloading

Cooling water in jacket reached boiling point after 600 rounds of rapid fire

Carrying handle

Flash hider suppresses flash from exploding propellant gases

Tripod leg

Shield for protecting gunner from enemy fire

Ammunition belt made of metal instead of fabric

Enlarged cap allowed water jacket to be filled with snow

Cooling water jacket

Drainage cap

Recoil booster

Carriage wheel

▲ SCHWARZLOSE MODEL 07/12

Date	1912
Origin	Austria-Hungary
Barrel	20¼in (52.6cm)
Caliber	8mm Mannlicher

The Schwarzlose was the only heavy machine-gun to use an unlocked recoil-operated system, better suited to pistol-caliber ammunition. In this system, the weight and stiffness of the working parts (bolt and return spring) were chosen to achieve exactly the right rate of fire—around 400–580 rounds per minute. Massively over-engineered, it proved almost indestructible in normal use.

▲ RUSSIAN MAXIM MODEL 1910

Date	1910–42
Origin	Imperial Russia
Barrel	28½in (72.1cm)
Caliber	7.62 × 54mm

The Imperial Russian arsenal at Tula, Russia, began manufacturing their own version of the Vickers "New Light" model in 1910; it stayed in production until 1942. The guns were mounted on Sokolov wheeled carriages, each of which incorporated a turntable, while some, such as this one, were fitted with shields. The Model 1910 fired 500 rounds in a minute.

HEAVY MACHINE-GUNS (1911–45)

The heavy machine-guns of the two world wars proved their effectiveness when used against vehicles. Many were made in calibers of a sufficient size to penetrate light armor. These weapons, such as the gas-operated ones seen here, could also be used at long ranges—the Degtyarev DSHK1938 had a range of about 1¼ miles (2km), for instance. This helped to compromise the massing of enemy troops prior to attacks.

▶ **HOTCHKISS M1914**

Date 1914

Origin France

Barrel 31in (78.7cm)

Caliber 8 × 50mm

Weighing over 36kg (80lb), complete with its tripod, the Hotchkiss MLE 1914 (see p.195) was a massive gas-operated weapon. While it was normal for machine-gun crews to sit or lie behind their weapons, in some instances they had to stand. This variant of the MLE 1914 is equipped with a shoulder brace and a tripod allowing its use from such a position.

Shoulder brace

Gas port and expansion chamber for driving the operating piston rearwards

Rear sight

Spade grip

Elevation adjustment knob

Ejected case deflector keeps away spent cases

108mm-long cartridge

Steel ammunition belt

Elevating quadrant

Antiaircraft mounting

Rear sight

Grip

Water jacket
to cool barrel

Internal magazine held
50 rounds in five trays

Elevation
crank

▲ FIAT-REVELLI MODEL 1914

Date 1914

Origin Italy

Barrel 25¼in (65.4cm)

Caliber 6.5mm Mannlicher-Carcano

This model employed a delayed recoil-operated
system. The delay in breech unlocking allowed
a better tolerance for higher breech pressures
and more powerful shots than normal recoil-
operated systems. Rounds were fed from a
50-round stack magazine and oiled on their
way to the chamber. The oiled rounds picked
up dust and dirt, causing the gun to jam
frequently. This weapon's rate of fire was
500 rounds per minute.

Elevating
quadrant

Tripod leg

Foresight

Muzzle brake diverts exploding
propellant gases sideways to reduce recoil

Fins on barrel
to dissipate heat

Gas tube
carrying piston

▲ DEGTYAREV DSHK1938

Date 1938

Origin Soviet Union

Barrel 39½in (100cm)

Caliber 12.7 × 108mm

Employed as the Red Army's heavy
machine-gun, the gas-operated
DShK1938 resembled the .50in
Browning M2 (see p.192). It enjoyed
similar longevity—some units are
still in service. It fired 600 rounds
per minute.

Rear
sight

Ammunition
belt feedway

Grip

Regulator to adjust the gas
volume used to drive the
operating piston

Elevating
quadrant

▲ BREDA MODELLO 37

Date 1937

Origin Italy

Barrel 50in (127cm)

Caliber 8 × 59mm

Adopted by the Italian Army in
1937, the Breda was a gas-operated
machine-gun (see pp.194—95) fed
by 20-round ammunition strips, and
later belts. Its primary disadvantage
was that the cartridges had to be
lubricated with oil prior to firing.
Stoppages caused by dust or dirt
were therefore a problem. Its low
cyclic rate (450 rounds per minute),
however, was an advantage for
accurate support fire.

Tripod leg

LIGHT MACHINE-GUNS (1902–15)

Trench warfare and stagnant lines were the norm on World War I battlefields, and the development of easily carried machine-guns became a necessity for raids and the strengthening of positions under fire. Some light machine-guns were developed strictly for use in aircraft, for which weight was a primary design consideration. During the first years of its use, the light machine-gun proved to be invaluable both as a defensive and offensive weapon, thereby leading to its further refinement as World War I progressed.

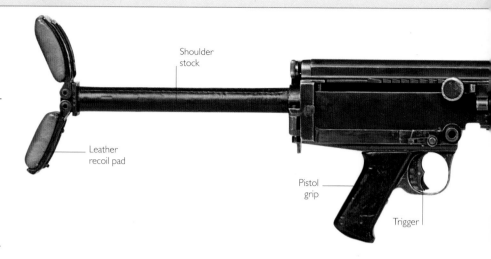

Shoulder stock

Leather recoil pad

Pistol grip

Trigger

▲ **MADSEN MEDIUM LMG**

Date 1902

Origin Denmark

Barrel 23in (58.4cm)

Caliber 7 × 57mm

Developed by Julius Rasmussen and Theodor Schouboe, the Madsen was introduced into service in 1902. It had an effective cyclic rate of 450 rounds per minute and was noted for its reliability. It was, however, expensive to manufacture and therefore had a limited clientele.

Barrel casing

Operating handle

Safety lever

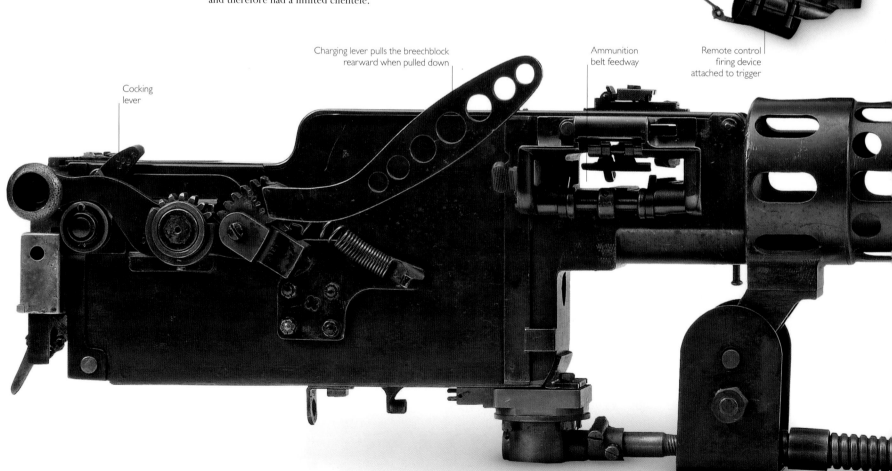

Cocking lever

Charging lever pulls the breechblock rearward when pulled down

Ammunition belt feedway

Remote control firing device attached to trigger

Perforated
barrel shroud

Flash
hider

**▲ DREYSE
MASCHINENGEWEHR 13**

Date 1914

Origin Germany

Barrel 28¼in (71.7cm)

Caliber 7.92 × 57mm Mauser

Carrying handle

The *Maschinengewehr* 13 (MG13) was developed from
a weapon designed by the famous German gunmaker
Louis Schmeisser and produced by Nikolaus von Dreyse
from 1909. That gun was water-cooled, but the MG13
swapped the water jacket for a perforated shroud—for
air-cooling—and gained a tubular shoulder stock and
a pistol grip and trigger group. The trigger allows
switching between firing modes—its top half is for
semiautomatic mode and bottom half for fully
automatic mode.

Bipod leg

Perforated
barrel shroud

Rear sight

Drum
magazine

Wooden
butt

▲ CHAUCHAT MLE 1915

Date 1907

Origin France

Barrel 19in (48.26cm)

Caliber 8 × 50mm

More properly described as a machine-rifle,
since it was intended for use by one person
and could be fired in semiautomatic mode,
the Chauchat has the dubious distinction of
being known as the worst light machine-gun
ever made. It was prone to jamming and
the thin-walled pressed steel magazines
were far too delicate for field use.

Foresight

Perforated
barrel shroud

FULL VIEW

**▲ SPANDAU 08/15 AIRCRAFT
MACHINE-GUN**

Date 1915

Origin Germany

Barrel 28¼in (71.9cm)

Caliber 7.92 × 57mm Mauser

Though it was also used by infantrymen,
fitted with a butt and pistol grip, the
LMG08/15 was developed as a fixed
gun for use in aircraft. In this form,
it had a synchronizer cable linked to
an interrupter gear, which allowed
it to fire forward—right through
the propeller's arc.

Synchronizer cable

LIGHT MACHINE-GUNS (1916–25)

Although some light machine-guns continued to be fitted with water-cooling jackets, these models were intended for high-volume fire. When used simply to provide cover in short bursts, air-cooled weapons such as the Bergmann became the norm. These machine-guns had the benefit of easy portability because of the reduced weight, and they had less cumbersome accessories, thus requiring smaller crews.

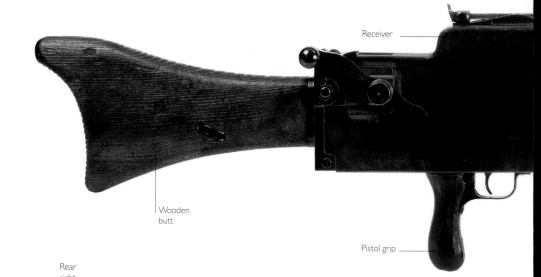

Receiver

Wooden butt

Pistol grip

Butt plate

Rear sight

Ammunition belt feedway

Trigger

Pistol grip

▲ BERGMANN LMG 15NA

Date 1916

Origin Germany

Barrel 28½in (72.6cm)

Caliber 7.92 × 57mm Mauser

Bergmann's LMG was adopted in 1910, but it was not until the appearance of a modified version in 1916 that it found favor. Its ammunition was contained in a metal link belt, fed from a drumlike container.

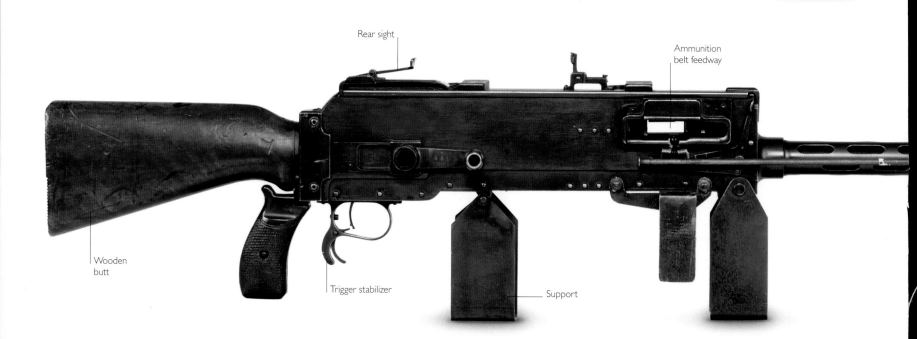

Rear sight

Ammunition belt feedway

Wooden butt

Trigger stabilizer

Support

Cooling jacket holds 4 quarts (4 liters) water

Flash hider

Ammunition belt feedway

▲ MAXIM MASCHINENGEWEHR 08/15

Date 1917

Origin Germany

Barrel 28¼in (71.9cm)

Caliber 7.92 × 57mm Mauser

Germany's first, hurried attempt to produce a light machine-gun saw the DWM MG08 (see p.196) fitted with a butt, a pistol grip, and a conventional trigger, resulting in the Maxim 08/15. This improved version of the MG08 had a recontoured receiver to reduce the gun's weight and an integral bipod with a shortened ammunition belt contained in a drumlike container. Weighing 30¾lb (14kg), it was still far too heavy. Around 130,000 units were produced, and it became the principal support weapon for the stormtroopers of the *Reichswehr*—Germany's interwar armed forces.

Integral bipod

Foresight

Barrel has a perforated shroud to air-cool it

Carrying handle

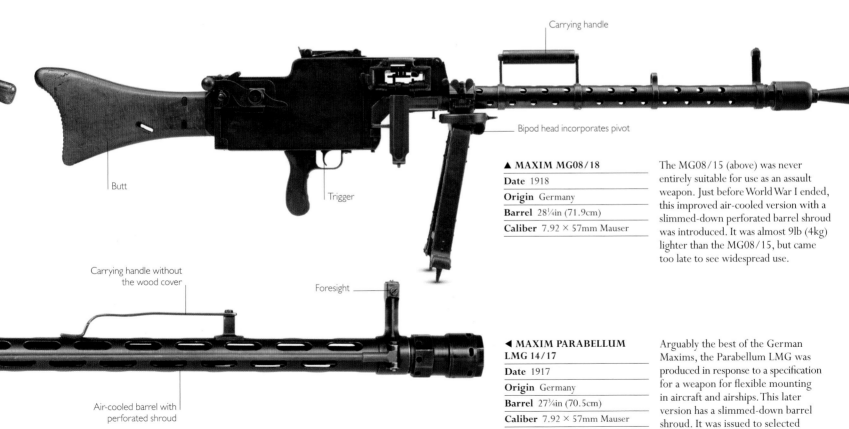

Butt

Bipod head incorporates pivot

Trigger

Foresight

▲ MAXIM MG08/18

Date 1918

Origin Germany

Barrel 28¼in (71.9cm)

Caliber 7.92 × 57mm Mauser

The MG08/15 (above) was never entirely suitable for use as an assault weapon. Just before World War I ended, this improved air-cooled version with a slimmed-down perforated barrel shroud was introduced. It was almost 9lb (4kg) lighter than the MG08/15, but came too late to see widespread use.

Carrying handle without the wood cover

Air-cooled barrel with perforated shroud

◄ MAXIM PARABELLUM LMG 14/17

Date 1917

Origin Germany

Barrel 27¾in (70.5cm)

Caliber 7.92 × 57mm Mauser

Arguably the best of the German Maxims, the Parabellum LMG was produced in response to a specification for a weapon for flexible mounting in aircraft and airships. This later version has a slimmed-down barrel shroud. It was issued to selected infantry units in this form toward the end of the war.

LIGHT MACHINE-GUNS (1926–45)

From the 1920s onward, light machine-guns were redesigned with a view to reducing the size of their crews. While earlier LMGs, such as the Maxim 08/15 (see p.203), required a crew of four, newer LMGs such as the Bren could be operated by a one- or two-man crew. This reduction in the crew size was made possible by changing the ammunition feed system from belts, which needed an additional user for ensuring proper loading, to box magazines, which could be loaded and changed by the main user only.

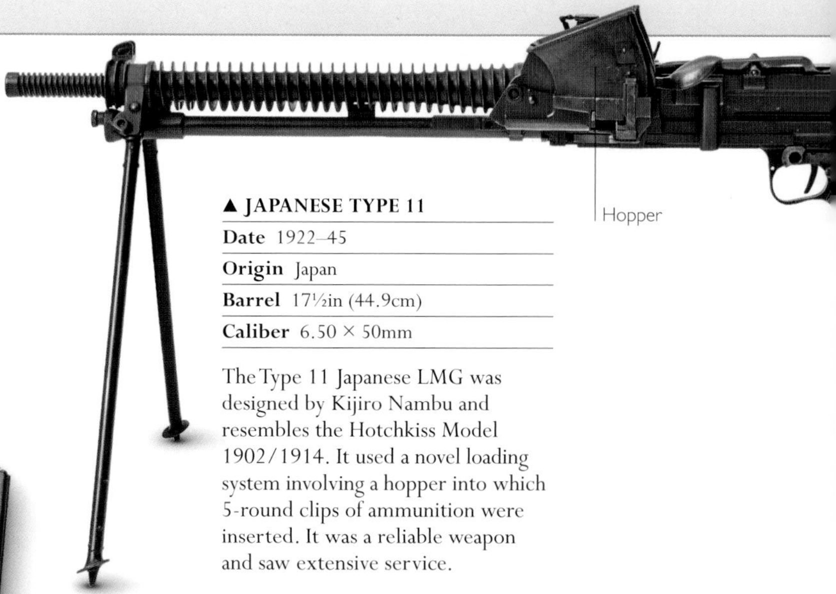

▲ **JAPANESE TYPE 11**

Date 1922–45

Origin Japan

Barrel 17½in (44.9cm)

Caliber 6.50 × 50mm

The Type 11 Japanese LMG was designed by Kijiro Nambu and resembles the Hotchkiss Model 1902/1914. It used a novel loading system involving a hopper into which 5-round clips of ammunition were inserted. It was a reliable weapon and saw extensive service.

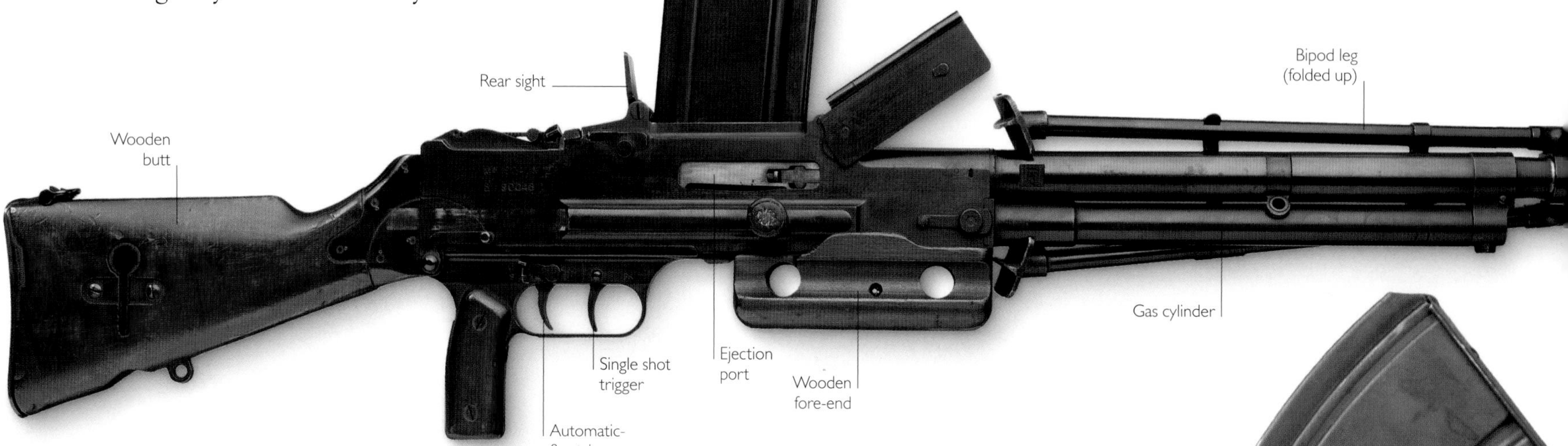

Hopper

Top-mounted magazine

Bipod leg (folded up)

Rear sight

Wooden butt

Gas cylinder

Single shot trigger

Ejection port

Wooden fore-end

Automatic-fire trigger

▲ **CHÂTELLERAULT MODÈLE 1924/29**

Date 1929

Origin France

Barrel 19¾in (50cm)

Caliber 7.5 × 54mm

The MLE 1924 was designed as a light machine-gun replacement for the terrible Chauchat MLE 1915 (see p.201) from World War I, but was let down by poor ammunition. The cartridge was redesigned, along with parts of the gun, to produce the MLE 1924/29, which served through World War II and into the 1950s. The gun was unusual in having a dual-trigger arrangement—the forward trigger was for single-shot firing and the rear-set trigger for continuous fire.

30-round detachable box magazine

Rear sight

Body locking pin

Left-hand grip

BREN Mk II

INGLIS 1945

Cocking handle

Tripod attachment point

Wooden butt

30-round detachable box magazine

Barrel cooling fin

Foresight

Wooden butt

Bipod leg

**▲ VICKERS BERTHIER
.303-IN LMG**

Date 1930s

Origin UK

Barrel 24in (60.9cm)

Caliber .303in

The British armaments firm Vickers purchased the rights to manufacture a modified version of the French Berthier (see p.155) in the early 1930s. The resulting arm, which superficially resembles the Bren gun (below), was adopted by the Indian Army in 1933 and still remains in reserve service.

Rear sight

Breech

Flash hider

Wooden butt

Folding magazine

▲ BREDA MODELLO 30

Date 1930

Origin Italy

Barrel 20½in (52cm)

Caliber 6.5 × 54mm

The standard light machine-gun of the Italian Army, the Breda Modello 30 utilized a novel 20-round metallic strip feed system, but proved chronically unreliable and too delicate for battlefield conditions.

Bipod leg

Carrying handle

Foresight

Barrel band

Adjustable gas regulator

▲ BREN

Date 1938

Origin UK

Barrel 25in (63.5cm)

Caliber .303in

Developed at Brno in the Czech Republic and modified at Enfield, London (hence its name), the Bren gun was the British Army's principal light support weapon from its introduction until the 1970s, latterly in 7.62mm NATO chambering. If it had a deficiency, it lay in its ammunition having a protruding rim around the .303in cartridge base, a feature corrected in the 7.62mm NATO round.

FULL VIEW

EUROPEAN SUBMACHINE-GUNS (1915–38)

Although trench warfare during World War I involved static lines facing each other, night-time raids across "No Man's Land" were frequent. Intended to probe weak points or to secure prisoners for interrogation, the taking of an enemy trench was fraught with danger. Limited manoeuvrability restricted the use of rifles and most actions were fought hand-to-hand. To counter this, arms designers developed submachine-guns—reduced-length, fully-automatic weapons using pistol cartridges. The choice of ammunition made the submachine-gun an intrinsically short-range weapon, but it was ideal for close-quarters trench conditions. Submachine-guns continued to be significant up to the eve of the next world war.

▼ **BERGMANN MP18/1**

Date 1918

Origin Germany

Barrel 7¾in (19.6cm)

Caliber 9mm Parabellum

The strong, sturdy MP18/1 was the first effective *maschinen-pistole* (machine-pistol—the German name for a submachine-gun). It was chambered for the Parabellum round Luger had developed for the P.08 pistol (pp.170–71), although that resulted in feed problems until a simpler box magazine was designed. Shown to the right is the original drum magazine.

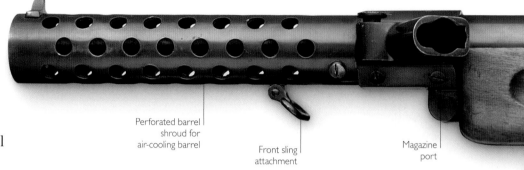

Perforated barrel shroud for air-cooling barrel

Front sling attachment

Magazine port

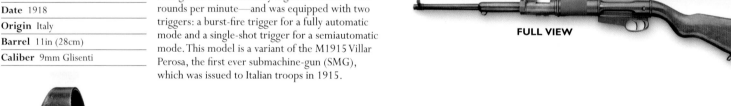

Foresight

Magazine catch

Magazine port

Cocking sleeve was pulled rearward to cock the weapon

Front sling attachment

Barrel shroud

▲ **VILLAR PEROSA M1918**

Date 1918

Origin Italy

Barrel 11in (28cm)

Caliber 9mm Glisenti

This gun had an extremely high rate of fire—900 rounds per minute—and was equipped with two triggers: a burst-fire trigger for a fully automatic mode and a single-shot trigger for a semiautomatic mode. This model is a variant of the M1915 Villar Perosa, the first ever submachine-gun (SMG), which was issued to Italian troops in 1915.

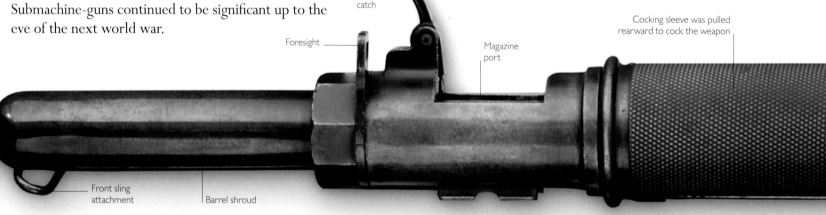

FULL VIEW

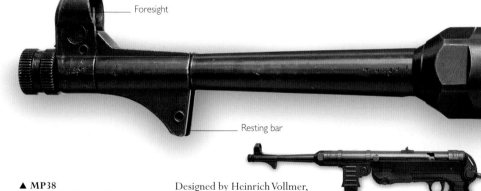

Foresight

Cocking handle

Resting bar

▲ **MP38**

Date 1938

Origin Germany

Barrel 10in (25.1cm)

Caliber 9mm Parabellum

Designed by Heinrich Vollmer, the MP38 submachine-gun closely resembles its famous successor, the MP40, which would use simple steel pressings, die-cast parts, and plastics. However, the MP38 can be easily distinguished by its machined steel receiver and longitudinally grooved receiver tube. Since the gun's barrel became extremely hot during firing, it was fitted with an aluminum or Bakelite resting bar beneath it, forward of the magazine.

FULL VIEW

Magazine

32-ROUND "SNAIL" DRUM MAGAZINE USED BY BERGMANN MP18/1

Graduated rear sight

THEODOR BERGMANN ABT.WAFFENBAU.SUHL

Wooden butt

Trigger

Rear sling swivel

Single-shot trigger

Burst-fire trigger

Small of stock is gripped in hand

Rear sight

Skeleton butt

Longitudinally grooved receiver tube

Trigger guard

Pistol grip

EUROPEAN SUBMACHINE-GUNS (1939–45)

The submachine-gun (SMG) was one of World War II's primary offensive weapons. Light in weight and capable of delivering a massive amount of fire if needed, the submachine-gun was favored by shock troops and those operating in cramped quarters. Soviet forces used the PPSH-41 in extensive numbers when attacking, simply because of the volume of fire it could deliver against enemy formations.

Compensator reduces muzzle lift

▲ PPSH-41

Date	1939
Origin	Soviet Union
Barrel	10½in (27cm)
Caliber	7.62mm

Georgi Shpagin's "Peh-Peh-Sheh," reliable and simple both to manufacture and to maintain, was to become the mainstay of the Red Army after it stopped the German advance into the Soviet Union. At least five million examples of this sturdy weapon had been produced by 1945. During World War II, entire units were armed with the PPSH so that its firepower could be used against Axis forces.

Carrying sling

Mainspring

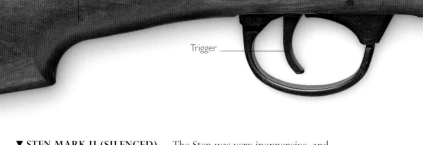

▼ LANCHESTER SMG

Date	1941–45
Origin	UK
Barrel	8in (20.3cm)
Caliber	9mm Parabellum

The Lanchester SMG was one of the more robustly built SMGs of World War II. Developed for use by the Royal Air Force in 1940, it was later adopted for boat crews by the Royal Navy and saw extensive action in that service. It was equipped with either a 32- or 50-round magazine. In all, some 95,000 guns were made.

Small of stock is gripped in hand

Trigger

Rear sling attachment

Fore grip insulated against heat

▼ STEN MARK II (SILENCED)

Date	1941
Origin	UK
Barrel	35¼in (91cm)
Caliber	9mm Parabellum

The Sten was very inexpensive, and naturally had its faults, but it was an effective way of putting devastating short-range firepower into the hands of inexperienced combatants. This version had an integrated noise- and flash-suppressor.

Noise/flash suppressor

Magazine port

Breech bolt

Pressed and stamped steel body

Rear sight

Fixed steel butt

▲ STEN MARK II

Date	1941
Origin	UK
Barrel	7¾in (19.7cm)
Caliber	9mm

Cheap and easy to manufacture, the Sten Mark II was a stop-gap weapon that was to prove itself an effective submachine-gun. The gun was fitted with a 32-round magazine.

Rate-of-fire selector

71-ROUND DRUM MAGAZINE

Barrel shroud

Bolt

Bayonet lug

Finger groove

Foresight

High-quality wooden butt

Double trigger for automatic and single-shot fire

Extended 40-round magazine

Rear sight

Fixed skeleton butt

Trigger

▲ **BERETTA MODELLO 1938/42**

Date 1942

Origin Italy

Barrel 8½in (21.3cm)

Caliber 9mm

One of the finest weapons of its type to see service during World War II, the M38/42 was well-made, reliable, and, for a submachine-gun, surprisingly accurate.

AMERICAN SUBMACHINE-GUNS (1920–45)

Originally intended for trench warfare, the submachine-gun achieved notoriety in the US during the "Roaring Twenties" as the weapon of choice for gangsters. Used by criminals such as Clyde Barrow, the Thompson submachine-gun became associated with rum running and violence. During World War II, its usefulness in the field was appreciated by commandoes and infantry facing dogged resistance in all theaters of operation.

Cutts Compensator prevents muzzle rising

Rear sight adjustable for windage and elevation

Receiver machined from solid steel billet

Cocking handle

Cooling fin

Forward pistol grip

Magazine release catch

Rear pistol grip

▲ THOMPSON M1921

Date	1921
Origin	US
Barrel	10½in (26.7cm)
Caliber	.45in ACP

US General John Tagliaferro Thompson began by designing an unsatisfactory self-loading rifle in 1916, but by 1919, he had produced an early version of what would be known universally as the Tommy Gun. The M1921 was the first to come to the market, but it was not until 1928 that the US government adopted it, in small numbers, for the Marine Corps.

50-ROUND DRUM MAGAZINE

Flat key for winding the internal spiral magazine spring

Cocking-handle cover acts as safety catch

Barrel locking nut

Retractable skeleton butt

Pistol grip

Flash hider

30-round detachable box magazine

▲ M3A1

Date	1940s
Origin	US
Barrel	8in (20.3cm)
Caliber	.45in ACP

The M3 "Grease Gun," and the improved M3A1 version, were cheap to produce and simple to strip, clean, and maintain. The M3A1 fired the same heavy pistol round used in the Colt M1911A1 (see p.169).

Rear sight

Walnut butt

Receiver take-down release to disassemble the lower receiver

Trigger

Semi-pistol grip

Cocking handle

Detachable butt

Pistol grip

Box
magazine

◄ THOMPSON MODEL 1928A1

Date 1935

Origin US

Barrel 30.5cm (12in)

Caliber .45in

This model was fitted with a Cutts
Compensator that allowed combustion
gases generated during firing to be vented
at the barrel's muzzle, thereby reducing
the weapon's tendency, common in
submachine-guns, to rise in fully
automatic mode. This gun is a simplified
version of earlier Thompson models and
lacks cooling ribs and a forward
pistol grip.

Rear sling
attachment

Wooden butt

Rear sight

Cocking
handle

Wooden
forestock

Wooden butt
removable in
some models

Rear sling
attachment

Box magazine

▲ THOMPSON M1

Date 1941–42

Origin US

Barrel 10in (25.4cm)

Caliber .45in

To speed up production during
wartime and reduce costs, the
Thompson was further simplified by
losing the compensator, foresight, and
cooling ribs to produce the M1. This
gun featured a simple rear sight.

▼ THOMPSON M1A1

Date 1942–45

Origin US

Barrel 10in (25.4cm)

Caliber .45in

The M1A1 was a slight variation of the
Thompson M1 (right). Additions included
a foresight and a shrouded rear sight. The
M1A1 saw wide service in virtually every
Allied army and theater of war.

Shrouded rear sight

Cocking handle

Foresight

Wooden
butt

Box
magazine

Rear sling
attachment

Pistol grip

**▼ UD42
SUBMACHINE-GUN**

Date 1942

Origin US

Barrel 11in (28cm)

Caliber 9mm Parabellum

Designed by Gus Swebelius of
the High Standard Arms Company,
the UD42 was an extremely simple
submachine-gun that could be
manufactured at a relatively low
cost. It was distributed primarily
to resistance forces operating in
Occupied Europe.

Barrel

Two 20-round
magazines
clamped
together for
faster reload

Forward
pistol grip

FULL VIEW

SHOWCASE

THOMPSON SUBMACHINE-GUN MODEL 1928

This iconic submachine-gun shot to fame because of its use by gangsters such as "Machine-gun Kelly" before attaining respectability in the hands of US military and federal agencies. Recoil-operated (see p. 305), this weapon could fire either single shots or continuously in automatic mode, at a rate of 600–700 rounds per minute. A devastating weapon at close quarters, it employed the powerful .45in ACP cartridge.

Compensator slots

Cutts Compensator

▲ **BARREL ASSEMBLY AND RECEIVER**
The barrel fits into the receiver. It features fins that radiate heat and cool it during operation. The receiver is a hollow steel channel that holds the sliding bolt assembly.

▲ **CUTTS COMPENSATOR**
The Cutts Compensator, a device designed by Richard Cutts in 1926, is screwed onto the muzzle. Unlike a regular muzzle compensator, it consists of a cylinder with slots in its upper half to divert the muzzle blast upward and force the muzzle downward. This prevents the muzzle from rising, especially when the gun is fired in automatic mode.

Flat key for winding the internal spiral magazine spring

Forward pistol grip is mounted in front of the receiver

◀ **DRUM MAGAZINE**
For this gun, 50- and 100-round drum magazines were available to provide extended fire capability. To load a new cartridge into a magazine, the magazine had to be dismantled and then wound like a clock, compressing the internal spiral magazine spring.

THOMPSON SUBMACHINE-GUN MODEL 1928

Date 1928

Origin US

Barrel 12in (30.5cm)

Caliber .45in ACP

This weapon was invented by John T. Thompson. Its success is attributed to its compactness and high rate of fire. This model was adopted by the US Navy in 1928 and was a slight upgrade of the Thompson M1921 (see p.210). The Model 1928 was fitted with a Cutts Compensator and a straight forestock, which replaced the forward pistol grip for US Navy use, although some units were also produced with the grip.

Cocking handle

Removable butt

Lower receiver

20-round box magazine, an alternative to the drum magazine

DRUM MAGAZINE

FULL VIEW

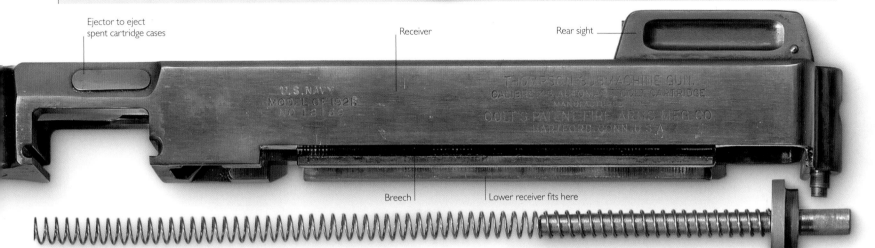

Ejector to eject spent cartridge cases

Receiver

Rear sight

Breech

Lower receiver fits here

▶ **BLISH "H" PIECE**
The Blish "H" piece connects the cocking handle with the bolt. It prevents the bolt from moving backward before the bullet has left the gun. The pressure generated on firing a cartridge pushes the "H" piece downward, locking the bolt in position and closing the breech. When the pressure drops, the "H" piece slides back upward, allowing recoil force to push the bolt backward.

Cocking handle

▼ **COCKING HANDLE**
To cock the gun for firing, the cocking handle is pulled backward, moving the bolt to the rear. When the trigger is pulled, the bolt moves forward, chambering and firing a cartridge.

▲ **MAINSPRING**
The recoil force generated by firing a cartridge pushes back the bolt, compressing this spring. It then springs forward, advancing the bolt and preparing the gun to fire the next round.

Slot for "H" piece

Slot for "H" piece

Firing pin placed inside

◀ **BOLT**
When firing in automatic mode, the bolt is locked and unlocked repeatedly, moving forward and backward. As a result, spent cartridge cases are continuously ejected from the ejection port and new ones are chambered from the magazine.

Fire selector lever

Magazine attaches here

Magazine release catch

Safety catch

Rear pistol grip

▶ **LOWER RECEIVER**
Also known as the frame, the lower receiver houses the basic firing mechanism—the trigger, the fire selector lever, the safety catch, the housing in front of the trigger guard which the magazine slides into, and the magazine-release catch. A rearward extension has the fitting onto which the removable butt is attached. It also carries the rear pistol grip.

▲ **REMOVABLE BUTT**
To allow the gun to be made even more compact for ease of carrying, or for concealment, the user could easily detach the butt by depressing a catch and sliding it rearward.

Folding sight

Muzzle brake

Tubular bayonet
in carrying position

Wooden
forestock

Bipod legs

SELF-LOADING AND FULLY AUTOMATIC RIFLES

Machine-guns were well established by the early 20th century, but semiautomatic and automatic rifles were not as universally accepted. However, the outbreak of World War II in 1939 caused a profound change in firearms technology. Self-loading, or semiautomatic, military rifles (those firing one round at a time), which had been treated with some caution by military authorities, were now rapidly accepted for general use. The speed with which this took place is clearly demonstrated by the development of what was to become the M1 Carbine in only 13 days. Equal attention was paid to the design of fully automatic rifles, capable of discharging multiple rounds continuously while the trigger was kept pulled. By 1943, nearly every nation involved in the conflict had either adopted or tested automatic rifles and used them on the battlefield to devastating effect.

Folding stock

Rear sight

▼ STURMGEWEHR 44 WITH KRUMMLAUF DEVICE

Date	1944
Origin	Germany
Barrel	16½in (41cm)
Caliber	7.62 × 33mm

The Sturmgewehr 44, or StG44 (see pp.176–77), was christened by Adolf Hitler and first issued to German troops in 1944. It was the first true assault rifle (see pp.244–45), capable of switching between semiautomatic and fully automatic modes. It was first deployed on the Eastern Front to counter the Soviet infantry armed with the PPSH-41 (see pp.208–09). Some examples of this weapon were equipped with curved barrels (the *Krummlauf* device) so that they could be fired indirectly at targets out of the user's direct line of sight by means of a prismatic sight. This device would prove especially useful in house-to-house fighting.

Magazine
housing

30-round
magazine

Folding
rear sight

20-round
box magazine

Slanting
pistol grip

Metal butt

◀ FG42 AUTOMATIC RIFLE

Date 1943

Origin Germany

Barrel 19¾in (50.2cm)

Caliber 7.92 × 57mm Mauser

The FG42 was a fully automatic
weapon designed to provide long-
range firepower to paratroopers on
the ground. It pioneered a "straight-
line" butt-to-muzzle layout. Its gas-
operated rotating bolt mechanism,
also seen in the semiautomatic M1
Carbine (see p.177), was unusual
among automatic arms. The bolt
was unlocked by the carrier, which
had a slot that caused the bolt to
turn as it was driven rearward.

Rear sight

Forestock

▲ M1A1 CARBINE WITH FOLDING STOCK

Date 1942

Origin US

Barrel 18in (45.7cm)

Caliber .30in

The M1 Carbine (see p.177) had already
proved popular with soldiers who needed
a lightweight weapon. For airborne
forces, this special M1A1 variant was
produced, complete with a folding stock
for use during parachute drops.

Detachable 15-round
box magazine

Gas
cylinder

Foresight

Perforated
barrel jacket

Bent barrel
attachment
(*Krummlauf*)

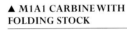

FULL VIEW

ARTILLERY (1885–96)

In 1855, British engineer William Armstrong developed the first effective breech-loading, rifled field gun. While breech-loading was quicker than loading via the muzzle, rates of fire increased dramatically after 1885 with the introduction of integrated ammunition. This ammunition consisted of primer, propellant charge, and projectile, all contained in a brass cartridge case, was similar to the small-arms rounds developed only a few years before. Rapidly firing artillery using these new cartridges were described as "Quick-Fire" or "QF" guns. Other breech-loaders used no cartridge case—the explosion of the propellant was contained by a special seal, or obturator, on the breechblock. Projectiles fired by artillery pieces in the smoothbore era were spherical and had predictable weights. For example, a 6.4in caliber weapon always fired a 32lb (14.5kg) projectile and was called a "32-pounder." With the coming of rifled artillery, projectiles could be made in a range of shapes and weights for a given caliber. Yet some weapons continued to be described in terms of the weight of the solid projectiles they would shoot if they were smoothbore.

▶ HOTCHKISS QF 3-POUNDER NAVAL GUN

Date	1885
Origin	France
Length	(Barrel) 6½ft (2m)
Caliber	47mm
Range	2¼ miles (3.6km)

The breech-loading Hotchkiss QF 3-pounder was used by the British Royal Navy from 1885, as well as the French, Russian, and US navies. These guns, made by a division of the Armstrong armaments business, were designed to fire at fast torpedo boats. Operated by two men, they could achieve a rate of fire of about 25 steel shells per minute, an incredibly high rate for the period.

Traversing ring

Naval pintle mounting

Steel barrel

Carriage wheel

▶ BREECH-LOADING 15-POUNDER 7CWT

Date	1892
Origin	UK
Length	(Barrel) 7ft (2.13m)
Caliber	76.2mm
Range	3¼ miles (5.26km)

This light field gun could fire eight rounds per minute. It had a barrel weight of 7 cwt (7 hundredweight/784lb). It was equipped with an early recoil device—its spade was connected to a spring recoil buffer. When fired, the gun was aligned in such a way that the spade dug into the ground, compressing the spring. The elasticity of the spring stopped the rearward movement of the gun and pushed it back to its original position. Stability during operation meant that the gun fired its projectile at the intended angle, and the crew was not injured by the entire piece leaping backward.

FULL VIEW

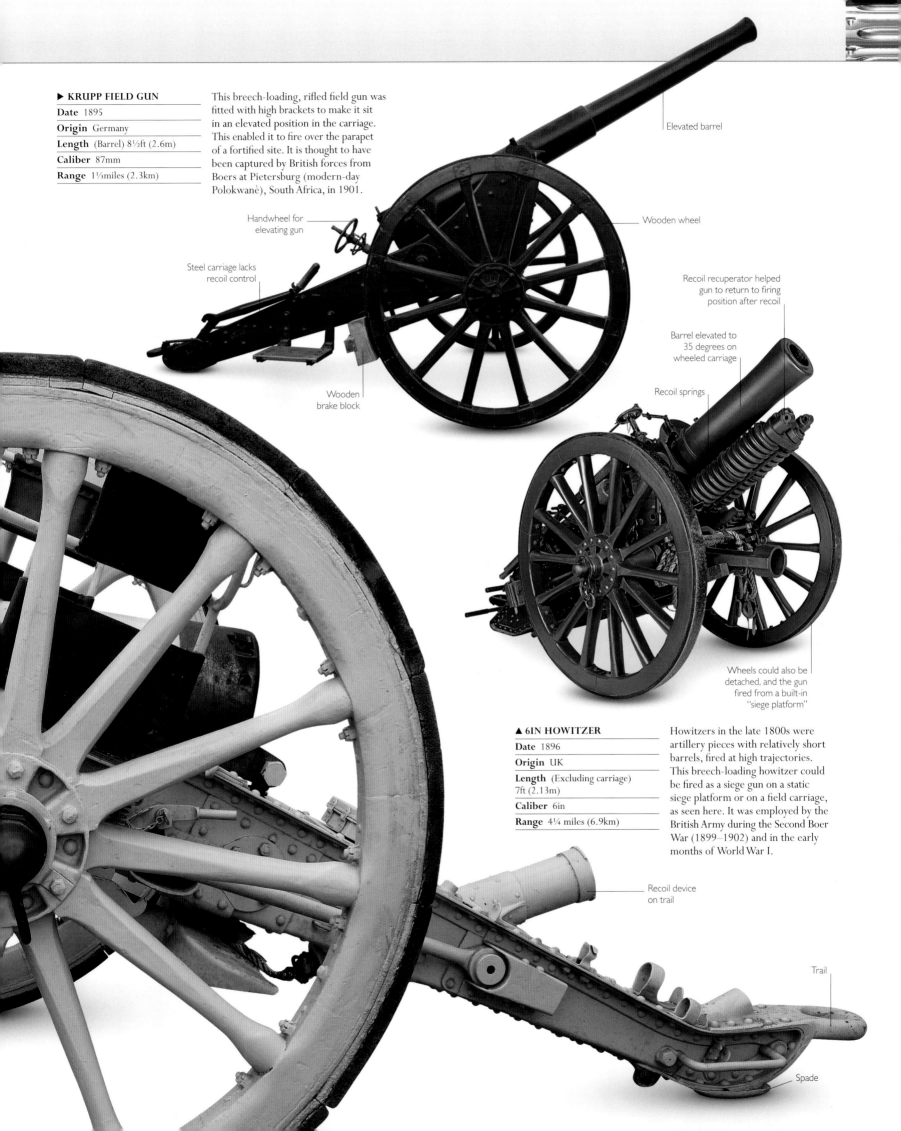

▶ KRUPP FIELD GUN

Date	1895
Origin	Germany
Length	(Barrel) 8½ft (2.6m)
Caliber	87mm
Range	1⅓miles (2.3km)

This breech-loading, rifled field gun was fitted with high brackets to make it sit in an elevated position in the carriage. This enabled it to fire over the parapet of a fortified site. It is thought to have been captured by British forces from Boers at Pietersburg (modern-day Polokwanè), South Africa, in 1901.

Elevated barrel

Handwheel for elevating gun

Steel carriage lacks recoil control

Wooden wheel

Wooden brake block

Recoil recuperator helped gun to return to firing position after recoil

Barrel elevated to 35 degrees on wheeled carriage

Recoil springs

Wheels could also be detached, and the gun fired from a built-in "siege platform"

▲ 6IN HOWITZER

Date	1896
Origin	UK
Length	(Excluding carriage) 7ft (2.13m)
Caliber	6in
Range	4¼ miles (6.9km)

Howitzers in the late 1800s were artillery pieces with relatively short barrels, fired at high trajectories. This breech-loading howitzer could be fired as a siege gun on a static siege platform or on a field carriage, as seen here. It was employed by the British Army during the Second Boer War (1899–1902) and in the early months of World War I.

Recoil device on trail

Trail

Spade

ARTILLERY (1897–1911)

In Europe there were some key requirements that guided the development of field guns at the end of the 19th century. Almost all artillery was horse-drawn, which limited the weight of the gun and its mobility. Armed forces also demanded greater range and accuracy. To achieve this, mechanisms to control the recoil of the gun were developed so that the trail and wheels were still while firing, and all the force of the exploding charge was directed forward. At the same time, Quick-Fire guns (see p.216) evolved, achieving rates of fire of 20 rounds per minute or more.

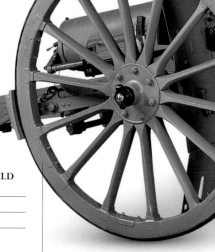

Trail spade managed recoil and ensured that the gun remained stable while firing

FULL VIEW

Rollers at muzzle, part of the recoil device

Carriage wheel

▲ FRENCH M1897 75MM FIELD GUN "SOIXANTE QUINZE"

Date	1897
Origin	France
Length	(Excluding carriage) 14¾ft (4.5m)
Caliber	75mm
Range	4¼ miles (6.9km)

Wooden carriage wheel

This Quick-Fire gun incorporated a hydropneumatic recoil mechanism, which kept the gun's trail and wheels still during the firing sequence. In addition, the gun had a rapid-opening screw breech. These factors allowed it to achieve a rate of fire of 15 rounds per minute.

Barrel could be depressed to -15 degrees and elevated to +22 degrees

▲ FRENCH CANON DE 75MM MODÈLE 1897

Date	1897
Origin	France
Length	(Barrel) 8¾ft (2.7m)
Caliber	75mm
Range	4¼ miles (6.9km)

The Canon de 75mm Modèle 1897 used a hydropneumatic recoil mechanism that worked like a shock absorber and kept the trail and wheels stationary when firing. Widely regarded as the first modern artillery gun, it could fire 15 rounds per minute.

FULL VIEW

Carriage wheel

Recuperator wrapped with rope

Dial sight for precise angular position during indirect fire

Muzzle

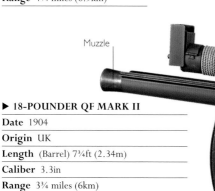

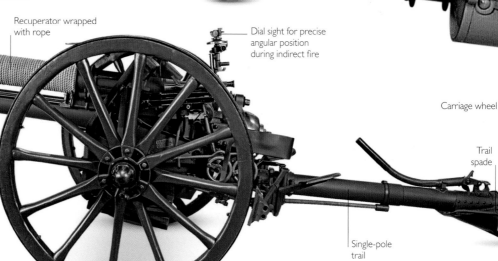

▶ 18-POUNDER QF MARK II

Date	1904
Origin	UK
Length	(Barrel) 7¾ft (2.34m)
Caliber	3.3in
Range	3¾ miles (6km)

The standard British field gun for almost four decades, the 18-pounder (which fired projectiles weighing 18lb/8.17kg) was first introduced in 1904. It fired a wide variety of projectiles, including high explosive, shrapnel, gas, and armor-piercing rounds. Its six-man crew could fire 20 rounds per minute for short periods.

Trail spade

Single-pole trail

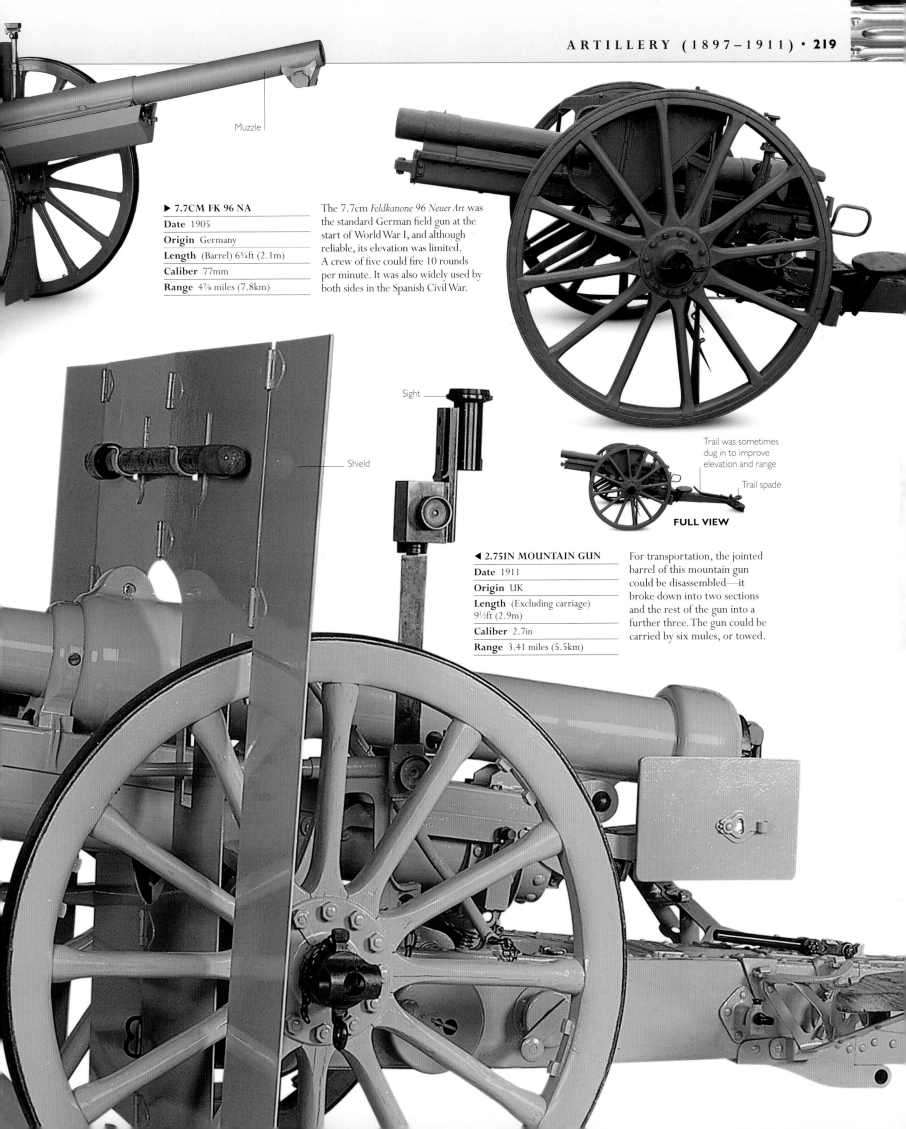

Muzzle

▶ 7.7CM FK 96 NA

Date 1905

Origin Germany

Length (Barrel) 6¾ft (2.1m)

Caliber 77mm

Range 4⅞ miles (7.8km)

The 7.7cm *Feldkanone 96 Neuer Art* was the standard German field gun at the start of World War I, and although reliable, its elevation was limited. A crew of five could fire 10 rounds per minute. It was also widely used by both sides in the Spanish Civil War.

Shield

Sight

Trail was sometimes dug in to improve elevation and range

Trail spade

FULL VIEW

◀ 2.75IN MOUNTAIN GUN

Date 1911

Origin UK

Length (Excluding carriage) 9½ft (2.9m)

Caliber 2.7in

Range 3.41 miles (5.5km)

For transportation, the jointed barrel of this mountain gun could be disassembled—it broke down into two sections and the rest of the gun into a further three. The gun could be carried by six mules, or towed.

SPECIAL-PURPOSE GUNS

Special-purpose firearms range from those designed for personal defence, such as the Dolne Apache Pistol which combines a revolver, dagger, and knuckle-duster, to silenced weapons intended for clandestine operations. Also in this category are single-shot, large-bore pistols that fire pyrotechnic smoke cartridges for signaling, or flares to illuminate a night sky.

Hammer

Barrel

Brass body

Six-round cylinder

Trigger guard

► DOLNE APACHE PISTOL

Date 1890

Origin Belgium

Barrel No barrel

Caliber 7mm

Developed in the 1870s by Louis Dolne, a Belgian gunmaker, the Apache pistol was a pure street weapon. It consisted of a barreless pin-fire revolver—only of value at point-blank range— to which was attached a hinged knife blade at the lower front edge of the cylinder frame. Its handle doubled as a set of knuckle-dusters.

Knuckle-duster

▲ WEBLEY AND SCOTT FLARE PISTOL

Date 1882–1919

Origin UK

Barrel 4in (10cm)

Caliber 1in

Visual signals are an important means of communicating during military actions. This was never more the case than during World War I, when the din of battle was ever-present. Breaking open for loading like a shotgun, this brass Webley and Scott Flare Pistol could fire smoke charges or flares to illuminate the battlefield at night.

Barrel

Trigger

27MM FLARE CARTRIDGE

10 Signal-Patronen mit gelben Doppelstern

FLARE CARTRIDGE PACKET

Cocking handle

Barrel

▲ FLARE PISTOL

Date 1907

Origin Germany

Barrel 4in (10¼cm)

Caliber 27mm

Trigger guard

This flare pistol is of simple steel and wood construction. The firing mechanism consists of a sprung cocking handle, which acts as a firing pin when released by the trigger.

Slide grips

Barrel

External suppressor

**▲ WEBLEY AND SCOTT PISTOL
WITH SUPPRESSOR**

Date 1907

Origin UK

Barrel 9¼in (23cm) with suppressor

Caliber 7.65 × 17mm

The Webley and Scott 1907 was one of
several automatic pistols manufactured
by Webley in the first decades of the
20th century. Fitted with a silencer,
this gun was carried by agents of
British covert forces in World War II.

Checkered
pistol grip

Rear sight

Ejection port

External
suppressor

Trigger

**▲ VZ 27 PISTOL
WITH SUPPRESSOR**

Date 1927

Origin Czechoslovakia

Barrel 8in (20.3cm)
with suppressor

Caliber 7.65 × 17mm

The VZ 27 (*vzor* or Model 27) was a
compact self-loading pistol designed
by Josef Nickl of the Ceska Zbrojovka.
The VZ 27 remained in production
until 1955. During World War II, the
German intelligence service (*Abwehr*)
used VZ 27s fitted with sound
suppressors (shown here). Later,
they were used by the Czech
intelligence services.

External
suppressor

◀ LUGER P.08 WITH SUPPRESSOR

Date 1940s

Origin Germany

Barrel 11¼in (28cm) with suppressor

Caliber 9mm Parabellum

This Luger was used by some British
covert forces during World War II.
It is fitted with a suppressor for use
as an assassination weapon. In many
ways, the Luger was best suited to
covert, police, and security work,
since its mechanical system was
vulnerable to the dirt of battlefield use.

Open receiver

Breech bolt with
grasping ribs

Top-folding
stock

Magazine
housing

Trigger
guard

▲ WELGUN SMG

Date 1943

Origin UK

Barrel 6½in (16.5cm)

Caliber 9mm Parabellum

The Welgun was a light and compact experimental
submachine-gun developed for British covert
operations use, but also as an intended airborne
forces weapon, a replacement for the troublesome
Sten (see p.208). It had a top-folding stock and was
fed from a 32-round vertical magazine.

SPY AND COVERT FORCES GUNS

The Special Operations Executive (SOE) was a British organization specializing in covert operations. Along with its American counterpart, the Office of Strategic Services (OSS), the SOE inserted commandoes and agents into Occupied Europe during World War II. These forces were frequently armed with weapons featuring sound suppressors (silencers) that allowed stealth tactics to be implemented. Often, the OSS dropped cheap, single-use pistols, such as the Liberator, from aircraft to arm partisan forces until they could secure standard-issue weapons from enemy forces.

Trigger guard

Firing mechanism

Wrist strap

Barrel

Fixed butt

633

Trigger guard

Combined foresight and trigger guard

Detachable magazine

Hand-operated breechblock

Trigger

Pressed-steel body

▲ HIGH STANDARD MODEL B WITH SILENCER

Date	1932
Origin	US
Barrel	9in (23cm)
Caliber	.22in

Of the guns made by the High Standard Manufacturing Company, one of the first was the Model B. It was a highly accurate .22in handgun designed for casual target shooting, but also found military applications. Unlike the Model A target pistol, which was similar but had adjustable sights, the Model B had fixed sights. This gun was used by OSS agents in World War II.

▶ WRIST PISTOL

Date	1939–45
Origin	UK
Barrel	1in 2.54cm)
Caliber	.25in

This small, .25in-caliber firing device was designed to be worn on the wrist of SOE personnel, so that it was readily available without having to be held. It was fired by a string attached to the inside of a shirt or jacket.

▲ DE LISLE CARBINE

Date	1942
Origin	UK
Barrel	8¼in (20.9cm)
Caliber	.45in

Designed by William Godfray de Lisle, this carbine is recognized as one of the quietest firearms ever made. It incorporates an integral sound suppressor around its barrel, and the report made when it is fired is inaudible except to the user. Though made in severely limited quantities, it saw service with British commandoes during World War II, as well as afterward.

◀ FP-45 LIBERATOR PISTOL

Date	1942
Origin	US
Barrel	4in (10cm)
Caliber	.45in

Designed by the OSS as a simple and very cheap gun, the Liberator was intended to be paradropped to resistance groups. It had 10 rounds of ammunition and was delivered with illustrated strip instructions for use.

Blade
foresight

Sound
suppressor

Bowl

▼ PIPE PISTOL

Date	1939–45
Origin	UK
Barrel	Not known
Caliber	.22in

Common items carried on the person were capable of being transformed into lethal firing devices. This device from World War II was designed for use by SOE personnel. It was fired by removing the mouthpiece and twisting the bowl while grasping the barrel.

Barrel

Muzzle housed
within cigarette

Firing string

**◄ SINGLE-SHOT
CIGARETTE PISTOL**

Date	1939–45
Origin	UK
Barrel	Not known
Caliber	.22in

This device disguised as a cigarette was developed at an SOE laboratory. The device was fired when the user pulled on a string with his teeth. Because of its short barrel it had a limited range.

Rear
sight

Forestock

Barrel is surrounded by
integral sound suppressor

Front sling
attachment

Rear
sight

Foresight

Barrel containing
baffles and wipes
to suppress sound

**▲ WELROD
SILENCED PISTOL**

Date	c.1943
Origin	UK
Barrel	12in (30.5cm)
Caliber	9mm

Developed at Station IX—a secret SOE factory—the Welrod was an exceptionally quiet assassination weapon, firing subsonic ammunition (ammunition having a muzzle velocity less than 1,100ft/335m per second). The sights were sometimes marked with fluorescent paint for low-light conditions.

Trigger

Pistol grip containing
six-round magazine

SPORTING AND HUNTING FIREARMS

In this period, as previously, hunters required firearms of differing natures for different environments and types of game. A small-caliber repeating rifle firing a revolver cartridge might have been ideal for some circumstances, such as hunting small game, but a heavy-caliber rifle firing powerful cartridges was essential when dealing with large, dangerous animals such as rhinos or elephants. While a higher rate of fire made lever-action guns popular for sporting and hunting, bolt-action weapons were more robust and reliable, and easier to maintain.

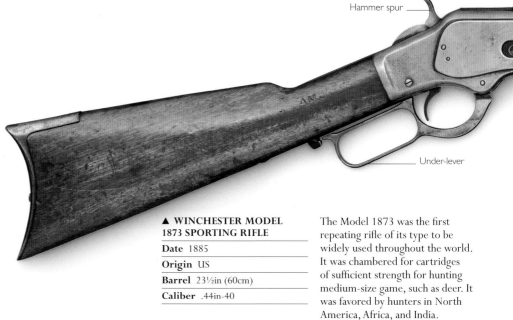

Hammer spur

Under-lever

▲ WINCHESTER MODEL 1873 SPORTING RIFLE

Date	1885
Origin	US
Barrel	23½in (60cm)
Caliber	.44in-40

The Model 1873 was the first repeating rifle of its type to be widely used throughout the world. It was chambered for cartridges of sufficient strength for hunting medium-size game, such as deer. It was favored by hunters in North America, Africa, and India.

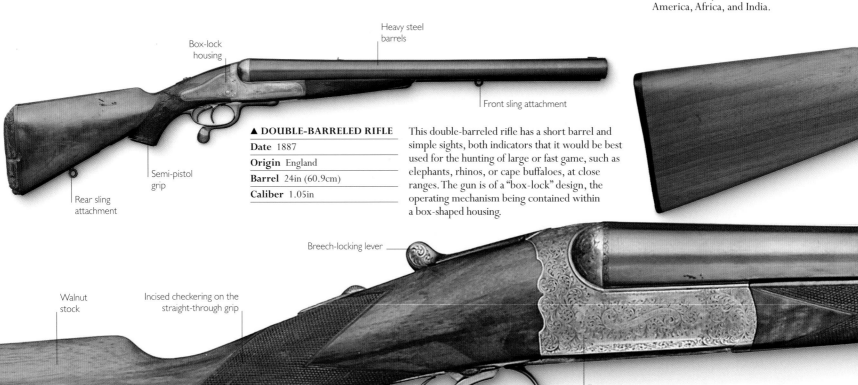

Box-lock housing

Heavy steel barrels

Front sling attachment

Semi-pistol grip

Rear sling attachment

▲ DOUBLE-BARRELED RIFLE

Date	1887
Origin	England
Barrel	24in (60.9cm)
Caliber	1.05in

This double-barreled rifle has a short barrel and simple sights, both indicators that it would be best used for the hunting of large or fast game, such as elephants, rhinos, or cape buffaloes, at close ranges. The gun is of a "box-lock" design, the operating mechanism being contained within a box-shaped housing.

Breech-locking lever

Walnut stock

Incised checkering on the straight-through grip

Single trigger

Engraved lock cover

Breech

Metal-reinforced stock

Under-lever

Fine-grained stock

▲ GIBBS-FARQUHARSON RIFLE

Date	c.1890
Origin	UK
Barrel	25in (63.5cm)
Caliber	.22in Hornet

This rifle was made for famous hunter F. C. Selous in .400in/.450incaliber. The grip is fitted with steel plates, a customization requested by Selous to strengthen the gun. The original barrel has been replaced by one made to take a .22in-caliber Hornet round. Despite this small caliber, the velocity of the bullet was ideal for shooting game such as deer.

Forestock

Receiver

Safety catch

Bolt

Rear sight

Tubular magazine

Incised checkering on semi-pistol grip

Turned-down bolt handle

Five-round integral box magazine

▲ MAUSER BOLT-ACTION RIFLE

Date	1890
Origin	Germany
Barrel	25in (63.5cm)
Caliber	7.9 × 57mm

Waffenfabrik Mauser (see pp.164–65) came to dominate the world market for bolt-action rifles for both civilian and military applications, and its hunting rifles set the standard for the type. This rifle employs the action of the Model 1888 infantry rifle as modified for the carbine, with a flattened, turned-down bolt handle. The five-round magazine is of the pattern developed by Steyr-Mannlicher (see pp.290–91).

Under-lever

Tubular magazine

▲ WINCHESTER MODEL 1894 SPORTING CARBINE

Date	1894
Origin	US
Barrel	20in (50.8cm)
Caliber	.30in-30

In 1883, a young gunmaker named John Browning (see pp.180–81) began working for Winchester. His first task was to revamp the action of the company's under-lever rifle to allow it to use new types of ammunition, and he supplemented the toggle-jointed bolt designed by American gunmaker Benjamin Tyler Henry with additional vertical locking bars. The system was perfected in the Model 1894.

Abbreviated forestock

Steel barrels

FULL VIEW

▲ WESTLEY RICHARDS DOUBLE-BARRELED HAMMERLESS SHOTGUN

Date	c.1930
Origin	UK
Length	26½in (67.5cm)
Caliber	.74in

Master gunmaker Westley Richards produced various notable and highly innovative sporting guns and rifles. This bird-hunting example of a double-barreled hammerless ejector gun has a patent one-striker mechanism and locks that can be detached by hand. A press-button mechanism enables each barrel to be fired independently. Available in a choice of finishes, the gun could be tailored to suit the individual tastes of purchasers.

Forestock

Bolt handle

Bolt

Rear sight

Tall foresight blade

Safety catch

Front sling attachment

Internal five-round box magazine

Incised checkering on semi-pistol grip

▲ RIGBY MAUSER RIFLE

Date	1925
Origin	UK
Barrel	27½in (70cm)
Caliber	.375in

Rigby's began making guns in Dublin, Ireland, in the 18th century. In 1900, now in London, the company was appointed Mauser's UK agent, and began producing bolt-action rifles to its design in a variety of calibers. John Rigby, the company's head, oversaw the design of the British Army's bolt-action rifles.

ELEPHANT-BACK SAFARI
Fine-quality firearms have traditionally been made for nobles and wealthy sportsmen. Pictured here in Nepal, c.1910, is the Prince of Wales, later King Edward VIII, standing in the front of the howdah on an elephant, ready to hunt tigers with his English double-barreled hammerless rifle.

ARTILLERY (1914–36)

Howitzers and field guns remained in use during this era. Howitzers had first been developed in the 17th century as weapons intermediate in range and firing angle between a mortar and a field gun. By World War I, some had grown to become huge, long-range weapons mounted on rails. Mortars, in contrast, had become light weapons usually operated by infantry, rather than artillerymen. During World War I, large howitzers were used to engage targets in the rear of enemy positions. British long-range guns tended to use a bag-charge propellant system, while the Germans used heavy-caliber brass cartridges.

Barrel

Screw jack handles for raising and lowering the gun carriage

Stepping ladder

Traverse turntable

Barrel clamp

Muzzle

▲ MODEL 12IN HOWITZER MARK I ON RAILROAD MOUNTING

Date	1916
Origin	UK
Length (Excluding carriage) 18¾ft (5.71m)	
Caliber	12in
Range	6¼ miles (10.17km)

Manufactured by the Elswick Ordnance Company for the British Army, 12in railroad howitzers were operated in pairs by the British Royal Garrison Artillery. The short-barreled Mark I was soon superseded by the longer-barreled Mark III, which had 40 percent greater range, and the Mark V, which had much-improved traverse, or horizontal, field of fire.

Carriage wheel

Crew step for front seat

◀ SKODA HEAVY FIELD HOWITZER M1914/16

Date	1916
Origin	Austria-Hungary
Length (Excluding carriage) 14¾ft (4.5m)	
Caliber	149mm
Range	5½ miles (8.75km)

This gun was produced for the Austro-Hungarian Army. A skilled crew could fire two 90¼lb (41kg) shells a minute for a limited period of action. Large numbers of the gun were handed over to the Italian Army in World War II.

Shield protects the
crew against enemy fire

◀ KRUPP L/12 HOWITZER

Date	1914
Origin	Germany
Length	(Excluding carriage) 19¼ft (5.88m)
Caliber	12in
Range	9¼ miles (15km)

The Germans used this heavy
howitzer made by Krupp at the
beginning of World War I to
bombard the Belgian forts at
Liege. Only two weapons were
in use at the outset of the war,
but a further 10 were built.
The gun came to be called
"Big Bertha."

▼ BL 6IN MARK 1 26CWT HOWITZER

Date	1917
Origin	UK
Length	(Barrel) 7¼ft (2.21m)
Caliber	6in
Range	6½ miles (10.42km)

This British howitzer was built
during World War I, (seen here
without a carriage) and over
4,000 were made. British forces
continued to use it during World
War II. It used one of the first
hydropneumatic recoil systems in
British service.

◀ BRITISH 3IN MORTAR

Date	1930
Origin	UK
Length	(Excluding stand) 4½ft (1.4m)
Caliber	3.2in
Range	1 mile (1.6km)

Sight

This mortar was officially
known as the 3in Mark II.
While it was a sturdy and
reliable weapon, its range
was not as good as its
equivalent—the German
8cm Granatwerfer 34. In
the early years of World War
II, it required a change in the
ammunition propellant to
increase the weapon's range.

Tails

MORTAR BOMB

◀ 50MM LIGHT MORTAR 36

Date	1936
Origin	Germany
Length	(Excluding stand) 7¼ft (1.14m)
Caliber	50mm
Range	¼ mile (0.52km)

Carrying
handle

Despite its designation as a light
mortar, with the tube and
baseplate combined, the M36,
at 30¾lb (14kg), was a somewhat
heavy mortar, and its complex
and costly design led to it being
phased out of service from 1941.

ARTILLERY (1939–45)

Field artillery continued to play an important role during World War II. While artillery manufacture was handled by commercial companies in Germany, in countries such as Britain, artillery was built by the state. A lot of British artillery tactical thinking was still based on ideas from World War I—centered around improving twists in rifling and fire controls—and this restricted the speedy development of new designs. While howitzers and mortars continued to be used, new threats spurred the development of antitank (see pp.232–33) and antiaircraft (see pp.234–35) guns.

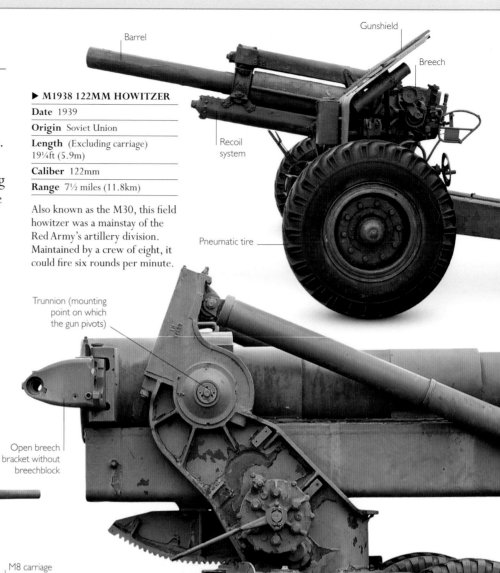

▶ M1938 122MM HOWITZER

Date	1939
Origin	Soviet Union
Length (Excluding carriage) 19¼ft (5.9m)	
Caliber	122mm
Range	7½ miles (11.8km)

Also known as the M30, this field howitzer was a mainstay of the Red Army's artillery division. Maintained by a crew of eight, it could fire six rounds per minute.

Barrel

Gunshield

Breech

Recoil system

Pneumatic tire

Trunnion (mounting point on which the gun pivots)

Open breech bracket without breechblock

M8 carriage

▶ BRITISH 7.2IN BL HOWITZER MARK III ON US M8 CARRIAGE

Date	1940
Origin	UK
Length (Excluding carriage) 45ft (13.71m)	
Caliber	7.2in
Range	more than 7 miles (11.26km)

This gun had originally been designed for a two-wheeled box trail carriage. It was found to be too powerful when using a full propellant charge and so was mounted on the more stable M8 gun carriage. The gun was introduced in 1943 and became the main heavy gun of the British Army.

FULL VIEW

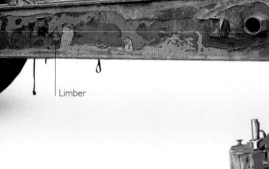

Limber

Trail

Steel wheel

M8 carriage

Pneumatic tires

Muzzle of short howitzer barrel

◀ M1A1 PACK HOWITZER

Date	1940
Origin	US
Length (Excluding carriage) 12ft (3.68m)	
Caliber	75mm
Range	1½ miles (2.56km)

This lightweight howitzer was developed for use on rough terrain, where it could be broken down into separate pieces and carried by pack animals. It was also successfully assigned to US airborne forces.

Trail spades (here in traveling position) managed recoil and ensured that the gun remained stable while firing

FULL VIEW

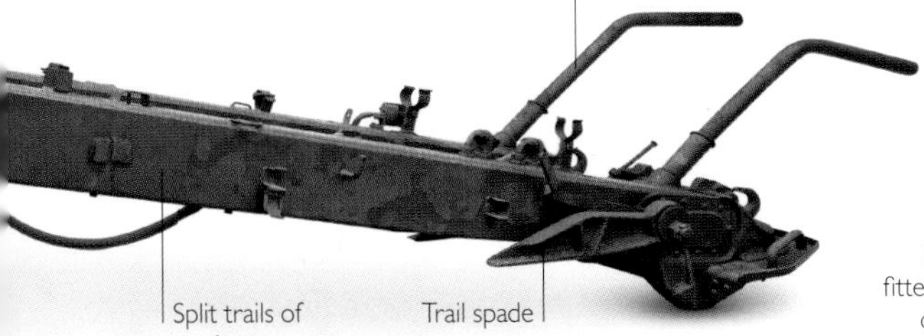

Long barrel raised in firing position

Trail handle

Split trails of carriage

Trail spade

Road wheels fitted in traveling configuration

Barrel

Wheel

▲ M1A1 155MM GUN

Date	1941
Origin	US
Length	24ft (7.36m)
Caliber	155mm
Range	14½ miles (23.22km)

The M1A1 was the principal gun of US long-range artillery during World War II. It was capable of firing a 95lb (43kg) high-explosive shell at a speed of 2,800ft (853m) per second. It could also fire other ammunition, including smoke and antitank rounds.

▼ BL 5.5IN MEDIUM GUN MARK III

Date	1942
Origin	UK
Length	(Excluding carriage) 24½ft (7.52m)
Caliber	5.5in
Range	10¼ miles (16.55km) with 80lb (36.2kg) shell

After several design problems, this gun was introduced in 1942. British forces used it in the Western Desert Campaign in Africa and until the end of World War II. At over six tons in weight, it was difficult to maneuver and deploy without a heavy tractor.

Breechblock operating lever assembly

Split trail carriage

Barrel

▼ BRITISH 4.2IN MORTAR

Date	1942
Origin	UK
Length	6¾ ft (2.1m)
Caliber	4.2in
Range	2½ miles (3.75km)

Unlike most mortars, which were infantry weapons and did not require artillery crews to operate them, the 4.2in Mortar—the British Army's heavy mortar—was manned by crews from the Royal Artillery.

Tripod for support

ANTITANK ARTILLERY

The rapid development of the tank during World War I spurred a parallel development in antitank weapons. Most of the designs from before World War II were of small caliber and used a solid projectile fired at high velocity to smash through a tank's defensive armor. In the years leading up to World War II, tank armor became thicker, prompting the need for larger caliber weapons, often using explosive rounds, to counter it. It was not uncommon for weapons designed for other purposes to be used as antitank weapons, the German Flak 36 being an example used in the first years of World War II.

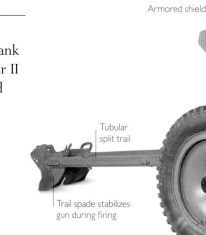

Armored shield

Tubular split trail

Trail spade stabilizes gun during firing

▲ PAK 36 ANTITANK GUN

Date 1934	
Origin Germany	
Length (Excluding carriage) 11ft (3.4m)	
Caliber 37mm	
Armor penetration 1½in (38mm) at 400 yards (365m)	

Designed for warfare in the 1930s, the light PAK 36 was obsolete by 1940. It was nicknamed the "door knocker" for the way its shells bounced off the armor of Allied tanks.

Double-baffle muzzle brake

▶ ZIS-3 M1942 FIELD/ ANTITANK GUN

Date 1942	
Origin Soviet Union	
Length (Excluding carriage) 20ft (6.1m)	
Caliber 76.2mm	
Armor penetration 3¾in (98mm) at 545 yards (500m)	

Although designed as a divisional field gun, the M1942 could also destroy armor with high-explosive and armor-piercing rounds. The gun's recuperator helped its barrel to return to the firing position after recoil.

Recuperator

Shield to protect crew from enemy fire

Split trail

▼ 6-POUNDER ANTITANK GUN

Date 1943	
Origin UK	
Length (Excluding carriage) 15¾ft (4.8m)	
Caliber 57mm	
Armor penetration 3in (80mm) at 1,000 yards (915m)	

The 6-pounder Antitank Gun replaced the ineffective 2-pounder in 1942. It was widely used in all theaters of the war. A version (shown here) was made with jointed trail legs so it could be carried in an aircraft.

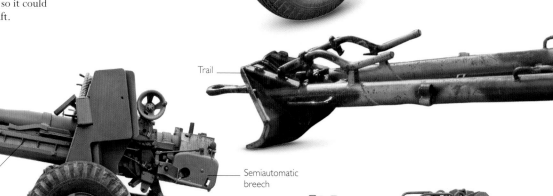

Trail

Muzzle brake

Recuperator

Gun slide

Semiautomatic breech

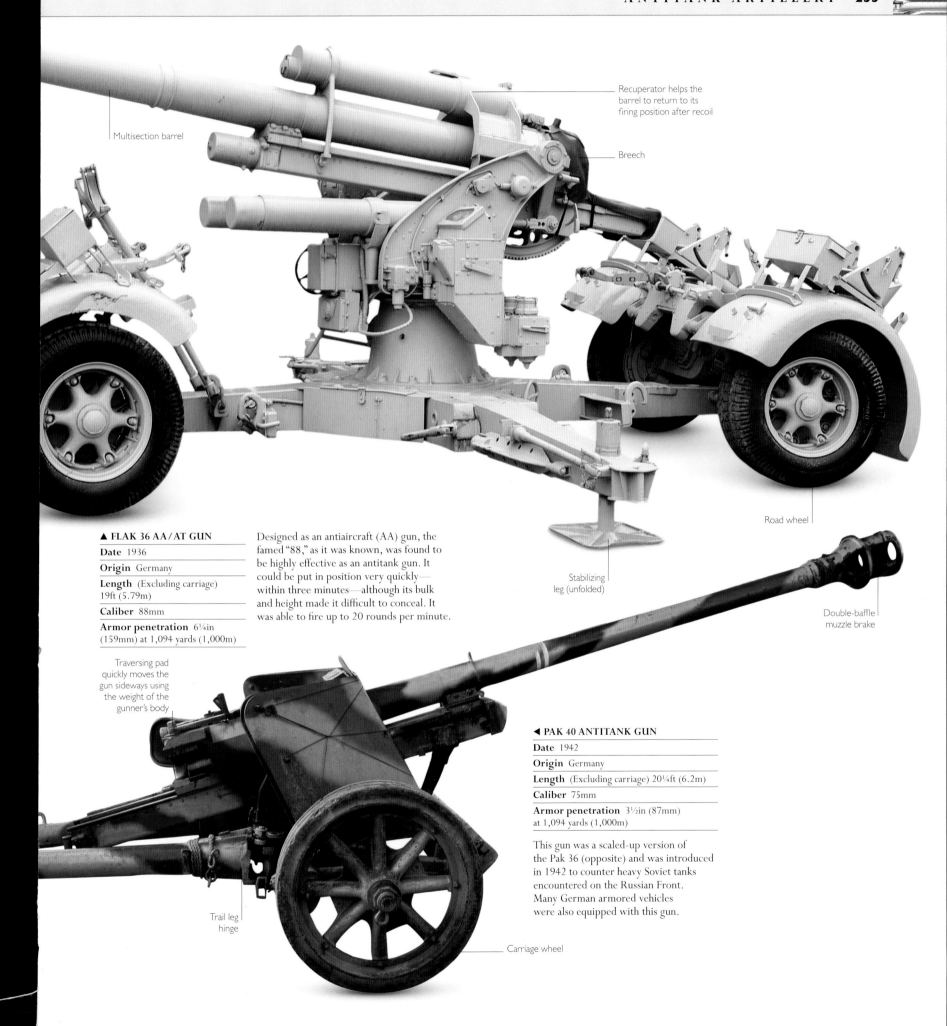

Multisection barrel

Recuperator helps the
barrel to return to its
firing position after recoil

Breech

Road wheel

Stabilizing
leg (unfolded)

▲ FLAK 36 AA/AT GUN

Date 1936

Origin Germany

Length (Excluding carriage)
19ft (5.79m)

Caliber 88mm

Armor penetration 6¼in
(159mm) at 1,094 yards (1,000m)

Designed as an antiaircraft (AA) gun, the
famed "88," as it was known, was found to
be highly effective as an antitank gun. It
could be put in position very quickly—
within three minutes—although its bulk
and height made it difficult to conceal. It
was able to fire up to 20 rounds per minute.

Traversing pad
quickly moves the
gun sideways using
the weight of the
gunner's body

Double-baffle
muzzle brake

◀ PAK 40 ANTITANK GUN

Date 1942

Origin Germany

Length (Excluding carriage) 20¼ft (6.2m)

Caliber 75mm

Armor penetration 3½in (87mm)
at 1,094 yards (1,000m)

This gun was a scaled-up version of
the Pak 36 (opposite) and was introduced
in 1942 to counter heavy Soviet tanks
encountered on the Russian Front.
Many German armored vehicles
were also equipped with this gun.

Trail leg
hinge

Carriage wheel

ANTIAIRCRAFT GUNS

Specialized antiaircraft guns were developed as soon as
aircraft became a perceived threat at the beginning of World
War I. By the outset of World War II, aircraft had become a
major threat to ground forces, and heavy guns were designed
to fire projectiles at a high altitude for high-flying aircraft,
while light-caliber guns fired rapidly at low-flying aircraft.
The target height was measured by optical instruments on
the ground. Antiaircraft guns fired shells with fuses timed
to explode when they reached target height. Aircraft were
not usually brought down by direct hits, but by shrapnel from
these bursting shells, which came to be known as "flak."

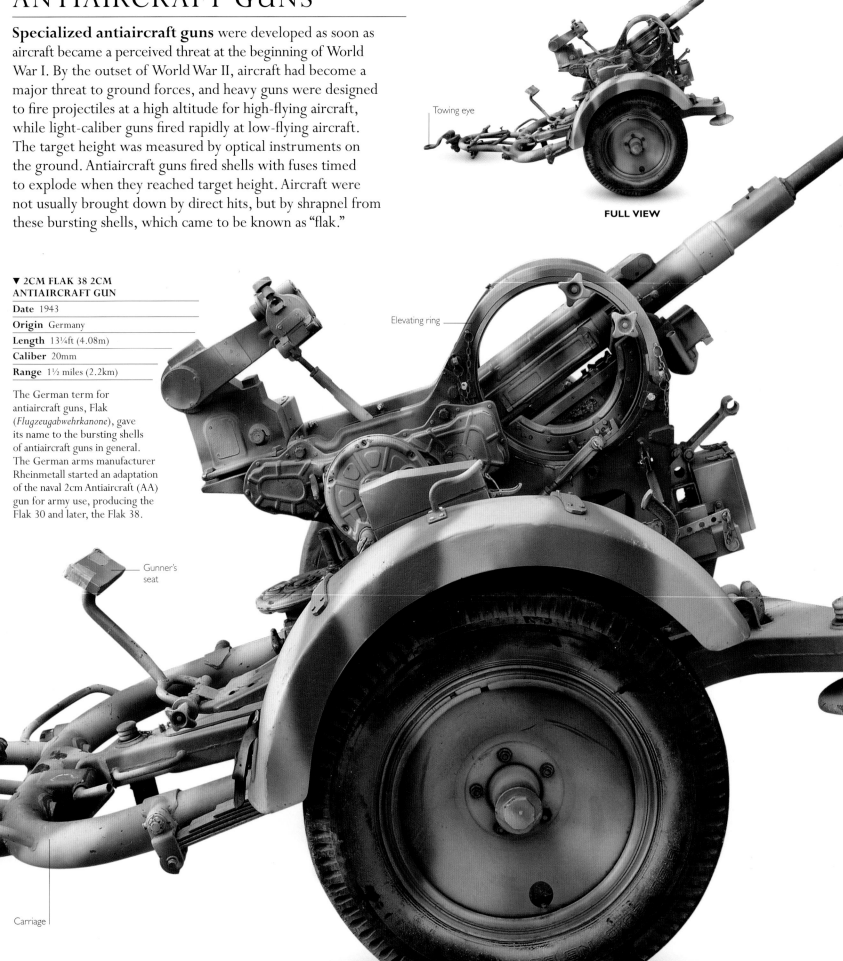

Towing eye

FULL VIEW

▼ 2CM FLAK 38 2CM
ANTIAIRCRAFT GUN

Date	1943
Origin	Germany
Length	13¼ft (4.08m)
Caliber	20mm
Range	1½ miles (2.2km)

The German term for
antiaircraft guns, Flak
(*Flugzeugabwehrkanone*), gave
its name to the bursting shells
of antiaircraft guns in general.
The German arms manufacturer
Rheinmetall started an adaptation
of the naval 2cm Antiaircraft (AA)
gun for army use, producing the
Flak 30 and later, the Flak 38.

Elevating ring

Gunner's
seat

Carriage

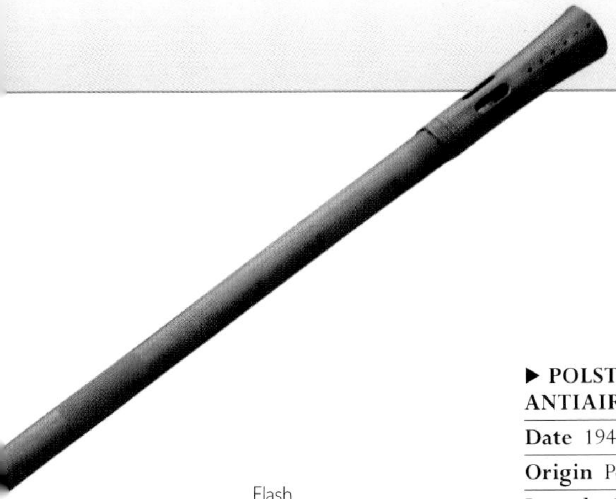

Flash
hider

Single
20-mm barrel

Sight
bracket

▶ POLSTEN QUAD 20MM ANTIAIRCRAFT GUN

Date	1944
Origin	Poland
Length	6¾ft (2.1m)
Caliber	20mm
Range	1¼ miles (2.02km)

The Polsten was a Polish AA gun similar to the 20mm German Oerlikon gun. The quad version of the Polsten (with four mounted barrels) could fire at a rate of 450 armor-piercing bullets or explosive shells per minute. The elevating and traversing action was hydraulically controlled, which enabled the gunner to have immediate control at his fingertips.

Drum
magazine

Sight

▶ BOFORS 40MM ANTIAIRCRAFT GUN

Date	1934
Origin	Sweden
Length	(Excluding carriage) 20ft (6.24m)
Caliber	40mm
Range	4½ miles (7.2km)

Considered to be one of the finest antiaircraft guns of World War II, the Bofors combined combining accuracy, range, and a decent-sized exploding projectile. It was exported throughout the world, and used by both Axis and Allied armies.

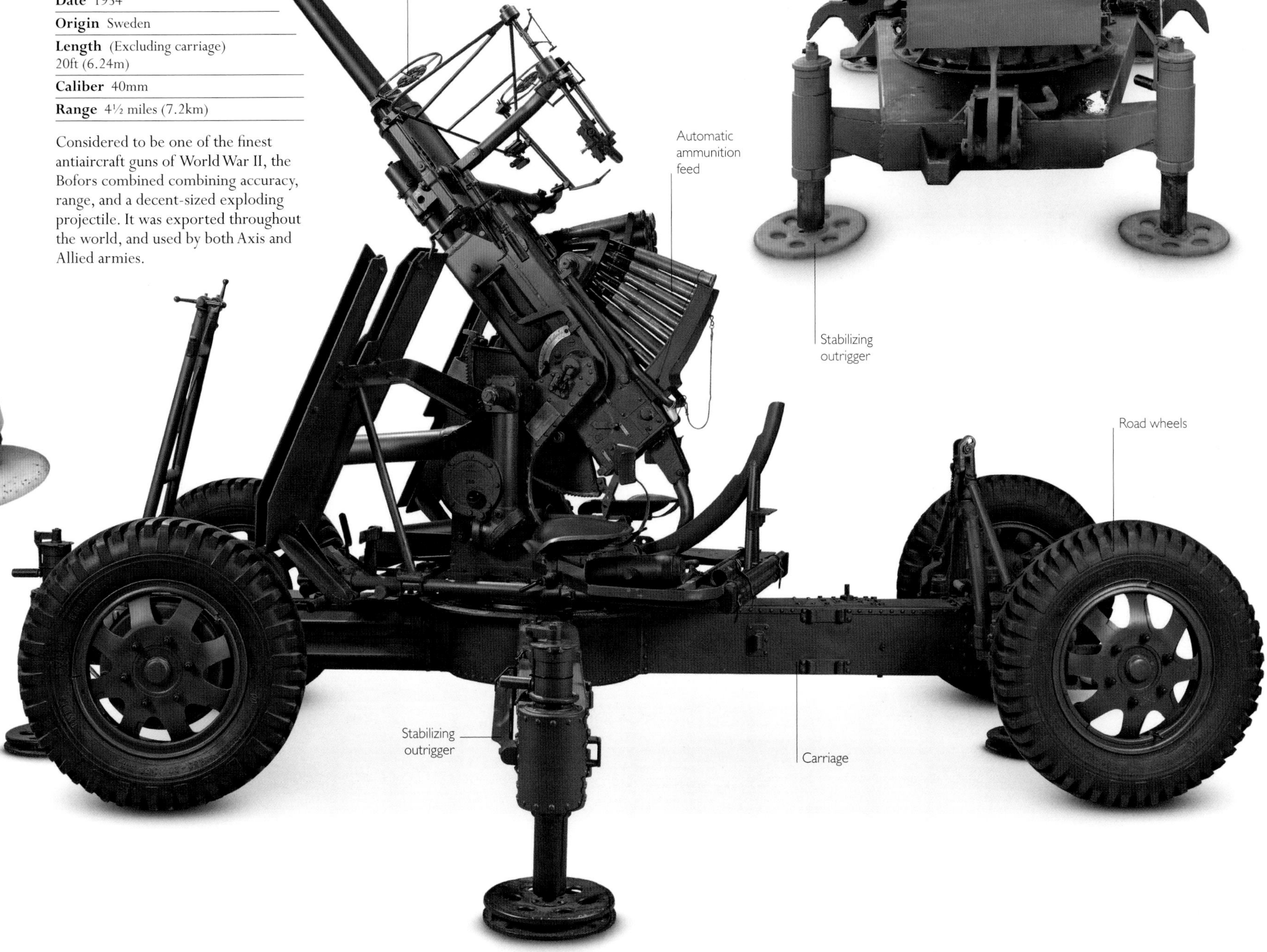

Automatic
ammunition
feed

Stabilizing
outrigger

Road wheels

Stabilizing
outrigger

Carriage

MAN-PORTABLE ANTITANK WEAPONS (1930–39)

The first portable antitank rifle was developed by
Germany in World War I. It was called the Mauser 1918
T-Gewehr and was chambered for 13.2mm cartridges. German
forces used this long, heavy weapon effectively against British
tanks. Antitank weapons required a heavily constructed breech
and barrel to fire a sufficiently heavy and high-velocity round
to penetrate armor. All of the designs developed prior to World
War II were heavy and needed a support, such as a bipod, so
that the operator could fire the weapon.

Oil bottle

Five-round
box magazine

Cheek rest

Left-hand
grip

Pad absorbs
some recoil

Pistol grip

Gas
regulator

Recoil
pad

Rear grip
support

Gas cylinder, into which propellant
gas was bled off to drive piston
and bolt rearward to cycle action

▲ **SOLOTHURN S18-100
ANTITANK RIFLE**

Date 1930

Origin Switzerland

Barrel 35½in (90cm)

Caliber 20mm

Armor penetration 1½in
(35mm) at 109 yards (100m)

The Solothurn Antitank rifle fired a
base-fused shell (an artillery round
in miniature) that gave acceptable
results against light armor. This gun
had a gas-operated, self-loading action
similar to that of many self-loading
small-arm rifles. An upgraded version
of this one, the S18-1000, saw service
with the German Army as the PzB41.

Perforated jacket
to air-cool barrel

Gas
cylinder

Spiked
bipod feet

FULL VIEW

Harmonica
muzzle brake

Recoil pad

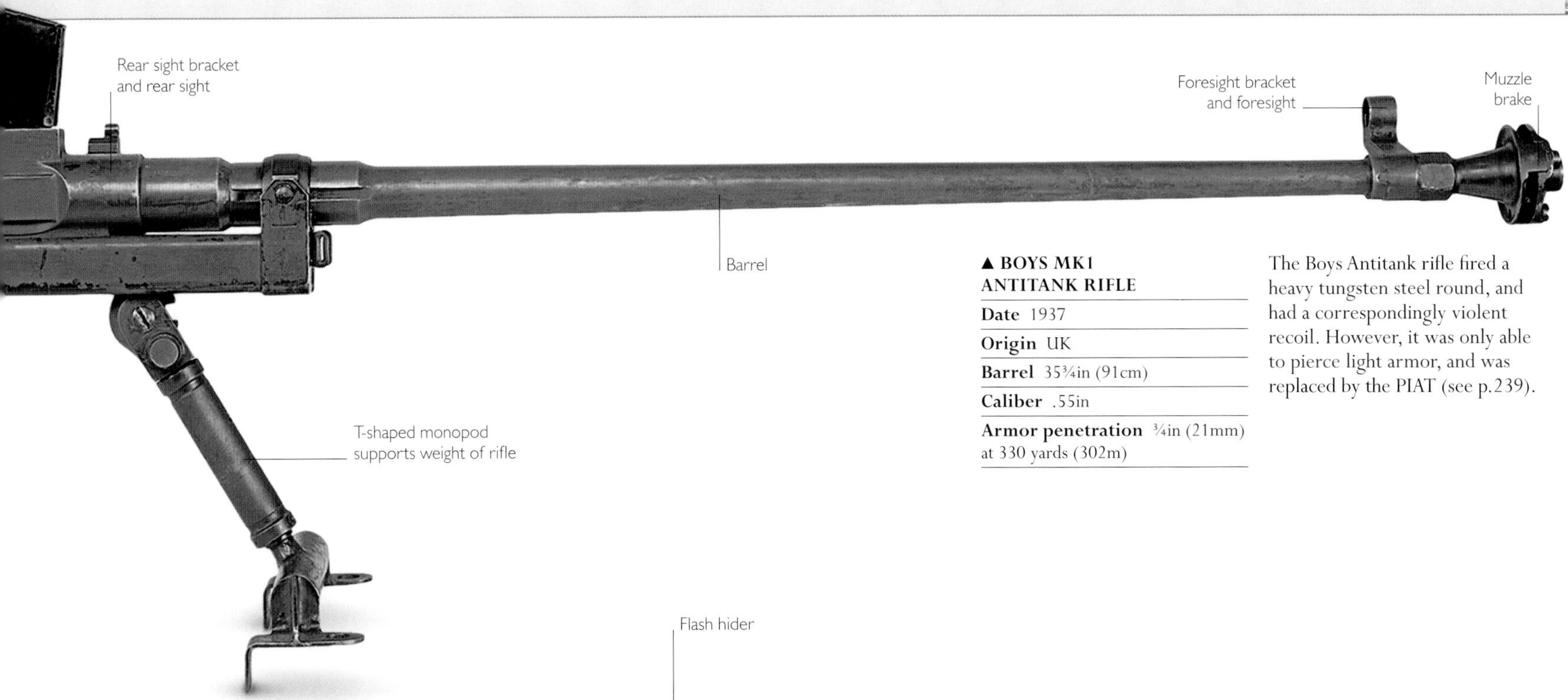

Rear sight bracket
and rear sight

Foresight bracket
and foresight

Muzzle
brake

Barrel

▲ BOYS MK1
ANTITANK RIFLE

The Boys Antitank rifle fired a heavy tungsten steel round, and had a correspondingly violent recoil. However, it was only able to pierce light armor, and was replaced by the PIAT (see p.239).

Date 1937

Origin UK

Barrel 35¾in (91cm)

Caliber .55in

Armor penetration ¾in (21mm) at 330 yards (302m)

T-shaped monopod
supports weight of rifle

Flash hider

Muzzle brake

▼ LAHTI L39
ANTITANK RIFLE

The L39's enormous size and weight gave it the nickname "Elephant Gun." The Finnish Army used it against Soviet tanks to good effect during the Winter War of 1939–40.

Date 1939

Origin Finland

Barrel 4¼ft (1.3m)

Caliber 20 × 138mm

Armor penetration 1¼in (30mm) at 110 yards (100m)

10-round
box magazine

Rear sight

Plywood skis
for balance

Pistol grip

MAN-PORTABLE ANTITANK WEAPONS (1940–42)

Portable antitank weapons continued to be developed as World War II progressed. Some systems, such as the PIAT, relied on a spring-driven firing pin to ignite a propellant charge attached to the base of a self-propelled projectile. Others, such as the bazooka, released projectiles with solid rocket motors. In both cases, when the projectile met its target, a shaped-charge warhead helped to focus the effect of the explosive's energy so that it could penetrate armor effectively. This made launchers lighter and easier to make. As tanks evolved and their armor became thicker, older designs of antitank rifle, such as the PTRD, became obsolete, as they could rarely knock out a tank even at a very short range.

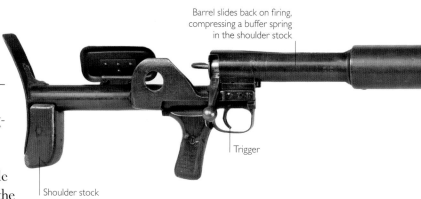

Barrel slides back on firing, compressing a buffer spring in the shoulder stock

Trigger

Shoulder stock

Foresight

Trough to hold bomb before launch

Tubular receiver contains mortar and driving spring

Propellant charge in body tube

PIAT 3LB (1.36KG) BOMB

Shaped-charge warhead

Shrouded stabilizing fins

Supporting monopod

Trigger guard

Rectangular frame front sight

▼ **PANZERBÜSCHE 39 ANTITANK RIFLE**

Date	1940
Origin	Germany
Barrel	3½ft (1.08m)
Caliber	7.92 × 94mm
Armor penetration	1in (25mm) at 330 yards (300m)

The Panzerbüsche 39 relied on its very high muzzle velocity and tungsten-cored bullet to penetrate enemy armor. It was, however, expensive to manufacture, and was only produced in small numbers.

Rear sight

Foresight

Folding stock (extended)

Trigger

Barrel with integral recoil mechanism

Carrying handle

Barrel

Foresight

Bipod leg

▲ PTRD ANTITANK RIFLE

Date 1941

Origin Soviet Union

Barrel 4ft (1.23m)

Caliber 14.5mm

Armor penetration 1.3–1.5in (35–40mm) at 110 yards (100m)

The PTRD was a more complicated weapon than it appeared. It had a barrel that recoiled into the receiver and unlocked the bolt in the process. The bolt was held back when the barrel returned to its original position, opening the breech and ejecting the spent round. A fresh round was then introduced by the loader and the bolt closed by hand.

▼ PIAT

Date 1942

Origin UK

Length 3ft (0.99m)

Caliber 89mm

Armor penetration 3in (75mm) at 120 yards (110m)

The PIAT (Projector, Infantry, Antitank), like the Sten (see p.208), was a wartime expedient design that put function before form. It was actually a special mortar that fired a bomb with a shaped-charge warhead.

Canvas covering

Shoulder pad

Rear sight

Shoulder rest containing battery for electrical launch

Tail latch holds the rocket in firing position

Rocket inserted at rear

Lightbulb to test the circuit

Trigger is the switch in a battery-powered circuit

Shaped-charge warhead

▲ M1A1 BAZOOKA

Date 1942

Origin US

Length 4½ft (1.37m)

Caliber 60mm

Armor penetration 4¾in (120mm) at 150 yards (138m)

The Bazooka was essentially a tube that launched a solid-fuel rocket with a shaped-charge warhead. It was operated by two men—one who fired and one who loaded.

M1A1 3½LB (1.54KG) ROCKET

COLT M4 CARBINE

THE MODERN ERA

1945–PRESENT DAY

After 1945, the construction and manufacture of firearms changed in key ways—parts made of wood became parts of polymer or synthetic composite materials, and detailed castings replaced components previously machined from blocks of steel. Guns became more robust and production costs dropped. Some truly distinct types of firearm, such as assault rifles and advanced submachine-guns, evolved and became widely used.

SELF-LOADING RIFLES

Drawing upon the designs developed during World War II, and the performance of the arms made during that conflict, postwar designers further refined self-loading rifles. Improvements were made to their locks, or actions, synthetic materials began to replace wood stocks, and pressed metal components were introduced to reduce weight. Importantly, most of these rifles, which were all gas-operated (including those featured here), were chambered for standardized cartridges adopted by defense unions, such as NATO.

▲ SIMONOV SKS-45 CARBINE

Date	1945
Origin	Soviet Union
Barrel	20½in (52cm)
Caliber	7.62 × 39mm

Designed by Sergei Gravilovich Simonov, the SKS entered service in 1945, and variants have been sold throughout the world. It was adopted as China's primary battle rifle. Some variants, such as this example, were equipped with permanently attached bayonets that folded rearward when not in use.

Flash hider

Fire selector switch

▲ FN FAL PROTOTYPE

Date	1950
Origin	Belgium
Barrel	23½in (60cm)
Caliber	.280in

Originally developed to fire a .280in caliber cartridge, the FAL proved to be an immediate success. It was later modified for use with the 7.62 × 51mm NATO round, which was developed as a standard for small arms among NATO countries. This rifle has seen service throughout the world.

Ribbed walnut forestock

Detachable 20-round box magazine

Trigger

Magazine release catch

Rear sight

Folding butt

▼ L1A1

Date	1954
Origin	UK
Barrel	21in (53.3cm)
Caliber	7.62 × 51mm NATO

The L1A1, manufactured by the Royal Small Arms Factory, Enfield, UK, was the standard British service rifle until its replacement by the L85A1 (see p.250) in 1985. It was adapted from the Belgian FN FAL (above), but with minor changes to the specifications, to facilitate manufacture in the UK.

Pistol grip

Trigger guard

Detachable box magazine

Gas regulator

Wooden forestock

Twenty-round detachable box magazine

Flash hider (a device that reduces flash from the exploding propellant gases after the gun is fired, preventing the user from being blinded in low-light conditions)

Rear sight

Bayonet

Rear sling swivel

Magazine catch

Detachable 20-round
box magazine

▲ M14 RIFLE

Date 1957

Origin US

Barrel 22in (55.8cm)

Caliber 7.62 × 51mm NATO

Designed to use the then-standard NATO
round, the US M14 replaced the old M1
rifle (see p.176). The M14 possessed fully
automatic fire capability and was equipped
with a larger magazine. By the late 1960s,
it was replaced by the M16 (see p.245).

Gas cylinder

Flash hider

Detachable 30-round
box magazine

Butt

Rear sling swivel

Wooden
butt

**▲ STONER 63
ASSAULT RIFLE**

Date 1963

Origin US

Barrel 20in (50.8cm)

Caliber 5.56 × 45mm NATO

Designed as a modular firearm,
the Stoner 63 can be assembled
to produce different variants that
include a carbine, an assault rifle
(shown here), and several
machine-gun configurations.

▼ STERLING LIGHT AUTO RIFLE

Date 1970s

Origin UK

Barrel 19¾in (50cm)

Caliber 5.56 × 45mm NATO

Sterling produced this light automatic
rifle in the 1970s, by which time
the 5.56 × 45mm NATO round was
becoming established as a standard
cartridge. The Sterling gun featured
a patent folding butt to improve the
gun's portability.

Vented housing
for gas cylinder

Flash hider

► HECKLER AND KOCH G3A3

Date 1964

Origin Switzerland

Barrel 17¾in (45cm)

Caliber 7.62 × 51mm NATO

The G3 series of rifles was developed jointly
by Heckler and Koch (see pp.256–57) and
Spanish design and development agency
(CETME). The rifle's firing mechanism
is an improvement on that found in
the German StG45 designed by Ludwig
Vorgrimler, who worked on the G3. The
designation G3A3 refers to the version
fitted with a polymer stock.

Foresight

Rate-of-fire
selector

Rear sight

Flash hider

Fixed polymer
stock

Detachable
20-round box
magazine

Rear sling
attachment

Carrying
handle

Safe, semi,
burst, and fully
automatic settings

Rear sling
attachment

◄ HECKLER AND KOCH G41

Date 1981

Origin Germany

Barrel 17¾in (45cm)

Caliber 5.56 × 45mm NATO

The G41 was a rechambered version
of Heckler and Koch's 7.62mm G3
rifle. The G41 was designed to take
the 5.56 × 45mm NATO round and
could be fitted with other NATO
standard features including a universal
sight mount and magazine. The gun
wasn't much used by armed forces.

Flash hider

Detachable
30-round box
magazine

High-impact
polymer butt

TURNING POINT

ASSAULT RIFLES

Just as the breech-loading repeating rifle had brought about a change in warfare following its introduction in the late 19th century, the development of reliable self-loading military arms during the 1930s altered tactics again—now a single infantryman could deliver fire equivalent to a squad of 10 or 12. In 1944, the assault rifle magnified this effect almost 50-fold as it mimicked a machine-gun. Easy to use, an assault rifle allowed anyone to become an effective adversary, transforming warfare from a clash between trained armies on a battlefield to a contest between masses, often street-to-street or even house-to-house.

▲ ASSAULT RIFLE
An assault rifle is a short-barreled rifle, intended for use by infantry, and capable of selective fire—switching between semiautomatic and automatic modes. It chambers medium- and small-caliber cartridges with short cases. It has a high-capacity magazine that can carry 20 or more rounds. Shown here is a 1954 AK47, which fires 7.62 × 39mm cartridges.

Conflicts at the turn of the 20th century saw the development of groundbreaking weaponry. Firearms were modernized with the invention of the Maxim gun—the first machine-gun (see pp.184–85)—which spurred the refinement of automatic weapons technology at a furious pace. Heavy machine-guns were followed by medium- and light machine-guns, as armies felt need to provide groups of soldiers with portable, automatic firepower. It was not until the invention and use of the assault rifle during World War II (1939–45) that this deadly objective was fully achieved.

EARLY EXPERIMENTS
The precursor to the modern assault rifle—Burton's automatic rifle of 1917—had twin, 20-round magazines for use by a single rifleman. It chambered short-cased, high-velocity cartridges and was a selective-fire weapon—it could be used as a single-shot,

▲ 5.56 × 45MM AND 7.62 × 51MM CARTRIDGES
To prevent heavy recoil, assault rifles fire short-cased, small-caliber or "intermediate" cartridges (left) instead of long-cased, large-caliber rifle cartridges (right).

self-loading arm or fired in bursts like a machine-gun. Except for its barrel length, it matched all the modern criteria for a weapon to be deemed an assault rifle. However, the design was ahead of its time and was never adopted for production. The first mass-produced assault rifle was the German Sturmgewehr 44, or StG44 (see p.176). It was used extensively in World War II on both the Eastern and Western fronts and provided the German troops with an effective countermeasure to the Soviet submachine-gun, the PPSH-41 (see p.208). Between 1945 and 1946, Soviet arms dealer Mikhail Kalashnikov designed a modern assault rifle, and in 1947, he unveiled the AK47 (see pp.248–49).

MODERN ASSAULT RIFLES
The AK47 embodied all the features typical of assault rifles; it had a short barrel, a high-capacity magazine, and full- and semiautomatic fire controls. In the West, development of the assault

> "I created a weapon to **defend the borders** of my **motherland**. It's **not my fault** that it's being used where **it shouldn't be …**"

MIKHAIL KALASHNIKOV,
SOVIET AK47 DESIGNER

KEY **FIGURE**

Frank F. Burton
(1871–1939)

Frank F. Burton was the son of the famed civil engineer Col. James Henry Burton. He joined the Winchester Repeating Arms Company as a designer in the 1890s. He designed his assault rifle in response to a need for a light automatic arm for observers in aircrafts prior to the introduction of synchronized machine-guns.

» **BEFORE**

Prior to the development of the assault rifle, concentrated fire in volume could only be delivered by machine-guns. Their long medium-caliber rounds were capable of accuracy at up to 3,000ft (900m).

• **SOME LIGHT MACHINE-GUNS**, such as the 1918 Browning Automatic Rifle (BAR), were intended to replace heavy machine-guns for small groups of soldiers. However, they were heavy and unwieldy.

• **SUBMACHINE-GUNS** were intended to be an ideal replacement for the machine-gun. In practice though, their reliance on pistol cartridges meant that they were effective only at close range and were not able to fulfill the functions of a multipurpose combat weapon.

BURTON'S AUTOMATIC RIFLE

• **BURTON'S AUTOMATIC RIFLE**, designed in 1917, was the ancestor of assault rifles. It used a .345-caliber cartridge and was capable of selective fire.

BROWNING AUTOMATIC RIFLE

rifle proceeded at a much slower pace. In 1956, firearms designers Eugene Stoner and L. James Sullivan developed a small-caliber rifle for the Armalite company of the Netherlands. This became the M16—the US Army's standard assault rifle. The US Army used it in the 1960s against North Vietnamese Communist forces armed with the AK47 in the Vietnam War.

The M16 was lighter, more accurate, and fired more quickly than the AK47, but was prone to jamming in adverse conditions. However, it provided the US troops with a fitting response to the unstoppable AK47 in a bloody jungle war.

THE AK47 AND ITS AFTERMATH

The AK47 was reliable in war conditions—it continued to fire despite exposure to sand, water, and weather. Easy to maintain and simple in design, its workings could be grasped in minutes and, even in untrained hands, it became a formidable weapon that changed the rules of modern warfare. It demystified the gun and its usage for ordinary people, and gave untrained warriors the ability to wield immense firepower. It brought about a new

trend in warfare in which irregular combatants (guerillas) and terrorists could hold out against well-trained armies.

The assault rifle has emerged as the main weapon in modern warfare—from civil wars in Africa, to conflicts in the Middle East, to local turf wars—in the hands of militaries, terrorists, militias, and even child soldiers.

▲ **THE VIETNAM WAR**

The M16 was deployed for warfare in South Vietnam in 1965. Its ability to focus a large volume of fire on a target made it quite effective, especially at close quarters against enemy guerilla tactics. Seen here are US soldiers armed with M16s in a Vietnamese jungle.

AFTER ≫

Modern assault rifles can provide accurate fire in volume at distances well in excess of 1,600ft (500m). Short-cased, small-caliber cartridges continue to be used. The assault rifle's deadly combination of a light machine-gun's firepower and a machine-pistol's portability makes it a popular weapon with untrained combatants.

● **NEW PRODUCTION METHODS** developed. With the incorporation of synthetic materials into its construction, the modern assault rifle is far less likely to suffer a catastrophic failure of its components due to stress and wear.

● **FIRE CONTROL MECHANISMS** improved. This allowed modern assault rifles to fire a specific number of cartridges in a single burst, increasing accuracy and making the weapons deadlier than ever.

● **THE "BULLPUP" CONFIGURATION** (see pp.250–51), as seen in the Famas F1 assault rifle, served two purposes. It lessened a weapon's overall length and placed the user totally in line with the barrel, thus reducing the effects of recoil.

FAMAS F1 ASSAULT RIFLE

● **HIGH CASUALTIES** have become the norm of modern warfare with the use of the assault rifle. Its move from the battleground to the streets has triggered a debate about its usage by nonmilitary personnel.

ASSAULT RIFLES (1947–75)

If there is a quintessential firearm of the post-World War II period, it is the assault rifle (see pp.244–45). Chambered for short-case, medium- or small-caliber cartridges, the assault rifle is distinguished by its high-capacity magazine and ability to function in semi- or full-automatic modes. Though the idea was first developed at the end of World War I, the assault rifle was technically born in 1949 when the AK47 (see pp.248–49), designed by Soviet arms engineer Mikhail Kalashnikov, entered service. Now the weapon of choice on five continents, the assault rifle has become so well-known that even its blacked-out profile is immediately recognized by most people.

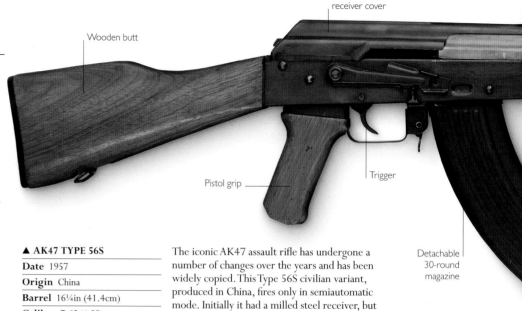

Wooden butt

Pressed steel receiver cover

Pistol grip

Trigger

Detachable 30-round magazine

▲ AK47 TYPE 56S

Date	1957
Origin	China
Barrel	16¼in (41.4cm)
Caliber	7.62 × 39mm

The iconic AK47 assault rifle has undergone a number of changes over the years and has been widely copied. This Type 56S civilian variant, produced in China, fires only in semiautomatic mode. Initially it had a milled steel receiver, but was later adopted for use with a stamped version.

Fire control lever

Rear sight

30-round detachable box magazine

Tubular butt folds to the left

▲ AK74

Date	1974
Origin	Soviet Union
Barrel	16¼in (41.5cm)
Caliber	5.45 × 39mm

In 1974, the design of the Kalashnikov (AK47) was modified to improve its performance. The caliber was reduced to 5.45mm, stamped components replaced those that had been previously machined from solid steel, and a plastic magazine was substituted for the earlier metal version. This resulted in a much lighter rifle that still had the reliability of its predecessor.

FULL VIEW

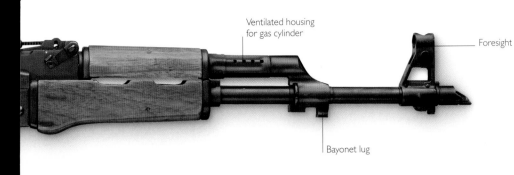

Ventilated housing
for gas cylinder

Foresight

Bayonet lug

▼ CZ58

Date 1959

Origin Czechoslovakia

Barrel 15½in (39cm)

Caliber 7.62 × 39mm

Though superficially similar to the famous AK47, and later the AKM, the Czech CZ58 is structurally quite different. Designed by Jiri Cermak, it uses a short-stroke piston to cycle the action. Its gas port has a fixed diameter and so the full force of combustion gases is directed toward the piston, driving it rearward. This gun is readily identifiable by its wood-impregnated plastic butt.

Wood-impregnated
plastic butt

Magazine
catch

Detachable 30-round
magazine

Gas
regulator

Flash hider

Gas cylinder

Foresight

Flash hider

Cocking handle

Gas cylinder

Magazine
catch

Detachable 35-round
box magazine

Bipod
mounting point

Flash hider

▲ GALIL ASSAULT RIFLE

Date 1972

Origin Israel

Barrel 18in (46cm)

Caliber 5.56 × 45mm NATO

The Galil is based on the Finnish Valmet M62, itself derived from the AK47. It replaced the FN Fal (see p.242), which was used extensively by the Israeli Army. The Galil was much shorter and weighed less. It was also unaffected by dust or sand, an issue with the FN Fal. The Galil comes in a number of variants that include standard assault rifle, light machine-gun, and sharpshooter rifle configurations.

SHOWCASE

AK47

Designed by Mikhail Kalashnikov between 1945 and 1946, the *Avtomat Kalashnikova 47*, or AK47, is the most famous assault rifle in the world. This gun has a gas-operated auto-loading mechanism (see p.305). Its low number of moving parts has helped greatly to reduce its production costs. The AK47 has been adopted by more than 100 armies throughout the world, and its variants are built in more than 30 countries. Amazingly, more than 75 million units have been produced.

▶ MAINSPRING
The mainspring fits inside the rear portion of the bolt carrier (the bolt carrier is covered by the action cover). The mainspring's rear is fitted with a ribbed lug that serves as a locking piece for the action cover. When the lug is pushed, the mainspring moves slightly forward so that the cover can be removed.

Ribbed lug

Rear mainspring guide

Mainspring

Steel cross pin

Piston

▲ BOLT CARRIER AND PISTON
The bolt carrier houses the bolt. The piston is attached to the bolt carrier by a steel cross pin. The piston fits in the gas cylinder. When the gun is fired, some of the exploding gases are vented toward the piston, pushing it rearward, driving the bolt backward, and extracting the spent cartridge.

Bolt holder

Bolt carrier

Stem

Locking lug

Cartridge case extractor pulls out spent case from chamber

◀ BOLT
Noteworthy for its extremely simple construction, the bolt has a narrow rear stem that fits into the lower part of the bolt carrier. Its head is machined with locking lugs, which slightly retard the rearward movement of the bolt to avoid loss of combustion gas pressure (and consequent bullet velocity) before the bullet leaves the muzzle.

Safety lever pivot

Safety lever

Trigger

Magazine-release catch

Butt

Pistol grip

▲ RECEIVER AND BARREL ASSEMBLY
Although initial experiments with pressed steel receivers failed, renewed attempts at producing such receivers after World War II were successful and these became standard production items. The distinctive feature of the barrel is its chromium-plated bore; the chromium minimizes wear and protects against corrosion. The hand guard serves to protect the user's hand from the heat dissipated through the barrel and gas cylinder.

AK47

Date 1954

Origin Soviet Union

Barrel 12in (30.5cm)

Caliber 7.62mm

The AK47 has earned a reputation for being a near-perfect military weapon due to its low cost of production, durability, and simplicity. More AK47s have been produced than any other assault rifle. The rifle entered service in 1949 and was used extensively by Soviet forces from the 1950s, gaining significant popularity during the conflicts of the Cold War. The unit seen here was manufactured in 1954.

FULL VIEW

Ejection port is closed

◄ ACTION COVER

To prevent dirt from getting into the moving parts of the rifle's mechanism (bolt, mainspring, and trigger assembly), the uppermost part of the receiver is fitted with a removable pressed steel cover. It is held in place by spring tension from the mainspring. When the safety lever is in the uppermost position, the action cover blocks dirt from entering the rear part of the action.

Front guide retainer

▼ GAS CYLINDER

Some of the exploding gases released on firing a cartridge are vented from the barrel, through the gas port, into the gas cylinder, which contains the piston. The pressure of the exploding gases drives the piston and the bolt backward against the mainspring. This withdraws the empty case from the chamber and ejects it, cocking the weapon ready for the next round to be fired. When the bolt begins to advance again, driven by the mainspring, it feeds a new cartridge into the chamber from the magazine.

Piston rings

Hand guard latch

Rear face of the piston tube

Ejection port

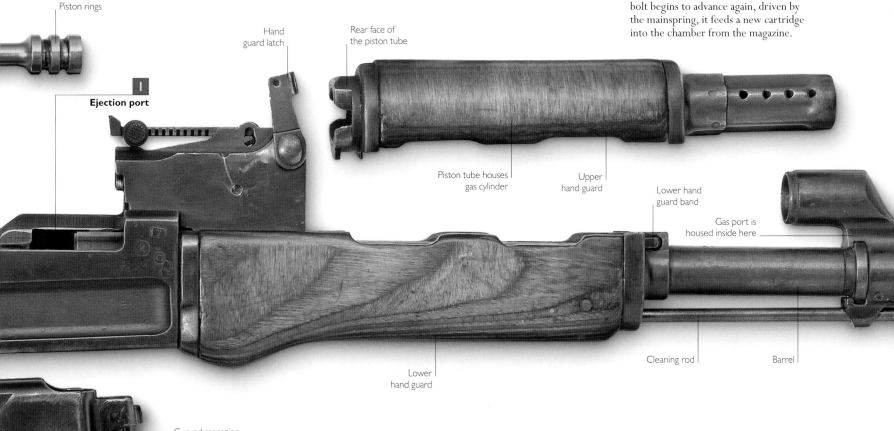

Piston tube houses gas cylinder

Upper hand guard

Lower hand guard band

Gas port is housed inside here

Cleaning rod

Barrel

Lower hand guard

Curved magazine carries 30 rounds

◄ MAGAZINE

The AK47 uses a relatively short cartridge. The cartridges, when stacked, form a tight curve, resulting in the pronounced curve of the magazine. The magazine-release catch is a simple pressed steel lever, easy to operate when wearing gloves, and situated just in front of the trigger guard.

◄ EJECTION PORT (OPEN)

The ejection port is the cutaway part of the action cover positioned above the lower receiver. It remains closed during firing. After firing, when the bolt moves rearward, the ejection port opens to eject the spent cartridge case.

ASSAULT RIFLES (1976—PRESENT)

During the final quarter of the 20th century, assault rifles increasingly utilized what is known as the "bullpup" configuration. This involved placing the bolt and the recoil mechanism in the butt so that the magazine could be placed behind the trigger. In addition to reducing the overall length of the firearm, this design also reduced muzzle rise considerably since the force of recoil was more fully absorbed by the shooter's shoulder. As with other arms of the period, these new designs utilized plastics to a greater degree than ever before.

▼ **STEYR AUG**

Date 1978

Origin Austria

Barrel 20in (50.8cm)

Caliber 5.56 × 45mm NATO

Dating back to the 1970s, the futuristic and highly successful AUG was among the first assault rifles to combine an integral optical sight, plastic components, and a bullpup configuration.

Flash hider

Carrying handle containing sights

Flash hider

Front grip

▶ **FAMAS F1**

Date 1978

Origin France

Barrel 19¼in (48.8cm)

Caliber 5.56 × 45mm NATO

A bullpup design, the FAMAS F1 is a very compact weapon and has been used by the French armed forces since the late 1970s. Like many modern assault rifles, it makes use of plastics and stamped metal components.

Ejection port

Bipod (folded)

25-round detachable box magazine

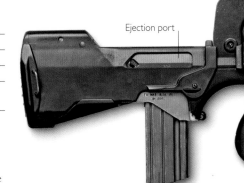

Optical sight with low-light capability and 4× magnification

Eyepiece with protective rubber shroud

▼ **L85A1**

Date 1985

Origin UK

Barrel 20½in (51.8cm)

Caliber 5.56 × 45mm NATO

The L85A1 was the last weapon system to be developed and produced at the Royal Small Arms Factory, Enfield, UK, before it closed in 1988. It was dogged with problems during the development stage, and trials continued even after its adoption in 1985. It was designed from the start to use an optical sight. The body and many other parts are steel stampings. All the furniture is high-impact plastic.

Release catch for dismounting action

Stamped steel body

Large trigger guard for gloved hand

Pistol grip with high-impact plastic molding

Detachable 30-round magazine compatible with other NATO weapons

Optical sight adjustment knob

1.5× magnification optical sight

Ejection port

Receiver/ butt

Trigger

Magazine catch

Detachable 42-round box magazine

Rear sling swivel

Optical sight

Butt plate

Picatinny rail (a rail for mounting accessories on the gun)

Foresight

Flash hider

Forward vertical hand grip

Flash hider

Detachable 30-round box magazine

Plastic pistol grip

◄ SA80

Date 1985–1994

Origin UK

Barrel 20½in (51.8cm)

Caliber 5.56 × 45mm NATO

Developed at the Royal Small Arms Factory, Enfield, UK, until 1988 and then British Aerospace (BAE) until 1994, the SA80 represented the culmination of a design program that had begun in the late 1940s. Aside from its use of plastic, the SA80 is also notable for its incorporation of sheet metal parts.

Rear aperture of sight cover

Forward opening of sight cover

► FN2000 BULLPUP RIFLE

Date 2001

Origin Belgium

Barrel 16in (40.6cm)

Caliber 5.56 × 45mm NATO

The FN2000 is undoubtedly one of the most futuristic-looking weapons to have been developed. Of modular construction, it consists of a barrel/receiver unit attached to a frame by a single pin. The rifle is fitted with an optical sight and has a chromed barrel to resist wear and corrosion.

Receiver assembly

Detachable box magazine

Trigger

Barrel

SNIPER RIFLES (BOLT ACTION)

Whether used by military forces or the police, bolt-action sniper rifles represent the epitome of accuracy. Though some, such as the US M40, are quite plain and closely resemble sporting arms, others are equipped with stocks that can be adjusted to the personal preferences of their users and bipods to provide steady support. For normal field use, they are chambered for standard-issue cartridges that are loaded to precise specifications, including weight of charge, and bullet type and weight. Long-range sniper rifles are normally chambered for .50in BMG cartridges, first developed for the Browning machine-gun in the late 1910s.

Optical sight

Unsupported barrel allows firing vibrations to dissipate without restriction

▲ M40 SNIPER RIFLE

Date 1966

Origin US

Barrel 24in (61cm)

Caliber 7.62 × 51mm NATO

A military version of the Remington 700 sporting rifle, the M40 was first used by the US Marine Corps in the Vietnam War. Subsequent models were equipped with a fiberglass stock.

6x Kahles ZF69 optical sight

Magazine is housed here

Synthetic stock

▲ STEYR SSG-69

Date 1969

Origin Austria

Barrel 25½in (65cm)

Caliber 7.62 × 51mm NATO

Developed for the Austrian army, the SSG also proved popular with police organizations. The SSG-69 was unusual in its use of a five-round rotating spool magazine housed within the rifle body.

Optical sight

Raised comb stock

Heavy barrel

▲ ENFIELD L42A1

Date 1970

Origin UK

Barrel 27½in (70cm)

Caliber 7.62 × 51mm NATO

The L42A1 was a British Army sniper rifle in production between 1970 and 1985, but still in use well into the 1990s. It was built using the standard Lee-Enfield action, but was fitted with a heavy barrel chambered for the 7.62 × 51mm NATO cartridge.

Saddle cheek piece helps the user to brace the gun against his cheek

Polymer stock

Bolt handle

Five-round detachable magazine

6x optical sight

Unsupported
stainless-steel barrel

Bipod in folded position

Attachment
point for sling

Polymer
stock

Ten-round
detachable
box magazine

Hooded
foresight

▲ L96A1

Date 1986

Origin UK

Barrel 25¾in (65.5cm)

Caliber 7.62 × 51mm NATO

The British Army's L96A1 sniper rifle,
in service since 1986, was the first to
be developed specifically for sniping;
earlier versions had been based on
various models of the Lee-Enfield.
It has an aluminum frame to which its
components are attached. Each rifle is
individually fitted with a Schmidt and
Bender six-power optical sight.

Heavy barrel

10x optical sight

Muzzle brake

Rear
monopod

Bipod leg

▲ HECATE II SNIPER RIFLE

Date 1993

Origin France

Barrel 27½in (70cm)

Caliber .50in BMG

As with other Western long-range sniper rifles,
the Hecate II fires the .50in BMG (12.7 ×
99mm NATO) round. It is based around a
skeleton stock developed by PGM, France,
and has a high-efficiency muzzle brake.

Optical sight

Weight-reducing
helically fluted barrel

▲ C14 TIMBERWOLF

Date 2005

Origin Canada

Barrel 26in (66cm)

Caliber .338in Lapua Magnum

The C14 began as a hunting rifle,
but was then developed for sniper
use because of its accuracy. In
sniper use, it is chambered for the
powerful .338in Lapua Magnum
antipersonnel round, which extends
the rifle's effective range to more
than 1,300 yards (1,200m).

FULL VIEW

Bipod leg

SNIPER RIFLES (SELF-LOADING)

In common with their single-shot counterparts, self-loading sniper rifles are designed to provide accurate fire at long distances—up to 1,000 yards (900m) in the hands of a well-trained marksman. Sniper rifles are identifiable by their optical sights and a butt with adjustable cheek rests. Self-loaders have, in addition, a cycling action that autoloads ammunition from a magazine. Such rifles are capable of firing multiple rounds in quick succession, and on the battlefield they can be used to disrupt enemy command posts at long range.

PSO-1 optical sight

Battery compartment

Cheek pad helps user to brace the gun against his cheek

Skeleton wooden butt

Safety catch

Magnification selector

Nimrod optical sight

Wooden butt

Adjustable comb

Pistol grip

Forestock

Detachable 25-round steel box magazine

Bipod leg

▲ **GALIL 7.62MM SNIPER RIFLE**

Date 1960s

Origin Israel

Barrel 20in (50.8cm)

Caliber 7.62 × 51mm NATO

The semiautomatic Galil Sniper Rifle features a folding butt with an adjustable comb, as well as a folding bipod and a 25-round box magazine. The example illustrated is equipped with a six-power Nimrod optical sight.

Shielded cover over objective lens

▼ DRAGUNOV SVD

Date 1963

Origin Soviet Union

Barrel 24in (61cm)

Caliber 7.62 × 54mm

The SVD came to be used as a sharpshooter platoon-support weapon by Warsaw Pact armies in the 1960s. Its four-power PSO-1 optical sight has limited infrared capability.

Gas cylinder

Gas regulator

FULL VIEW

Muzzle brake and flash hider

Cocking handle

Perforated barrel shroud for air-cooling barrel and insulating user's hands

10-round detachable box magazine

Magnification selector, 2.5–10x

Windage adjustment

Shielded cover over objective lens

Bipod in folded position

Ejection port

Six-round detachable box magazine

Thumb hole

▲ WALTHER WA2000

Date 1978

Origin Germany

Barrel 25½in (65cm)

Caliber .300in Win Mag/7.62 × 51mm NATO

Developed primarily for police use, the WA2000 employed a "bullpup" configuration (see p.250) and a semiautomatic action fed by a six-round magazine. High manufacturing costs ended its production in 1988.

Barrel

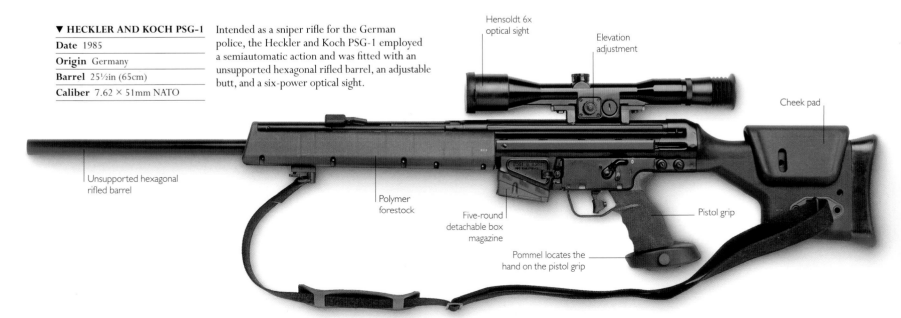

▼ HECKLER AND KOCH PSG-1

Date 1985

Origin Germany

Barrel 25½in (65cm)

Caliber 7.62 × 51mm NATO

Intended as a sniper rifle for the German police, the Heckler and Koch PSG-1 employed a semiautomatic action and was fitted with an unsupported hexagonal rifled barrel, an adjustable butt, and a six-power optical sight.

Hensoldt 6x optical sight

Elevation adjustment

Cheek pad

Unsupported hexagonal rifled barrel

Polymer forestock

Five-round detachable box magazine

Pistol grip

Pommel locates the hand on the pistol grip

GREAT GUNSMITHS

HECKLER AND KOCH

Rooted in the long tradition of German firearms manufacture, Heckler and Koch was founded by three former Mauser engineers after World War II. A major contract to provide a rifle for the German Federal Army brought the company early success, and it has been a significant force in weapons production ever since. Products such as the G3 and HK33 rifles have sold very widely and spawned numerous variants, making the Heckler and Koch brand one of the most familiar in the world of weapons.

THEODOR KOCH

In the years following World War II, the Allied forces (UK, US, and others) put severe restrictions on industry in Germany and, although some of these curbs were soon lifted, the ban on arms production remained well into the 1950s. The Mauser weapons factory at Oberndorf was shut down by the French occupying forces, but three former Mauser employees, Edmund Heckler, Theodor Koch, and Alex Seidel, salvaged some of the machinery. All three were seasoned engineers with experience in firearms manufacture and the metalworking industry, and they needed all their skill and adaptability in the tough economic conditions of postwar Germany. Their new business—originally named after Heckler, but renamed Heckler and Koch—began as a manufacturer of bicycles, machine tools, and precision parts for items such as sewing machines. Many of their workers had formerly been Mauser employees.

▼ **OBERNDORF FACTORY**
Part of the Heckler and Koch factory at Oberndorf, Germany, consisted of low-rise prefabricated buildings put up in the period after the end of World War II.

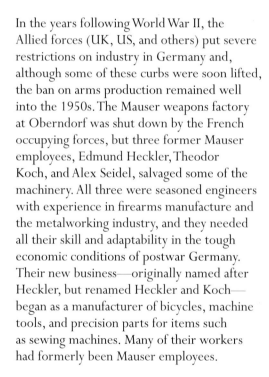

"The **MP5** deserves its reputation for excellence."

CHRIS MCNAB, **THE SAS TRAINING MANUAL**

IN THE BEGINNING
When Germany began to reconstruct its economy after the war, there was a large demand for the items originally produced by Heckler and Koch. But the founders' roots were in the firearms business and they waited patiently for a chance to return to the industry in which they had once flourished. The opening did not come until the mid-1950s, when the ban on weapons production was finally lifted. The big opportunity for Heckler and Koch arrived in 1956, when tenders were invited to produce a new assault rifle for the infantry of the German Federal Army. The successful weapon was based on a rifle that had been developed at the old Mauser factory in the 1940s, before being modified by the Spanish design and development agency CETME and then refined

still further by Heckler and Koch. The army preferred their design to the competitors' on offer at that time—one rifle from America and another from Switzerland—and in 1959, Heckler and Koch were awarded a contract to produce the rifle, which became known as the G3 (see p.243). The G3 was based on a roller-delayed recoil action developed by the engineer Ludwig Vorgrimler. The weapon has a modular design, allowing the user to swap parts at speed to reconfigure the rifle. In addition, Heckler and Koch made a host of variants on the basic design. Versions with different trigger groups, sights, stocks, deflectors, and other parts have been produced, making the G3 highly versatile and helping it to become widely used.

ADVANCES IN TECHNOLOGY
The G3 provided Heckler and Koch with a hugely successful start in firearms manufacturing. Armed forces from Norway to South Africa have bought it, the weapon has seen service all over the world, and some models remain in production today. It also provided the basis for further firearms that proved highly successful for Heckler and Koch. There are four main groups of these, each sharing the G3's roller-delayed action, but each chambered for a different cartridge and consisting of a large subfamily of weapons. A prime example is the MP5 submachine-

HECKLER AND KOCH G3A3, 1964

HECKLER AND KOCH MP5A5, 1966

HECKLER AND KOCH G41, 1981

1945 Occupying French forces dismantle the Mauser weapons factory at Oberndorf, Germany.

1949 Heckler and Koch begins to manufacture items for non-military use, such as components for domestic appliances and bicycles.

1959 The contract for the new infantry rifle for the West German army is awarded to the company. The G3 follows, and later, the G3A3 (see p.243).

1966 The MP5 is developed. The MP5A5 (see p.292) follows.

1968 The HK33 assault rifle is launched. It is a 5.56mm weapon intended for the export market.

1981 The G41 rifle (see p.243), originally designed as a replacement for the HK33, is introduced.

1990 The company's long-running project to develop the G11 assault rifle, with high-velocity caseless

ammunition, is canceled due to political changes surrounding Germany's reunification.

1991 The British company Royal Ordnance purchases Heckler and Koch.

2002 Heckler and Koch is sold to private investors and receives substantial orders for the British SA80 assault rifle (see p.251) and other firearms.

gun, which, like the G3, is a modular design so that the user can adapt it with ease; it has spawned many variants. The MP5 has been bought by military and law-enforcement customers all over the world and is one of the most ubiquitous submachine-guns.

The company also worked with materials which were new and unusual for firearms, such as polymers. While these materials had

been used for nonstructural parts such as grips, Heckler and Koch (as well as companies such as Glock) pioneered their use for gun frames, making huge weight savings, and once the precision molds for the parts had been made, savings in manufacturing costs, too. Polygonal rifling is another technology in which Heckler and Koch have expertise. This old idea had fallen out of favor, but

Heckler and Koch applied it to modern weapons, replacing the traditional grooved barrel with a rounded polygonal internal surface to give a better gas seal around the projectile. Heckler and Koch have successfully tethered these technological ideas to the development of versatile families of weapons, making them one of the leading firearms manufacturers of the 21st century.

▶ MP5 IN USE
Members of the US Special Operations Response Team (SORT), who operate in prisons and are specialists in handling tense and dangerous situations among the inmates, were frequent users of the MP5 between 2000 and 2010.

LIGHT MACHINE-GUNS (1945–65)

The development of light machine-guns in the years following World War II drew heavily on designs that had been created during the war, particularly in Germany. This is most evident in the US M60 and the Mauser-CETME arms, which parallel the wartime German MG42 (see p.193), StG44 (see p.177), and StG45. These light machine-guns also began to use sheet metal stampings and light-weight metal alloys extensively in their construction.

Hinged shoulder rest in open position

Recoil spring housing

Rate-of-fire selector and safety catch

Ammunition belt feedway

Laminated wooden butt

▲ DEGTYAREV RP46

Date 1946

Origin Soviet Union

Barrel 23¾in (60.5cm)

Caliber 7.62 × 54mm

The Red Army adopted the Degtyarev DP in 1928. It was modified in 1945, and the following year, it received a heavier barrel and was adapted to take belts as well as drum magazines, evolving into the RP46. It was still not entirely satisfactory, however, and was soon replaced by the RPD.

Ammunition belt

Rear sight

► FN MAG

Date 1958

Origin Belgium

Barrel 21½in (55cm)

Caliber 7.62 × 51mm NATO

The MAG (*Mitrailleuse à Gaz*, meaning gas-operated machine-gun), produced by FN, used a modified form of the locking system developed by John Browning for his Automatic Rifle (see p.194); this was married to the feed mechanism of the MG42. This gun could fire 650–1,000 rounds per minute and was adopted by the British Army as their General-Purpose Machine-Gun (GPMG).

Gas cylinder

Pistol grip

Butt plate

Tripod leg

Elevation gears

Ammunition box

Butt-receiver attachment sleeve pin

Receiver

Rear sight

Rear sling attachment aperture

Butt-receiver attachment sleeve plate

Selector switch

Ammunition feed

Barrel jacket

Flash hider

Ammunition belt feedway

Gas tube

Foresight

Butt plate

Butt release pin catch

Bipod leg

▲ L7A2 LIGHT MACHINE-GUN

Date 1960

Origin UK

Barrel 27½in (70cm)

Caliber 7.62 × 51mm NATO

The British L7A2 light machine-gun is essentially a copy of the Belgian FN MAG (far left) made under license in Britain. It is a platoon support weapon of considerable versatility since it can also be used with fixed mounts on vehicles.

Carrying handle

Receiver cover

Ammunition belt feedway

Heat shield

Foresight

Bipod foot

Receiver

Bipod (folded)

Pistol grip

▲ M60 LIGHT MACHINE-GUN

Date 1963

Origin US

Barrel 23½in (59.9cm)

Caliber 7.62 × 51mm NATO

In the early 1960s, the US Army replaced its Browning M1917 (see p.188) derivatives with a new, gas-operated GPMG whose rate of fire are 500–600 rounds per minute. The M60 used the feed system of the MG42 (see p.193) and the locking system of the German FG42 assault rifle (see p.215). It was unsatisfactory to begin with, because it was heavy, bulky, had poor balance and a complex barrel changing system. In early versions, some components, such as the bolt, experienced failure due to wear. Modifications were carried out over the next two decades to correct most of the gun's faults.

Gas tube

Foresight

Gas tap-off point

Fore hand grip

▲ MAUSER–CETME LMG

Date 1960s

Origin Spain / Germany

Barrel 23¼in (59cm)

Caliber 7.62 × 51mm NATO

The Mauser–CETME light machine-gun was a joint German-Spanish development of the German MG42, although chambered for the 7.62 × 51mm NATO round. The gun was not a success with this chambering, because the fluted chamber caused spent cartridge cases to stick—in some instances, the extractor would pull the base of a spent case off its body—a major problem in the field. CETME later achieved a good workable design in their 5.56 × 45mm NATO Ameli machine-gun.

LIGHT MACHINE-GUNS (1966–PRESENT)

Modern light machine-guns are either gas- or recoil-operated. They continue to be characterized by their extensive use of plastic or resin-impregnated components, stamped parts, and light weight. With a few exceptions, they are designed for individual use to provide squad support fire. Increasingly they have been fitted with optical sights to improve their effectiveness in the field. While the Gatling Minigun was intended for use from a fixed mount, its short overall length qualifies it as a light machine-gun.

Ammunition feed

Optical sight

▲ GATLING MINIGUN M134

Date 1960s

Origin US

Barrel 22in (56cm)

Caliber 7.62 × 51mm NATO

The M134 is a Gatling-type rotary weapon that is powered by an electric motor to achieve extremely high rates of fire—up to 6,000 rounds per minute, although typically the rate is limited to around 4,000 rounds per minute. The weight and bulk of the external power source mean that the gun is usually used in helicopters, on armored vehicles, or on boats.

Butt plate

Folding shoulder support

Secondary grip

Pistol grip

Trigger guard

Ammunition belt

Detachable 30-round box magazine

Carrying handle

▲ PKM

Date 1969

Origin Soviet Union

Barrel 25¼in (64cm)

Caliber 7.62 × 54mm

A General-Purpose Machine-Gun (GPMG), the PKM is gas-operated, belt-fed, and air-cooled. Its rate of fire is around 650–750 rounds per minute. It is an improved variant of the Mikhail Kalashnikov-designed PK. Its butt plate is hinged.

Tubular butt

▶ FN MINIMI

Date 1975

Origin Belgium

Barrel 18¼in (46.5cm)

Caliber 5.56 × 45mm NATO

An outstanding gas-operated, air-cooled light machine-gun, the Minimi has a rate of fire of around 700–1,150 rounds per minute. It was adopted by the British Army and the US Army, among others. In the US Army, it was designated the M249 Squad Automatic Weapon (SAW).

Mounting fixture

Flash hider

Ammunition belt container

Bipod leg

Composite
shoulder stock

45-round
box magazine

▲ RPK74

Date 1976

Origin Soviet Union

Barrel 23¼in (59cm)

Caliber 5.45 × 39mm

The light machine-gun version
of the infantryman's AK74 assault
rifle (see p.246), this weapon
features a heavier barrel, which
is chrome-lined like the band of
the AK74. It also has a modified
receiver, a bipod, and an extended
magazine. It fires up to 650 rounds
per minute.

Bipod (folded)

▼ STEYR AUG LMG

Date 1980

Origin Austria

Barrel 24½in (62cm)

Caliber 5.56 × 45mm NATO

By fitting a bipod and a heavy barrel, Steyr produced a
light machine-gun from its AUG assault rifle (see p.250).
The AUG LMG can be fitted either with the AUG's
standard optical sight/carrying handle combination (as
seen here) or without the handle for fitting of a different
sight on a rail. It fires around 680–750 rounds per minute.

Ejection port

Bipod

Front grip

Barrel support

Foresight

**◄ L86A1 LIGHT
SUPPORT WEAPON**

Date 1986

Origin UK

Barrel 25½in (64.5cm)

Caliber 5.56 × 45mm NATO

The L86A1 has a heavier and larger barrel than the
earlier L85A1 (see p.250), and a rear grip to aid
sustained firing. There is no quick-change barrel,
so the gun must be fired in short, controlled bursts
to prevent overheating. It fires around 610–775
rounds in one minute.

Flash hider

▲ NEGEV

Date 1988

Origin Israel

Barrel 18in (46cm)

Caliber 5.56 × 45mm NATO

Israel Military Industries' Negev
is one of the breed of lightweight
automatic weapons that has blurred
the distinction between LMG and
GPMG. Chambered for the SS109
NATO round in 5.56mm caliber,
it can deliver automatic fire at 700
or 900 rounds per minute.

Pistol grip

▼ MG43

Date 2001

Origin Germany

Barrel 18¾in (48cm)

Caliber 5.56 × 45mm NATO

A rival to the FN Minimi (left), the
MG43 is a belt-fed light machine-
gun that features a foldable butt and
a quick-change barrel. Its rate of fire
is about 880 rounds per minute.
A slightly modified form was
adopted by the German Army
in 2001 and renamed MG4.

Optical sight with 4x magnification
and low-light capability

Foldable
butt

Flash hider

Plastic forestock

Trigger
guard

Molded plastic
pistol grip

MODERN REVOLVERS

Despite the fact that their basic lock work was designed in the 19th century, revolvers remain extremely popular to this day. The reasons for this are their dependability, the ease with which they can be loaded, and their compact size. As self-defense weapons, their major assets are their light weight and the fact that they can be readily concealed. In addition, their construction allows them to use powerful cartridges that would place unacceptable strains on semiautomatic arms.

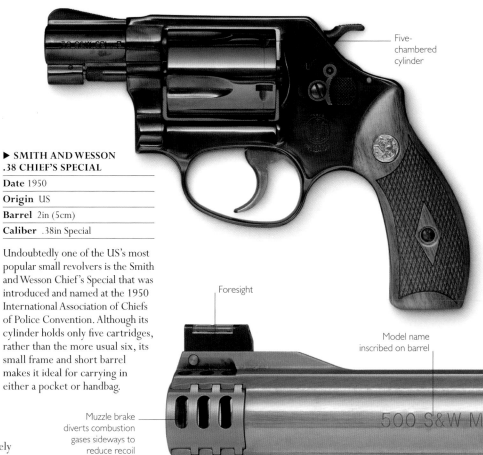

Five-chambered cylinder

**▶ SMITH AND WESSON
.38 CHIEF'S SPECIAL**

Date	1950
Origin	US
Barrel	2in (5cm)
Caliber	.38in Special

Undoubtedly one of the US's most popular small revolvers is the Smith and Wesson Chief's Special that was introduced and named at the 1950 International Association of Chiefs of Police Convention. Although its cylinder holds only five cartridges, rather than the more usual six, its small frame and short barrel makes it ideal for carrying in either a pocket or handbag.

Foresight

Model name inscribed on barrel

Muzzle brake diverts combustion gases sideways to reduce recoil

500 S&W MAG

Cylinder axis rod

**▲ SMITH AND WESSON
AIRWEIGHT**

Date	1952
Origin	US
Barrel	2in (5cm)
Caliber	.38in Special

Most gunmakers produced "pocket" revolvers. These were lighter in weight than semiautomatic pistols chambered for the same ammunition, and to ensure easy concealment, they were fitted with an extremely short barrel. Smith and Wesson's Centennial range, which included the Airweight, carried five rounds and had shrouded hammers. One version of the Airweight was made with an aluminum frame to reduce its weight.

Adjustable rear sight

Rear sight

Hammer

Ventilated barrel rib

▲ COLT PYTHON

Date	1953
Origin	US
Barrel	8in (20.3cm)
Caliber	.357in Magnum

Introduced in 1953, the Python was Colt's first Magnum revolver driven by double action—its hammer could be cocked manually or by pulling the trigger. Though initially designed primarily for target shooting, and therefore equipped with a ventilated sighting rib, the model was also made with short barrels to be issued to police.

Checkered grip

Gold inlays

Trigger guard

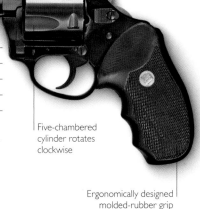

**▶ CHARTER ARMS
POLICE BULLDOG**

Date	1971
Origin	US
Barrel	4in (10.1cm)
Caliber	.357in Magnum

Built on a heavy frame, this gun was also available with a 2in (6.5cm) barrel. Revolvers of either barrel length were chambered for .357in Magnum or .44in Special ammunition. The molded rubber grip reduced the amount of recoil transferred to the user's hand.

Five-chambered cylinder rotates clockwise

Silver decoration on grip

Ergonomically designed molded-rubber grip

Adjustable rear sight

Foresight

Trigger guard

Checkered grip

▲ SMITH AND WESSON MODEL 29

Date 1980s

Origin US

Barrel 8¾in (22cm)

Caliber .44in Magnum

Introduced in 1955, the Model 29 was one of Smith and Wesson's N-frame revolvers, specially designed for shooting heavy loads. It came with a variety of barrel lengths, from 4in (10cm) up to 10½in (27cm), and all featured adjustable rear sights since the .44in Magnum cartridge was accurate at ranges well beyond those of standard pistol cartridges.

▼ RUGER GP-100

Date 1987

Origin US

Barrel 4in (10.2cm)

Caliber .357in Magnum

Sturm, Ruger and Co. was a latecomer to the world of gun manufacture, opening for business in 1949. The double-action GP-100 is a well-built revolver that incorporates an automatic hammer safety to prevent accidental discharges and an ergonomic grip that makes it easier to hold.

Cylinder-locking bolt recess

Six-chambered cylinder

Pistol grip

Cylinder release catch

Five-chambered cylinder

Trigger guard

▲ SMITH AND WESSON TIFFANY MAGNUM

Date 1989

Origin US

Barrel 6in (15cm)

Caliber .44in Magnum

Smith and Wesson has produced various decorated "Tiffany-style" revolvers. This gun, based on a .44in Magnum Model 29 (above), features a grip decorated in silver, and a gold-inlaid barrel.

▲ MODEL 500 X-FRAME

Date 2003

Origin US

Barrel 8¾in (22cm)

Caliber .500in Smith and Wesson Magnum

This massive five-shot revolver is the largest commercially made handgun in the world. Weighing 72½oz (2kg) unloaded, it fires a bullet weighing ¾oz (22.7g), designed for use against the heaviest of game. The barrel is equipped with a muzzle brake to reduce recoil.

Pistol grip

Gold-plated hammer

Gold-plated cylinder

▲ SMITH AND WESSON .357 MAGNUM

Date 2000

Origin US

Barrel 4¾in (12 cm)

Caliber .357in Magnum

Trigger

This Smith and Wesson revolver has, apart from exquisite grip decoration, a gold-plated cylinder, trigger, and hammer. The barrel and much of the frame remain conventional, undecorated Smith and Wesson parts. As with most Smith and Wesson special editions, the revolver is fully functional.

SELF-LOADING PISTOLS (1946–80)

In the years following World War II, the design of self-loading handguns more or less followed the patterns set down earlier. By the 1970s, however, these pistols began to take on more streamlined profiles such as those seen in Heckler and Koch's VP70M. At the same time, components made from investment castings—wax models placed in molds so that finely detailed castings can be produced in metal—began to appear. Concurrently, plastic became the material of choice for pistol grips due to its stability in all weather conditions.

Safety catch

Slide

▲ M20 SILENCED
Date 1950s

Origin China

Barrel 9in (23cm) (including silencer)

Caliber 7.62 × 25mm

The M20 was a Chinese copy of the Soviet 7.62 × 25mm Tokarev TT Model 1933 (see p.174). It differed from the original in having more slide grip cuts. The model here features a silencer.

Magazine base

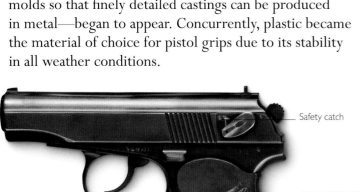

Butt houses detachable eight-round box magazine

◀ MAKAROV PM
Date 1950s

Origin Soviet Union

Barrel 3¾in (9.7cm)

Caliber 9mm Makarov

The Tokarev TT Model 33 (see p.174) was replaced by this copy of the Walther PP as the Red Army's standard sidearm. It was a double-action weapon and had a two-stage safety device. Its ammunition was about as powerful as could safely be used in a recoil design at that time.

Muzzle

Serial number

▲ HELWAN
Date 1965

Origin Egypt

Barrel 4¼in (11cm)

Caliber 9mm Parabellum

The Helwan is an Egyptian licensed version of the Beretta Model 1951 Brigadier, a single-action (the hammer has to be cocked manually) 9mm automatic handgun with an eight-round magazine capacity.

Integral silencer

▲ TYPE 67
Date 1968

Origin China

Barrel 3½in (8.9cm)

Caliber 7.62 × 17mm

The Type 67 was a recoil pistol with an integral suppressor, or silencer. It featured a manual slide locking system, which stopped ejection of the spent cartridge after firing, making the pistol quieter during operation.

Magazine inserted into grip

External
silencer

Enclosed
hammer

Burst-fire
selector

▶ HECKLER AND KOCH VP70M

Date 1970s

Origin Germany

Barrel 4½in (11.6cm)

Caliber 9mm Parabellum

The VP70M, the first pistol to make extensive use of plastic, was an attempt to produce a fully automatic handgun, although limited to firing three-round bursts. The mechanism that controlled this was housed in the detachable butt; when it was removed, the pistol reverted to normal semiautomatic operation.

FULL VIEW

Fiber-reinforced
polymer butt

Push-button
safety catch

Butt houses
18-round magazine

Slide

Slide stop

CZ75B CAL. 9 LUGER

▶ CZ75

Date 1975

Origin Czechoslovakia

Barrel 4¾in (12cm)

Caliber 9mm Parabellum

The CZ75 had several derivatives, such as the CZ97 in .45in caliber and the CZ75 P-07 featuring a polymer frame rather than a steel one. These models quickly established reputations for reliability, and they were adopted by a number of military and police forces.

Barrel (visible)

Cutaway slide top

Muzzle

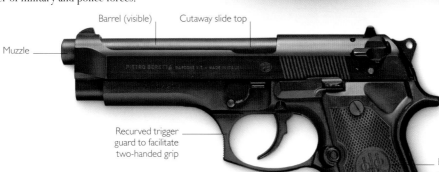

Recurved trigger
guard to facilitate
two-handed grip

Butt houses
detachable
13-round box
magazine

▶ BERETTA MODEL 92FS

Date 1976

Origin Italy

Barrel 4¼in (10.9cm)

Caliber 9mm Parabellum

The Beretta 92 was chosen as the US military's official sidearm to replace the Colt M1911A1 (see p.169) in the 1980s. Its frame was forged from aluminum to reduce weight. The slide top was cut away to allow single rounds to be loaded manually.

SELF-LOADING PISTOLS (1981–90)

Self-loading pistols from this period all display the squared profile that has become the accepted norm for these weapons. Structurally, they increasingly incorporated components made of lightweight metal alloys or synthetic polymers. The use of the latter initially caused unease among both users and law enforcement officials. Users feared that parts made entirely of polymers would not withstand the stresses generated during firing, while the police were worried that such arms would be invisible to metal detectors. But these concerns proved to be unfounded—the so-called "plastic pistols" were here to stay.

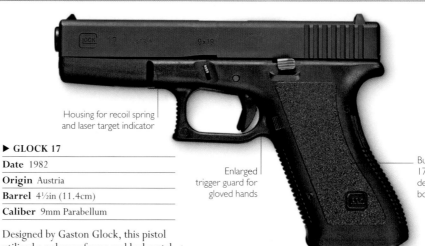

Housing for recoil spring and laser target indicator

Enlarged trigger guard for gloved hands

Butt houses 17-round detachable box magazine

▶ GLOCK 17

Date 1982

Origin Austria

Barrel 4½in (11.4cm)

Caliber 9mm Parabellum

Designed by Gaston Glock, this pistol utilized a polymer frame and had metal parts treated with a proprietary formula finish that prevented surface oxidation. It also had three independent safety locking systems, including the Browning locking system (see p. 270), that prevented accidental firing. Though treated with skepticism when introduced, the Glock is now used worldwide by police forces and military personnel.

Elevation adjustment

Optical sight

Muzzle brake

Interchangeable barrel

▲ IMI DESERT EAGLE

Date 1983

Origin Israel

Barrel 10in (25.4cm)

Caliber .44in Magnum (as shown here)

Unlike almost all other self-loading pistols, the Desert Eagle, made by Israel Military Industries (IMI), was gas-operated (see p. 305), and of modular design. Its standard frame was able to accept sets of components for different ammunition, from .357in Magnum to .5in Action Express (AE), and barrels of different lengths.

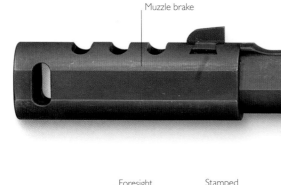

Foresight

Stamped slide

Grooves allow slide to be gripped

Decocking device

Internal barrel bushing

Magazine catch

▶ SIG-SAUER 9MM P226

Date 1984

Origin Switzerland

Barrel 4¼in (11cm)

Caliber 9mm Parabellum

Developed in Switzerland by SIG, the SIG-Sauer is manufactured by J. P. Sauer and Sohn in Germany and in the US. Early versions had stamped slides but later production examples have slides milled from steel billets. It features a decocking device that allows the hammer to be safely lowered with a loaded cartridge in the chamber for carrying, so that the pistol is ready for immediate use when it is loaded.

Butt houses detachable box magazine

Adjustable rear sight

Hammer

Extended barrel

▲ LAR GRIZZLY MK IV

Date	1985
Origin	US
Barrel	6½in (16.5cm)
Caliber	.44in Magnum

The LAR Grizzly handgun was developed as a high-power hunting or target shooting weapon. It is based upon the classic Colt M1911 (see pp.178–79), most of the differences being related to size and minor external features (such as the form of the trigger guard, the spur on the rear grip strap, and the forward grip strap). The Mk 1 came with caliber conversion kits; the Mk IV, by contrast, is available only in .44in Magnum.

Magazine release catch

Checkered front grip

Adjustable eyepiece

Hammer

Milled cocking grip

Safety catch

Adjustable rear sight

Slide

Removable barrel weight

▲ BERETTA 89 TARGET

Date	1989
Origin	Italy
Barrel	6in (15cm)
Caliber	.22in

The Beretta 89 is an automatic recoil-powered handgun designed for competitive target shooting. It is a single-action gun (its hammer must be cocked manually) and is built for high accuracy, with a heavy barrel and an adjustable rear sight.

Recurved trigger guard to facilitate two-handed grip

Slide catch/release

Foresight

Recoil spring housing

Butt houses nine-round removable magazine

▶ IMI JERICHO 941

Date	1990
Origin	Israel
Barrel	4¾in (12cm)
Caliber	9mm/.41in AE

The Jericho 941 entered production with IMI in 1990. The "941" designation refers to the way it was originally supplied with interchangeable barrels, magazines, and recoil springs to swap between 9mm and .41in AE cartridges.

AMPHIBIOUS FIREARMS
The creation of the ADS Amphibious Rifle by Russian engineers was made public in 2009. Amazingly, this assault rifle for combat divers can fire under water—by using a special cartridge filled with a powder that releases oxygen on ignition, allowing the powder to burn.

SELF-LOADING PISTOLS (1991–PRESENT)

Modern self-loading pistols differ little from their predecessors visually. However, their construction now involves an increased use of carbon composites, plastics, and lightweight metal alloys. Another key development is that their grips are designed to allow the use of high-capacity magazines capable of holding up to 20 rounds. The profile of the forward trigger guard bow has also become more vertical and grooved, a configuration that allows shooters to hold a pistol securely with both hands.

Forward portion of slide houses end of mainspring

Double-action trigger

Butt houses 15-round box magazine

Frame-mounted safety catch

▲ COLT ALL AMERICAN 2000

Date 1991

Origin US

Barrel 4½in (11cm)

Caliber 9mm Parabellum

The All-American emerged from Colt in 1991, the brainchild of Reed Knight Jr. and Eugene Stoner. It was a 9mm gun with a frame made of either polymer or aluminum, hence it was extremely light. Colt ceased production of the gun in 1994.

▲ SIG-SAUER P226

Date 1991

Origin Switzerland

Barrel 4½in (11.5cm)

Caliber 9mm Parabellum

The SIG-Sauer P226 is a development of the SIG P220, one of the postwar period's finest semiautomatic handguns. The P226's higher-capacity magazines store up to 20 9mm Parabellum cartridges in a staggered column. This example is decorated with white gold, blue enamel, and 1,517 diamonds.

Vertical forward bow of trigger guard facilitates two-handed shooting

Rear sight

Ejector

Enlarged trigger guard

▲ HECKLER AND KOCH USP

Date 1993

Origin Germany

Barrel 4¼in (10.7cm)

Caliber 9mm Parabellum

The Universal Service Pistol (USP) was Heckler and Koch's answer to the Glock 17 (see p.266), and it, too, was largely made of plastic and employed the tried-and-tested Browning locking system. The USP could be configured in nine different ways—for instance, the trigger assemblies and magazines could be changed quickly.

Butt houses 10-round box magazine

Butt houses 17-round box magazine

▲ SMITH AND WESSON SIGMA

Date 1994

Origin US

Barrel 4in (10cm)

Caliber .40in Smith and Wesson

Smith and Wesson developed its Sigma pistol during 1993 and 1994. It features a frame made from a high-strength polymer and has an ergonomic grip containing a 17-round magazine. In common with some modern pistols, the frame has an integral accessory rail.

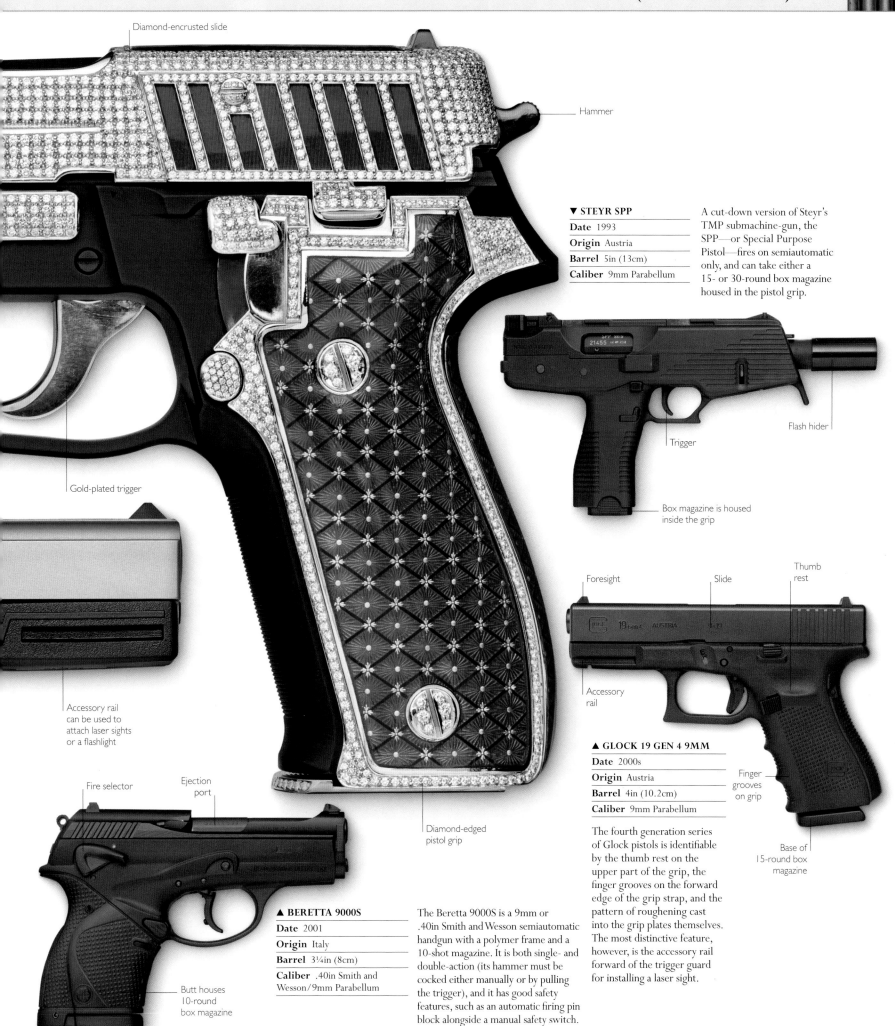

Diamond-encrusted slide

Hammer

Gold-plated trigger

Accessory rail can be used to attach laser sights or a flashlight

Fire selector

Ejection port

Butt houses 10-round box magazine

Diamond-edged pistol grip

▼ STEYR SPP

Date 1993

Origin Austria

Barrel 5in (13cm)

Caliber 9mm Parabellum

A cut-down version of Steyr's TMP submachine-gun, the SPP—or Special Purpose Pistol—fires on semiautomatic only, and can take either a 15- or 30-round box magazine housed in the pistol grip.

Trigger

Flash hider

Box magazine is housed inside the grip

Foresight

Slide

Thumb rest

Accessory rail

▲ GLOCK 19 GEN 4 9MM

Date 2000s

Origin Austria

Barrel 4in (10.2cm)

Caliber 9mm Parabellum

Finger grooves on grip

Base of 15-round box magazine

The fourth generation series of Glock pistols is identifiable by the thumb rest on the upper part of the grip, the finger grooves on the forward edge of the grip strap, and the pattern of roughening cast into the grip plates themselves. The most distinctive feature, however, is the accessory rail forward of the trigger guard for installing a laser sight.

▲ BERETTA 9000S

Date 2001

Origin Italy

Barrel 3¼in (8cm)

Caliber .40in Smith and Wesson/9mm Parabellum

The Beretta 9000S is a 9mm or .40in Smith and Wesson semiautomatic handgun with a polymer frame and a 10-shot magazine. It is both single- and double-action (its hammer must be cocked either manually or by pulling the trigger), and it has good safety features, such as an automatic firing pin block alongside a manual safety switch.

SUBMACHINE-GUNS (1946–65)

In the years following World War II, submachine-gun design was focused on the reduction of weight through the use of stampings, normally reinforced by ribbing. The French MAT 49, with its pivoting magazine, is an excellent example of this idea in use. Though most submachine-guns were chambered for the 9mm Parabellum cartridge, police versions, such as the Czech Skorpion, were usually designed for use with the less powerful 7.65mm pistol round. One of the more unusual designs was the Russian Stechkin APS, which, due to its modest weight, proved to be almost uncontrollable during use.

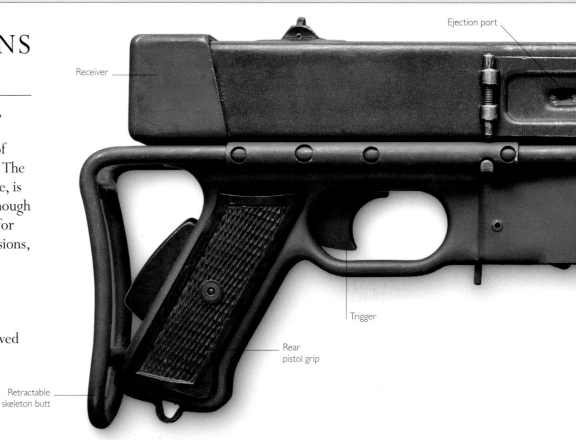

Ejection port

Receiver

Trigger

Rear pistol grip

Retractable skeleton butt

Rear sight

▼ UZI 9MM STEEL STOCK

Date	1950
Origin	Israel
Barrel	10¼in (26cm)
Caliber	9mm Parabellum

While the original version of the UZI (right) was fitted with a conventional wooden butt, this proved unwieldy in confined quarters, such as aircraft or armored vehicles. Consequently, a modified model was designed that had a collapsible metal butt that greatly reduced the firearm's overall length when folded.

ACTION ARMS. LTD

Phila.Pa.

SA 69741

FULL VIEW

Collapsible metal butt

Trigger guard

Perforated barrel shroud for air-cooling barrel and insulating user's hands

Foresight shroud

◀ MANUFACTURE NATIONALE D'ARMES DE TULLE (MAT) 49

Date 1950s

Origin France

Barrel 9in (23cm)

Caliber 9mm Parabellum

The MAT 49's distinctive feature is its pivoting magazine housing; in addition to making the weapon easier to conceal, it's a very positive safety device because it takes the magazine out of the firing position. The gun saw widespread combat use during the First Indochina War (1946–54) and the Algerian War (1954–62), as well as in the 1956 Suez Crisis.

32-round box magazine

Pivoting magazine housing doubles as fore grip

Cocking handle

Pressed-steel receiver

Rear sight in protective shroud

Replaceable barrel

Barrel-locking nut

Molded-plastic fore grip

Forward sling swivel

▲ UZI

Date 1950s

Origin Israel

Barrel 10¼in (26cm)

Caliber 9mm Parabellum

The secret of the UZI's legendary stability lies in its bolt being wrapped around its barrel; this brings the center of gravity forward and helps to cure the tendency for the barrel to rise during automatic fire. Heavy moving parts keep its rate of fire to a manageable 600 rounds per minute.

Rigid wooden butt

Cocking handle

Foresight

Barrel extension for use with sound suppressor

Combined safety and rate-of-fire selector

Skeleton stock folded forward

▶ SKORPION VZ61

Date 1959

Origin Czechoslovakia

Barrel 4½in (11.43cm)

Caliber 7.65mm

The VZ61, or Skorpion, submachine-gun was designed by Miroslav Rybar. It was intended for use by security personnel and police. By incorporating a telescoping bolt, Rybar was able to produce a weapon that was short overall, so it was ideal for use in cramped spaces or for carrying beneath clothing. Its vertically folding stock further minimized its length.

Trigger

Pistol grip

10-round or 20-round double-column box magazine in butt

▲ STECHKIN APS

Date 1960s

Origin USSR

Barrel 5in (12.7cm)

Caliber 9mm Makarov

The Stechkin was an unsuccessful attempt to produce a fully automatic pistol for use by security forces. Like the Makarov (see p.264), it was an unlocked recoil design based on the American Walther PP. In automatic mode, firing 750 rounds per minute, it was virtually uncontrollable.

20-round double-column box magazine in butt

SUBMACHINE-GUNS (1966–PRESENT)

In this period, **some of the guns** took on a futuristic look that almost masked their real purpose. The ability to conceal a gun became a prime factor in their construction. Consequently, many submachine-guns were little larger than pistols so that police SWAT and military personnel could carry them beneath civilian clothing. Heckler and Koch's MP5 (see p.257) is probably one of the most iconic submachine-guns produced at this time, and it has been employed in more than 40 countries. It gave way to the MP7 seen here.

Foldable skeleton stock

Pistol grip

▲ SKORPION VZ83

Date	1990s
Origin	Czechoslovakia
Barrel	4½in (11.5cm)
Caliber	9mm Kurz

The Skorpion VZ61 (see p.273) was modified following its introduction to accept larger cartridges, including 9mm Kurz and 9mm Parabellum, but did not go into production. In the 1990s, the rechambered versions were introduced officially. The version using the 9mm Kurz cartridge was called the VZ83.

Trigger guard

Sling

25- or 30-round detachable box magazine

▲ STEYR MPI 81

Date	1990s
Origin	Austria
Barrel	10¼in (26cm)
Caliber	9mm Parabellum

The MPi 81 has a conventional cocking handle that allows the bolt to be manually drawn rearward to cock the gun. This gun is a 9mm recoil-operated weapon with fire selection via trigger pressure—light pressure fires single shots while heavy pressure produces automatic fire, shooting 700 rounds per minute.

Rear sight

Picatinny rail (a rail for mounting accessories on the gun)

Retractable butt

Pistol grip

Optical sight

Muzzle

Transparent 50-round
detachable box magazine

Injection-molded plastic
butt contains receiver,
bolt, and lock

Trigger

▲ **FN P90**

Date 1990

Origin Belgium

Barrel 10¼in (26.3cm)

Caliber 5.7 × 28mm

A ground-breaking personal defense
weapon (PDW), the FN P90's non-
mechanical body components are
all molded from plastic, and its unique
horizontal ammunition feed allows the
magazine to be incorporated within
the receiver.

Advanced collimator
(red-dot) sight

Foresight

End of action body

Ambidextrous
control

Folding vertical
fore grip

Flash
hider

▲ **HECKLER AND KOCH MP7**

Date 2001

Origin Germany

Barrel 7in (18cm)

Caliber 4.6 × 30mm

Similar in concept to the FN P90 (above), the MP7
is a "personal defense weapon" that fires one of the
new-generation reduced caliber, high-velocity
rounds (950 rounds per minute), in this case the
4.6 x 30mm cartridge. It has a fully ambidextrous
design—having controls, such as the safety switch
and decocking device, on both sides, accommodating
both left-and right-handed operators.

Finger
grooves

FULL VIEW

SHOWCASE

MAC M-10

Manufactured by the Military Armaments Corporation, the M-10 submachine-gun was designed by Gordon Ingram in 1964. Although it was only in production from 1970 to 1973, its stamped steel components, compact design, and two-stage sound suppressor provided a successful blueprint for future arms design. This weapon was extensively used by military special forces because of its light weight and highly effective sound suppressor—features that made it a perfect fit for clandestine operations.

FULL VIEW (RIGHT SIDE)

MAC M-10

Date 1970–1973

Origin US

Barrel 2in (5cm)

Caliber 9mm Parabellum

This weapon is officially called the M-10, but since many gun collectors and writers used the name "Mac-10," this designation has become more common. The reason for the gun's popularity lay in its sound suppressor, which made it so quiet that the bolt could be heard functioning. The gun was widely used by US special forces and CIA agents during the Vietnam War (1955–75).

▶ **UPPER RECEIVER AND BARREL ASSEMBLY**

The upper receiver contains the cocking handle, bolt housing, and recoil spring. It also houses the ejection port along the right side, corresponding to the placement of the magazine beneath it. Mounted on the upper receiver is an unusual threaded barrel. The thread supports the sound suppressor, which can be easily screwed on to reduce the sound of firing without affecting the velocity of a bullet.

▶ **SHOULDER STOCK FOLDED AND UNFOLDED**

The M-10 is fitted with a hinged tubular steel shoulder stock that slides into the lower receiver assembly. The stock can be pulled out by pressing the release button at the bottom of the assembly, and it can be folded downward to act as a shoulder support, steadying the gun during firing.

1

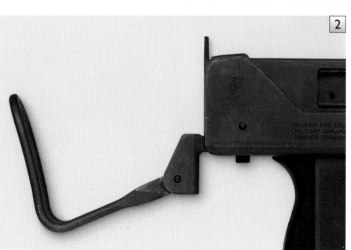

2

Recoil spring

Rear sight

Bolt guide

Recoil spring and guide attachment plate

INGRAM M10, CAL 9MM PAR
MILITARY ARMAMENT CORP
POWDER SPRINGS, GA, USA

Shoulder stock release button

1 2

Shoulder stock attaches here

Detachable 32-round box magazine

◄ SOUND SUPPRESSOR

The sound suppressor is fitted onto the barrel and has a two-stage design. The first stage consists of a large cylinder that is fed into the second stage, which is a longer, slimmer cylinder. This two-stage design baffles the air from rushing into the barrel directly, which greatly reduces the sound emitted on firing a cartridge. The sound suppressor does not add much to the weight of the gun, allowing it to be fired single-handed.

► COCKING HANDLE

The cocking handle is situated along the top of the receiver. A notch cut through the handle ensures an unobstructed line of sight between the user and his target. The user pulls the cocking handle backward to ready the gun for firing the first time. The handle can be turned through 90-degrees to lock the bolt when the weapon is not in use.

Notch

Foresight

3

Sound suppressor fits onto the threaded barrel

Ejection port

Bracket for attachment of sling strap, which helps to control muzzle rise during fully automatic fire

◄ BOLT AND RECOIL SPRING

This is an "open-bolt" recoil-action gun, in which the bolt is held at the rear when the gun is not firing. The bolt is driven to the rear by moving the cocking handle backward. On pulling the trigger, the recoil spring drives the bolt forward. As it advances, the bolt strips a cartridge, chambers it, and fires it, then flies back, ejecting the spent cartridge. This cycle is repeated automatically during fully automatic fire (when the trigger is kept pulled). When firing from an open bolt, the ejection port is left open to release gases during the firing process. This prevents the breech chamber from overheating. Open-bolt guns, however, are not as accurate as closed-bolt guns, in which the bolt is closed and chambered at rest. As in the case of most automatic guns, this weapon relies more on rate of fire (1,090 rounds per minute in this case) than accuracy. It was originally designed for covert operations, especially during the Vietnam War.

Housing contains bolt

◄ LOWER RECEIVER ASSEMBLY

Made from steel stampings, the lower receiver assembly incorporates the magazine as part of the grip. A simple rear sight is attached to the uppermost rear part of the assembly.

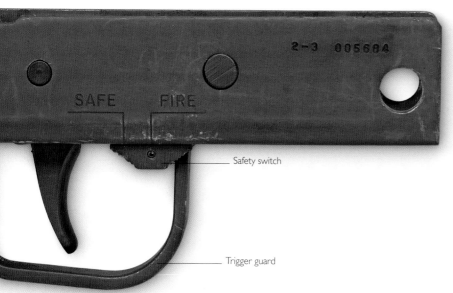

Safety switch

Trigger guard

HUNTING RIFLES (BOLT ACTION)

Although bolt-action sporting rifles have changed little since they were introduced in the 19th century, they continue to be extremely popular. This is primarily because these guns are very dependable and rarely malfunction, a consideration of some importance when hunting dangerous game. Cosmetically, some modern sporting rifles differ from their predecessors in the use of synthetic materials for their stocks. This eliminates any possibility of breakage, which is sometimes encountered with wood.

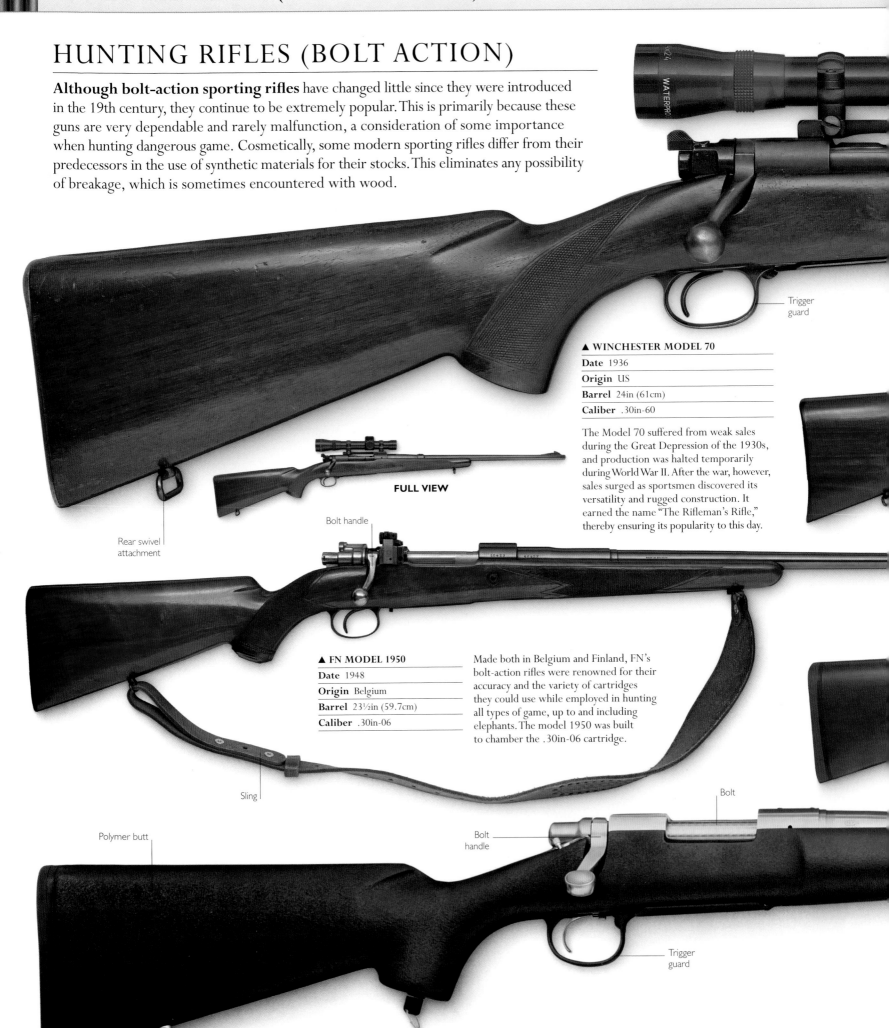

Trigger guard

▲ **WINCHESTER MODEL 70**

Date	1936
Origin	US
Barrel	24in (61cm)
Caliber	.30in-60

The Model 70 suffered from weak sales during the Great Depression of the 1930s, and production was halted temporarily during World War II. After the war, however, sales surged as sportsmen discovered its versatility and rugged construction. It earned the name "The Rifleman's Rifle," thereby ensuring its popularity to this day.

FULL VIEW

Rear swivel attachment

Bolt handle

▲ **FN MODEL 1950**

Date	1948
Origin	Belgium
Barrel	23½in (59.7cm)
Caliber	.30in-06

Made both in Belgium and Finland, FN's bolt-action rifles were renowned for their accuracy and the variety of cartridges they could use while employed in hunting all types of game, up to and including elephants. The model 1950 was built to chamber the .30in-06 cartridge.

Sling

Bolt

Polymer butt

Bolt handle

Trigger guard

Optical sight

Checkered forestock

Front swivel attachment

Optical sight

Abbreviated forestock

Double set trigger

Detachable magazine

▲ BRNO MODEL 465

Date	1949
Origin	Czechoslovakia
Barrel	23in (58.4cm)
Caliber	.22in Hornet

This bolt-action, Mauser-style rifle, which derives its action from the Mauser Model 1898 (see p.153), was designed for hunting light game or vermin with either open or telescopic sights. Its lightweight and attractive profile made it a favorite weapon among hunters. Featuring a detachable magazine, it could be loaded and fired with considerable speed. It had a double set trigger. This system increased accuracy by minimizing physical movement at the time of firing. Pulling the rear trigger held the sear, following which the slightest pressure on the forward trigger caused the sear to disengage, releasing the firing pin.

Foresight

Elevation adjustment

Fixed rear sight

Checkered semi-pistol grip

Fluted barrel

▲ RUGER 77

Date	1983
Origin	US
Barrel	22in (55.8cm)
Caliber	7 × 57mm

The Sturm, Ruger, and Company Model 77 is truly a product of modern technology. It is built using wax investment castings that require a minimum amount of machining. More importantly, the barrel is rifled using a proprietary process that makes the rifle very accurate.

Front sling swivel

▲ REMINGTON MODEL 700 ETRON-X

Date	2005
Origin	US
Barrel	26in (66cm)
Caliber	.243in Winchester

The Model 700 Etron-X features electric primer ignition. Pulling the trigger sends a pulse of electricity that ignites the cartridge's electric-sensitive primer. This essentially eliminates any movement during the firing process, significantly increasing the gun's accuracy as well as its lock time.

HUNTING RIFLES (OTHER TYPES)

Repeating rifles employing bolt action are commonly used by hunters. Other kinds of hunting rifles include repeaters operated by lever action (see pp.114–15), self-loading rifles (see pp.176–77), and even some that fire only single shots. Some rifles, such as the venerable Winchester Model 94, continue to be extremely popular despite having been in production for over a century. Others, the Sturm Ruger No. 1 being a prime example, incorporate designs that reflect new methods of construction and manufacture. Some recent rifles have been built using nylon components or operating systems developed in the late 1900s.

Wooden butt

▼ WINCHESTER MODEL 1894

Date	1945
Origin	US
Barrel	20in (50.8cm)
Caliber	.30in WCF

The durability of this deer-hunting rifle has been appreciated by hunters since its introduction in 1894. Since then, very few changes have been made to its design aside from cosmetic modifications, such as its finish. This particular unit was produced in 1945. Easy to use and lightweight, this gun has proven its worth in the forests of North America, the African veldt, and even the vastness of Siberia. Loaded by a swift movement of the wrist to lower and then raise the operating lever, the Model 1894 can be fired quickly if the need arises.

Hammer

Loading port

Under-lever

Receiver

Safety catch

Trigger guard

Recoil pad fitted to butt

Synthetic butt

Optical sight

Foresight

Trigger guard

Detachable box magazine

Checkered forestock

▲ WINCHESTER MODEL 100

Date	1961
Origin	US
Barrel	22in (55.8cm)
Caliber	.308in Winchester

Fed by a detachable box magazine, the Model 100 was one of the first successful self-loading sporting rifles. Chambered for the .308in Winchester cartridge, it has proved to be a very popular rifle for deer hunting in some parts of North America.

Barrel band

Magazine tube

▼ REMINGTON NYLON 66

Date	1959
Origin	US
Barrel	19½in (49.5cm)
Caliber	.22in

FULL VIEW

In 1959, the Remington Arms Company broke with tradition and introduced a self-loading rifle with a stock made entirely from the Dupont Chemical Corporation's Zytel-101 nylon. Offered in three colors (Mohawk Brown, Apache Black, and Seneca Green), the new firearm weighed just 4lb (1.8kg). It ushered in a new era in gunmaking because of its light weight and use of new materials.

Adjustable rear sight

Zytel-101 nylon stock

Optical sight

Blued barrel

Foresight

Hammer

Forestock

Under-lever

Lever latch

▲ STURM RUGER NO. 1

Date	c.1999
Origin	US
Barrel	24in (61cm)
Caliber	.375in Magnum

This gun was designed by William B. Ruger. Built using wax investment castings (see p.264), the No. 1 had improved lock-work and a safety meeting the more stringent requirements of today's regulations, such as the presence of two concurrent safety mechanisms—one preventing the hammer from moving and the second blocking trigger movement. This weapon incorporates blocks for the hammer and trigger. Older arms usually had one or the other.

DOUBLE-BARRELED SHOTGUNS

Since the 18th century, double-barreled shotguns have been characterized by a pair of barrels placed horizontally next to each other. By aligning them carefully, the shot patterns created during firing can be made to converge at some specific point forward of the muzzle, such as 50 yards (46m). Recently, over-and-under guns (shotguns having their barrels set vertically one above the other) have gained popularity, especially among trapshooters and skeet shooters. The shot patterns of over-and-under guns can be made to converge as well, albeit vertically, thus allowing shooters used to rifles more opportunities of hitting a clay pigeon or a live bird.

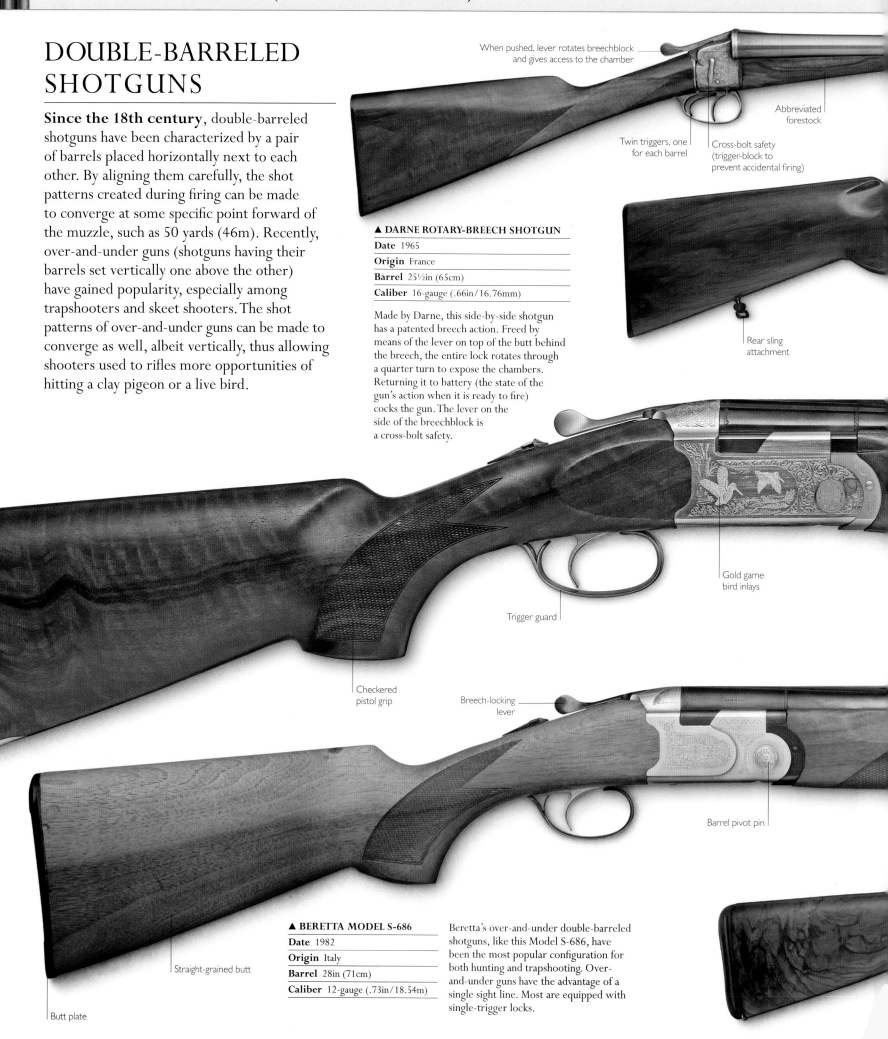

When pushed, lever rotates breechblock and gives access to the chamber

Twin triggers, one for each barrel

Cross-bolt safety (trigger-block to prevent accidental firing)

Abbreviated forestock

Rear sling attachment

▲ DARNE ROTARY-BREECH SHOTGUN

Date	1965
Origin	France
Barrel	25½in (65cm)
Caliber	16-gauge (.66in/16.76mm)

Made by Darne, this side-by-side shotgun has a patented breech action. Freed by means of the lever on top of the butt behind the breech, the entire lock rotates through a quarter turn to expose the chambers. Returning it to battery (the state of the gun's action when it is ready to fire) cocks the gun. The lever on the side of the breechblock is a cross-bolt safety.

Gold game bird inlays

Trigger guard

Checkered pistol grip

Breech-locking lever

Barrel pivot pin

Straight-grained butt

▲ BERETTA MODEL S-686

Date	1982
Origin	Italy
Barrel	28in (71cm)
Caliber	12-gauge (.73in/18.54m)

Beretta's over-and-under double-barreled shotguns, like this Model S-686, have been the most popular configuration for both hunting and trapshooting. Over-and-under guns have the advantage of a single sight line. Most are equipped with single-trigger locks.

Butt plate

Right barrel

Breech-locking lever

Ventilated barrel rib (for air-cooling the barrel)

One barrel on top of the other

Checkered forestock

Trigger guard

▲ ANSCHUTZ–MIROKU OVER/UNDER SHOTGUN

Date 1998

Origin Japan

Barrel 28in (71cm)

Caliber 12-gauge (.73in/18.54mm)

To reduce manufacturing costs, a number of Western arms companies partnered with the Miroku Corporation of Nankoku, Kochi Prefecture in Japan, to produce rifles and shotguns bearing their names. One such cooperative product is the Anschutz-Miroku shotgun. This moderately priced sporting arm is highly regarded because of its solid construction and ease of maintenance.

Checkered forestock

Ventilated barrel rib

▲ BERETTA ULTRA LIGHT DELUXE

FULL VIEW

Date 1998

Origin Italy

Barrel 28in (71cm)

Caliber 12-gauge (.73in/18.54mm)

This attractive gun was designed for shooting upland birds, such as pheasants and quail. It has an aluminum frame that makes the gun light enough for hunters to carry around all day. The strength of the action, however, is not compromised because the breech face and shoulders are made of titanium. To increase demand for the gun, it features machine-cut engraving and gold inlays.

Ventilated barrel rib

Incised checkering on abbreviated forestock

Checkered forestock

Trigger guard

Checkered pistol grip

▲ BERETTA 686 ONYX PRO

Date 2003

Origin Italy

Barrel 26in (66cm)

Caliber 12-gauge (.73in/18.54mm)

This shotgun features laser-cut checkering on the pistol grip and forestock. Although designed for hunting, its barrels are equipped with screw-in chokes that modify the bore diameter to change shot patterns, which makes the gun fit for other purposes, too, such as trapshooting or skeet shooting.

SHOTGUNS (REPEATING AND SELF-LOADING)

Repeating shotguns, usually equipped with tubular magazines carrying 3–11 cartridges, can fire several rounds in quick succession. The repeating action is commonly a slide, or a pump—a slide bar attached to the forestock which moves the breechblock back and forth. Some shotguns are self-loading, driving their autoloading cycle by gas or recoil operation. Repeating and self-loading shotguns have several applications. For sporting purposes, they allow a hunter to fire several rounds in quick succession at rising birds. This feature also makes them ideal for military or police use, when multiple attackers might be met at close quarters.

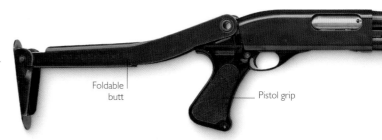

Foldable butt

Pistol grip

▲ REMINGTON WINGMASTER PUMP-ACTION SHOTGUN

Date	1951
Origin	US
Barrel	20in (51cm)
Caliber	13-gauge (.748in/19mm)

Fitted with a folding stock and rear pistol grip, this shotgun epitomizes the American police shotgun. Compact and easily stored, it can be quickly brought into service if needed. Its extended magazine also allows it to be loaded with about 4–5 more cartridges than similar sporting versions.

Ventilated barrel rib (for air-cooling the barrel)

▲ WINCHESTER MODEL 50

Date	1954
Origin	US
Barrel	30in (76.2cm)
Caliber	13-gauge (.748in/19mm)

Designed jointly by J. L. Lochhead and David M. Williams, the Winchester Model 50 was a recoil-operated weapon. The gun harnessed the recoil energy of the fired round to power its self-loading cycle.

Ejection port

Wooden butt

Recoil pad

Recoil pad

▲ STEVENS MODEL 77E

Date	1960s
Origin	US
Barrel	20in (51cm)
Caliber	12-gauge (.73in/18.5mm)

The Stevens 77E was a popular combat shotgun during the Vietnam War. It was a 12-gauge weapon, and its robust pump action could withstand the worst of the jungle environment. In total, 69,700 77Es were produced for military use in Southeast Asia during the 1960s.

Rear sling attachment

Stock folds upward through 180 degrees

Bolt

Slide handle/forestock

Foresight

Tubular eight-round magazine

Section of stock folds down to become a shoulder piece

▲ FRANCHI SPAS 12

Date	1978
Origin	Italy
Barrel	21½in (54.5cm)
Caliber	12-gauge (.73in/18.5mm)

Developed as a close-combat weapon for both police and military, the Special Purpose Automatic Shotgun (SPAS) is a gas-operated, semiautomatic (with an optional pump mode) and holds eight rounds in an under-barrel tubular magazine. Military or police guns frequently had folding stocks, which allowed the guns to be stored in confined spaces, such as armored vehicles or squad cars.

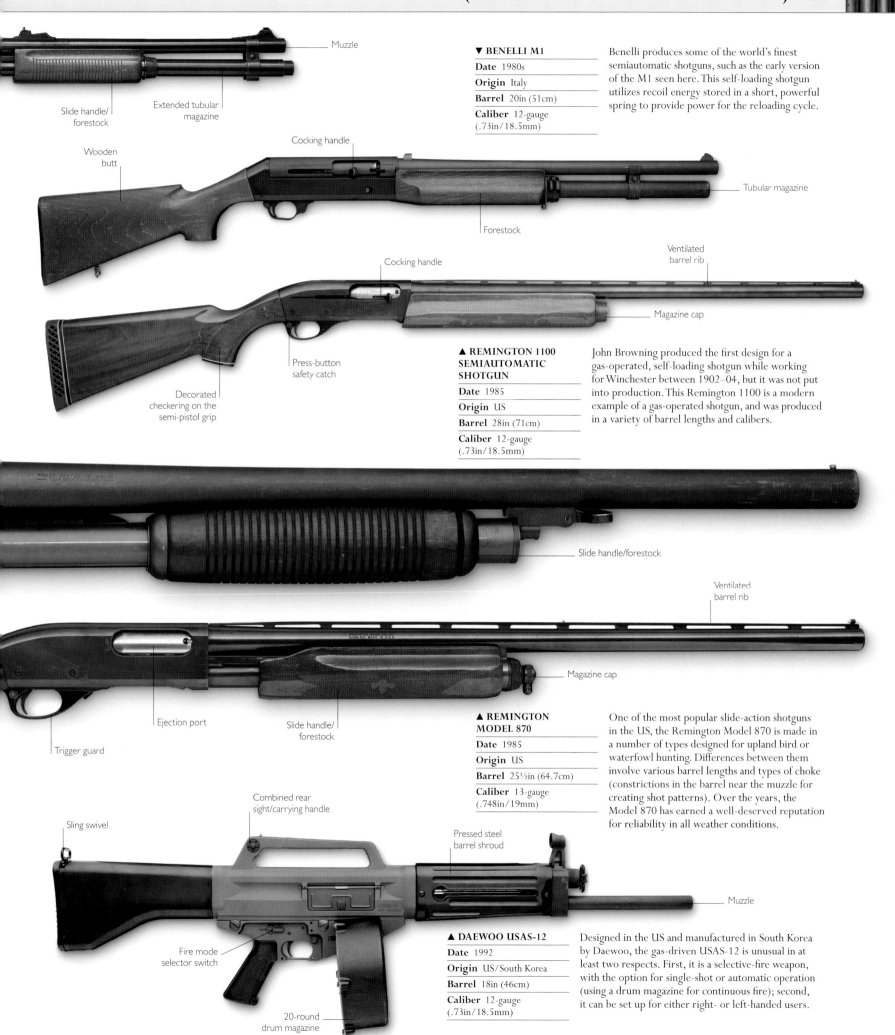

Muzzle

Slide handle/forestock

Extended tubular magazine

▼ BENELLI M1

Date	1980s
Origin	Italy
Barrel	20in (51cm)
Caliber	12-gauge (.73in/18.5mm)

Benelli produces some of the world's finest semiautomatic shotguns, such as the early version of the M1 seen here. This self-loading shotgun utilizes recoil energy stored in a short, powerful spring to provide power for the reloading cycle.

Wooden butt

Cocking handle

Tubular magazine

Forestock

Cocking handle

Ventilated barrel rib

Magazine cap

Decorated checkering on the semi-pistol grip

Press-button safety catch

▲ REMINGTON 1100 SEMIAUTOMATIC SHOTGUN

Date	1985
Origin	US
Barrel	28in (71cm)
Caliber	12-gauge (.73in/18.5mm)

John Browning produced the first design for a gas-operated, self-loading shotgun while working for Winchester between 1902–04, but it was not put into production. This Remington 1100 is a modern example of a gas-operated shotgun, and was produced in a variety of barrel lengths and calibers.

Slide handle/forestock

Ventilated barrel rib

Trigger guard

Ejection port

Slide handle/forestock

Magazine cap

▲ REMINGTON MODEL 870

Date	1985
Origin	US
Barrel	25½in (64.7cm)
Caliber	13-gauge (.748in/19mm)

One of the most popular slide-action shotguns in the US, the Remington Model 870 is made in a number of types designed for upland bird or waterfowl hunting. Differences between them involve various barrel lengths and types of choke (constrictions in the barrel near the muzzle for creating shot patterns). Over the years, the Model 870 has earned a well-deserved reputation for reliability in all weather conditions.

Sling swivel

Combined rear sight/carrying handle

Pressed steel barrel shroud

Muzzle

Fire mode selector switch

20-round drum magazine

▲ DAEWOO USAS-12

Date	1992
Origin	US/South Korea
Barrel	18in (46cm)
Caliber	12-gauge (.73in/18.5mm)

Designed in the US and manufactured in South Korea by Daewoo, the gas-driven USAS-12 is unusual in at least two respects. First, it is a selective-fire weapon, with the option for single-shot or automatic operation (using a drum magazine for continuous fire); second, it can be set up for either right- or left-handed users.

MODERN SHOTGUNS
Established in 1835 in London, Holland and
Holland produces some of the most coveted
modern sporting rifles and shotguns. It is known
for the restrained elegance of its arms, whether
gold inlaid or engraved, as seen on this shotgun.

IMPROVISED ARMS

During insurgencies and revolutions, some combatants may not have production arms at their disposal. They may use handmade arms that have been produced based on necessity. These firearms vary enormously in their quality and performance—from crude guns made of metal pipes to sophisticated submachine-guns. These weapons are often poor in construction and are generally unable to withstand the pressure developed during the ignition of a cartridge. This makes them likely to blow up when in operation.

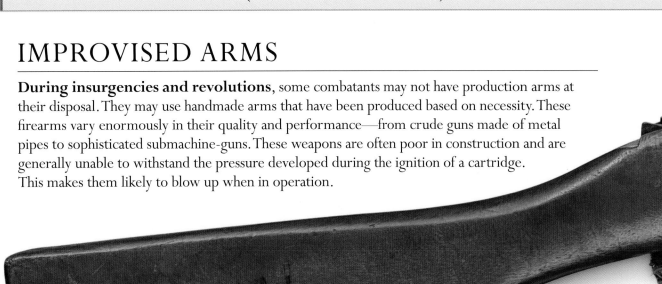

Trigger

Bolt handle

Stock reminiscent of a Lee-Enfield

Cartridge case from 20mm cannon shell serves as barrel

Hole used to ignite charge

Muzzle

Wire wrapping secures barrel to stock

Perforated barrel shroud serves as the fore grip

Smoothbore barrel

Foresight

▶ EOKA PISTOL

Date 1950s

Origin Cyprus

Barrel 4¼in (11cm)

Caliber 12-gauge (.73in/18.54mm)

The *Ethniki Organosis Kyprion Agoniston*, or National Organization of Cypriot Fighters (EOKA), fought a guerrilla campaign against British colonial rule on the Mediterranean island of Cyprus from 1955 to 1959. During that time, they created small numbers of crude guns. This pistol is so crudely fashioned that it barely qualifies for the name. The barrel is a spent 20mm caliber cartridge case, secured to a rough-hewn wooden frame. Since it had no rifling, the most effective way of firing would have been by putting the "muzzle" up against the enemy's body before the gun was discharged.

Roughly carved wooden grip

Rear sight

Trigger

Cocking handle

Barrel

Break-open hinge

Pistol grip

◀ EOKA SHOTPISTOL

Date 1950s

Origin Cyprus

Barrel 4¼in (11cm)

Caliber 12-gauge (.73in/18.54mm)

Eoka built this weapon in the 1950s. Made from iron piping, it has a simple break-open action. It fires a shotgun cartridge by means of a spring-loaded plunger.

Barrel band
and rear sight

Unrifled barrel

FULL VIEW

Sling

▲ MAU-MAU CARBINE

Date 1950s

Origin Kenya

Barrel 20¼in (51.2cm)

Caliber .303in

Somewhat more sophisticated than many of its type, this short-barreled, bolt-action, single-shot carbine was made in Kenya during the time of the Mau-Mau insurrection against British rule in the 1950s. Most of the improvised weapons made by the rebels, the majority of whom were from the Kikuyu people, exploded when they were fired.

Magazine
port

Magazine
release catch

Square-section
receiver

Safety catch

▲ LOYALIST SUBMACHINE-GUN

Date 1970s

Origin UK

Barrel 7¾in (20cm)

Caliber 9mm Parabellum

Modeled on the vintage Sten gun from World War II, this homemade machine-pistol was produced by a loyalist paramilitary group in Northern Ireland. The barrel shroud and receiver have been fashioned from square-framed tubing. This gun uses a magazine from an L2 Stirling submachine-gun.

Pistol grip

Barrel-retaining
band

Rear sight

Hammer

Trigger

Retaining
bolt

Trigger

◄ SOUTH AFRICAN PISTOL

Date 1980s

Origin South Africa

Barrel 8¾in (22cm)

Caliber Not known

This homemade pistol, recovered in South Africa, is rather more sophisticated than it appears at first sight. It has a simple, single-action lock linking trigger and hammer, perhaps derived from a child's toy pistol, and can be used single-handedly. It would have been so inaccurate as to render the rudimentary sights redundant.

FERDINAND RITTER VON MANNLICHER

STEYR-MANNLICHER

Steyr-Mannlicher, a celebrated Austrian firearms manufacturer, began as a very traditional maker of weapons, but has also embraced innovation and change. The company's founder, Josef Werndl, came from a family of metalworkers, so he could draw on experience stretching back over many generations. However, his company made rapid progress in the 1860s, when Werndl began to collaborate with Austrian designer Ferdinand Ritter von Mannlicher, especially on innovative rifle designs.

The city of Steyr, near the confluence of the Enns and Steyr rivers in Upper Austria, has been a metalworking center since at least the 13th century. Weapons manufacture became a major industry in the area around the time of the Thirty Years' War (1618–48), when the region supplied muskets and pistols to the Hapsburg Army. During the 19th century, this tradition continued, and one Steyr metalworker, Leopold Werndl, sent his son Josef to the US to learn about the latest ideas in firearms production. By the late 1860s, Josef was in control of the family firm and was delivering thousands of breech-loading rifles to the Austro-Hungarian Army.

ROOTS IN TRADITION

Josef Werndl's company, the Österreichische Waffenfabriksgesellschaft (Austrian Weapons Manufacturing Company), prospered in the second half of the 19th century, combining modern production methods with a traditional use of craft skills. A turning point came in 1885, when the Austro-Hungarian Army adopted its new bolt-action rifle, which was the brainchild of Ferdinand Ritter von Mannlicher. Mannlicher, who also invented the en bloc clip for loading cartridges, eventually became the company's chief designer, and the firm's name changed to Steyr-Mannlicher. He was successful again with the Mannlicher Schönauer full-stock rifle, a hunting weapon that he designed with Otto Schönauer, the director

of the company. By this time, the company had established a prime position in both sporting and military markets.

Mannlicher died in 1904, but the company continued to build on its tradition and introduced new models, notably pistols, including the self-loading M1912, and also built a new factory, much larger than its predecessor and with the latest machinery. This new plant enabled the company to turn out firearms in large numbers, and was in place just in time to fulfill the huge surge in demand triggered by World War I. The firm

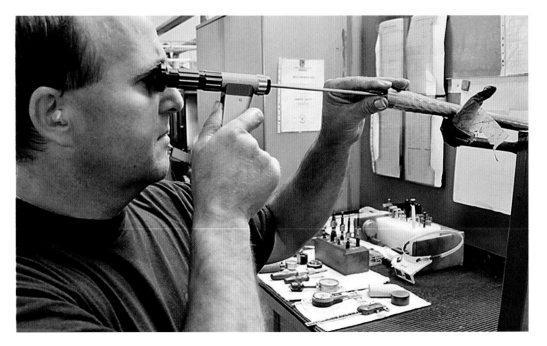

▲ QUALITY CONTROL
Careful quality control is at the heart of successful firearms production. Here a worker undertakes a manual check on a gun barrel at the Steyr-Mannlicher factory.

soon employed around 15,000 people and even branched out into products such as bicycles and aircraft engines. However, the postwar treaty signed by Austria severely diminished the country and imposed economic limitations on it. The size of its army and the production of weapons were restricted. As a result, Steyr-Mannlicher faced difficulties. It only staved off bankruptcy by concentrating on products other than weapons, particularly bicycles and cars, which it had begun to manufacture during the war.

THE MODERN COMPANY

Large-volume production of firearms began again at Steyr during World War II, but the factory suffered damage from Allied bombing. After the war, the production of weapons was

"There is no figure in the history of **firearms** who can approach the great Austrian inventor, **Ferdinand Ritter von Mannlicher …**"

ATTRIBUTED TO **W. H. B. SMITH, AUTHOR OF *"SMALL ARMS OF THE WORLD"***

M1905

SSG-69, 1969

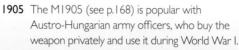

AUG, 1978

1864 Josef Werndl and his brother Franz found their first company (Österreichische Waffenfabriksgesellschaft), which later becomes Steyr-Mannlicher.

1867 The Austro-Hungarian Army begins to take delivery of Werndl's breech-loading rifles.

1885 Mannlicher's bolt-action rifle is accepted by the Austro-Hungarian Army.

1905 The M1905 (see p.168) is popular with Austro-Hungarian army officers, who buy the weapon privately and use it during World War I.

1914 On the eve of World War I, Steyr-Mannlicher completes its large new factory building.

1915 In a move toward diversification, Steyr begins to manufacture automobiles.

1969 The SSG-69 (see p.252) sniper rifle features a cold hammer-forged barrel and rotary five-round magazine.

1978 The Steyr AUG assault rifle (see p.250) is launched; it will spawn a huge number of variants and see very wide service.

curtailed, but in 1950, the company received the go-ahead for the manufacture of hunting rifles. Since then, it has built up an impressive range of weapons for hunters, together with a number of sporting rifles and pistols. When it

▼ MILITARY USE
Some militaries in Southeast Asia use Steyr rifles. Women members of the Royal Malaysian Air Force can be seen marching with Steyr AUG assault rifles during the 48th Malaysian Independence Day celebrations in 2005.

reentered the field of military weapons, it produced a new assault rifle—a "bullpup" design making extensive use of synthetic materials. In Austria, this model became known as the StG 77, while in foreign markets it is the AUG (*Armee Universal Gewehr*) (see p.250). The company has produced this firearm in a range of models, along with sniper rifles such as the Steyr SSG-69 (see p.252); submachine-guns such as the Steyr MPI 81 (see p.274); and

pistols such as the Steyr SPP (see p.271). To take full commercial advantage of these products, Steyr-Mannlicher adapted to the business conditions of the late-20th century by adopting an international approach—licensing production overseas (for example, to Australia and Malaysia) and exporting widely. As a result, the company continues to be a prominent player in the 21st-century firearms market.

SPECIALIZED AND MULTIPURPOSE ARMS

Multipurpose firearms have existed since the 17th century, when pistols and long arms were used for launching grenades for the first time. What has changed over the intervening centuries is the lethality of those projectiles and the need to launch them farther to protect the firer. Other specialized arms were built ruggedly for survival in the event of aircraft crashes, or other similar incidents where a virtually indestructible firearm might be needed. Precision target shooting also demands arms specifically designed for that purpose, and often they bear little resemblance to other firearms. One example of such a weapon is the Hammerli 162, which is fired by an electronic trigger.

Receiver

10-round magazine

Skeleton stock

▲ M59/66 WITH GRENADE-LAUNCHER

Date	1949
Origin	Soviet Union
Barrel	20in (50.8cm)
Caliber	7.62 × 39mm
Grenade range	330ft (100m)
Grenade type	Antitank

This was the Red Army's standard antitank grenade launcher during the 1950s. Mounted on the self-loading M59/66 assault rifle, it employed an overpowered blank cartridge to launch a grenade. While effective, it proved unpopular due to the disastrous effect of mistakenly chambering a regular live round while the grenade is still attached.

Rear aperture sight

Bolt handle

Barrel unit

Magazine

Hollow butt

▲ AR7 EXPLORER ARMALITE SURVIVAL RIFLE

Date	1958
Origin	US
Barrel	16in (40cm)
Caliber	.22in

The AR7 was designed by Eugene Stoner in 1959 as a survival rifle for USAF aircrew. A semiautomatic .22in weapon, it ingeniously breaks down into four main parts—the barrel, action, magazine, and water-resistant stock (which can float in water).

Receiver cover

Butt

Rifle trigger

30-round magazine

Foresight in annular shroud

Mounting for standard NATO sights

◀ HECKLER AND KOCH MP5A5

Date	1966
Origin	Germany
Barrel	8¾in (22.5cm)
Caliber	9mm Parabellum
Grenade range	450ft (137m)
Grenade type	Antipersonnel

The MP5A5 is a plastic-stock version of the MP5 (see p.257). Here the multipurpose arm is featured in combination with a mounted grenade-launcher built by the British company ISTEC.

Grenade-launcher safety catch

Safety catch and rate-of-fire selector

Stabilizing tail fins

Shaped-charge warhead

Simonov grenade

Padded cheek rest

Stock/action hinge

▼ ITHACA M6 SURVIVAL RIFLE

Date 1975

Origin US

Barrel 14in (35.5cm)

Caliber .22in/.410in

The Ithaca M6 survival rifle combines a rifled .22in upper barrel with a lower .410in shotgun barrel, the stock having storage capacity for 15 .22in cartridges and four shotgun shells. The gun originally had a folding design, while current models break down into two pieces. This rifle typifies survival arms in its extremely simple construction and collapsible form, which minimizes weight as well as storage size.

Upper barrel

Lower barrel

Forestock with launcher mounted on underside

Launcher foresight in the folded position

Foresight

Rifled grenade-launcher tube

Pistol grip

Rifle trigger

Magazine

▲ M16A1 WITH M203A2 GRENADE-LAUNCHER

Date 1990s

Origin US

Barrel 12in (30.5cm)

Caliber 5.56 × 45mm

Grenade range 500ft (150m)

Grenade type Antipersonnel

This version of the M16 (see pp.244–45) is equipped with an M203A2 grenade-launcher. By fitting a standard infantry rifle with a grenade-launcher, a two-fold purpose is served—providing direct fire (as a rifle) and allowing projectiles to be fired over long range (via the grenade-launcher).

Upper hand guard

Gas tube

Muzzle brake for venting propellant gas emitted by firing of cartridge

БГ15NА61429

Grenade-launcher trigger

Rifled grenade-launcher tube

GP25 GRENADE

▲ AK74 WITH GP25 GRENADE-LAUNCHER

Date 1978

Origin Soviet Union

Barrel 16¼in (41.5cm)

Caliber 5.45 × 39mm

Grenade range 500ft (150m)

Grenade type Antipersonnel

The AK74 (see p.246) is an improved version of the AK47, rechambered for the high-velocity intermediate 5.45 × 39mm cartridge. The example shown here has been equipped with a GP25 grenade-launcher. Aside from being an infantry arm, the AK74 with the GP25 is a multipurpose weapon designed for defensive and offensive actions.

Match grade foresight

Contoured grip

Rear sight

HAMMERLI

Trigger guard

▲ HAMMERLI 162 TARGET

Date 1992

Origin Switzerland

Barrel 11in (28cm)

Caliber .22in

Hammerli make a range of high-accuracy .22in target pistols. The 162 features an electronic trigger system with a hair-trigger adjustment, and is powered by batteries that hold enough power for around 10,000 discharges.

GRENADE-LAUNCHERS

The highly fluid character of modern warfare
has necessitated mortars that are portable or even
handheld infantry weapons. More often termed
grenade-launchers, these mortars are designed to
provide immediate support fire. The simplest are
the American M79 and the South African Mechem.
In contrast, the Russian AGS-17 almost enters the
artillery class with its heavy fixed mount. The Rocket
Propelled Grenade (RPG) launcher is now the most
common launcher due to its simplicity and effectiveness.
Its shaped-charge projectiles allow a single combatant
to disable or destroy armored vehicles and fixed
positions such as buildings.

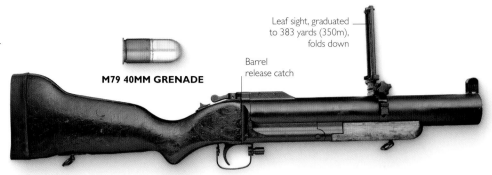

M79 40MM GRENADE

Leaf sight, graduated
to 383 yards (350m),
folds down

Barrel
release catch

▲ M79 "BLOOPER"

Date	1961
Origin	US
Barrel	12in (30.5cm)
Caliber	40mm
Grenade range	328 yards (300m)

Nicknamed the "Blooper" because of the distinctive
sound it makes when fired, the M79 grenade-launcher
bridged the gap between short-range hand grenades
and the long-range mortar. In addition to firing
high-explosive grenades, the M79 could fire
antipersonnel, smoke, and illuminating rounds.
During the Vietnam War, two M79s were issued to
each US infantry squad consisting of nine men.

Rifle barrel
has cooling fins

FULL VIEW

Drum contains 29
30mm grenades in a
non-disintegrating belt

▼ RPG-7V

Date	1961
Origin	Soviet Union
Barrel	37½in (95cm)
Caliber	40mm
Grenade range	547 yards (500m)

The RPG-7V can be used with a variety of
grenades, including antipersonnel, fuel-air
explosive, and high-explosive antitank ones.
Regardless of the grenade type, the projectiles
have two propelling charges, one for launching
and the other for flight.

Barrel contains tail of
missile, with launching
cartridge and stabilizing
fins folded

Optical sight graduated
to 547 yards (500m)

Exhaust gas
collector/diffuser

Muzzle,
in which
projectile
is loaded

Trigger

Wooden heat shield to
protect operator's shoulder

FULL VIEW

Laser designator

▲ **MECHEM MGL MK 1**

Date 1990

Origin South Africa

Barrel 12in (30.5cm)

Caliber 40mm

Grenade range 383 yards (350m)

A scaled-up version of a shotgun of similar design, the MGL MK 1 is a six-shot revolver grenade-launcher. Rotation of the cylinder is performed by a spring, wound by rotating the cylinder manually when it is swung out of the frame for loading.

Cylinder holds six 40mm grenades

Optical sight graduated to 1 mile (1.7km)

Cocking handle has toggle attached

◀ **AGS-17 "PLAMYA"**

Date 1975

Origin Soviet Union

Barrel 11¾in (30cm)

Caliber 30mm

Grenade range 1 mile (1.7km)

This recoil-operated gun is the Soviet equivalent of the American 40mm M19 that was first used in the Vietnam War. Like the M19, the AGS-17 is a belt-fed, air-cooled launcher. Such weapons are commonly mounted in ground vehicles, boats, and hovercraft, and aboard helicopters and fixed-wing aircraft.

Horizontal grips on both sides of receiver

Elevating quadrant

Elevation screw

Tripod leg clamp

RECOIL-LESS ANTITANK WEAPONS

Antitank weapons have diversified since the World Wars. Developed in the 1930s, the recoil-less rifle has evolved into the towed and handheld types seen today. It is a lightweight artillery weapon that diverts the exhaust gases of the propellant backward to counteract the recoil of a gun. Gun carriages for it were designed to face forward, toward the barrel. The next major development after the recoil-less rifle has been the creation of portable guided missile systems in the latter half of the 20th century. These can be launched by a single operator, often firing from mounts in helicopters.

▼ **MILAN ANTITANK MISSILE LAUNCHER**

Date	1972
Origin	France, West Germany
Length	4ft (1.2m)
Caliber	125mm
Range	1¼ miles (1.95km)

The *Missile d'Infanterie Léger Antichar*, or MILAN, is an antitank guided missile that is directed to its target via signals sent along wires that reel out behind it as it flies. Seen here is its launcher. Although many MILANs are vehicle-mounted, they can be deployed by a two-man infantry crew.

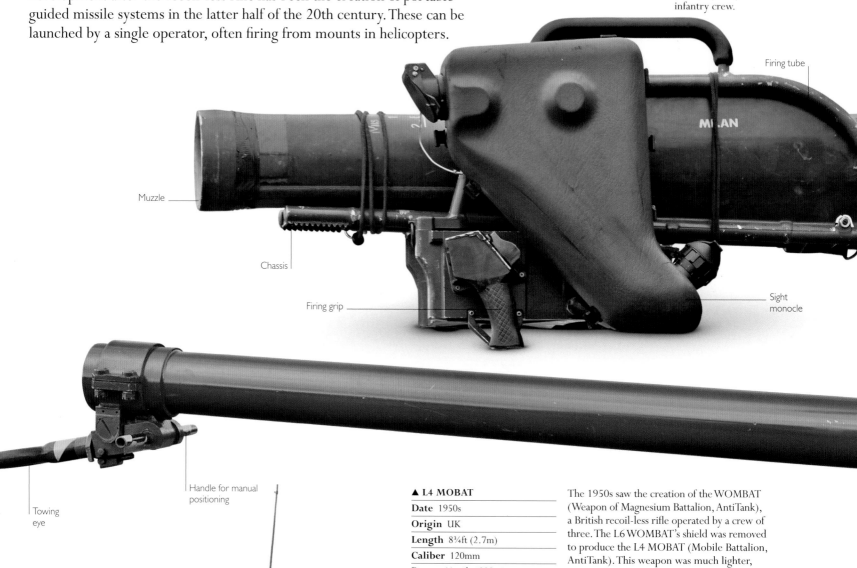

Firing tube

Muzzle

Chassis

Firing grip

Sight monocle

Towing eye

Handle for manual positioning

FULL VIEW

▲ **L4 MOBAT**

Date	1950s
Origin	UK
Length	8¾ft (2.7m)
Caliber	120mm
Range	½ mile (800m)

The 1950s saw the creation of the WOMBAT (Weapon of Magnesium Battalion, AntiTank), a British recoil-less rifle operated by a crew of three. The L6 WOMBAT's shield was removed to produce the L4 MOBAT (Mobile Battalion, AntiTank). This weapon was much lighter, and it was designed to be towed by a specially adapted Land Rover.

Carriage with split trails

▶ CARL GUSTAV RECOIL-LESS RIFLE

Date 1946

Origin Sweden

Length 3½ft (1.1m)

Caliber 84mm

Range ½ mile (700m)

The Carl Gustav is a man-portable multirole recoil-less rifle produced in Sweden by Saab Bofors Dynamics. It was first tested in 1946, and different versions have been adopted by armies all over the world. It is usually operated by a two-man crew, one for carrying the weapon and another for carrying high-explosive (HE) rounds.

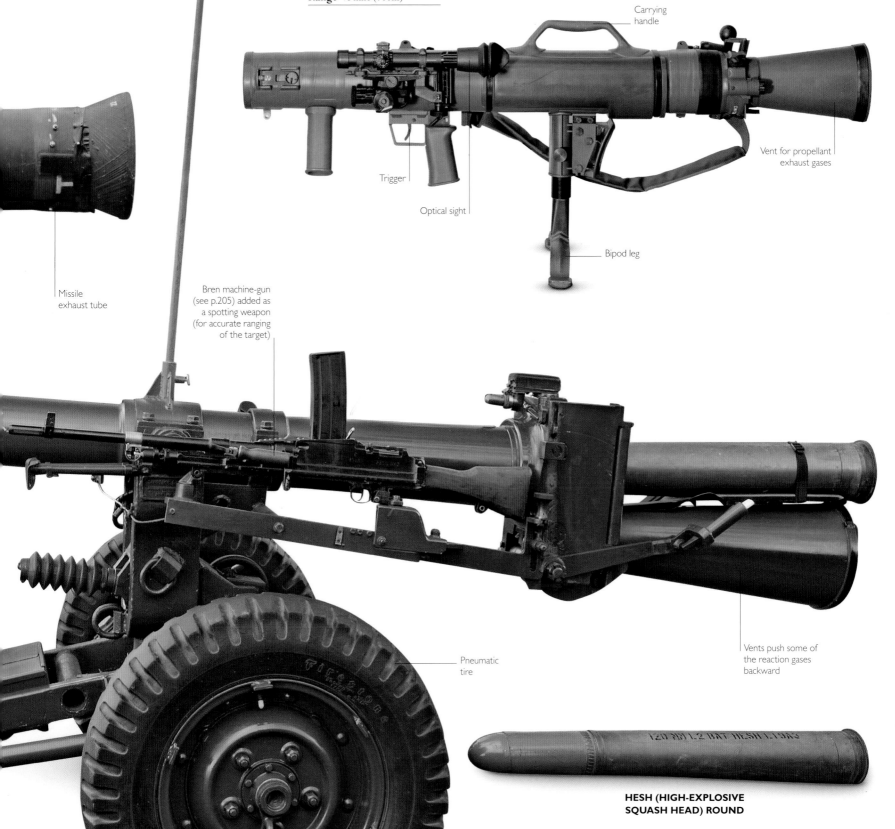

Carrying handle

Vent for propellant exhaust gases

Trigger

Optical sight

Bipod leg

Missile exhaust tube

Bren machine-gun (see p.205) added as a spotting weapon (for accurate ranging of the target)

Pneumatic tire

Vents push some of the reaction gases backward

HESH (HIGH-EXPLOSIVE SQUASH HEAD) ROUND

MODERN ARTILLERY (1946–PRESENT)

Since World War II, artillery in fixed positions has died out due to the threat of being destroyed from the air. Modern artillery is mobile—either towed, self-propelled, or even air-portable by helicopter, as in the case of the lightweight M777. Conventional artillery (that firing shells rather than rockets) includes howitzers and field guns. Towed artillery is generally 4.13–6.10in (105–155mm) in caliber and has become ever more precise in its targeting, using indirect fire—where the target cannot be seen—and benefitting from technologies such as the Global Positioning System (GPS). This is especially useful for longer guns, which can now achieve ranges of up to 30 miles (50km). Despite these advances, most artillery weapons used in conflicts today are designs that originated in the Soviet Union. Examples such as the D20 are simple, robust, and reliable.

▼ **D20**

Date	1950s
Origin	Soviet Union
Length	28½ft (8.7m)
Caliber	152mm
Range	15 miles (24km) with rocket-assisted projectile

Soviet-made artillery is commonly used in conflicts around the world. The rugged D20 is a manually loaded towed howitzer. The gun's barrel is mounted on a cradle, which houses a recoil system. This includes a recuperator, which enables the gun's barrel to return to its firing position after recoil.

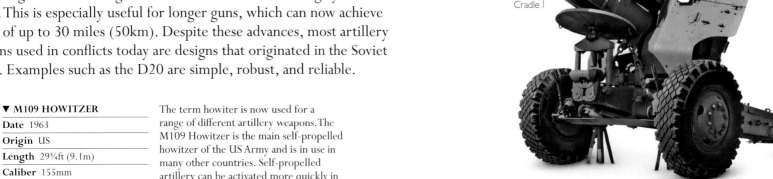

Cradle

▼ **M109 HOWITZER**

Date	1963
Origin	US
Length	29¾ft (9.1m)
Caliber	155mm
Range	18½ miles (30km) with rocket-assisted projectile

The term howiter is now used for a range of different artillery weapons. The M109 Howitzer is the main self-propelled howitzer of the US Army and is in use in many other countries. Self-propelled artillery can be activated more quickly in battle than towed artillery.

Commander's cupola

Barrel mounted on armored vehicle

Fume extractor

Muzzle brake

Elevation handwheel

Trunnion to elevate or lower barrel

Caterpillar tracks

Assistant gunner's display

Trail spade

Trail

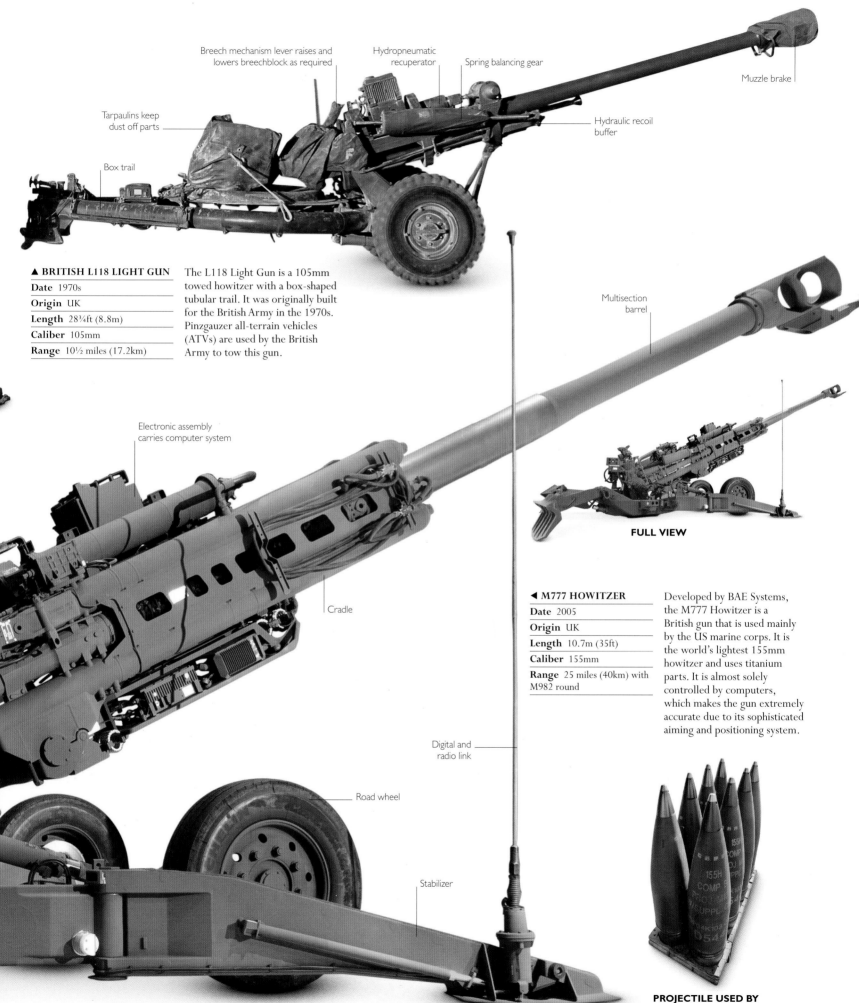

Breech mechanism lever raises and
lowers breechblock as required

Hydropneumatic
recuperator

Spring balancing gear

Muzzle brake

Tarpaulins keep
dust off parts

Hydraulic recoil
buffer

Box trail

▲ BRITISH L118 LIGHT GUN

Date	1970s
Origin	UK
Length	28¾ft (8.8m)
Caliber	105mm
Range	10½ miles (17.2km)

The L118 Light Gun is a 105mm towed howitzer with a box-shaped tubular trail. It was originally built for the British Army in the 1970s. Pinzgauzer all-terrain vehicles (ATVs) are used by the British Army to tow this gun.

Multisection
barrel

Electronic assembly
carries computer system

Cradle

FULL VIEW

◄ M777 HOWITZER

Date	2005
Origin	UK
Length	10.7m (35ft)
Caliber	155mm
Range	25 miles (40km) with M982 round

Developed by BAE Systems, the M777 Howitzer is a British gun that is used mainly by the US marine corps. It is the world's lightest 155mm howitzer and uses titanium parts. It is almost solely controlled by computers, which makes the gun extremely accurate due to its sophisticated aiming and positioning system.

Digital and
radio link

Road wheel

Stabilizer

**PROJECTILE USED BY
M777 HOWITZER**

DISGUISED FIREARMS

Since the 16th century, attempts have been made to disguise firearms as other objects (see pp. 222–23). Although early ignition systems (wheel-lock and flintlock) prevented any degree of effective disguise, the introduction of the self-contained metallic cartridge made it possible. As a result, from the mid-19th century onward, firearms have been made in the form of canes, umbrellas, pens, and so forth. These arms are effective only at close range, and civilian use of them is frowned upon by authorities because the weapons could be utilized for nefarious purposes, such as assassinations.

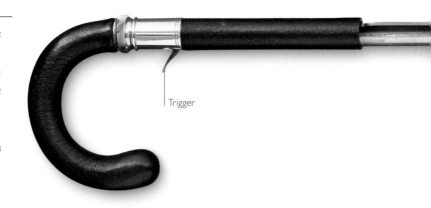

Trigger

Muzzle

Trigger

◀ CIGARETTE LIGHTER PISTOL

Date	1970s
Origin	Not known
Barrel	1½in (4cm)
Caliber	.22in

What appears to be a cigarette lighter actually contains a single-shot pistol. The trigger is of a clasp type and runs up the side of the "gun" body. It is not known which country produced this firearm, but it was made in the 1970s.

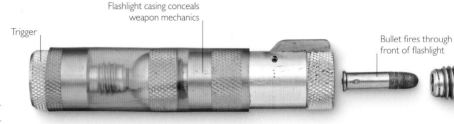

Flashlight casing conceals weapon mechanics

Trigger

Bullet fires through front of flashlight

▲ FLASHLIGHT STINGER

Date	1980s
Origin	US
Barrel	2in (5cm)
Caliber	.22in

This covert weapon is disguised as a flashlight and actually contains a .22in single-shot firearm. The bullet is loaded behind the flashlight's bulb section and is fired by depressing the light switch.

Leather-bound shaft

Trigger

Chamber

▲ WILSON UMBRELLA GUN

Date	1985
Origin	UK
Barrel	30in (76.2cm)
Caliber	.410in

Umbrellas lend themselves well to concealed firearms. This example comes under the category of "gentry guns," along with the Wilson cane gun above. The purpose of gentry guns such as these is somewhat ambiguous, since they are impractical for hunting and are of limited power for self-defense. This umbrella gun has a center-fire mechanism around its barrel. However, it is not licensed for sporting use in the US.

▲ WILSON CANE GUN

Date 1984

Origin UK

Barrel Not known

Caliber .410in

This cane gun is a "gentry gun" produced by the same gunmaker who made the Wilson umbrella gun (below). With a caliber of .410in and a range of up to 25 yards (23m), it was probably used for poaching.

Barrel housed in shaft of cane

Cocking mechanism

Barrel

▲ PEN PISTOL

Date 1990s

Origin Lebanon

Barrel 2in (5cm)

Caliber .22in

This pen pistol is of extremely lightweight—2½oz (70g)—hence it uses the .22in cartridge. However, it would require careful handling if the pistol was not to endanger the user as well as the target.

Trigger

Barrel

◄ RING PISTOL

Date 1990s

Origin Switzerland

Barrel 1in (2.5cm)

Caliber .22in

This is possibly the ultimate concealed weapon. It has an overall length of only 1¾in (4.3cm) and the barrel is scarcely longer than the .22in cartridge that it fires. Penetration from such a gun would be a matter of an inch or two, so the firing range would need to be point-blank.

Muzzle

Cloth umbrella

Knife grip

Hammer

Trigger

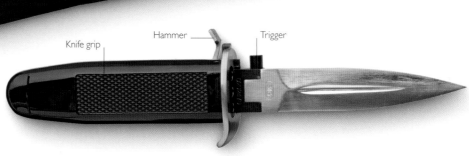

▲ KNIFE PISTOL

Date 2000s

Origin China

Barrel 1in (2.5cm)

Caliber .22in

This modern weapon originated in China in the 2000s, and would be intended for criminal or covert use. It features a folding knife integrated with a three-shot pistol firing .22in ammunition. The .22in round is ideal for small weapons such as this firearm, since it produces negligible recoil.

HOW GUNS WORK

BEFORE THE 19TH CENTURY

Early guns were tubes of bronze or iron, loaded at the muzzle with a propellant (main charge of gunpowder) and a projectile (ball of lead or stone). The barrel had a small hole—a vent, or touchhole—at the breech, into which a user placed priming powder (a small amount of gunpowder). Igniting this priming powder, usually with smoldering match-cord, caused flames to pass down the vent and fire the propellant in the barrel. The vents of later hand-cannon were on the right of the breech, with a shelf, or pan, for the priming powder. Next came devices that ignited the priming powder mechanically. These mechanisms were called locks, because their workings resembled the lock mechanism on a door or chest. The first was the matchlock.

▲ FIRING ARTILLERY
Until the 19th century almost all artillery was fired by match-cord, usually held at the end of a rod (linstock) to allow the gunner to stand away from the recoiling gun. In the late 19th century, gunners were able to fire instantly using "friction tube" primers—copper tubes containing fine gunpowder placed directly into the vent. It was operated by a lanyard, as seen here, which was a length of cord with a hook.

Wooden tiller, which was used to adjust aim

Vent

Wrought-iron barrel

▲ HAND-CANNON
Hand-cannon were the earliest guns small enough to be carried and fired by one user. They had no mechanical firing mechanism— the user touched a smoldering match-cord on the vent manually.

Matchlock

A user loaded a charge of gunpowder and a lead ball at the muzzle, then poured a small amount of finer-grained gunpowder into the priming pan, before closing the pan cover. He would then place a piece of match-cord, its end already smoldering, in the jaws of a snake-shaped match-holder called a serpentine. The user might test the position of the end of the match by gently squeezing the trigger to lower the serpentine, to make sure the match was positioned over the center of the closed pan.

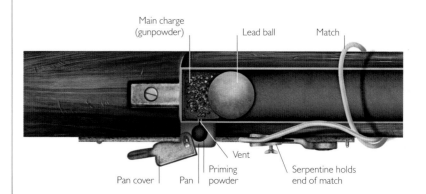

Main charge (gunpowder)

Lead ball

Match

Vent

Pan cover

Pan

Priming powder

Serpentine holds end of match

OVERHEAD VIEW OF MATCHLOCK MECHANISM

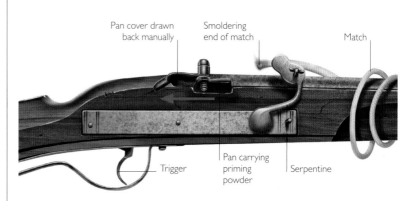

Pan cover drawn back manually

Smoldering end of match

Match

Trigger

Pan carrying priming powder

Serpentine

1 Before firing, the user readies the gun by blowing on the already-smoldering match to enliven it, and by moving the pan cover aside.

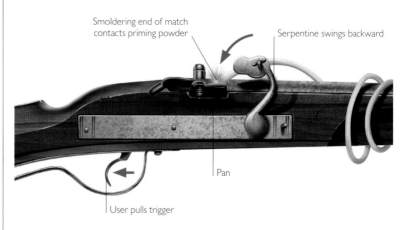

Smoldering end of match contacts priming powder

Serpentine swings backward

Pan

User pulls trigger

2 Pulling the trigger rotates the serpentine, plunging the burning match into the pan with the priming powder. This produces a flash that ignites the main charge via a vent in the side of the barrel.

Wheel-lock

The wheel-lock used a rotating steel wheel to strike sparks from a piece of iron pyrite. After loading the barrel, the user rotated the wheel with a key about three-quarters of a turn, until it was held by the trigger mechanism. Then he placed the priming powder in the pan. The top of the wheel passed up through a slot in the bottom of the priming pan, so that sparks produced when the iron pyrite contacted the wheel fell into the priming powder.

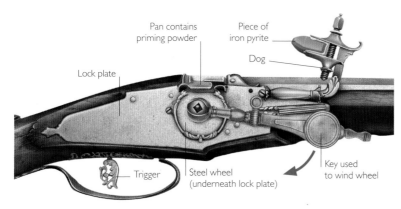

Pan contains priming powder | Piece of iron pyrite
Dog
Lock plate
Trigger | Steel wheel (underneath lock plate) | Key used to wind wheel

1 A spring-loaded arm called a dog, retained in position by the dog spring, holds a piece of iron pyrite in its jaws. The user spans the lock—winding the steel wheel using a key, which compresses the mainspring (underneath lock plate).

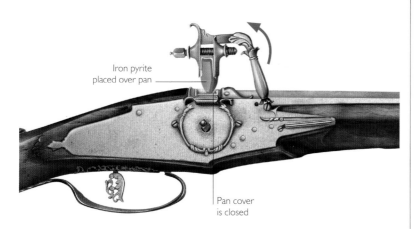

Iron pyrite placed over pan
Pan cover is closed

2 Before firing, the user moves the dog manually, placing it onto the pan cover, which is shut.

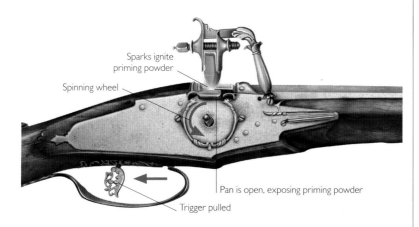

Sparks ignite priming powder
Spinning wheel
Pan is open, exposing priming powder
Trigger pulled

3 Pulling the trigger releases the wheel, which starts spinning. The pan cover opens automatically, bringing the iron pyrite into contact with the wheel. The friction creates sparks, which ignite the priming powder, causing a flash that ignites the main charge in the barrel.

Flintlock

The flintlock had a simpler design than the wheel-lock. It used the impact of natural flint on hardened steel to strike sparks. The cock held a flint, which was propelled forward by a spring to strike a steel part called the frizzen, which was a combined striking plate and pan cover. The impact forced the steel back, opening the pan cover. Sparks fell into the priming powder to ignite it.

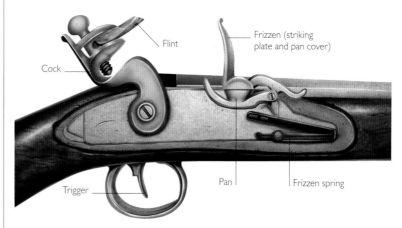

Flint | Frizzen (striking plate and pan cover)
Cock
Trigger | Pan | Frizzen spring

1 Before firing, the cock is held by a hooked part called a sear (inside the gun). A frizzen spring holds the frizzen closed over the pan.

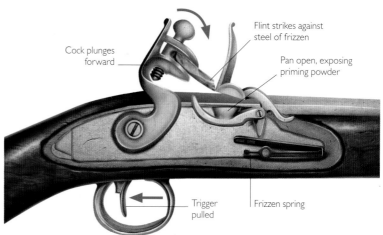

Flint strikes against steel of frizzen
Cock plunges forward
Pan open, exposing priming powder
Trigger pulled | Frizzen spring

2 Pulling the trigger retracts the sear, allowing the cock to spring forward to scrape the face of the steel. This impact forces the steel back, opening the attached pan cover and exposing the priming powder.

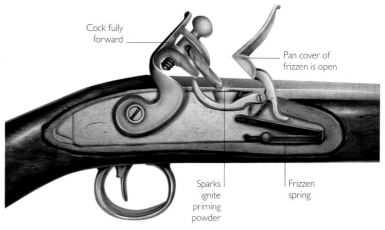

Cock fully forward
Pan cover of frizzen is open
Sparks ignite priming powder | Frizzen spring

3 Sparks caused by the flint striking the steel fall into the pan to ignite the priming powder. This produces a flash that ignites the main charge in the barrel via a vent in the side of the barrel.

HOW GUNS WORK

FROM THE 19TH CENTURY

The invention of percussion caps provided firearms with an instantaneous method for the chemical ignition of the propellant (gunpowder). By the 1870s, these caps were contained within fully integrated metallic cartridges. These cartridges carried a projectile, propellant, and a primer in one compact package. Cartridges could be loaded quickly at the breech of the gun—with the cartridges being fed into the chamber by bolt action. Soon, cartridges were being fed repeatedly from magazines. The automation of this loading process, from magazines or belts, using a recoil-operated or a gas-operated action, led to semi-automatic (self-loading) and fully automatic weapons.

Percussion cap

A percussion cap is formed of two layers of copper foil with a mixture of fulminate of mercury, potassium chlorate, and sulfur or antimony between them. The composition catches fire when the hammer strikes it.

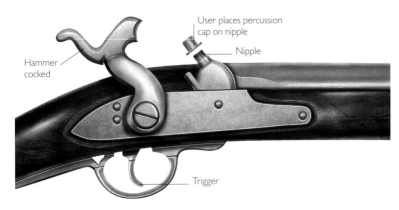

1 A sear (a hooklike part inside the gun) holds the hammer in the cocked position. The sear connects to the trigger. The user places the percussion cap on the nipple, the bore of which leads to the propellant in the barrel.

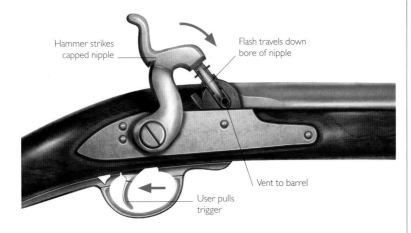

2 Pulling the trigger trips the sear, releasing the hammer and driving it onto the nipple. The primer in the cap ignites. The flame passes down the bore in the nipple and through a vent into the main charge in the barrel, igniting it.

Bolt action

Bolt action, essentially based on the device that holds a garden gate closed, is a sure and effective design of breech-loading firearm. The mechanism was used with the first repeater rifles, which were the first guns with magazines. The magazines contained cartridges ready to be loaded and fired.

1 The user lifts the bolt handle, rotating the body of the bolt and freeing its locking lugs, and draws it fully to the rear. This opens the breech of the gun. As the user moves the bolt forward, it picks up a cartridge from the magazine and chambers it.

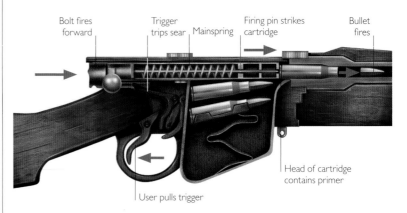

2 As the user returns the bolt handle to the closed position, seating the locking lugs and sealing the breech, the mainspring and firing pin are held back by the sear, which keeps the bolt cocked. Pulling the trigger trips the sear and releases the firing pin. As the mainspring decompresses, the pin flies forward and impacts the primer at the head of the cartridge, detonating it and firing the bullet.

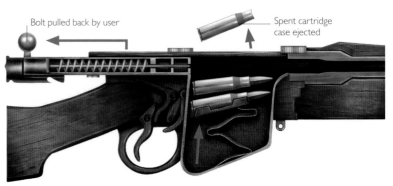

3 As the user withdraws the bolt, it extracts the spent cartridge case by means of a hook on the bolt head, which engages with the rim of the case. The recoil force generated pushes the bolt backward, compressing the mainspring, which then springs forward once more. The movement pushes up the next cartridge.

Recoil reloading

Every action, Isaac Newton's Third Law of Motion tells us, has an equal and opposite reaction. The action—ignition of the propellant—in a firearm—propels the bullet down the barrel and on toward its target. The reaction, known as the recoil, drives the gun into the shoulder or hand of the user. Recoil-operated action drives the auto-loading action of many semiautomatic pistols and automatic guns, such as machine-guns.

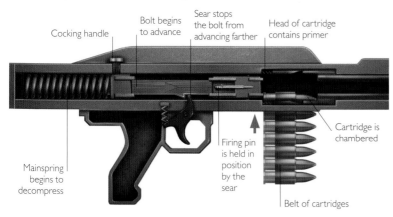

1 First, the user draws the cocking handle back against the mainspring, compressing it. As the mainspring rebounds, it pushes the bolt forward, stripping a cartridge from the magazine and chambering it. The sear is connected to the trigger and now holds the bolt and the firing pin in position.

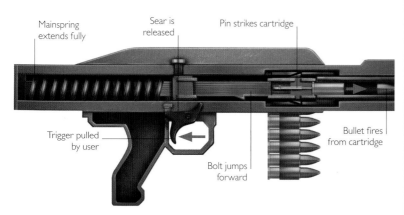

2 Pulling the trigger releases the sear. The mainspring extends fully, pushing the bolt fully forward and sending the firing pin flying toward the cartridge. The pin impacts the primer in the head of the cartridge and detonates it, igniting the propellant and firing the bullet.

3 The recoil from firing the cartridge sends the bolt backwards, ejecting the empty cartridge case and allowing a new cartridge to enter the chamber. If the trigger remains depressed, the cycle continues.

Gas reloading

As an alternative to harnessing the force of the gun's recoil, it is possible to use some of the energy of the violently expanding gases that propel the bullet down the barrel. Some of that gas can be tapped off after the bullet has passed and employed to reload the gun by driving the breechblock or bolt to the rear. In automatic weapons, this action is cycled to produce continuous fire.

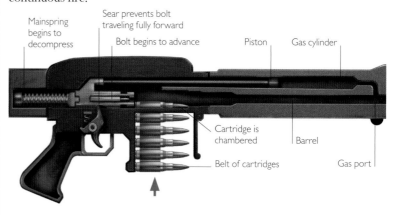

1 First, the user draws back the bolt against the mainspring. The mainspring pushes it forward again and as the bolt begins to advance, it strips a cartridge from the magazine and chambers it. The bolt is attached to a piston in a cylinder running parallel to the barrel. At the head of the cylinder is a gas port.

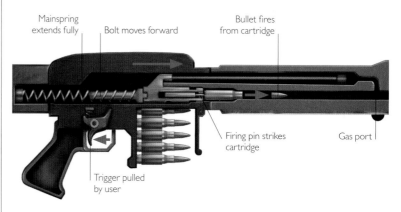

2 Pulling the trigger releases the sear. The mainspring extends, pushing the bolt forward. The firing pin impacts with the primer in the head of the cartridge, detonating it, igniting the propellant and firing the bullet.

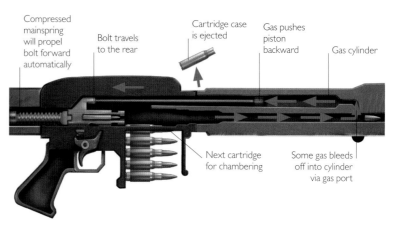

3 As the bullet passes the gas port, some of the gas produced by burning the propellant bleeds through the port, forcing the piston backward. As the bolt travels to the rear, it ejects the spent cartridge case. The mainspring then extends, pushing the bolt ahead and chambering a new cartridge. If the trigger remains depressed, the cycle continues.

AMMUNITION BEFORE 1900

Smoothbore guns and rifles were loaded at the muzzle with lead balls and a separate propellant (gunpowder), ignited by fine gunpowder acting as primer. Guns became easier to load with the advent of the cartridge, a package carrying the lead ball and propellant. While early paper cartridges had to be torn open, later ones could be loaded whole. It was the unitary metallic cartridge (see pp.112–13), a combination of cartridge and primer in one case, that made breech-loading quick and simple.

The powder-and-ball era

To achieve any sort of accuracy, the ball fired from a smoothbore gun had to be spherical and of an exact size. Rifling improved matters, but made the weapon slow to load; the problem was solved by the expanding bullet (see pp.98–99).

Rifle belt

MUSKET/RIFLE BALLS
The size of the ball was expressed in "bore," being the number of balls of that size that could be cast from 1lb (0.45kg) of lead.

BELTED BALL
Some balls, such as the Brunswick ball (see p.98), were belted to slide into the grooves in a gun's rifled barrel.

Skirt

Groove

MINIÉ BULLETS
These bullets had a hollow base. The force of the propellant detonating caused the bullets' skirts to expand and grip the rifling.

GROOVED MINIÉ BULLET
Greased grooves in the bullet lubricated the barrel as the bullet gripped the rifling.

Percussion cap

PERCUSSION CAPS
The percussion cap (see pp.80–81) provided an easier way to ignite the propellant by using a chemical primer. It was a thin, copper cap shaped to fit over a hollow plug attached to the breech of the gun. The chemical in it exploded when struck by the gun's hammer. Percussion caps could be used with powder and ball, as well as the earliest cartridges.

Early cartridges

Early 19th-century cartridges carried a measured quantity of gunpowder and a bullet. Wrapped in paper, skin, or fabric, these cartridges posed a problem for breech-loading guns, whose breeches had to be sealed to prevent leakage of gases produced by the ignited propellant. To propel the bullet efficiently, a gas-tight seal was needed at the breech. The solution lay in the metallic cartridge, which was able to seal the breech perfectly. At the same time, metallic cartridges became "unitary" cartridges by integrating the primer, along with the propellant and projectile, within their metal shell. Metallic cartridges for rifled arms have longer ranges than those of handguns. They are usually longer than pistol cartridges, contain more propellant, and are designed for longer barrels, which allow bullets to be fully accelerated. This provides more velocity and energy to the bullet, increasing its range and penetration power.

Ball held at one end

PAPER CARTRIDGES
The first cartridges were nothing more than paper packages containing a measured charge of powder and a ball. They were used with both flintlock and percussion systems.

Pin

PIN-FIRE CARTRIDGE
Invented in the 1830s, the pin-fire was an early version of the unitary metallic cartridge. When the trigger was pulled, the gun's hammer fell on a pin projecting from the base of the cartridge. The force of impact drove the pin into the primer contained within the cartridge's base, igniting the primer and firing the gun.

WESTLEY RICHARDS "MONKEY TAIL" CARTRIDGE
This paper-wrapped cartridge had a greased felt wad at the rear, which remained in the breech until pushed forward for removal before a new round was loaded. Doing so cleaned the bore and reduced fouling.

SNIDER-ENFIELD BOXER CARTRIDGE
This was an early experiment at producing a center-fire cartridge, in the 1860s, with the primer at the center of the base. This cartridge for the Snider-Enfield rifle had a perforated iron base and walls built up from coiled brass foils.

.56IN-50 SPENCER (1860)
The rim-fire was another early type of metallic cartridge. This rim-fire round was fired by the first effective repeater rifle—the Spencer carbine—from the Civil War-era.

11MM CHASSEPOT (1871)
After the Franco-Prussian War (1870–71), the cartridge developed for the Mauser M71 rifle was adapted for the Chassepot rifle, which was converted to take it.

.30IN-30 WINCHESTER (1895)
This cartridge was the first "civilian" round to be charged with smokeless powder (see pp.142–43), a new propellant. It contained 30 grains (1.94g) of it.

.303IN MK V (1899)
The British Army's Lee-Metfords and Lee-Enfields were chambered for this blunt-nosed rifle bullet from 1899.

CARTRIDGE BOX FOR REPEATING RIFLES (1871)
Manufacturers of firearms preferred owners to use their own brand of ammunition. This pack of Winchester rifle cartridges is typical of the late 1800s.

BULLET BOX FOR MATCH RIFLES (1872)
To maintain consistent shooting, competitors in long-range "match" rifle-shooting contests demanded great precision in the manufacture of ammunition components. Swaged, or pressure-formed, bullets were individually weighed.

TOOLS

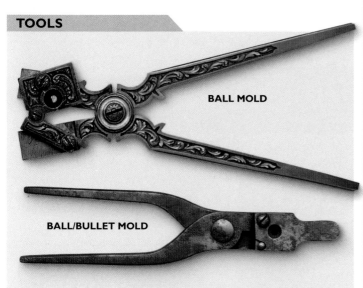

BALL MOLD

BALL/BULLET MOLD

CASTING BULLETS
Until the sale of loose bullets became common, firearms were supplied with molds, with cavities into which molten lead was poured via channels. The metal solidified in the molds, producing ammunition of the correct size. Excess metal that solidified in the channels was termed sprue. Seen here are two molds. The upper mold has an automatic sprue cutter, which simply sliced off the sprue as the mold was opened. The lower mold has a more usual pivoting sprue cutter, which would cut off the sprue when knocked to one side.

CAPPER/
DECAPPER

RELOADING PRIMERS
This tool was used to remove fired primers—a special form of percussion cap—and install fresh ones in the heads of metallic center-fire cartridges.

Pistol cartridges
Pistols fire over a shorter range than rifles, and they use shorter cartridges that contain less powder and are less powerful. Shorter barrels mean a lower bullet velocity and lower penetrating power. Like rifle cartridges, they developed from rim-fire to the better center-fire design in the 1860s.

.44IN HENRY (1860)
This rim-fire round had primer arranged around the base of its case. It was soon superseded by the center-fire cartridge.

.44IN ALLEN AND WHEELOCK (1860s)
Allen and Wheelock revolvers were chambered for "lip-fire" cartridges (similar to rim-fire), chiefly in small calibers.

.45IN COLT (BÉNÉT 1865)
Colonel S V Bénét's 1865 version of the center-fire cartridge formed the basis for Berdan's popular center-fire metallic cartridge.

.45IN COLT (THUER 1868)
Alexander Thuer developed a method of converting Colt "cap-and-ball" revolvers to fire this tapering brass cartridge.

.44IN SMITH AND WESSON RUSSIAN (1870)
This center-fire cartridge was supplied to the Russian Army for Smith and Wesson revolvers.

.577IN WEBLEY (1880s)
Many small-caliber cartridges lacked the explosive power to stop a man. Webley addressed this with a .577in cartridge.

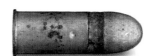

.476IN WEBLEY (1881)
The .577in revolver was unwieldy and a replacement in .476in caliber was adopted instead. It, too, was short-lived.

10.4MM BODEO (1889)
This revolver cartridge, used by the Italian Army from 1891, produced a muzzle velocity of 837ft (255m) per second—higher than most cartridges of the time.

.455IN WEBLEY (1891)
Webley's first smokeless-powder cartridge was more powerful than earlier types. As a lighter bullet with a more powerful charge, it could travel faster and inflict more damage.

7.63MM BERGMANN (1896)
The first cartridges made for the Bergmann No 3 pistol in 1896 were rimless and grooveless, with a sharp nose.

Shotgun cartridges
Only the very largest shotgun cartridges were made entirely of brass. Others had cardboard bodies.

10-BORE PIN-FIRE
Production of most pin-fire cartridges ceased in the 1860s. However those for shotguns, continued until the 1920s.

WILDFOWL CARTRIDGE
Large cartridges such as this were loaded with up to ¾oz (20g) of gunpowder and 3½oz (100g) of shot.

AMMUNITION AFTER 1900

Following the development of the unitary brass cartridge, which combined all three essential elements (primer, propellant, and projectile) in one package, it only remained for the nature of those elements to be improved. Primers became more effective and bullets became more aerodynamic and capable of accuracy at long ranges. However, the most important developments were in propellant. In the final decade of the 19th century, propellants evolved, with the advent of smokeless powder and later of a nitroglycerine-based mixture generally known as cordite. This replaced gunpowder entirely.

Rifle cartridges

In the late 19th century, rifle bullets acquired a sharply pointed nose and a taper toward the tail. The shape minimized air resistance in flight, which almost doubled their effective range and improved their accuracy. In these examples, both velocity and energy are measured at the muzzle. The heavier the bullet and the higher its velocity, the greater is its energy.

8 × 58MM KRAG (1889)
This option for the Krag-Jørgensen rifle was adopted by the Danish Army. This 195-grain (12.7-g) bullet had a muzzle velocity of 2,525ft (770m) per second.

7.7 × 56MM JAPANESE (1889)
This fully rimmed cartridge—in which the rim was significantly wider than than the base of the cartridge—was used by the Arisaka rifle. It had a 175-grain (11.35g) bullet and a muzzle velocity of 2,350ft (716.3m) per second.

7.62 × 54MM RUSSIAN (1891)
This "3-line" cartridge was loaded with a 150-grain (9.65-g) bullet that left the muzzle at 2,855ft (870m) per second. The "line" is a caliber measure approximating one-tenth of an inch.

7.92 × 57MM MAUSER (1905)
Also called the SmK cartridge, this was loaded with a steel-jacketed 177-grain (11.5-g) bullet that left the muzzle at 2,745 ft (836.6m) per second. The boat-tail (tapered end) of the bullet reduced the size of the vacuum at the base of the bullet, and increased its accuracy.

.30IN-06 SPRINGFIELD (1906)
The .30in-06 remained in US service from 1906 until 1954. Its 152-grain (9.85-g) bullet left the muzzle at 2,910ft (887m) per second, with 2,820ft-lb (3,823J) of energy.

.470IN NITRO EXPRESS (1907)
"Nitro" refers to the propellant, while "Express" refers to the bullet, which was first produced in 1907. The bullet is hollow at the tip— on hitting the target, the bullet expands, reducing its penetration but increasing the tissue damage. Muzzle velocity of the bullet is 2,150ft (655.3m) per second, with 5,130ft-lb (6,955J) of energy.

7.7 × 56MM ITALIAN (1910)
The Italian 7.7mm cartridge had a 173-grain (11.25-g) bullet and a small charge with a muzzle velocity of 2,035ft (620.3m) per second.

.303IN MKVII (1910)
This version of the Lee-Enfield cartridge, with a 180-grain (11.66-g) bullet, had a muzzle velocity of 2,460ft (804.6m) per second and 2,420ft-lb (3,281J) of energy.

.50IN BROWNING /12.7MM M2 (1916/17)
Developed for the M2 machine-gun and adopted as a rifle round, this cartridge has a 710-grain (46-g) bullet and a muzzle velocity of 2,800ft (853.4m) per second.

.22IN HORNET (1920s)
One of very few high-velocity miniature rounds, the .22in Hornet was developed in the 1920s. Its 45-grain (2.9-g) bullet leaves the muzzle at 2,690ft (820m) per second.

7.92 × 33MM KURTZ (1938)
This was the first effective intermediate cartridge—less powerful than a typical battle rifle cartridge, such as the 7.62 × 54mm Russian, but significantly more powerful than pistol cartridges. It was developed in Nazi Germany and was copied by the Soviet Union in slightly smaller dimensions. It had a range of around 1,950ft (595m).

.257IN WEATHERBY MAGNUM (1944)
This is loaded with an 87-grain (5.31-g) "varmint" bullet— for rifles used to shoot small mammals, such as rodents. The cartridge achieves a muzzle velocity of 3,825ft (1165.8m) per second and delivers 2,826ft-lb (3,832J) of energy.

.30IN M1 CARBINE (1940)
This intermediate round developed for the American World
War II-vintage M1 Carbine is loaded with a 110-grain (7.13-g)
blunt-nosed bullet, effective at up to 600ft (180m).

7.62 × 51MM NATO (1954)
When NATO chose a new rifle and machine-gun cartridge
in the early 1950s, it opted for one based on the .30in-06.

.458IN WINCHESTER MAGNUM (1956)
Developed in 1956 as a "big game" round, with a 500-grain
(32.4-g) bullet, it has a muzzle velocity of 2,040ft (621.8m)
per second and 4,620ft-lb (6,264J) of energy.

.338IN WINCHESTER MAGNUM (1958)
First produced in 1958, this cartridge was developed for large
North American game. It can be loaded with a variety of bullets,
from 175 to 300 grains (11.34g to 19.44g) in weight.

SS109 5.56MM (1962)
The NATO-standard SS109 5.56mm round has a steel-tipped
projectile, which allows it to penetrate steel effectively. The
cartridge weighs 61.7 grains (4g) and achieves a muzzle
velocity of 3,085ft (940.3m) per second.

7MM REMINGTON MAGNUM (1962)
Loaded with 62 grains (4,02g) of propellant and a 150-grain
(9.72-g) spitzer bullet, this produces a muzzle velocity of 3,100ft
(944.8m) per second and 3,220ft-lb (4,365J) of energy.

.416IN REMINGTON MAGNUM (1988)
A development of a cartridge produced by John Rigby and Company
in 1911, the .416in Remington produces a muzzle velocity of 2,400ft
(731.5m) per second and 5,115ft-lb (6,935J) of energy.

.243IN WINCHESTER MAGNUM (2003)
This short-case round delivers less power than a normal cartridge: a
100-grain (6.48-g) bullet leaves the muzzle at 2,960ft (902.2m) per
second with 1,945ft-lb (2,637J) of energy.

Pistol cartridges

The only significant change in the
character of pistol ammunition after
1900 was the introduction of the
high-performance Magnum load.

.38IN S&W (1877)
This is the least powerful .38in cartridge. It
gives the 145-grain (9.4-g) bullet a muzzle
velocity of 685ft (208.7m) per second and
150ft-lb (203J) of energy.

.32IN LONG (1896)
Though a popular caliber for revolvers,
the original .32in cartridge was low on
power. A longer version was produced
in 1896.

.45IN MARS (1899)
This was the most powerful pistol
ammunition in the world prior to
the arrival of the .44in Magnum. The
bullet had a muzzle velocity of 1,200ft
(370m) per second and 700ft-lb (950J)
of energy.

.32IN AUTO (1899)
A popular caliber for small self-loading
pistols, the .32in has a 60-grain (3.89-g)
bullet and produces 125ft-lb (169J)
of energy.

9MM MARS (1899)
Severely bottlenecked cartridges (with
necks narrower than the rest of the case)
are unusual in pistols, but the designer
insisted on a heavy propellant load for
the 9mm Mars.

.380IN ENFIELD/WEBLEY (1900)
Made for the Enfield Mk 1 revolver, the
200-grain (12.96-g) bullet was almost as
powerful as the .455in it replaced.

9MM PARABELLUM (1901)
Also known as 9mm Luger, this is the most
common cartridge in the world. Countless
firearms have been chambered for it.

8MM NAMBU (1902)
The Japanese officer's pistols issued from
1909 onward were the only weapons ever
made for this powerful round.

.45IN ACP (1904)
An iconic pistol cartridge, the .45in
Automatic Colt Pistol round was
developed for the John Browning-
designed Colt M1911.

9MM STEYR (1911)
There are many varieties of 9mm
revolver cartridge. This one was
developed for a pistol designed
by Mannlicher.

.357IN MAGNUM (1935)
Developed by Smith and Wesson and
Winchester, this cartridge has been
produced in many varieties. Average
muzzle velocity is around 1,300ft
(396.2m) per second.

.44IN MAGNUM (1954)
This round was originally developed for
revolvers, but later adopted for rifles and
carbines as well. A 240-grain (15.55-g)
bullet leaves the muzzle at 1,500ft
(457.2m) per second with 1,200ft-lb
(1,627J) of energy.

.50IN ACTION EXPRESS (1988)
Developed for the Desert Eagle pistol, its
325-grain (21-g) bullet leaves the muzzle
with 1,415ft-lb (1,918J) of energy.

GLOSSARY

Action
The mechanism of a gun involving the loading and firing of a cartridge and the ejection of the spent cartridge.

Artillery
Guns that are too big and heavy to be fired by hand, including cannon, and also smaller weapons, such as swivel guns.

Assault rifle
A short-barreled, easily portable rifle capable of selective fire—semiautomatic or automatic fire—and utilizing a high-capacity magazine with medium- and small-caliber cartridges with short cases.

Automatic
Describes a firearm that will load and fire continually while the trigger is kept pulled.

Barrel shroud
A covering attached to the barrel of a firearm that insulates the user's hands from the hot barrel.

Battery
A group of artillery weapons—usually four to eight.

Bayonet
A blade designed to fit into, over, under, or around the muzzle end of a firearm, enabling it to be used as a close-combat weapon.

Blowback
A type of firearm operation in which the loading cycle is driven by the motion of the spent cartridge case as it is pushed backward by the exploding gases, which are produced by the ignition of the propellant.

Blunderbuss
A muzzle-loading firearm with a short barrel and a flared muzzle.

Bolt
In bolt-action weapons, the rod-shaped part that closes and seals the breech. It loads and extracts cartridges and carries the firing pin. It is also present in recoil- and gas-operated self-loading weapons.

Bolt action
A mechanism for loading a firearm at its breech. In guns featuring this action, the bolt is manually moved using a small handle. The breech opens, and the spent cartridge case is ejected while a fresh round is chambered.

Bore
The internal diameter of a gun's barrel.

Box-lock
A variant of the flintlock mechanism in which the cock was placed centrally inside the pistol. In later firearms, the term is used to describe a firing mechanism enclosed within a box-shaped housing in the breech.

Break-open
An action in which the barrel hinges downward before the trigger guard for loading at the breech of the firearm.

Breech
The rear part of the bore of a firearm or artillery piece.

Breechblock
An iron or steel component that slides or hinges to expose the breech of a barrel to allow reloading, and against which the cartridge rests while being fired.

Breech-loader
A firearm in which the propellant and projectile are loaded at the breech of the barrel.

Bridle
A piece of metal projecting from the pan of a flintlock to support the head of the frizzen's pivot screw; also, a bridging piece inside a gunlock to stabilize the inner end of the axle of the tumbler (part of the sear mechanism).

Bullpup
A type of rifle configuration in which the firing mechanism is set in the butt, allowing for a normal-length barrel in a relatively short weapon. It also allows the magazine to be housed behind the trigger.

Butt
The part of a long gun held to the shoulder or the part of a pistol held in the hand.

Caliber
The internal diameter of a weapon's barrel; also used to describe specific cartridge types.

Carbine
A short-barreled rifle or musket. Among muzzle-loading firearms, a carbine was often of lighter caliber than a long musket.

Cartridge
A wrapping of paper containing a measured charge of gunpowder and a ball or bullet (in muzzle-loading firearms); a tube, usually metallic, containing propellant, primer, and projectile (in breech-loading guns).

Center-fire
Describes a self-contained cartridge carrying the chemical primer in the center of its head. It is the most modern form of metallic cartridge.

Chamber
The part of a firearm from which the projectile is fired.

Cleaning rod
A metal device used to clean residue in the barrel.

Cock
The clamp that holds the flint in a flintlock gun; the act of pulling back a hammer, bolt, or cocking handle to ready a gun for firing.

Cycle
The series of operations necessary to fire a round and return the gun to its firing position.

Cyclic rate
An estimated rate of fire of an automatic weapon.

Cylinder
The part of a revolver that holds cartridges in separate chambers usually placed parallel to a central axis.

Discharger cup
A cup fixed to the end of a musket or rifle to accept grenades or missiles for firing.

Dog
The spring-loaded arm that holds the iron pyrite in a wheel-lock gun.

Double-action
An action type, typical of a revolver, in which the hammer can be cocked either automatically by pulling the trigger, or manually.

Extractor
The moving part of a firearm that removes spent cartridge cases from the chamber after firing.

Field gun
A portable artillery piece that was towed alongside infantry and cavalry on the battlefield. In the 18th and 19th centuries, it fired solid shot, explosive shells, and canister shot (shot made of smaller balls). Modern field guns fire shells.

Firing pin
A thin rod that strikes the primer of a center-fire cartridge when the trigger is pulled. It can be moved by an external hammer on the gun or, in firearms with bolts, positioned at the end of the bolt.

Flash hider
A device that conceals the flash of burning gases exiting the muzzle on firing a gun.

Flint
A piece of stone with a sharp edge that is capable of producing sparks when that edge is struck against hardened steel.

Flintlock
A firing mechanism in which a flint strikes a hardened steel surface, creating sparks that ignite the priming powder.

Forestock
The part of the stock of a firearm under the barrel and forward of the trigger guard.

Frizzen
In the flintlock mechanism, a curved metal plate, formed by the union of the pan cover and striking steel that is usually hinged and struck by a flint.

Fulminate
A detonating chemical used as a primer to ignite the main powder charge in the case of percussion locks and all subsequent types of firing mechanism.

Gas operation
A type of autoloading action in which the loading cycle is driven by the gases produced by igniting the propellant.

General-purpose machine-gun (GPMG)
A multipurpose machine-gun that works either as a light or a medium machine-gun and is mounted on a bipod or tripod.

Grenade
A small bomb that can be fired by grenade-launchers and also by some rifles. In the case of rifles, the grenade is mounted on the muzzle and propelled by firing a blank cartridge down the barrel.

Gunlock
The firing mechanism on a small arm.

Gunpowder
A mixture of saltpetre, charcoal, and sulfur. Until the 1880s, the sole propellant used in small arms and artillery.

Halberd
A weapon with a short, wide, axlike blade, a spearpoint, and a back pike for penetrating armor.

Hammer
An externally-mounted spring-driven part that is cocked by hand. When released by the trigger, it struck the cap on the nipple of a percussion firearm, or the cartridges of revolvers and earlier kinds of breech-loading sporting guns and rifles.

Hand-cannon
A small, crude, cannonlike firearm dating from the early 15th century. It was equipped with a wooden tiller to direct it.

Harquebus
A man-portable firearm that evolved from the hand-cannon. It was equipped with a wooden stock to rest it against the user's shoulder, arm, or chest, and was originally fired by a handheld match-cord.

Heavy machine-gun
A machine-gun chambered for a round of larger-than-rifle caliber, usually 12.7mm. It was usually fired from a fixed mount.

Hinged frame
A pistol in which the barrel can be hinged down to expose the chamber.

Hold-open device
A catch that holds back a long gun's bolt if there is no cartridge to be chambered; it also holds the slide of a self-loading pistol back so that the weapon may be dismantled.

Howitzer
A high-angle, long-range artillery piece, fitted with a shorter barrel than a field gun, used for destroying fortifications and trench systems. After World War I, howitzers come to include longer-barreled weapons.

Hydropneumatic recoil
A type of recuperator mechanism for artillery. Metal tubes below the barrel were partially filled with liquid. As the barrel recoiled on firing, the liquid was forced back in the tubes, compressing the air, which acted as a natural spring to return the barrel to its rest position.

Iron pyrite
A natural mineral that was used to produce sparks for igniting the priming powder in the wheel-lock mechanism.

Lanyard ring
A ring on the butt of a pistol or revolver by which the user can attach the weapon to his body using a cord or strap.

Lever action
A mechanism for loading a gun at its breech. The lever is used to open the breech chamber.

Light machine-gun (LMG)
A machine-gun chambered for rifle-caliber ammunition, but not capable of sustained fire.

Lock plate
An iron or steel plate around which a gun's lock mechanism is built; the main part of many forms of gunlock.

Machine-gun
A fully automatic weapon intended for sustained fire from an ammunition belt or magazine.

Mainspring
The principal spring of a gunlock mechanism. In early gunlocks, it powered the wheel or cock, and in later mechanisms, the hammer, striker, or firing pin.

Magazine
A storage device, detachable or integral, in a gun for holding and feeding the ammunition. Forms include box, drum, or tube.

Magnum
A long version of a standard cartridge. Its increased length helps to accommodate more powder for higher velocity, power, and range.

Matchlock
A firing mechanism incorporating a match-cord (or "slow-match") that ignites the priming powder when the trigger is pulled.

Match-cord
A hemp cord which was used to ignite gunpowder in early firearms.

Medium machine-gun
A machine-gun chambered for rifle-caliber ammunition and capable of sustained fire.

Metallic cartridge
A cartridge with a metallic case. Most are self-contained—propellant, projectile (bullet), and chemical primer are held within the case.

Miquelet
A type of flintlock mechanism—prevalent in the Mediterranean between the late-16th and mid-19th centuries—in which the mainspring is on the outside of the gun.

Mortar
A short-barreled, muzzle-loading artillery piece that fires projectiles at high angles. Mortars have evolved from weapons firing solid projectiles of stone to those firing special self-propelled explosive projectiles.

Musket
A smoothbore, muzzle-loading long arm that fires a spherical lead ball; the standard military weapon carried by infantry from the 16th to the mid-19th century.

Muzzle brake
A device that reduces the muzzle's tendency to lift or swing. Also known as a compensator.

Muzzle-loader
A firearm in which the propellant and projectile are loaded from the gun's muzzle.

Nipple
A small tube screwed into the breech of a percussion firearm's barrel. It was hollow and allowed the burning gases from the primer to reach the breech.

Open frame
A revolver design in which the cylinder is not contained by a top-strap of metal and can be removed easily for cleaning.

Pan
The receptacle for holding the priming powder of either a matchlock, wheel-lock, or flintlock gun.

Parabellum
The 9 × 19mm cartridge developed by Georg Luger for his self-loading pistol.

Patchbox
A compartment in the stock of a firearm; used for storing tools and patches of greased cloth, in which the ball of a muzzle-loading rifle was wrapped before it was loaded in order to grip, clean, and lubricate the bore.

Pepperbox
A popular name for a type of revolver, usually percussion, which had no separate barrel. Instead the chambers of the cylinder were extended to form a group of barrels.

Percussion-cap mechanism
A firing mechanism featuring a small cap containing fulminate that serves as a primer.

Pin-fire
Describes a self-contained cartridge that includes a metal pin, which strikes and ignites the primer within the cartridge when hit by the weapon's hammer.

Pistol
A nonrepeating, repeating, or semiautomatic small arm designed to be fired from one hand.

Prawl
A bump or a knob on the frame of a small arm to prevent the user's hand from slipping.

Pricker
A pointed metal tool used to clean out residual gunpowder from a gun's touchhole.

Primer
A substance lit by a firing mechanism to ignite the main charge in the barrel. Priming powder (gunpowder) and a detonating chemical, such as fulminate, are both examples of a primer.

Priming powder
The small amount of fine gunpowder lit by a firing mechanism to ignite the main charge in the barrel.

Projectile
A bullet, ball, grenade, or shot (group of small lead balls), fired by a firearm.

Propellant
The chemical substance, such as gunpowder, which imparts movement to the projectile in a firearm. Also called the main or powder charge.

Ramrod
A wooden or metal rod employed in charging the weapon by ramming the wad and bullet or shot down the barrel against the powder charge.

Recoil
The rearward movement of the barrel (or weapon) in reaction to the forward motion of the bullet.

Recoil operation
A type of firearm action in which the loading cycle is driven by the recoil of the barrel or breechblock after the firing of a cartridge.

Recoil spring
A coil spring attached to the slide or other type of breech component of a self-loading or automatic firearm. It initially absorbs the recoil, then returns the slide or breech mechanism to the closed position, readying the gun for firing.

Recuperator
A device that enables an artillery piece's barrel to return to its firing position after recoil.

Repeating rifle
A rifle that can discharge multiple consecutive shots using cartridges loaded from a magazine.

Revolver
A gun that carries ammunition in a rotating cylinder.

Rifle
A long-barreled firearm with spiral grooves in the barrel.

Rifling
The spiral grooves cut into the barrel that induce spin on the bullet.

Rifled musket
A musket which has been rifled by adding grooves in its barrel to impart a spin to the bullet.

Rim-fire
Describes a self-contained cartridge that carries the primer in its rim. The primer is ignited when the firing pin strikes and crushes the rim when hit by the weapon's hammer.

Safety catch
A mechanism which helps prevent the accidental discharge from a firearm, ensuring safe handling.

Sear
An often hooklike part of the firing mechanism that connects the trigger to the cock, hammer, or striker.

Selective fire
The system in some firearms for switching between semiautomatic and automatic firing mode. The preferred mode can be activated by means of a selector.

Self-loading
Describes a weapon that employs recoil force or the force of exploding propellant gases to eject a spent cartridge and chamber a new one. Also known as auto-loading.

Semiautomatic
Describes weapons that go through one cycle of firing and self-loading on each pull of the trigger, but do not perform continuous fire. Also known as self-loading. See also *Automatic*.

Serpentine
An S-shaped piece of metal with a central pivot attached to the side of a matchlock gun. It held a slow match that was lowered onto the priming pan on pulling the trigger.

Shot
A measured quantity of small lead pellets.

Shrapnel
Fragments or debris thrown out by an exploding shell, grenade, or bomb.

Single-action
An action type, typical of a revolver, in which the hammer must be cocked manually prior to each shot.

Silencer
A device that reduces, but rarely silences, the sound, flash, and recoil of a fired round.

Single-shot rifle
A rifle that has to be manually reloaded after every shot.

Slide action
A firearm mechanism in which the rearward and forward motion of a sliding sleeve ejects the spent cartridge case, loads a new cartridge, and cocks the gun. Also known as pump action.

Smokeless powder
A smokeless propellant, used almost universally now, that is composed of a mixture of nitrocellulose and other chemicals and is shaped into thin flakes before being loaded into a cartridge. Unlike black powder (gunpowder), it does not give away a concealed shooter's position.

Smoothbore
Describes a gun barrel lacking a rifled interior.

Snaphance
An early flintlock mechanism featuring a separate pivoting striking surface made of steel, and a sliding pan-cover. Sometimes spelled "snaphaunce."

Solid frame
A revolver design in which the cylinder is held in a rectangular frame made by the top and bottom straps, the standing breech end, and the part of the frame forming the rear of the barrel.

Stock
The portion of a firearm that is held by the person firing it.

Submachine-gun
A handheld, fully automatic weapon firing pistol-caliber rounds; it is shorter than a rifle.

Suppressor
Another word for silencer.

Toradar
An Indian matchlock gun on which the barrel and the stock are fastened together by coils of rawhide or wire.

Touchhole
A hole in the breech of early cannon and small arms through which the main charge was ignited. Also known as the vent.

Trigger guard
A frame protecting the trigger from damage and unintentional pressure that could accidentally discharge the weapon.

Trunnion
A cylindrical protrusion on each side of the barrel of an artillery piece on which it pivots to lower or elevate its barrel.

Under-lever
A lever, placed under the barrel near the trigger guard, that is used to open the breech in most lever-action guns.

Wad
A piece of paper, cardboard, or felt, used to retain the charge in the cartridge or barrel.

Wheel-lock
A firing mechanism that provided a means for self-igniting a firearm for the first time. It featured a wheel that created sparks on rubbing against a piece of iron pyrite. The sparks then lit the priming powder.

INDEX

Page numbers in **bold** indicate major entries.

ACKNOWLEDGMENTS

Dorling Kindersley would like to thank the following for their help with making the book:

The Smithsonian Institution
David D. Miller III
Associate Curator in the Armed Forces History division at the National Museum of American History, Kenneth E. Behring Center, Smithsonian

Springfield Armory
National Historic Site
Alex MacKenzie
Acting Chief of Resource Management

Richard Colton
Park Ranger / Interpreter, Historian, Historic Weapons Safety Officer

Down East Antiques
joesalter.com

Joe Salter
Joe Salter Jr.
Peter Shirley
Jim Emo

The publisher would also like to thank: Rohan Sinha, Martyn Page, Ishani Nandi, Saloni Singh, Esha Banerjee, and Priyaneet Singh for editorial assistance; Jaypal Singh Chauhan for DTP assistance; Debra Wolter for proofreading; and Helen Peters for indexing.

The publisher would like to thank the following for their kind permission to reproduce their photographs:

(Key: a-above; b-below/bottom; c-center; f-far; l-left; r-right; t-top)

Front Endpapers: **Corbis**: Philip James Corwin (lr). **1 Dorling Kindersley**: © The Board of Trustees of the Armouries (c). **2–3 Boxall and Edmiston gunmakers**. **4 Dorling Kindersley**: Springfield Armory (br). **5 Alamy Images**: Interfoto (bl). **Dorling Kindersley**: Down East Antiques (br). **6 Alamy Images**: Stan Tess (bl). **Boxall and Edmiston gunmakers**: (br). **7 Alamy Images**: EN Field Sports (bl). **Dorling Kindersley**: © The Board of Trustees of the Armouries (br). **8 Dorling Kindersley**: Down East Antiques (ftl). **9 Dorling Kindersley**: Down East

Information on caliber (firearms)
Throughout this book, measurements are provided in US measurements and metric, except in the case of caliber.
In the muzzle-loading era, the gauge diameters, or calibers, of guns were often not standardized, so calibers are provided in both US and metric measurements for each weapon from this period. With the advent of the metallic cartridge, manufacturers provided specifications for caliber, which is expressed in either inches or millimeters only.
Calibers of shotgun are given by "gauge," since this type of firearm is still identified using a form of measurement created in the 17th century, based on the number of balls which could be cast from a single pound of lead.

Antiques (ftr); Springfield Armory. **10–11 Dorling Kindersley**: Springfield Armory. **12 Dorling Kindersley**: Fort Nelson (c); Courtesy of the Royal Museum of the Armed Forces and of Military History, Brussels, Belgium (t). **12–34 Dorling Kindersley**: © The Board of Trustees of the Armouries (ftl). **13 Dorling Kindersley**: Fort Nelson (t); The Tank Museum (c, br). **13–35 Dorling Kindersley**: © The Board of Trustees of the Armouries (ftr). **14 Dorling Kindersley**: © The Board of Trustees of the Armouries (cla); The Combined Military Services Museum (CMSM) (b). **14–15 Dorling Kindersley**: © The Board of Trustees of the Armouries (c). **15 Dorling Kindersley**: Armé Museum, Stockholm, Sweden (t, ca); The Tank Museum (b). **16–17 Dorling Kindersley**: Fort Nelson (t, c, cb). **16 Dorling Kindersley**: Fort Nelson (cla, ca, bl). **17 Dorling Kindersley**: Fort Nelson (t, ca, b). **18–19 Getty Images**: Peeter Snayers. **20–21 Dorling Kindersley**: © The Board of Trustees of the Armouries (t, ca, c, b). **22–23 Dorling Kindersley**: © The Board of Trustees of the Armouries (t, c, b); The Combined Military Services Museum (CMSM) (ca). **23 Dorling Kindersley**: © The Board of Trustees of the Armouries (ca, cla, cb). **24–25 Dorling Kindersley**: © The Board of Trustees of the Armouries (ca). **24 Dorling Kindersley**: © The Board of Trustees of the Armouries (bl, br). **25 Dorling Kindersley** © The Board of Trustees of the Armouries (b, t). **26–27 Getty Images**: (c). **26 Dorling Kindersley**: © The Board of Trustees of the Armouries (cla, tr). **27 Dorling Kindersley**: © The Board of Trustees of the Armouries (br). **Getty Images**: (cra). **28–29 Dorling Kindersley**: © The Board of Trustees of the Armouries (c, b, t). **29 Dorling Kindersley**: © The Board of Trustees of the Armouries (cb, br, ca). **30–31 Dorling Kindersley**: © The Board of Trustees of the Armouries (t, b, c). **31 Dorling Kindersley**: © The Board of Trustees of the Armouries (ca, bc, c). **32–33 Dorling Kindersley**: © The Board of Trustees of the Armouries (t, b). **32 Dorling Kindersley**: © The Board of Trustees of the Armouries (cla); Wallace Collection, London (cr). **33 Dorling Kindersley**: © The Board of Trustees of the Armouries (c); Warwick Castle, Warwick (ca). **34–35 Dorling Kindersley**: © The Board of Trustees of the Armouries (ca). **34 Dorling Kindersley**: © The Board of Trustees of the Armouries (cb). **35 Dorling Kindersley**: © The Board of Trustees of the Armouries (bc, br, crb). **36–37 Dorling Kindersley**: Down East Antiques. **38–39 Alamy Images**: North Wind Picture Archives. **38 Dorling Kindersley**: © The Board of Trustees of the Armouries (bl). **38–82 Dorling Kindersley**: © The Board of Trustees of the Armouries (ftl). **39 Dorling Kindersley**: Springfield Armory. **39–83 Dorling Kindersley**: © The Board of Trustees of the Armouries (ftr). **40–41 Dorling Kindersley**: © The Board of Trustees of the Armouries (t, b); The Combined Military Services Museum

(CMSM) (c). **41 Dorling Kindersley**: The Combined Military Services Museum (CMSM) (ca). **42 Dorling Kindersley**: © The Board of Trustees of the Armouries (clb). **42–43 Dorling Kindersley**: © The Board of Trustees of the Armouries (c). **43 Dorling Kindersley**: © The Board of Trustees of the Armouries (t, b). **44 Dorling Kindersley**: © The Board of Trustees of the Armouries (cla, br); Warwick Castle, Warwick (tr). **44–45 Dorling Kindersley**: © The Board of Trustees of the Armouries (c). **45 Dorling Kindersley**: © The Board of Trustees of the Armouries (cla); Ross Simms and the Winchcombe Folk and Police Museum (clb); Judith Miller / Wallis and Wallis (b). **46 Dorling Kindersley**: © The Board of Trustees of the Armouries (tr, br); Springfield Armory (crb). **46–47 Dorling Kindersley**: © The Board of Trustees of the Armouries (c). **47 Dorling Kindersley**: © The Board of Trustees of the Armouries (t, cb, b). **48 Dorling Kindersley**: © The Board of Trustees of the Armouries (tr, cl). **48–49 Dorling Kindersley**: © The Board of Trustees of the Armouries (c). **49 Dorling Kindersley**: © The Board of Trustees of the Armouries (tl, cra, bl, br); David Edge (cla). **50–51 Getty Images**: Hippolyte Lecomte. **52–53 Dorling Kindersley**: © The Board of Trustees of the Armouries (t); Springfield Armory (c). **53 Dorling Kindersley**: Springfield Armory (cl). **54–55 Dorling Kindersley**: © The Board of Trustees of the Armouries (cb); Springfield Armory (t, ca, c). **54 Dorling Kindersley**: © The Board of Trustees of the Armouries (b). **55 Dorling Kindersley**: © The Board of Trustees of the Armouries (clb, cb); Springfield Armory (t). **56–57 Dorling Kindersley**: © The Board of Trustees of the Armouries (t, c, cb). **56 Dorling Kindersley**: © The Board of Trustees of the Armouries (ca, b). **57 Dorling Kindersley**: © The Board of Trustees of the Armouries (cla, b). **58–59 Dorling Kindersley**: © The Board of Trustees of the Armouries (t, cb); Springfield Armory (c). **59 Dorling Kindersley**: © The Board of Trustees of the Armouries (ca, b). **62 © Copyright James A. Langone 2013** (c). **courtesy of the National Park Service**: Springfield Armory NHS / Historic Photograph Collection (tr). **63 Dorling Kindersley**: © The Board of Trustees of the Armouries (tl, tr); Springfield Armory (tc). **Courtesy of the National Park Service**: Springfield Armory NHS / Historic Photograph Collection (b). **64–65 Dorling Kindersley**: © The Board of Trustees of the Armouries (t, ca, c). **64 Dorling Kindersley**: © The Board of Trustees of the Armouries (cra, cb). **65 Dorling Kindersley**: © The Board of Trustees of the Armouries (t, cra, cb, b). **66–67 Dorling Kindersley**: Fort Nelson (t, c). **66 Dorling Kindersley**: Fort Nelson (ca, cl, bl). **67 Dorling Kindersley**: Fort Nelson (ca). **Courtesy of the Royal Artillery Historical Trust**: (cr). **68 Dorling Kindersley**: © The Board of Trustees of the Armouries (tr); Fort Nelson (cl, bc). **68–69 Dorling Kindersley**: Fort Nelson (tl). **69 Dorling**

Kindersley: © The Board of Trustees of the Armouries (tr); Fort Nelson (cr, b). **70–71 Dorling Kindersley**: Fort Nelson (c, t). **70 Dorling Kindersley**: Fort Nelson (bl). **71 Dorling Kindersley**: Fort Nelson (c). **72 Dorling Kindersley**: © The Board of Trustees of the Armouries (tl, clb). **74–75 Dorling Kindersley**: © The Board of Trustees of the Armouries (c, t, ca, b). **75 Dorling Kindersley**: © The Board of Trustees of the Armouries (c, cra, cb). **76–77 Corbis**: Stapleton Collection. **Dorling Kindersley**: © The Board of Trustees of the Armouries (t, ca, c, b). **77 Dorling Kindersley**: © The Board of Trustees of the Armouries (t, ca, bl). **78 Dorling Kindersley**: © The Board of Trustees of the Armouries (tr, ca, c). **78–79 Dorling Kindersley**: © The Board of Trustees of the Armouries (cb, b). **79 Dorling Kindersley**: © The Board of Trustees of the Armouries (tl, tr, c, clb). **80 Dorling Kindersley**: © The Board of Trustees of the Armouries (tr); Down East Antiques (bl). **80–81 The Bridgeman Art Library**: National Army Museum, London / Gibb, Robert (1845–1932) (b). **81 Dorling Kindersley**: Springfield Armory (br). **University Of Aberdeen**: Alexander John Forsyth, Belhelvie, Aberdeenshire, (cla). **www.historicalimagebank.com**: Military & Historical Image Bank (crb). **82 Dorling Kindersley**: © The Board of Trustees of the Armouries (t, cl). **82–83 Dorling Kindersley**: © The Board of Trustees of the Armouries (c). **83 Dorling Kindersley**: © The Board of Trustees of the Armouries (b). **Smithsonian Institution, Washington, DC, USA**: (ca, ca / Full View). **84–85 Dorling Kindersley**: Down East Antiques. **86–87 Dorling Kindersley**: © The Board of Trustees of the Armouries (t). **86 Dorling Kindersley**: © The Board of Trustees of the Armouries (c, bl). **86–138 Dorling Kindersley**: © The Board of Trustees of the Armouries (ftl). **87 Dorling Kindersley**: © The Board of Trustees of the Armouries (ca, c, bc). **87–139 Dorling Kindersley**: © The Board of Trustees of the Armouries (ftr). **88 Dorling Kindersley**: © The Board of Trustees of the Armouries (tr, cla). **88–89 Dorling Kindersley**: © The Board of Trustees of the Armouries (c). **89 Dorling Kindersley**: © The Board of Trustees of the Armouries (bl); Gettysburg National Military Park (t, br). **90–91 Dorling Kindersley**: © The Board of Trustees of the Armouries (t). **90 Dorling Kindersley**: © The Board of Trustees of the Armouries (br). **91 Dorling Kindersley**: © The Board of Trustees of the Armouries (t, cb, bl, br). **92 Dorling Kindersley**: © The Board of Trustees of the Armouries (tr, b). **92–93 Dorling Kindersley**: © The Board of Trustees of the Armouries (c). **93 Dorling Kindersley**: © The Board of Trustees of the Armouries (t, b). **94 Corbis**: Bettmann (bl). **Getty Images**: (tl). **95 Alamy Images**: AF archive (b). **Dorling Kindersley**: © The Board of Trustees of the Armouries (tl, tc, tr). **96 Dorling Kindersley**: Springfield Armory (t). **96–97 Dorling Kindersley**: © The Board of Trustees of the Armouries (ca);

Kindersley: © The Board of Trustees of the Armouries (c); Springfield Armory (t, crb, b). **98–99 Alamy Images:** Archive Images (b). **98 Dorling Kindersley:** © The Board of Trustees of the Armouries (clb, bl); Springfield Armory (tr). **99 Alamy Images:** Steven Milne (br). **Photoshot:** UPPA (cra). **100–101 Dorling Kindersley:** © The Board of Trustees of the Armouries (c, b). **100 Dorling Kindersley:** © The Board of Trustees of the Armouries (br, cla). **101 Dorling Kindersley:** © The Board of Trustees of the Armouries (tl, tr, cb, br, bl). **102–103 Dorling Kindersley:** © The Board of Trustees of the Armouries (ca, c). **102 Dorling Kindersley:** © The Board of Trustees of the Armouries (cb). **103 Dorling Kindersley:** © The Board of Trustees of the Armouries (t, b, cb). **104–105 Dorling Kindersley:** © The Board of Trustees of the Armouries. **104 Dorling Kindersley:** © The Board of Trustees of the Armouries (ca, bl, bc, br). **105 Dorling Kindersley:** © The Board of Trustees of the Armouries (ca, t, bl, cb). **106–107 Alamy Images:** INTERFOTO. **108 Dorling Kindersley:** Springfield Armory (t, ca, b). **109 Dorling Kindersley:** Springfield Armory (c, cr, clb, bl, br). **110–111 Dorling Kindersley:** © The Board of Trustees of the Armouries (t, c, b). **111 Dorling Kindersley:** © The Board of Trustees of the Armouries (ca, cb, bl). **112 Dorling Kindersley:** © The Board of Trustees of the Armouries (bl); Springfield Armory (tr); 95th Rifles and Re-enactment Living History Unit (cl). **112–113 The Bridgeman Art Library:** Art Gallery of New South Wales, Sydney, Australia (b). **113 Corbis:** Medford Historical Society Collection (cla). **Dorling Kindersley:** © The Board of Trustees of the Armouries (crb). **114–115 Dorling Kindersley:** © The Board of Trustees of the Armouries (c, b); Springfield Armory (ca). **115 Dorling Kindersley:** © The Board of Trustees of the Armouries (ca, cb); Springfield Armory (t). **116 Dorling Kindersley:** © The Board of Trustees of the Armouries (cla, cl). **116–117 Dorling Kindersley:** © The Board of Trustees of the Armouries (t, cb, b). **117 Dorling Kindersley:** © The Board of Trustees of the Armouries (cb); The Tank Museum (tr); The Combined Military Services Museum (CMSM) (b). **118–119 Getty Images:** De Agostini (b). **118 Dorling Kindersley:** © The Board of Trustees of the Armouries (ca). **Getty Images:** (tl). **119 Alamy Images:** Photos 12 (cr). **Dorling Kindersley:** © The Board of Trustees of the Armouries (tl, tr). **120–121 © The Board of Trustees of the Armouries:** © The Board of Trustees of the Armouries (b). **Dorling Kindersley:** © The Board of Trustees of the Armouries (t, ca, c). **121 Dorling Kindersley:** © The Board of Trustees of the Armouries (crb). **122–123 Dorling Kindersley:** © The Board of Trustees of the Armouries (tc, c, ca). **123 Dorling Kindersley:** © The Board of Trustees of the Armouries (t, b). **124–125 Dorling Kindersley:** © The Board of Trustees of the Armouries (t). **124 Dorling Kindersley:** Gettysburg National Military Park, PA (bl). **125 Dorling Kindersley:** © The Board of Trustees of the Armouries (bl); The Combined Military Services Museum (CMSM) (c, crb). **126 Dorling Kindersley:** © The Board of Trustees of the Armouries (tr, ca, cr, br); The Combined Military Services Museum (CMSM) (bl). **127 Dorling Kindersley:** © The Board of Trustees of the Armouries (t, cb, cla); The Combined Military Services Museum (CMSM) (br). **128 Getty Images:** (tl). **128–129 Getty Images:** Universal Images Group (b). **129 Dorling Kindersley:** © The Board of Trustees of the Armouries (tl, tc, tr). **Fairfax Media Management Pty Ltd.:** Wayne Taylor. **130–131 Corbis:** Bettmann. **132 Dorling Kindersley:** Fort Nelson (tr, c, br, bl). **133 Dorling Kindersley:** Fort Nelson (b); The Tank Museum (t). **134–135 Dorling Kindersley:** The Tank Museum (c). **134 Dorling Kindersley:** Fort Nelson (b). **135 Dorling Kindersley:** Fort Nelson (tr); The Tank Museum (b). **136 Dorling Kindersley:** Springfield Armory (tc, ftr, c). **136–137 Dorling Kindersley:** © The Board of Trustees of the Armouries (c). **137 Dorling Kindersley:** © The Board of Trustees of the Armouries (bl); Royal Artillery Historical Trust (tc); Courtesy of the Royal Artillery Historical Trust (bc). **138 Dorling Kindersley:** Courtesy of the Royal Artillery Historical Trust (bl). **140–141 Dorling Kindersley:** Down East Antiques. **142 Dorling Kindersley:** The Science Museum, London (clb). **Dreamstime.com:** Vladimir Tronin (tr). **Regis Dupont:** (br). **142–238 Dorling Kindersley:** © The Board of Trustees of the Armouries (ftl). **143 Corbis:** (b). **Dorling Kindersley:** The Tank Museum (tr). **143–239 Dorling Kindersley:** © The Board of Trustees of the Armouries (ftr). **144–145 Dorling Kindersley:** © The Board of Trustees of the Armouries (c, b); The Tank Museum (t). **144 Dorling Kindersley:** © The Board of Trustees of the Armouries (cla). **145 Dorling Kindersley:** © The Board of Trustees of the Armouries (ca, cb). **146–147 Dorling Kindersley:** © The Board of Trustees of the Armouries (t, c, b). **146 Dorling Kindersley:** © The Board of Trustees of the Armouries (cl). **147 Dorling Kindersley:** Courtesy of the Royal Artillery Historical Trust (ca); The Tank Museum (cb). **148–149 Dorling Kindersley:** © The Board of Trustees of the Armouries (t); The Combined Military Services Museum (CMSM) (cb). **149 Dorling Kindersley:** The Combined Military Services Museum (CMSM) (b). **150 Alamy Images:** PF-(wararchive) (b). **City of Cambridge Archives Photograph Collection:** (tr). **151 Dorling Kindersley:** Jean-Pierre Verney (tl); The Tank Museum (tr). **Getty Images:** John D McHugh (cr). **152–153 Dorling Kindersley:** © The Board of Trustees of the Armouries (t, ca, c, b). **153 Dorling Kindersley:** © The Board of Trustees of the Armouries (cla, cb). **154–cla Dorling Kindersley:** The Combined Military Services Museum (CMSM). **154–155 Dorling Kindersley:** © The Board of Trustees of the Armouries (cb, b); The Combined Military Services Museum (CMSM) (ca). **155 Dorling Kindersley:** © The Board of Trustees of the Armouries (c); The Combined Military Services Museum (CMSM) (t). **156–157 Dorling Kindersley:** © The Board of Trustees of the Armouries (t, ca, c, b); Imperial War Museum, Duxford (cb). **157 Dorling Kindersley:** © The Board of Trustees of the Armouries (cl). **158–159 Getty Images:** Time Life Pictures. **160–161 Dorling Kindersley:** © The Board of Trustees of the Armouries (c, b); Jean-Pierre Verney (t). **160 Dorling Kindersley:** © The Board of Trustees of the Armouries (c). **162–163 Dorling Kindersley:** © The Board of Trustees of the Armouries (c). **162 Dorling Kindersley:** © The Board of Trustees of the Armouries (tc, br, bc, tl); The Combined Military Services Museum (CMSM) (cl). **163 Dorling Kindersley:** © The Board of Trustees of the Armouries (tr, cra). **164 Alamy Images:** Interfoto (tl). **Dorling Kindersley:** © The Board of Trustees of the Armouries (cra). **Getty Images:** (bl). **165 Alamy Images:** AF archive (br). **Dorling Kindersley:** © The Board of Trustees of the Armouries (tl). **166–167 Dorling Kindersley:** © The Board of Trustees of the Armouries (t, c). **166 Dorling Kindersley:** © The Board of Trustees of the Armouries (ca). **167 Dorling Kindersley:** © The Board of Trustees of the Armouries (cra, br). **168 Dorling Kindersley:** © The Board of Trustees of the Armouries (tr, cl, bl); Springfield Armory (cla). **Smithsonian Institution, Washington, DC, USA:** (br). **169 Dorling Kindersley:** © The Board of Trustees of the Armouries (tl, tr, cra); The Tank Museum (c). **170 Dorling Kindersley:** Springfield Armory (ca, bc). **170–171 Dorling Kindersley:** Springfield Armory (c, b). **171 Dorling Kindersley:** Springfield Armory (tl, tc, cra, crb). **172 Corbis:** Sygma/Gianni Giansanti (bl). **Getty Images:** AFP (cr). **173 Dorling Kindersley:** © The Board of Trustees of the Armouries (tl, tc). **Getty Images:** (bl). **174 Dorling Kindersley:** © The Board of Trustees of the Armouries (cla, fcla, tr, bc, crb); H. Keith Melton, spymuseum.org (cl). **174–175 Dorling Kindersley:** © The Board of Trustees of the Armouries (c). **175 Dorling Kindersley:** © The Board of Trustees of the Armouries (tl, cr, tr); The Combined Military Services Museum (CMSM) (br). **176–177 Dorling Kindersley:** © The Board of Trustees of the Armouries (t, b). **176 Dorling Kindersley:** © The Board of Trustees of the Armouries (c); Springfield Armory (ca). **177 Dorling Kindersley:** © The Board of Trustees of the Armouries (bl, c, cb). **178 Dorling Kindersley:** © The Board of Trustees of the Armouries (cl); Springfield Armory (bl, br, cb). **178–179 Dorling Kindersley:** Springfield Armory (ca, c). **179 Dorling Kindersley:** Springfield Armory (bl, br, tc, tr). **180 Ogden Union Station Collection:** (tl, c). **181 Alamy Images:** AF archive (b). **Dorling Kindersley:** © The Board of Trustees of the Armouries (tl, tc). **182–183 Dorling Kindersley:** © The Board of Trustees of the Armouries (c, b, t). **183 Dorling Kindersley:** © The Board of Trustees of the Armouries (clb). **184 Dorling Kindersley:** © The Board of Trustees of the Armouries (tr). **184–185 The Royal Green Jackets Museum:** (b). **185 Alamy Images:** Lordprice Collection (cra). **Dorling Kindersley:** © The Board of Trustees of the Armouries (crb); Springfield Armory (br). **186 Dorling Kindersley:** By kind permission of The Trustees of the Imperial War Museum, London (tr); © The Board of Trustees of the Armouries (cl, bl). **187 Dorling Kindersley:** © The Board of Trustees of the Armouries (t, b). **188 Dorling Kindersley:** © The Board of Trustees of the Armouries (r); Springfield Armory (cl, clb). **189 Dorling Kindersley:** © The Board of Trustees of the Armouries (bc). **190–191 Corbis:** Hulton-Deutsch Collection. **192 Dorling Kindersley:** Courtesy of the Royal Artillery Historical Trust (bl); The Combined Military Services Museum (CMSM) (t). **192–193 Dorling Kindersley:** © The Board of Trustees of the Armouries (b). **193 Dorling Kindersley:** © The Board of Trustees of the Armouries (tc). **194 Dorling Kindersley:** © The Board of Trustees of the Armouries (cb, b). **194–195 Dorling Kindersley:** © The Board of Trustees of the Armouries (c). **195 Dorling Kindersley:** © The Board of Trustees of the Armouries (t, br). **196 Alamy Images:** INTERFOTO (cl). **Dorling Kindersley:** © The Board of Trustees of the Armouries (tr). **196–197 Dorling Kindersley:** The Tank Museum (c). **197 Dorling Kindersley:** Jean-Pierre Verney (tc). **198 Dorling Kindersley:** © The Board of Trustees of the Armouries (tr). **198–199 Dorling Kindersley:** The Tank Museum (c). **199 Dorling Kindersley:** The Tank Museum (b). **200 Dorling Kindersley:** © The Board of Trustees of the Armouries (c). **200–201 Dorling Kindersley:** © The Board of Trustees of the Armouries (b). **© Royal Armouries:** (t). **201 Dorling Kindersley:** © The Board of Trustees of the Armouries (bl); The Tank Museum (c). **202–203 Dorling Kindersley:** © The Board of Trustees of the Armouries (c); The Tank Museum (t). **© Royal Armouries:** (b). **203 Dorling Kindersley:** © The Board of Trustees of the Armouries (cb, ca). **204–205 Dorling Kindersley:** © The Board of Trustees of the Armouries (b). **204 Dorling Kindersley:** © The Board of Trustees of the Armouries (cl); The Combined Military Services Museum (CMSM) (tr). **205 Dorling Kindersley:** © The Board of Trustees of the Armouries (t, br); The Tank Museum (c). **206–207 Dorling Kindersley:** © The Board of Trustees of the Armouries (t, c); The Combined Military Services Museum (CMSM) (b). **206 Dorling Kindersley:** © The Board of Trustees of the Armouries (crb); The Combined Military Services Museum (CMSM) (bc). **207 Dorling Kindersley:** © The Board of Trustees of the Armouries (tc). **208–209 Dorling Kindersley:** © The Board of Trustees of the Armouries (t, b); The Combined Military Services Museum (CMSM) (c). **208 Dorling Kindersley:** The Combined

Military Services Museum (CMSM) (bl). **209 Dorling Kindersley:** © The Board of Trustees of the Armouries (tr); The Combined Military Services Museum (CMSM) (cb). **210–211 Dorling Kindersley:** Springfield Armory (t); The Tank Museum (b). **210 Dorling Kindersley:** © The Board of Trustees of the Armouries (ca, cr, cl). **211 Dorling Kindersley:** Springfield Armory (ca, cl); The Tank Museum (br). **212–213 Dorling Kindersley:** Springfield Armory (ca). **212 Dorling Kindersley:** Springfield Armory (bl). **213 Dorling Kindersley:** Springfield Armory (c, cb, crb, cb/Bolt, br, bl, tl, tc). **214–215 Dorling Kindersley:** The Tank Museum (t, b). **215 Dorling Kindersley:** The Combined Military Services Museum (CMSM) (c); The Tank Museum (bc). **216 Dorling Kindersley:** Fort Nelson (tr, bl). **216–217 Dorling Kindersley:** Fort Nelson (b). **217 Dorling Kindersley:** Fort Nelson (tc); Royal Artillery Historical Trust (cr). **218–219 Dorling Kindersley:** Royal Artillery Historical Trust (tc, b). **218 Dorling Kindersley:** Royal Artillery Historical Trust (cb); The Tank Museum (cl, cla, bc). **219 Dorling Kindersley:** Fort Nelson (tr, cla). **220 Dorling Kindersley:** The Combined Military Services Museum (CMSM) (tr); Robin Wigington, Arbour Antiques, Ltd., Stratford-upon-Avon (tc); Jean-Pierre Verney (cb, crb, b). **220–221 Dorling Kindersley:** © The Board of Trustees of the Armouries (c). **221 Dorling Kindersley:** © The Board of Trustees of the Armouries (t, b); H. Keith Melton (cra). **222–223 Dorling Kindersley:** The Tank Museum (c). **222 Dorling Kindersley:** © The Board of Trustees of the Armouries (tr, b); H. Keith Melton (ca). **223 Dorling Kindersley:** H. Keith Melton (tc); Ministry of Defence Pattern Room, Nottingham (b). **224–225 Dorling Kindersley:** © The Board of Trustees of the Armouries (c, t); Wallace Collection, London (cb). **224 Dorling Kindersley:** © The Board of Trustees of the Armouries (c). **225 Dorling Kindersley:** © The Board of Trustees of the Armouries (clb, b, ca, ca/Mauser). **226–227 Corbis:** Bettmann. **228 Dorling Kindersley:** Fort Nelson (cl); Royal Museum of the Armed Forces and of Military History, Brussels, Belgium (b). **228–229 RMN:** Modèle réduit de la Grosse Bertha Echelle 1/5 de l'obusier de siège allemand de type M, modèle 1914 07567/RMN – Grand Palais/Marie Bruggeman/Paris – Musée de l'Armée (t). **229 Dorling Kindersley:** The Combined Military Services Museum (CMSM) (bl, bc); Fort Nelson (crb). **230 Dorling Kindersley:** Fort Nelson (tr, cl); Royal Artillery Historical Trust (bl). **230–231 Dorling Kindersley:** Fort Nelson (cla). **231 Dorling Kindersley:** Fort Nelson (bc); Royal Artillery Historical Trust (tr, tc, br). **232 Dorling Kindersley:** Fort Nelson (b); Royal Artillery Historical Trust (tr, c). **233 Dorling Kindersley:** © The Board of Trustees of the Armouries (b); Royal Artillery Historical Trust (t). **234 Dorling Kindersley:** The Combined Military Services Museum (CMSM) (b, t). **235 Dorling Kindersley:** © The Board

of Trustees of the Armouries (tr); The Tank Museum (b). **236–237 Dorling Kindersley:** © The Board of Trustees of the Armouries (t); Ministry of Defence Pattern Room, Nottingham (b). **236 Dorling Kindersley:** © The Board of Trustees of the Armouries (c); Ministry of Defence Pattern Room, Nottingham (bl). **238–239 Dorling Kindersley:** © The Board of Trustees of the Armouries (t); Pitt Rivers Museum, University of Oxford (c). **238 Dorling Kindersley:** The Combined Military Services Museum (CMSM) (b); Pitt Rivers Museum, University of Oxford (clb). **239 Dorling Kindersley:** © The Board of Trustees of the Armouries (cb, b). **240–241 Dorling Kindersley:** Down East Antiques. **242–243 Dorling Kindersley:** © The Board of Trustees of the Armouries (c). **242 Dorling Kindersley:** © The Board of Trustees of the Armouries (bl, ca); The Combined Military Services Museum (CMSM) (tr). **242–300 Dorling Kindersley:** Down East Antiques (ftl). **243 Dorling Kindersley:** © The Board of Trustees of the Armouries (t, ca, b, crb). **243–301 Dorling Kindersley:** Down East Antiques (ftr). **244 Cody Firearms Museum:** (Original Winchester photograph from 1918–19) Rifle currently in the Cody Firearms Museum (bc). **Dorling Kindersley:** © The Board of Trustees of the Armouries (bl, c, c/left); Springfield Armory (tr). **Herb G Houze:** (br). **245 Dorling Kindersley:** The Tank Museum (br). **Press Association Images:** AP/Charles J. Ryan (t). **246–247 Dorling Kindersley:** © The Board of Trustees of the Armouries (t); The Tank Museum (c). **246 Dorling Kindersley:** The Tank Museum (bl). **247 Dorling Kindersley:** © The Board of Trustees of the Armouries (b); The Tank Museum (ca). **248–249 Dorling Kindersley:** Springfield Armory (t, cb). **248 Dorling Kindersley:** Springfield Armory (ca, c). **249 Dorling Kindersley:** Springfield Armory (bl, tr, bc). **250–251 Dorling Kindersley:** The Tank Museum (t). **250 Dorling Kindersley:** © The Board of Trustees of the Armouries (b); The Tank Museum (c). **251 Dorling Kindersley:** © The Board of Trustees of the Armouries (br); The Tank Museum (cb). **252 Dorling Kindersley:** © The Board of Trustees of the Armouries (tc, ca, cl). **252–253 Dorling Kindersley:** The Tank Museum (b). **253 Dorling Kindersley:** © The Board of Trustees of the Armouries (t); The Tank Museum (bl, ca). **254 Dorling Kindersley:** © The Board of Trustees of the Armouries (t, b). **255 Dorling Kindersley:** © The Board of Trustees of the Armouries (tr, c); Courtesy of the Ministry of Defence Pattern Room, Nottingham (b). **256 Heckler and Koch GMBH:** (tr, bl). **257 Alamy Images:** Mikael Karlsson (b). **Dorling Kindersley:** © The Board of Trustees of the Armouries (tc, tl, tr). **258 Dorling Kindersley:** © The Board of Trustees of the Armouries (tr, c). **258–259 Dorling Kindersley:** © The Board of Trustees of the Armouries (b). **259 Dorling Kindersley:** © The Board of Trustees of the Armouries (c); The Tank Museum (t). **260 Dorling Kindersley:** © The Board of Trustees of the Armouries (tc,

c, b); The Tank Museum (cr). **261 Dorling Kindersley:** © The Board of Trustees of the Armouries (t, cra, c, b). **262 Dorling Kindersley:** © The Board of Trustees of the Armouries (cla, cl, bl, br); Down East Antiques (tr). **262–263 Dorling Kindersley:** Down East Antiques (c). **263 Dorling Kindersley:** © The Board of Trustees of the Armouries (cra, bl). **© Royal Armouries:** (tl). **264–265 Dorling Kindersley:** © The Board of Trustees of the Armouries (t). **264 Dorling Kindersley:** © The Board of Trustees of the Armouries (cl, bl, bc). **265 Dorling Kindersley:** © The Board of Trustees of the Armouries (tr, tl, bc); Down East Antiques (c). **266 Dorling Kindersley:** © The Board of Trustees of the Armouries (tc, c); The Tank Museum (bl). **267 Dorling Kindersley:** © The Board of Trustees of the Armouries (t, cra, br). **268–269 Corbis:** Stocktrek Images/Tom Weber. **270 Dorling Kindersley:** © The Board of Trustees of the Armouries (bl); Down East Antiques (cr). **271 Dorling Kindersley:** © The Board of Trustees of the Armouries (bl, cra, crb). **272–273 Dorling Kindersley:** © The Board of Trustees of the Armouries (t); The Tank Museum (b). **272 Dorling Kindersley:** The Tank Museum (bl). **273 Dorling Kindersley:** © The Board of Trustees of the Armouries (c, br); The Tank Museum (bc). **274 Dorling Kindersley:** © The Board of Trustees of the Armouries (tr, cla). **274–275 Dorling Kindersley:** © The Board of Trustees of the Armouries (b). **275 Dorling Kindersley:** © The Board of Trustees of the Armouries (t, br). **276 Dorling Kindersley:** Springfield Armory (cla, cl, bl). **276–277 Dorling Kindersley:** Springfield Armory (b). **277 Dorling Kindersley:** Springfield Armory (tl, tc, cla, c). **278–279 Dorling Kindersley:** © The Board of Trustees of the Armouries (b); Down East Antiques (t). **278 Dorling Kindersley:** Down East Antiques (c, cla). **279 Dorling Kindersley:** Down East Antiques (ca, c). **280–281 Dorling Kindersley:** Down East Antiques (ca, c, b). **281 Dorling Kindersley:** Down East Antiques (t, cl). **282–283 Dorling Kindersley:** © The Board of Trustees of the Armouries (t, cb); Down East Antiques (c). **283 Dorling Kindersley:** Down East Antiques (clb, ca, b). **284–285 Dorling Kindersley:** © The Board of Trustees of the Armouries (t, c). **284 Dorling Kindersley:** © The Board of Trustees of the Armouries (b); Down East Antiques (ca). **285 Dorling Kindersley:** © The Board of Trustees of the Armouries (t, ca, b); Down East Antiques (cb). **288–289 Dorling Kindersley:** © The Board of Trustees of the Armouries (t, c, b). **288 Dorling Kindersley:** © The Board of Trustees of the Armouries (cb, bl). **289 Dorling Kindersley:** © The Board of Trustees of the Armouries (cla). **290 STEYR MANNLICHER GMBH:** (tl, cr). **291 Dorling Kindersley:** © The Board of Trustees of the Armouries (tl, tc); The Tank Museum (tr). **Getty Images:** AFP (b). **292–293 Dorling Kindersley:** © The Board of Trustees of the Armouries (t, cb). **292 Dorling Kindersley:** © The Board of Trustees of the Armouries (c). **293

Dorling Kindersley:** © The Board of Trustees of the Armouries (t, bl, crb, br). **294 Dorling Kindersley:** © The Board of Trustees of the Armouries (tr, cl, b). **294–295 Dorling Kindersley:** © The Board of Trustees of the Armouries (c). **295 Dorling Kindersley:** © The Board of Trustees of the Armouries (ca, tl). **296 Alamy Images:** Stocktrek Images, Inc (ca). **Dorling Kindersley:** The Tank Museum (bl). **296–297 Dorling Kindersley:** The Tank Museum (b). **297 Dorling Kindersley:** The Tank Museum (br). **Courtesy of U.S. Army:** (ca). **298 Alamy Images:** Stocktrek Images, Inc (cla). **Dreamstime.com:** Meoita (cra). **298–299 Courtesy of U.S. Army:** (b). **299 Alamy Images:** Stocktrek Images, Inc (t); ZUMA Press, Inc. (br). **Courtesy of U.S. Army:** (cr). **300–301 Dorling Kindersley:** © The Board of Trustees of the Armouries (t, b). **300 Dorling Kindersley:** © The Board of Trustees of the Armouries (cra, cl). **301 Dorling Kindersley:** © The Board of Trustees of the Armouries (br, ca). **302 Dorling Kindersley:** The Combined Military Services Museum (CMSM) (bl). **Palmerston Forts Society:** c. **302–320 Dorling Kindersley:** Down East Antiques (ftl). **303–319 Dorling Kindersley:** Down East Antiques (ftr). **306 Dorling Kindersley:** © The Board of Trustees of the Armouries (cl, cl/Belted Balls, bl, bl/opened, ca, cra, cr, c, cb, clb, bc, br); Down East Antiques. **307 Dorling Kindersley:** © The Board of Trustees of the Armouries (ca/Allen and Wheelock, c, cb/Theur, cb/.44in Smith and Wesson, cb, tr, tr/Bodeo, ca, cr, br/Wildfowl Cartridge, br); Down East Antiques (cl, clb, bl); (ca/.44in Henry); Springfield Armory (tl). **308 Dorling Kindersley:** © The Board of Trustees of the Armouries (cla, clb/7.62 × 54mm Russian (1891), bl, tr, cra/303 MKV, cr, cb, cb/7.92 × 33mm Kurtz (1938), br); (c, clb/7.92 × 57mm Mauser (1905)). **309 Dorling Kindersley:** © The Board of Trustees of the Armouries (cra/7.7 × 56mm Italian, tl, cla/7.62 × 51mm Nato, cla/.458in Winchester Magnum (1956), c, clb/7mm Remington Magnum rifle catridge, clb, bl, tc, tr/Parabellum, ca/Nambu, ca/.32 Long pistol cartridge, cr, cb/.32 Auto, cb/9mm Mars, bc, cra/.45in ACP, crb/.357in Magnum rifle cartridge, crb/.44in Magnum rifle cartridge, br). *Back Endpapers:* **Corbis:** Philip James Corwin (lr). **Dorling Kindersley:** © The Board of Trustees of the Armouries (Postcard 1), (Postcard 2).

All other images © Dorling Kindersley

For further information see:
www.dkimages.com

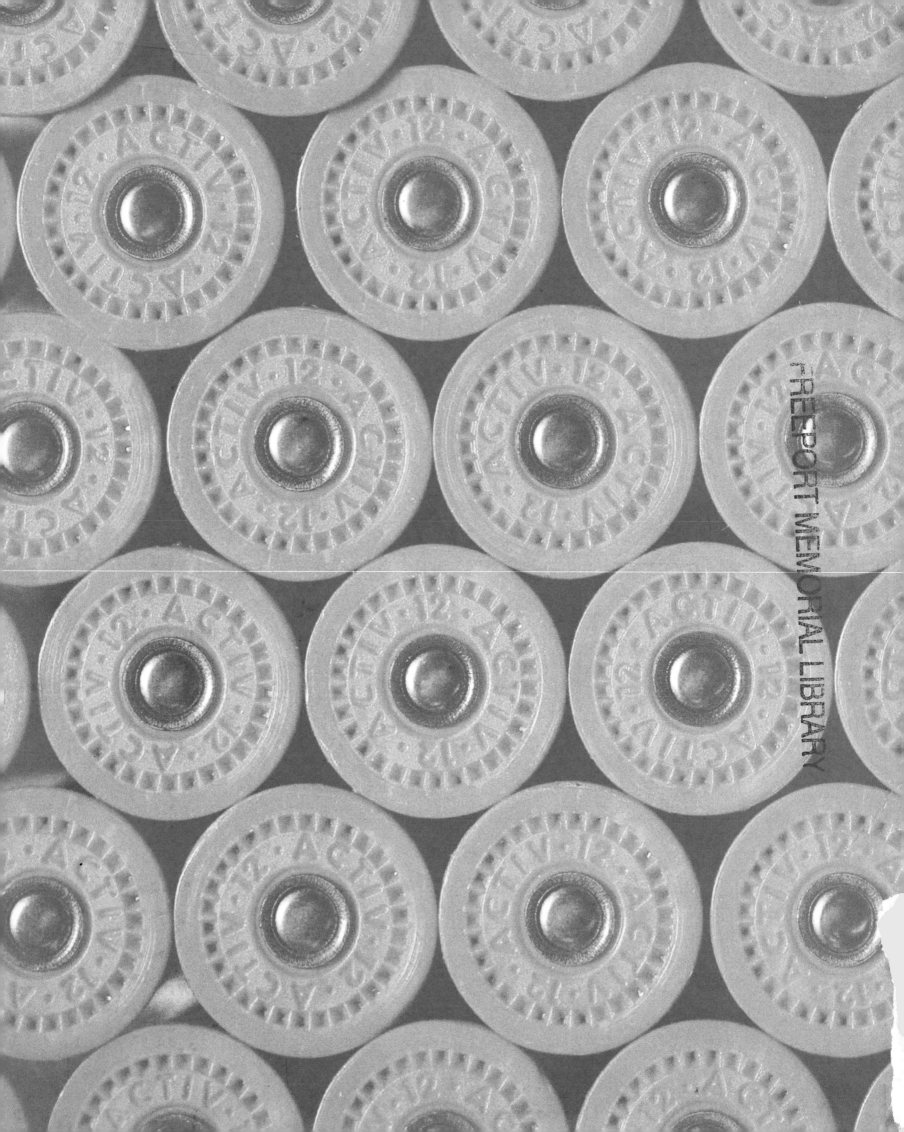